Introduction to Networking
Understanding Network Programs, Processes, and Protocols

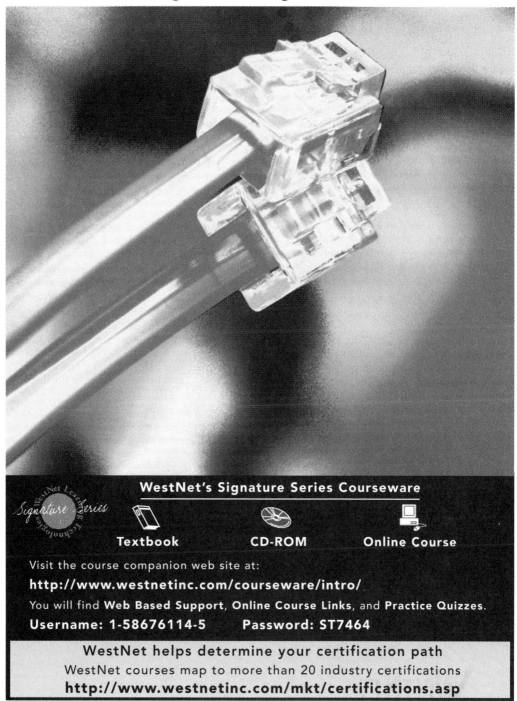

WestNet's Signature Series Courseware

Textbook   CD-ROM   Online Course

Visit the course companion web site at:

http://www.westnetinc.com/courseware/intro/

You will find **Web Based Support**, **Online Course Links**, and **Practice Quizzes**.

Username: 1-58676114-5   **Password: ST7464**

WestNet helps determine your certification path

WestNet courses map to more than 20 industry certifications

http://www.westnetinc.com/mkt/certifications.asp

CREDITS

Author and Development Editor: Kenneth D. Reed

Editorial and Production Manager: Marilee E. Aust

Book Design and Composition, and Copy Editor Manager: D. Kari Luraas, Clairvoyance Design

Illustrator: Lynn Siefken

Proofreader: Larry Beckett

Indexer: Amy Casey

Technical Writer and Editor: Kathy Russell

Copy Editor: Michelle Hanson, Clairvoyance Design

Associate Copy Editor: Sheryl Shapiro

Cover Design: David Jones

Printer: Johnson Printing

Revised edition © 2001 by WestNet Learning Technologies
Copyright © 1994–2000 by WestNet Learning Technologies

ISBN: 1-58676-114-5 (softcover)

Printed in the United States of America

Reed, Kenneth D.
Introduction to Networking
544 pp., includes illustrations and index

1. Computers and Software in Networks 2. Carrier Signals, Cable Types, and Network Topologies 3. Computer Protocols and Services 4. The OSI Model 5. LANs 6. Network Components 7. WANs 8. Integrating the Course Elements
WB77.0

For instructor-led training, self-paced courses,
turn-key curricula solutions, or more information contact:

WestNet Learning Technologies (dba: WestNet Inc.)
5420 Ward Road, Suite 150, Arvada, CO 80002 USA
E-mail: Info@westnetinc.com

To access the WestNet student resource site, go to
http://www.westnetinc.com/student

LEARNING TECHNOLOGIES

Preface

The *Introduction to Networking* course provides an introductory overview of the fundamental concepts of networking and data communications. This course is designed for those students who have basic experience using a computer, and would like a better understanding of how networks move information between computers.

This course brings together the acronyms, protocols and components that are essential to understanding how networks operate today. Students will learn how signals travel across different types of physical network structures, and how those signals carry useful data from one device to another. As you will see, the same key principles and components form the foundation of all networks, from the smallest peer-to-peer systems to the worldwide Internet. The knowledge gained in this course will serve as a firm foundation for a continued course of study in networking.

Key Topics

- Physical transmission media: copper wires, optical fibers, and radio waves
- Analog and digital signaling
- Communication protocols and services
- The OSI Reference Model
- Common transmission technologies for local area networks
- Popular network operating systems
- Networking devices
- Linking networks across a wide area
- Building local area networks

Course Objectives

- Identify the different types of networking hardware and software
- Explain how signals are transmitted over wires, fiber optic cables, and wireless systems
- Describe what protocols are, and why they are necessary
- Describe the different types of addresses that computers use to send and receive information
- Describe how information flows between two communicating computers
- Describe the technologies used in local area networks (LANs) and wide area networks (WANs)
- Identify the common types of networking devices, and explain the purpose of each one
- In simple terms, explain how the Internet works
- Build a small peer-to-peer network

Pedagogical Features

Several pedagogical features are included in this text to enhance the presentation of the materials so that you can easily understand the concepts and apply them. Throughout the book, emphasis is placed on applying concepts to real-world scenarios through end-of-lesson Activities, Extended Activities and other exercises and examples.

Learning Objectives, Unit Summaries, Discussion Questions, and Activities/Exercises

Learning objectives, unit summaries, discussion questions, and activities/exercises are designed to function as integrated study tools. Learning objectives reflect what you should be able to accomplish after completing each unit or chapter. Chapter summaries highlight the key concepts you should master. The discussion questions help guide critical thinking about those key concepts, and the Activities/Exercises provide you with opportunities to practice important techniques.

Key Terms

The information technology field includes many unique terms that are critical to creating a workable language when it is combined with the world of business. Definitions of key terms are provided in alphabetical order at the beginning of each unit and in a glossary at the end of the textbook.

Supplements

When this course is used in an academic or instructor-led setting, it is accompanied by an Instructor's Resource Tool Kit. The online-based kit includes an Instructor's Guide with the answers to Activities/Exercises, Lesson and Unit Quizzes and the End-of-Course Exam. It also includes PowerPoint presentations organized by lesson, unit and course. The Instructor's Resource site may also include sample syllabi, discussion topics, puzzles, cryptograms, and up-to-the-minute updates to the textbooks and supplemental course materials.

WestNet Learning Technologies' cutting edge Administrative Tools offer a unique online Windows-based exam software. The Online Course Exam engine includes lesson-, unit- and course-level questions. These exams can be accessed by individual students and is presented in randomized order, ensuring that no student ever gets the same question with the same sequence of answers. This feature allows you to create printed and online pretests, practice tests, and actual examinations.

Advancing Your Level of Technical Expertise

WestNet Learning Technologies envisions a new communications paradigm for the 21st century—a paradigm based on increased bandwidth and digital exchange. Moving forward, WestNet is integrating these capacities with data/telephony/IP educational solutions that will give its students a complete range of communications skills and knowledge.

Why Choose WestNet?

WestNet Learning Technologies offers comprehensive information technologies (IT) educational and certification programs and curricula to secondary schools, colleges and universities, as well as corporations, resellers and individual participants around the globe. These programs provide participants with the tools necessary to further their technical knowledge and skills, and to obtain hands-on experience. This unique program, which is vendor neutral, helps prepare participants to pursue IT careers, earn secondary and post-secondary educational degrees, and/or obtain industry certification.

WestNet Learning Technologies' programs are currently provided to more than 1,500 institutions around the world. Its programs also are being offered internationally in more than a dozen countries and five languages.

Contents

Unit 2
Carrier Signals, Cable Types, and Network Topologies 55

Lesson 4
Fiber Optic Cable 105

Lesson 5
Wireless Transmission 114

Lesson 6
Overview of a Structured Cable Plant 129

INTRODUCTION

This course is an introduction to computer networks and explains the technologies that are used to transmit information between computers, and ultimately between people. It is a fundamental course that provides a broad overview and foundation for understanding networks and working in the computer and networking industry. There are no prerequisites for this course other than basic experience using a personal computer.

WHAT IS A NETWORK?

A network can be defined as two or more computing devices that are connected to share data and other resources. Freestanding computers, that are not connected, can only exchange data by means of a portable storage medium such as a floppy disk or tape. But when computers communicate directly over some type of physical connection, they can share many resources beyond data, such as:

- Applications
- Peripherals, such as printers, scanners, or compact disk and read-only memory (CD-ROM) drives
- Storage
- Communication links, such as Internet connections

The devices that communicate over a network are often computers. However, a network can also include any device capable of sending or receiving electronic information. Thus, in addition to computers, networks can also connect:

- Printers

- Modems

- Devices that control the flow of network traffic

- Wireless access devices

Generically speaking, any communicating network device is called a "node." If you think of a connect-the-dots puzzle, nodes are the dots that the network must connect.

A network can consist of as few as two computers in the same room or millions of computers around the planet. No matter what their size, all networks have certain characteristics in common:

- A system of signaling to carry information from one node to another

- A physical communication medium over which signals can travel

- Communication rules, called "protocols," that give the signals meaning

- A system of controlling access to the communication medium to ensure orderly conversations

- A method of addressing so each node knows who is talking to whom and all data and messages arrive at their intended destinations

In this course we will explain each of these elements and show how they work together to allow machines and people to communicate.

Why Study Networking?

Not too long ago, networks were only used by large corporations. They were controlled by small groups of technical specialists and generally did not affect the daily lives of most people.

However, as the price of computer hardware has steadily fallen, both computers and networks have become common appliances. At the same time, the Internet has become both a worldwide communication system and a powerful entertainment medium. Even home users are setting up small networks to transfer files and share Internet connections.

Just because more people are now using networks does not mean that more people understand them. When science fiction author Arthur C. Clarke said, "Any sufficiently advanced technology is indistinguishable from magic," he could have been describing today's worldwide networks. Each day millions of computer users, even advanced users, log on to corporate networks and the Internet, with little or no understanding of the way those systems work.

This course will replace some of the magic with knowledge. When you complete this course you will understand how computers communicate across a room, building, city, or the world. You will be able to describe what happens when you use a browser to view a World Wide Web (Web) site. You will be able to set up a simple home or office network.

If you choose to end your study of networks after this course, you will know more about those systems than most computer users. You will understand the possibilities and limitations of networking technology and will be a smarter consumer.

If your goal is to be one of the essential people who maintain and design networks, this course will prepare you for more advanced study of network administration, analysis, and design. In this course you will learn the concepts and principles that you will use every day for the rest of your networking career.

Unit 1
Computers and Software in Networks

We begin this course by taking a look at the devices a network typically connects. The most common type of network endpoint is the computer; we will describe other types of network devices later in this course.

Computers come in all shapes and sizes, and are manufactured to serve different purposes. Some computers are made for single-user operation. Other computers support a small number of users in a workgroup environment, while still others support thousands of users in a large corporation.

But all computers, from small desktop computers to powerful mainframes, use the same basic structure and contain the same types of components. Before we consider how computers communicate with each other, it makes sense to first explain the basic concepts of how computers work. Thus, after we introduce the main types of computers, this unit will introduce the main components and features of computer systems, such as:

- Central processing unit (CPU) or microprocessor
- Memory
- Input/Output (I/O)
- Network interface card (NIC)
- Application software
- Operating system (OS) software
- Device drivers
- Network management software

Lessons

1. Devices on Networks
2. Internal Computer Components: CPU, I/O, Memory, and NICs
3. Software
4. Popular OSs

Terms

beta test—A beta test is the final stage of software testing in which volunteers use a new application or OS under real-world conditions.

binary—Binary refers to the base 2 numbering system used by computers to represent information. Binary numbers consist of only two values: 1 and 0. In a binary number, each position is two times greater than the position to its right.

bit—A bit, also referred to as a binary digit, is a single value that makes up a binary number. A bit can be either 1 or 0. See binary.

bits per second (bps)—The number of binary bits transmitted per second is measured in bps. For example, common modem speeds are 28,800 bps and 56,000 bps. Another way of writing 28,800 bps is 28.8 Kbps, because "kilo" means 1,000.

bus—An external bus connects a computer to its peripheral devices. An I/O bus connects the central processor of a PC with the video controller, disk controller, hard drives, memory, and other I/O devices. See serial bus and parallel bus.

byte—One byte is equal to eight bits. See bit.

client—A client is any program that requests a service or resource from another program, either on the same computer or a different one. This term is often used to refer to the computer that hosts the client program; however, a client program may also run on a computer that normally functions as a server. See server.

criminal hacker (cracker)—A cracker is someone who gets fun or profit from breaching a secure system and possibly stealing information or damaging data.

Extended Industry Standard Architecture (EISA)—EISA is a 32-bit bus technology for PCs that supports multiprocessing. EISA was designed in response to IBM's MCA; however, both EISA and MCA were replaced by the PCI bus. See Peripheral Component Interconnect and bus.

FireWire—FireWire is a new external bus that can connect up to 63 devices and transfer up to 400 Mbps. FireWire is good for real-time applications, such as video, because it transfers data at a guaranteed and predictable rate. FireWire is a trademark of Apple Computer, who developed the technology. Other companies market the same technology under different names.

hacker—A hacker is a very skilled, curious, experimental programmer. A hack is an unorthodox, often elegant, solution to a programming problem. See criminal hacker.

host—A host is any computer system that provides a resource over a TCP/IP network. A host may be a PC, UNIX workstation, networking device, or supercomputer.

Industry Standard Architecture (ISA)—ISA is an older PC bus technology used in IBM XT and AT computers. See bus.

local area network (LAN)—A network typically confined to a single building or floor of a building is referred to as a LAN.

megahertz (MHz)—One hertz equals one cycle of a wave per second. One MHz equals 1 million cycles per second.

open source—Open-source software is software that may be used and redistributed without paying a licensing fee, and includes a copy of its source code. Vendors may sell distributions that include both the open-source software and their own added-value components (including technical support). Open-source software is popular with large organizations that often need to customize an application or OS.

parallel bus—A parallel bus is an I/O bus that carries multiple bits simultaneously. See bus and serial bus.

peer—A device or process in one computer that has the same intelligence and functionality as a device or process in another computer is referred to as a peer.

peer-to-peer—A peer-to-peer relationship refers to two programs or processes that perform approximately the same function for their respective nodes. Neither process controls the other.

Peripheral Component Interconnect (PCI)—PCI is a 64-bit local bus that allows up to 10 expansion cards to be installed in a computer. PCI technology is capable of transferring data across a PC bus at very high rates.

peripherals—Peripherals are parts of a computer that are not on the primary board (motherboard) of a computer system. Peripherals include hard drives, floppy drives, and modems.

personal digital assistant (PDA)—PDAs are small, handheld devices that provide a subset of the operations of a typical PC. They are used for scheduling, electronic notepads, and small database applications.

redirector—A redirector is a client software component in a client/server network architecture. It is normally used in reference to Novell NetWare. A redirector decides whether a request for a computer service (for example, read a file) is intended for the local computer or a network server.

serial bus—An I/O bus that carries 1 bit at a time is referred to as a serial bus. See bus and parallel bus.

server—A server is any program that provides a service to a client program. This term is often used to refer to the computer that hosts the server program; however, a server program may also run on a computer that normally functions as a client. See client.

source code—Source code refers to the programming instructions a programmer writes using a programming language. The source code of most applications and OSs is compiled into a machine language format that computers can use (but people cannot read or alter). The compiled version of a program cannot be edited; however, the original source code can be changed and recompiled.

Universal Serial Bus (USB)—USB is an external bus that can transfer up to 12 Mbps. Up to 127 peripheral devices can be connected to a single USB port.

virus—A virus is a self-replicating, malicious program that spreads by attaching itself to a file. Viruses can spread quickly through a network, with effects that range from mildly irritating to highly destructive.

Lesson 1—Devices on Networks

In addition to the computers that people use directly, many types of electronic devices can communicate with each other over a network. Any device connected to a network is called a node. Each node has its own separate identity on the network, just as each house on a street has a different address. We will explain how this addressing system works later in the course. This lesson introduces the following types of nodes a network can interconnect:

- Desktop computers

- Mid-range computers and servers

- Mainframe computers

- Personal digital assistants (PDAs)

- Peripherals

- Internetworking devices

Objectives

At the end of this lesson you should be able to:

- Name and describe the types of devices that can be connected by a network

- Explain the main differences between desktop computers, mid-range computers, and mainframes

- Describe two ways to connect a peripheral device to a network

 **Key Point**

Computers are the most common endpoints of a network; they perform unique tasks based on their size.

Desktop Computers: PCs and Workstations

A desktop computer describes any computer used by a single individual. The term "personal computer (PC)," including both non-portable and laptop/notebook computers, is generally equivalent to the term "desktop computer."

Workstations are also used by individuals, and the difference between PCs and workstations is blurry. Generally, workstations and PCs differ in the OS software they use and their processing and graphics power.

PCs based on Intel processors typically run one of the Microsoft Windows OSs; Apple PCs run the Macintosh OS. A workstation typically runs a version of the UNIX OS. We will discuss these OSs later in this unit.

A workstation often features high-end hardware, such as large, fast disk drives, large amounts of processing memory, advanced graphics capabilities, and high-performance processors.

Mid-Range Computers and Servers

The term "mid-range" covers a wide range of computer systems that support more than one user, and may support many users. It covers an extensive range of computer systems, overlapping with desktop computers at one end and mainframe computers at the other end. Mid-range computers include:

- Computers with CPUs that use the high-end Reduced Instruction Set Computer (RISC) processors (IBM AS/400)
- Intel-based servers (such as Compaq, Dell, and Hewlett-Packard)

Server systems are commonly used in small to medium organizations, such as departmental information processing. The term "server" describes a powerful computer that provides a shared resource to multiple users. Typical server functions include:

- Finance and accounting applications used by an entire department
- Databases used by entire companies
- Print servers that process print jobs from multiple users
- Communications servers that provide remote network access for off-site users, or that share Internet connections for on-site users
- World Wide Web (Web) servers that display Web pages for Web users

Mainframe Computers

Mainframe computers, which include super computers, manage huge organization-wide networks by storing and ensuring the integrity of massive amounts of crucial data. Even though PCs and mid-range computers have become increasingly powerful, they cannot compete with the unique capabilities of leading-edge mainframe systems. Mainframe computers offer several advantages:

- Very high availability—Mainframes are designed to be operated around the clock every day of the year. The term "availability" describes the percentage of time a system is ready for use. The best mainframes can achieve "five nines" availability, that is, 99.999% availability.

- Rigorous backup, recovery, and security—Mainframes provide automatic and constant backup, tracking, and safeguarding of data.

- Huge economies of scale—The centralized nature of mainframes reduces the hidden costs associated with multiple small networks, such as administration and training, extra disk space, and printers. In other words, it is cheaper to manage one big machine than many small ones.

- High capacity I/O facilities—Mainframes can quickly and effectively transfer very high volumes of data so that thousands of clients can be served simultaneously.

PDAs

To satisfy a society that is increasingly mobile, PDAs, such as the PalmPilot, have become mainstream devices in the personal computing world. PDAs now offer enough memory and storage space to support scaled-down versions of popular desktop applications, such as electronic mail (e-mail), calenders, word processing, and spreadsheets. Simplified OSs, such as the Palm OS and Pocket PC, provide a graphical interface that makes efficient use of the device's limited memory and small display format.

There are two ways a PDA can communicate over a network:

- By physically connecting to a computer that is connected to a network. When a PDA is plugged into a desktop PC, it can exchange data with the larger computer. With the right software in place, it can also indirectly access network resources through the PC.

- By plugging into a special cradle attachment connected to a network. When snapped into a network cradle, a PDA functions as an independent network node.

Handwriting recognition is still the primary method of entering text directly into a PDA. However, some PDAs now support portable keyboard attachments. As the power and flexibility of these devices continues to increase, some highly mobile users are using their PDAs as their primary computing devices.

Peripheral Devices

One of the main reasons to have a network is to share peripheral devices among many users. A freestanding device, such as a printer, can directly connect to a network if it contains a NIC. Other devices, such as hard drives, tape drives, modems, or printers without NICs, are typically installed on a network-connected computer. The computer that provides one of these shared resources is called a server. Thus, a computer that stores data on large shared hard drives is a file server, a computer that hosts a shared modem is a communications server, and so on.

Internetworking Devices

Thus far, we have discussed network nodes that actively use a network to communicate. For example, some computers need information and other computers supply that information. Or a user on one computer transfers files or messages to a user on another computer. In this way, these network nodes are like buildings along city streets.

However, some form of traffic control is necessary to keep the traffic flowing smoothly between all the nodes. In other words, our network "streets" need intersections, traffic lights, and occasional safety barricades. A special category of network nodes, called internetworking devices, performs these functions.

Internetworking devices are part of the basic infrastructure of a network. When these devices are properly set up and managed, users never notice them. However, the choice and placement of these devices can have a big effect — good or bad — on the way a network performs. We will discuss these devices in more detail later in this course.

Activities

1. Match the characteristics with the computer type (choose all that apply).

    a. Desktop/PC

    b. Mainframe

    c. PDA

    d. Mid-range

    e. Workstation

    Nearly constant availability _____

    Single-user _____

    Mobility _____

    High-end graphics _____

    High-capacity I/O _____

    Functions as a server _____

2. The highest level of computer availability is commonly called "five nines," which means 99.999%. If a mainframe achieves this level of availability, how long will it typically be down during one year?

    _____

    _____

Extended Activities

1. Break into four groups to discuss computer types. Each group will choose one type of computer, research the applications for that type of device, and make a short presentation to the other groups.

    The computer types are:

    a. Desktop computers

    b. Mid-range computers (including server systems)

    c. Mainframe computers

    d. PDAs

2. Go to various Web sites and evaluate computer products in each of the categories presented in this lesson. Start with the following:

   a. Desktop computers (**http://www.compaq.com**, **http://www.dell.com**, **http://www.gateway.com**, and **http://www.micron.com**)

   _____

   _____

   _____

   b. Mid-range computers (**http://www.hp.com**, **http://www.ibm.com**, and **http://www.sun.com**)

   _____

   _____

   _____

   c. Mainframe computers (**http://www.ibm.com**, **http://www.amdahl.com**, and **http://www.hitachi.com**)

   _____

   _____

   _____

   d. Other computers (**http://www.3com.com**, **http://www.apple.com**, **http://www.hp.com**, **http://www.ncsa.uiuc.edu**, and **http://www.oracle.com**)

   _____

   _____

   _____

3. Conduct research to learn how mainframe computers are currently being used in corporate networks and the Internet. Summarize your findings in a brief report.

Lesson 2—Internal Computer Components: CPU, I/O, Memory, and NICs

Before we can learn how computers exchange data over a network, we must first understand how data moves within the computer itself. Users often blame a network for some type of poor performance, when one of the computer's internal systems is actually at fault. This lesson introduces the main components found in most computer systems, and outlines the basic principles of the way they work.

Objectives

At the end of this lesson you should be able to:

- Explain what a CPU is and what it does

- Describe the purpose of an I/O bus

- Name the various types of memory and explain the best use of each one

- Describe what a NIC is and explain why it is necessary

 **Key Point**

All internal computer components have various levels of speed and capacity.

CPU

A CPU is the brain of a computer. It executes the instructions contained in a computer program and directs the flow of information within the computer. At the heart of a CPU is a microprocessor (a highly complex integrated circuit chip), thus the terms "microprocessor" and "CPU" are often used interchangeably. There are two basic characteristics that differentiate microprocessors:

- Data bus size—The size of the bus refers to the number of data bits a CPU can work on in a single instruction.

- Clock speed—The clock speed indicates how many instructions per second the processor can execute. Each "tick" of the clock is called a cycle, thus clock speed is measured in thousands of cycles per second. A single cycle per second is called 1 hertz (Hz), 1,000 Hz is 1 kilohertz (kHz), 1 million Hz is 1 megahertz (MHz), and 1 billion Hz is 1 gigahertz (GHz). Thus, a CPU that runs at 400,000,000 cycles per second is a 400- MHz processor.

In both cases, the higher the value, the more powerful the CPU. If two processors have the same bus size, the one with the higher clock speed will perform more work in the same time. If two CPUs have the same clock speed, the one with the larger data bus can process more data during each cycle.

The vast majority of all IBM-type PCs incorporate a single Intel architecture processor, such as Pentium. Apple PCs are based on a different processor from Motorola. The difference in these processor architectures is why these two types of computers have fundamentally different characteristics. Although Intel is the world's largest microprocessor manufacturer, it does not have the entire PC processor market. For example, Advanced Micro Devices (AMD) manufactures processors comparable to the Intel Pentium processor.

I/O

Input refers to data that enters a computer from the outside, such as keystrokes from a keyboard, mouse movements, or incoming data from another device on a network. Output is data a computer sends to the outside world, such as print jobs, alert beeps, images on the monitor screen, or outgoing data to be sent to another part of the network.

The I/O of a computer is controlled by a program called the Basic Input/Output System (BIOS). This program contains the most basic instructions in the computer and is permanently written to an area of read-only memory (ROM) (described later).

I/O data travels over its own bus, which is a collection of wires that connects all internal computer components to the CPU, main memory, and each other. The I/O bus transmits incoming and outgoing data from one part of a computer to another. The term "local bus" usually refers to a fast internal bus that connects devices directly to a CPU. An "expansion bus" connects expansion boards to the CPU and memory, as illustrated on the Computer I/O Bus Diagram.

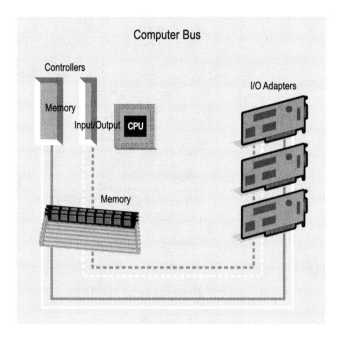

Computer I/O Bus

All buses consist of two parts: an address bus and a data bus. The data bus transfers actual data, and the address bus transfers information about where the data should go. There are two basic types of I/O bus:

• A serial bus streams data 1 bit at a time, like cars on a one-lane road.

• A parallel bus is like a multilane highway that transmits many bits simultaneously, using multiple transmission channels or wires. The size of a parallel bus, known as its width, is important because it determines how much data can be transmitted at one time. For example, a 16-bit bus can transmit 16 bits of data simultaneously, and a 32-bit bus can transmit 32 bits of data.

Every bus has a clock speed measured in MHz. A fast bus allows data to be transferred faster, making applications run faster. On PCs, the older 16-bit Industry Standard Architecture (ISA) expansion bus is being replaced by faster buses, such as the 32-bit

Peripheral Component Interconnect (PCI) bus. Newer PCs also include a local bus for data that requires especially fast transfer speeds, such as video data. The Bus Characteristics Table presents common bus technologies and their performance.

Bus Characteristics

Bus	Width (bits)	Speed (MHz)	Bandwidth (MB/sec)
8-bit ISA	8	8.33	8.3
16-bit ISA	16	8.33	16.6
Extended Industry Standard Architecture (EISA)	32	8.33	32
32-bit PCI	32	33	132
64-bit PCI	64	66	533.3
Universal Serial Bus (USB)	serial		1.2
FireWire	serial		80
USB 2.0	serial		12

The width of a bus describes the number of bits the bus can carry at one time. The term "bandwidth" describes the overall data-carrying capacity of a bus.

To find the bus bandwidth, multiply the bus width by the bus clock speed, then divide the result by the number of bits in a byte (8). The result is expressed in megabytes per second (MB/sec), which means 1 million bytes per second.

For example, the bandwidth of the PCI bus is 32 bits * 33 MHz = 1,056,000 bits per second (bps). Divide this figure by 8 bits, and the resulting bandwidth is 132 MB/sec.

Note: This is an instantaneous data burst rate figure; the average bandwidth is much lower.

Video Display

The most familiar type of computer output is its video display. A computer's video output usually does not affect the network, but may degrade the performance of an individual device by using excessive amounts of memory.

The type and quality of a monitor's image is determined both by the monitor itself, and by a circuit board called a "video adapter," "video card," or "graphics adapter." The monitor plugs into the video adapter, or video port, which generates the signals that produce the visible images.

Each combination of adapter and monitor supports a particular video display mode. From the 1970s to the present, the following display modes have been developed for Intel-based PCs:

- Monochrome—One-color text display.

- Color Graphics Adapter (CGA)—Four colors, with a maximum resolution of 320 pixels (horizontal) by 200 pixels (vertical).

- Enhanced Graphics Adapter (EGA)—Up to 16 colors, with resolution of 640 by 350 pixels.

- Video Graphics Array (VGA)—This standard allows resolution to trade off against the number of colors. For example, VGA supports 16 colors at 640 x 480 pixels, or 256 colors at 320 x 200 pixels. All Intel-based PCs support VGA, which is now considered the minimum level for PC video. Many VGA monitors are still in use.

- Extended VGA (XGA)—A later version, called XGA-2, provides 16 million colors at 800 by 600 pixel resolution, or 65,536 colors at 1,024 by 768 pixels.

- Super VGA (SVGA)—This standard, developed by the Video Electronics Standards Association (VESA), can support up to 16 million colors. However, the amount of available video memory determines the actual number of colors that can be rendered. The resolution also varies, with a choice of 800 by 600, 1,024 by 768, 1,280 by 1,024, or 1.600 by 1,200 pixels. Most computers now ship with SVGA adapters.

As we can see from this list, users who want a rich color display must pay a high price in memory. This problem is compounded by the fact that many users who need high-quality color displays also need high-speed graphics rendering that burdens a computer's CPU. For example, applications such as video or photo editing, computer-aided engineering, or scientific visualization are useless without extremely fast screen refresh times.

To remove this burden from the computer's CPU and main memory, many video adapter cards are equipped with their own dedicated memory. High-end adapters, called "video accelerators," also include a video coprocessor chip. Essentially, the coprocessor is a small CPU that only handles video display rendering.

Memory

A computer's memory holds data currently being worked on by the CPU; it is the computer's short-term storage. The term "memory" generally refers to random access memory (RAM), which comes in the form of integrated circuit chips that plug into the main circuit board (motherboard) of the computer. When we say "memory," we are often referring to the chips themselves. RAM is typically volatile, which means it needs a constant supply of electricity to hold data. If the power goes off, all data in RAM is lost.

The term "storage" is used to describe media that hold data for longer periods, even when the power goes off. Typically, computers use magnetic tapes or disks for long-term storage. However, in some cases, the concepts of memory and storage overlap. Some computers can use hard disk storage to supplement RAM in a system called "virtual memory." PDAs, and other small devices without a disk drive, often store data in programmable memory (described later).

When you run a program, it is read from storage, such as a hard drive or compact disk read-only memory (CD-ROM) drive, and put into memory for execution. After the program has completed or is no longer needed, it is typically removed from memory.

Every computer comes with a certain amount of RAM, and this supply can usually be increased by adding more memory chips. A computer that has 1 megabyte (MB) of RAM can hold approximately 1 million bytes of information. One byte can typically represent one letter of the alphabet or one numeral.

There are several different types of memory:

- RAM—RAM is the same as main memory. When used by itself, the term "RAM" refers to read and write memory; that is, you can both write data into RAM and read data from RAM. This is in contrast to ROM, which only permits a user to read data. Most RAM is volatile, which means it requires a steady flow of electricity to maintain its contents. As soon as the power is turned off, whatever data was in RAM is lost.

- ROM—Unlike RAM, ROM cannot be written to after it is initially programmed. However, the data contained in ROM is nonvolatile; data is not lost if the power is turned off. Computers almost always contain a small amount of ROM that holds instructions for starting up the computer.

- Programmable read-only memory (PROM)—A PROM is a memory chip on which you can store a program. After the PROM has been programmed, you cannot wipe it clean and reprogram it.

- Erasable programmable read-only memory (EPROM)—An EPROM is a special type of PROM that can be erased by exposing it to ultraviolet light. An EPROM can be reprogrammed and reused after it has been erased. If a computer's BIOS program is stored in EPROM, the BIOS can be upgraded when necessary.

- Electrically erasable programmable read-only memory (EEPROM)—This type of PROM can be erased and reprogrammed by an electrical signal, without having to remove the chip from its device. This makes it possible for a device to use EEPROM to record changeable data. However, although the number of times an EEPROM can be reprogrammed is large, it is also limited, thus it is not useful for main working memory.

- Flash ROM—This type of EEPROM is faster to erase and reprogram because it operates on large blocks of memory; in contrast, an EEPROM can alter individual bytes. Thus, Flash ROM is commonly used in devices that must store settings and messages, such as cell phones.

NICs

There are many types of plug-in expansion cards that add features to a computer. The one we are most concerned about in this course is the NIC. A NIC, also called a network adapter, is an expansion board that physically connects a computer to a network. A NIC fits into an expansion slot on a motherboard's I/O bus. A network cable attaches to the NIC, allowing the computer to both transmit and receive the signals that represent data as illustrated on the Connecting a NIC to the Network Diagram.

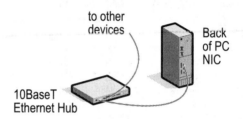

Connecting a NIC to the Network

The speed at which data may be transferred to and from a NIC is determined by many factors: the computer's I/O bus bandwidth and processor speed, design and quality of the NIC itself, computer's OS software, and type of network in use.

Different Networks, Different NICs

Each type of NIC is designed for a particular type of transmission medium (wire, radio signals, or optical fiber) and network transmission method. (We will discuss all of these a little later in this course.) Thus, a computer would need one type of NIC to send electrical signals over a copper-wired network, and a different NIC to send light pulses over a fiber optic system.

On a copper-wired network, a NIC varies the voltage level on the line in a precise pattern that represents data bits. On a fiber optic network, a NIC converts outgoing bits to flashes of light. On a wireless network, a NIC transmits bits by changing the pattern of a radio wave. In each case, the NIC also receives incoming signals as changing voltages, light flashes, or radio waves, and converts those signals into electrical bit patterns a computer can use.

Regardless of what physical medium a network uses, a NIC's job is to both generate and receive the signals that represent binary 1s and 0s. These signals must be precisely timed, thus the timing circuitry in sending and receiving NICs must be coordinated. The resulting sequence of bits is called a bit stream.

Each NIC is Unique

Each NIC contains a unique ID number which is built in at the factory. A central organization of computer manufacturers coordinates the assignment of these numbers to ensure that each ID is used by only one NIC anywhere in the world. Thus, in addition to physically transmitting and receiving signals, a NIC also uniquely identifies the device that contains it.

Each network node (computer, printer, or other device) must have a NIC to directly communicate with other nodes. However, if a resource, such as a printer, does not have a NIC, it can be indirectly connected to the network through a computer that does have a NIC. That computer can then be set to "share" its resource with other network nodes. All traffic to that printer would then pass through the computer, and not go to the printer directly.

In this way, a NIC is like a telephone. To "talk" directly with other nodes, a device must have its own communication equipment. However, if a device lacks that equipment, it can sometimes borrow it from another device, just as a person with a telephone may share it with a friend who does not have one.

Activities

1. The function of a CPU is to store programs. True or False

2. The amount of RAM determines the speed at which a CPU executes instructions. True or False

3. Look through a recent computer catalog and list the three fastest CPU speeds you find.

   _____

   _____

   _____

4. Explain the difference between RAM and ROM.

   _____

   _____

   _____

5. What is a NIC, and what is it used for?

   _____

   _____

   _____

6. Which device is associated with short-term storage: hard disk or RAM? (Circle one)

7. What determines the size of a bus: length or width? (Circle one)

8. Which is faster: an ISA bus or a PCI bus? (Circle one)

Extended Activities

1. Acquire the following computer components and use them for a "show-and-tell" session: motherboards, CPU chips, RAM chips, NICs and other expansion cards, network cabling, and anything else you might find interesting.

2. Go to any computer vendor's Web site or catalog and find prices for RAM. Pay particular attention to the various sizes offered, such as 8 MB, 16 MB, 32 MB, and 128 MB. Calculate the price per MB for the different sizes. Visit other Web sites for price comparisons.

   _____

   _____

   _____

3. Check vendors' catalogs or Web sites for memory terms such as SIMM, DIMM, EDO, SDRAM, SGRAM, then research the meaning of those terms. If you find any others, list those as well.

   _____

   _____

   _____

4. Look up information on "plug-and-play" devices. Can any type of expansion card be used in a plug-and-play environment?

   _____

   _____

   _____

5. Go to a Web site such as **http://www.webopedia.com** and find information on the accelerated graphics port (AGP) interface. Discuss how this is being used.

   _____

   _____

   _____

Lesson 3—Software

In general, software describes the changeable instructions carried out by the computing hardware. A software program does not work alone, but must cooperate with one or more other types of programs.

Software generally falls into the following broad categories:

- OSs provide a computer's basic functions.

- Networking software, included with an OS, controls network communication.

- Applications and utilities do work for users or other applications.

- Device drivers allow an OS to work with additional hardware.

- Network management tools help human administrators configure and maintain a network.

This lesson introduces each of these types of software and explains how they work together.

Objectives

At the end of this lesson you should be able to:

- Give several examples of what an OS does

- Explain what a device driver is and why it is necessary

- Explain the difference between peer-to-peer communication and client/server communication

- Describe what network management software is used for

 **Key Point**

To communicate over a network, a computer must use networking software.

Programs and Processes

The term "program" or "application" tends to mean a complete set of routines that provides a high-level function of some sort. For example, a word processing application performs the general task of creating documents.

However, that broad task is composed of many subprocesses, such as opening files, saving files, copying and pasting text, and deleting data. Therefore, in the literature of data communications, and at some points in this course, the term "process" will be used instead of "program," usually when we refer to some subset of functions (still possibly quite complex) that fits into a larger program or is part of a large system.

This distinction is important because some processes within a program are designed to communicate and cooperate with other processes over a network. Processes generally cooperate using three types of communication architectures:

- Master/slave

- Peer-to-peer

- Client/server

Master/Slave Communication

Master/slave communication often occurs when one node has much greater computing capacity than another. For example, in some networks a mainframe computer runs all the applications, stores all the data, and does all the processing. This powerful central computer is connected to a group of simple "dumb" terminals, which can only send data to the mainframe and receive responses in return.

For example, a typical master/slave relationship occurs in mainframe environments that use the IBM Systems Network Architecture (SNA). Each dumb slave client terminal has no data storage or real processing capability, but waits for the master mainframe to command it to send information. The slave merely displays text received from the master, and sends information to the master in the form of the operator's keystrokes. The Master/Slave Communications Diagram shows how a master mainframe, such as an IBM 3270, communicates with its dumb terminals through an intermediate cluster controller.

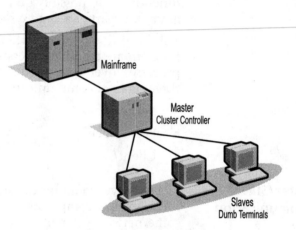

Mainframe

Master
Cluster Controller

Slaves
Dumb Terminals

Master/Slave Communications

Peer-to-Peer Communication

When two processes have roughly the same power and can perform approximately the same services for each other, we call them "peer" processes. When processes communicate as peers, neither one controls the other.

A typical neighborhood provides a good example of the way peer-to-peer communication works. Each neighbor is equal to every other neighbor, thus no single person can dictate rules to the others. However, each neighbor has unique capabilities or resources, thus they often cooperate as peers to help each other. For example, Fred can allow Joe to borrow his book, while Pat can cook a meal for Sue. Most important, there is no fixed pattern of communication among these neighbors. For example, Joe is not required to borrow books only from Fred. If Joe needs a different type of book, he can seek it from another neighbor.

A peer-to-peer computer network is created when we interconnect a group of computers of roughly equal power and function. This typically happens when a small office links the desktop computers of its employees. Each person's computer has a different set of applications and data, but the network connection allows various combinations of workers to share files, folders, applications, and printers. This type of relationship is illustrated on the Peer-to-Peer Communication Diagram.

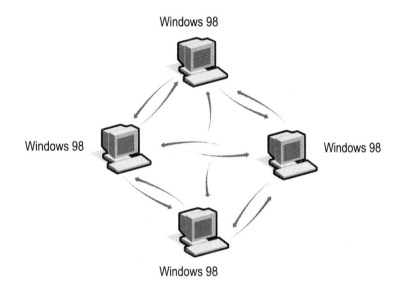

Peer-to-Peer Communication

No single computer sets the rules for these interactions. However, each computer's user can decide what resources to make available to other peer users.

**Client/Server
Communication**

Another way that processes can cooperate is for one process to take the role of client and the other that of server. Assume the neighborhood decides to store all of its books in a central lending library. Thus, instead of borrowing from each other, the neighbors can all get books from the central collection. The library functions as a "book server," and each neighbor who borrows a book is a client of that server. This arrangement is very common on networks, which often set aside computers as file servers. Everyone stores files on the common file server, which makes it easier to share data across an organization. This type of setup is presented on the Client/Server Communication Diagram.

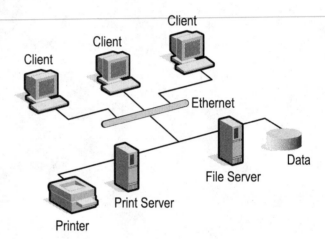

Client/Server Communication

Servers can also provide other types of resources, such as processing power, or access to peripheral devices or special applications. To see how this works, imagine that Pat opens a pizza delivery business. The entire neighborhood benefits from this efficient arrangement, because Pat has special pizza-making skills and equipment that the other neighbors do not have. All of the neighborhood's pizza-making expertise, equipment, and materials are now concentrated in Pat's Pizza Server. Now if Sue (the client) wants a pizza, she does not make it herself. Instead, she calls Pat (the server), who delivers one to her door.

Just as a customer orders a pizza, client and server processes interact with each other by transmitting request/reply pairs. The client process initiates an interaction by issuing a request to the server. The server process responds with a reply satisfying the request.

This request/reply communication essentially divides a task into two parts, and executes each part on a different system on the network. For example, the task of creating a report can be divided into two portions. In the client part of the task, a worker uses a desktop application to define what information a report should contain, then sends that report definition as a request to the server. (The user clicks a button to tell the server to generate the report.) When the server receives the request, it retrieves the requested data, formats the report, and replies by sending the information back to the client.

Both client and server processes are dedicated to their respective tasks, and those roles never reverse. In other words, the library does not borrow books from its users, and Pat will never ask one of the neighbors to cook a pizza for her. However, the same computing machine can run multiple processes. Some of those processes can be servers of some functions, and some can be clients of other servers. Thus, it is important to remember that "server" refers to a process, not necessarily a particular machine.

Also, peer-to-peer communication can still occur on a client/server network. If servers have been established for shared functions, such as file sharing or printing, this does not prevent two computers from exchanging data as peers.

Client/server architecture has two primary advantages:

- Distributed applications—Applications can be distributed on the network based on their requirements for resources. For example, an application that provides computing-intensive services can be installed on a computer with very high processing capacity, while the user's client application runs on a workstation that provides high-end graphic display capabilities.

- Resource sharing—A server process typically can serve many clients, thus client/server architecture is a good way to share many types of resources across an organization.

Peers, Servers, and Hosts

When a computer provides a resource to other computers, that computer is often called a "host." A host can be either a user's PC on a peer-to-peer network or a server in a client/server network. The term is often used to describe any computer capable of two-way communication over the Internet. However, in general, "host" refers to a computer that provides files, applications, or other resources.

Application Software

Applications are software programs used to perform work. Some applications are designed to be directly used by a person, while others interact only with other applications. In either case, each application is a tool made to do a specific job.

Applications can be divided into two basic categories: single-user applications and networked or multiuser applications. Some applications run primarily as single-user applications, and others run almost exclusively as networked applications. Some applications can run in both modes. Commonly used applications include:

- Word processors—A word processor is used to enter, edit, format, print, and save text documents, such as letters, memos, and reports.

- Desktop publishing—Desktop publishing goes beyond basic word processing. It is used to design professional publications, such as magazines, books, and newspapers.

- Graphics—Graphics programs are used to create images that are used by themselves or imported into other documents using programs such as desktop publishing packages.

- Databases—A database is an electronic filing system that categorizes data for quick retrieval. Database management applications create and maintain records for many types of organizations, from universities to small clubs.

- Spreadsheets—Spreadsheet applications are primarily used to organize numeric information for analysis and reporting. They make it possible to quickly analyze complex financial records.

- Web browsers—Web browsers are used to locate and retrieve information from the Web. They are primarily used to view Internet Web sites or search the Internet for specific information.

- Utilities—These tools are used to manage and configure the computer and its software. They do not help a user accomplish tasks, but they are necessary to keep the system itself in good working order. There are a huge number of utilities available, from screen savers to antivirus applications.

All of the applications listed above may be used in a single-user mode or a network (multiuser) mode, provided a particular software application is designed to support multiuser access. For example, a networked application can allow more than one user to view the same file simultaneously, and it will allow only one user to make changes at any one time. However, a single-user application does not have this capability.

Network Applications

There is also a category of "pure" networked applications, or client/server applications, that assume they will always be used by multiple users. These applications usually include two complementary applications: one for installation on the server, and one for installation on multiple client desktops.

These network applications often run on dedicated computers. There are many types of server applications; some of the most common are:

- Database server—A database server application controls multiple access to a single shared data repository. In response to requests from various clients, the central database management application can retrieve, add, delete, or update records.

- Print server—A print server allows multiple clients to efficiently share a single printer. All print requests are sent to the print server, so that each user's computer is freed for other work. The print server prints each job in turn, and notifies each client when its print job has been completed.

- Fax server—A fax server is similar to a print server, but allows multiple users to share a fax device.

- E-mail server—An e-mail server retrieves all users' mail messages from a company's Internet service provider (ISP), and stores them until each user is ready to read them. When a user logs on to the network and requests mail, the e-mail server transfers those e-mail messages to the user's computer.

- Web server—A Web server provides access to a Web site. When a distant browser (Web client) requests a Web page, the Web server application retrieves that page and transmits it back to the browser that requested it.

OSs

An OS is a suite of software programs that provide the basic functions of a computer, such as reading and writing files, running applications, and managing I/O. To understand what an OS does, imagine a very rich household. This family has so much money that they employ a large staff of servants to make their lives comfortable. The servants handle every detail of the home, from cooking meals to washing clothes, and even opening and closing windows. To get a household job done, the rich family simply calls on "the help." This arrangement leaves the family free to think about the stock market, parties, and golf.

Computer applications are like this rich family. Each application focuses on its particular task and does not concern itself with mundane (and demanding) chores, such as reading and writing to memory or disks, reading input from a keyboard, displaying output to a monitor, or printing a file. When an application needs to perform one of these jobs, it makes a request to the OS. Thus, an OS provides the basic infrastructure that supports any number of high-level applications.

The most common tasks of an OS include:

- Managing the operation of applications

- Controlling applications' access to memory

- Interpreting input from keyboard, mouse, and other input devices

- Displaying data to the computer screen

- Reading and writing files on disks

- Controlling peripheral devices, such as floppy disks, hard disks, and printers

Two Important Points

There are two important points about OSs. First, each OS is designed to control a particular type of computer CPU. Thus, an OS for an Intel Pentium platform cannot run on a computer such as an Apple Macintosh, that uses the PowerPC processor. Similarly, an OS designed for a 16-bit processor may not be able to run on a 32-bit processor; if it does run, it will only provide 16-bit performance. As we discuss particular types of OSs in the next lesson, you will see that some of them are called "32-bit applications." This means they are designed to control a 32-bit CPU.

Second, the services of an OS are not optional for the applications. In other words, an OS does not allow an application to directly read and write to memory, even if the application programmer wanted to do that. Back in the days when a computer ran only one application at a time, each application could use the system's resources much more freely. However, today's OSs run multiple applications simultaneously. To do this, the OS must strictly control each program's access to resources, such as memory or disk space. This feature, called "protected memory," prevents one program from interfering with any other.

GUIs

In older OSs, such as Microsoft Disk Operating System (MS-DOS) and UNIX, a user interacted with the OS through a set of typed commands. These instructions were accepted and executed by a part of the OS called the "command processor" or "command line interpreter." To use these command-line systems, a user had to learn and remember the syntax of each command.

Graphical user interfaces (GUIs) were added to OSs to allow a user to enter commands by pointing and clicking at objects and menu items on the screen. While this approach places more burden on computer resources, it made computers much easier to learn and use.

Basic OS Features

OSs can be classified according to which of the following features they support:

- Multitasking—Allows multiple programs to run on the CPU simultaneously. Preemptive multitasking allows multiple applications to request the attention of the user when necessary, so that one program does not always remain in the "foreground."

- Multithreading—Allows different parts of a single program to run simultaneously.

- Multiuser—Allows multiple users to run programs on the same computer simultaneously. Some OSs running on large-scale computers permit hundreds or even thousands of concurrent users.

- Multiprocessing—Supports running a program on more than one CPU at the same time.

Just as each OS is written to run on a particular CPU, each application program is written to run on a particular OS. Therefore, the choice of OS largely determines the applications a user can run.

Networking Features in OSs

OS software is also categorized according to the type of network communication it can enable:

- Peer-to-peer networking software is included with most popular desktop OSs. To create a simple peer-to-peer network, users physically connect their computers, then configure this software on each desktop machine. Each individual user configures software settings to allow or disallow the sharing of that computer's resources by other users. There is no central authority that decides what users may have access to what resources.

- A network OS (NOS), also called a client/server OS, has sophisticated features that identify individual computer users and assign them permission to access various resources. By far, the most common NOS packages are Novell NetWare and Microsoft Windows NT.

  Unlike a peer-to-peer network, a client/server NOS provides centralized control of all network resources. A network administrator can decide exactly what each user may see and do on the network.

  A key feature of a NOS is network redirection software that determines whether a request from a process is intended for a process on the same computer or a process on a computer across the network. Applications access network services through this redirection software. A NOS typically also provides client software, called System Status Messaging Services, to open windows for status messages from remote servers.

Device Drivers

A device driver is a special-purpose application that controls a specific hardware device, such as a hard disk drive, floppy disk drive, modem, printer, scanner, or NIC. Device drivers control the operation of a device and provide an interface for the computer's OS.

To understand how this works, think back to our analogy of the rich family (applications) with servants (the OS). Now imagine that the oldest son loves Italian cooking, so he hires a chef from Italy. None of the household staff (the OS) knows how to speak Italian, so no cooking gets done until they also hire an Italian translator. Now everyone is happy: the older son asks the household staff for lasagna, the staff passes the order to the translator, the translator instructs the chef, and the meal is cooked.

In a computer system, a device driver plays the role of the translator. A computer can be equipped with a nearly endless number of peripheral devices, and it is impossible for an OS to know how to communicate with all of them. Thus, each hardware device usually comes with a small software application (device driver), which contains all of the specialized instructions that allow the OS to use the device.

Each device manufacturer provides drivers for its own equipment. The major OSs often include device drivers for the most popular peripheral devices; however, those drivers were originally provided by the manufacturers.

Network Management Software

A network also requires software to manage and maintain the network itself. This type of software differs from application software in the fact that these programs are not used for individual productivity.

Network management and utility software is typically used by network administrators and information systems personnel. Communication and management software includes:

- Network security utilities
- Network management tools
- Network remote access services
- Network backup and recovery utilities

Network Security Utilities

In its broadest sense, network security means that network users have access to only the information and systems necessary to do their jobs. For example, only Human Resources personnel or supervisors should be able to view confidential employee records, and only the network administrators should be able to access the applications that control the network itself. NOSs include features to establish this level of security.

However, a network must also be protected from intentional attack from inside or outside an organization. Most businesses fail to recognize that the data flowing over their networks is an extremely valuable asset that is often easily accessible and exposed to various threats. Network security specialists classify these threats as follows:

- Criminal hackers (crackers)—Insiders or outsiders motivated by the thrill of breaching a secure system without detection. Crackers tend to be more concerned about developing subtle techniques for penetrating systems and are not necessarily interested in stealing data. In contrast, the term "hacker" generally refers to a highly skilled and clever programmer.

- Script kiddies—Unskilled intruders, often teenagers, who use readily-available programs or methods to exploit known weaknesses in Internet hosts. Unlike hackers, script kiddies have little understanding of the systems they penetrate and are more interested in getting attention.

- Bandits—Insiders or outsiders who use hacking techniques to steal data or disrupt systems for personal gain.

- Trojan horses—Covert programs hidden in system or application software that wait to suddenly destroy information using predetermined parameters. Once inside a system, some Trojan horses can also use e-mail messages to transmit confidential data out of an organization.

- Viruses—Self-replicating destructive programs designed to damage systems and networks by eroding executable programs until they are unusable.

Network security utilities are designed to prevent one or more of these threats. To prevent network failures and damage to an organization's assets, network administrators and information system managers often implement multiple layers of security utilities and other defenses.

Network Management Tools

Network management tools generally consist of the following functions:

- Configuration tools shape a network into logical areas, assign addresses to computers, and perform other organizational tasks.

- Troubleshooting tools measure network traffic and other conditions to help an administrator track down the cause of a problem.

- Event notification tools automatically alert an administrator when certain types of conditions occur. Network devices that use the Simple Network Management Protocol (SNMP) can be configured to notify the administrator of potential problems before they disrupt the network. (Protocols are discussed in the next unit.)

- Metrics and planning tools measure current network conditions and simulate the effect of proposed changes. For example, these tools can estimate how much traffic a network will carry if 50 more users are added.

Depending on the size and complexity of a network, these categories are all necessary to some degree.

Remote Access Services

Not only do users expect to have computers at their desks, but they also expect to have remote network connectivity. Print services, file services, and other special local area network (LAN) applications are essential for telecommuters, traveling professionals, and mobile users. The ability to work anywhere at any time is creating the need for secure remote LAN access.

Early remote access methods merely took control of a dedicated PC on a corporate network; however, this solution is very inefficient. More recently, network modems and multiuser communication servers have emerged to provide more efficient and secure access to an organization's electronic resources and network services.

Backup and Recovery Utilities

The information stored on servers and individual hard drives is the lifeblood of a company. The loss of critical information can be devastating. Therefore, a network manager is usually responsible for ensuring that all company data is regularly backed up and safely stored, and that procedures are in place to restore that data quickly in case of a disaster or emergency.

Backup and recovery software simplifies this important process by allowing an administrator to automatically run a complete system backup when the network is unused or lightly used, often in the middle of the night.

Activities

1. An application does not need to use the services of an OS, as long as the application is written to perform those tasks on its own. True or False

2. _____ means that an OS can allow one program to run on multiple CPUs.

3. _____ means that an OS can allow more than one program to run at a time.

4. A _____ OS allows many concurrent users.

5. List at least three tasks performed by OSs.

   _____

   _____

   _____

6. Controlling peripheral devices, such as floppy disks, hard disks, and printers. A _____ _____ controls an item of add-on hardware.

7. List at least three network server applications.

   _____

   _____

   _____

   _____

8. How would you go about getting the latest version of a device driver for a 3Com 3C905 NIC?

   _____

   _____

   _____

9. For each task below, indicate whether computers are using peer-to-peer communication, master/slave communication, or client/server communication.

   a. Mary saves a file to Joe's hard disk.

   _____

   b. Frank retrieves information from the company's central database.

   _____

   c. A data entry clerk uses a dumb terminal to update records.

   _____

   d. You use a Web browser to visit your favorite Web site.

   _____

   e. In a small office, three users share the same printer.

   _____

   f. In a large office, the shared printer is attached to a computer on the network. Print jobs from all users are sent to that computer, which controls the printing.

   _____

10. List at least five functions typical of network management programs.

    _____

    _____

    _____

    _____

    _____

Extended Activities

1. Go to **http://www.netcraft.com** and list the usage rates for the various Web server software programs.

   _____

   _____

2. What are the major database products? Where are these typically being used (for example, large organizations or small businesses)?

   _____

   _____

3. On the Web, go to **http://www.easydos.com** and use the DOS command index to learn how to enter a DOS command. For each of the tasks listed below, provide the name of the DOS command to use.

   a. Copy a file

   _____

   b. Delete a file

   _____

   c. Display the current directory

   _____

   d. Move to a different directory

   _____

   e. Create a new directory

   _____

   f. Delete a directory

   _____

4. If your PC is running Windows, this exercise will help you appreciate the value of a GUI. First, create a file, such as a word processing document. (The content of the file is not important.) Now, double-click the MS-DOS Prompt icon to open a DOS window. Perform the following tasks using the DOS commands you just learned. Have a partner record how much time you need to complete these steps using DOS commands.

   a. Display the contents of the current directory.

   b. Create a new subdirectory called "TEST."

   c. Move to the directory that contains the test file you just created.

   d. Copy your test file to the TEST directory.

   e. Move to the TEST directory.

   f. Display the contents of the TEST directory.

   g. Delete the test file.

   h. Remove the TEST directory.

   i. Close the DOS window by typing EXIT, then pressing Enter.

   Now perform the same tasks using Windows Explorer. Once again, have your partner record how much time you need to complete these steps using the graphical interface.

Lesson 4—Popular OSs

In the last lesson, we discussed the main functions of an OS. In this lesson, we introduce the most common OSs used in LANs today. As we look at the features of each of these OSs, you will see that some support peer-to-peer networking, while others are full NOSs.

Objectives

At the end of this lesson you should be able to:

- Name the two most popular NOSs

- Explain how an embedded OS is different from a typical computer OS

- Discuss some of the reasons why Linux is becoming a strong competitor to commercial OSs

 **Key Point**

Microsoft Windows is installed on most desktop computers; however, other OSs are also popular on network servers.

Microsoft Windows

Microsoft has dominated the desktop PC OS market more or less since its foundation, first with its disk operating system (DOS) for Intel processors, and then with the Windows user interface.

Windows Desktop OSs

Windows began as a GUI for Intel-based PCs that ran on top of DOS. Early versions of Windows were unreliable until the 1990 launch of Windows 3, which became the industry-standard platform for the desktop PC market. That 16-bit OS has since been succeeded by a series of upgraded and redesigned products:

- Windows for Workgroups 3.11 was Microsoft's first peer-to-peer NOS. It was a combination of Windows 3.1 and the Microsoft Windows Network software (which provided the peer-to-peer networking capability), with enhancements such as improved disk I/O performance, connectivity and remote access, and a range of features intended to appeal to the network manager.

- Windows 95, Microsoft's next peer-to-peer OS, was a major departure from Windows 3.*x*. It was the first true Windows OS, not just a GUI added onto DOS. To take advantage of the new 32-bit processors, Windows 95 provided preemptive multitasking and multiple threads for 32-bit applications. Windows 95 also ran 16-bit DOS and Windows applications; however, those applications did not get the full performance benefits of the new OS. Windows 95 was the first OS to support the Plug-and-Play (PnP) standard, which greatly simplified hardware installation. Other enhancements included improvements to the user interface, long file names, video playback, better fax and modem support, improved system administration, and remote network access.

- Windows 98 was an enhancement to Windows 95. It added the Active Desktop, which integrates a Web browser (Internet Explorer 4.0) with the underlying OS. From the user's point of view, there is little difference between accessing a document on the user's hard disk, or on a network server or Web server halfway across the world.

  Windows 95 and 98 are not processor-independent. For example, they will not run on the Apple's PowerPC processor. Those features are provided with the Windows NT OS (described later).

- Windows Millennium Edition (Windows ME) is the latest enhancement of Windows 98. It added features targeted to home users and families, such as Internet communication tools, online games, support for broadband Internet connections (such as cable modems), and tools to manage and edit digital images and music.

Windows NT

Windows NT, Microsoft's 32-bit client/server OS, was first launched in July 1993. It was targeted at advanced business network environments, and can be run on virtually every major processor including Intel, Alpha, and PowerPC. It is substantially more stable and reliable than Windows 98/ME, and offers graphical administration utilities that make it easier to manage than the dominant NOS at that time, Novell NetWare.

Windows NT includes two products:

- Windows NT Workstation offers the same user interface as Windows 98/ME, but with enhanced stability and security features.

- Windows NT Server is a client/server OS designed for heavily used network servers. By running each application in a strictly-separate memory space, this OS ensures that one application can crash without bringing down the others.

Windows 2000

For marketing purposes, many companies released new products near the turn of the new century. Microsoft was no different; however, it did have legitimate reasons for creating the Windows 2000 suite of OSs.

It had been 10 years since the release of Windows 3.*x*, which set the technical assumptions and methods that shaped all of the desktop OS releases through Windows ME. Likewise, Windows NT was seven years old, which is a very long time in the computing world. In the decade since 1990, PCs had undergone staggering increases in speed and storage. Applications were doing things with the new capacity that were unheard of in 1990, and computer users had learned to expect those extremely sophisticated features to work flawlessly.

Rather than upgrade Windows NT 4 to version 5, Microsoft decided to use the Windows NT version 5 technology as the basis for its next major departure in both desktop and server OSs. As you can see on the Windows Product History Diagram, all new Microsoft OSs are based on the more secure, more stable Windows NT technology.

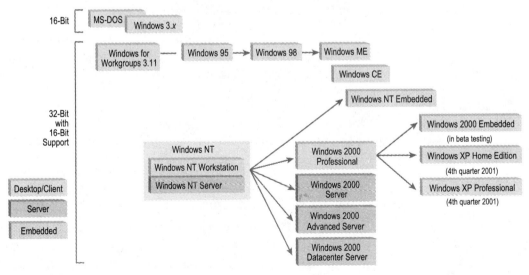

Windows Product History

The Windows 2000 family (which are limited to Pentium-compatible platforms) includes four OSs:

- Windows 2000 Professional is a desktop OS for individuals and businesses of all sizes. It includes improved security and enhancements for laptop computers.

- Windows 2000 Server is for Web servers or office servers in small- to medium-sized businesses.

- Windows 2000 Advanced Server is for larger business servers, especially those that host large databases.

- Windows 2000 Datacenter Server is designed for the very largest corporate databases (called data warehouses) and other applications requiring high-speed computation and large data storage.

At this writing, Microsoft has announced plans to release two new desktop OSs in late 2001. The Windows XP OS will be the first one that offers one version for business applications and one version specifically designed for home users.

Embedded OSs

During the late 1990s, the number of home computers grew dramatically, mainly due to falling hardware prices. Although this aspect of computing got most of the public's attention, a quieter revolution was already under way.

A new generation of small, intelligent devices was emerging, ranging from PDAs to cable television set-top controllers, and cell phones to industrial sensors. These devices needed an OS tailored to the demanding requirements of their compact hardware design. The primary needs of small platforms include the following:

- Widely varying services from the OS—Unlike computers, which all perform essentially the same jobs, these small devices are very different from one another. For example, a PDA must write to a very small screen, but a television set-top box or industrial gauge does not even have a display.

- Little or no writable storage—On a computer, the OS is stored on a hard drive and it can use that hard drive to record changing settings as it works. However, a compact device may have no writable disk storage at all. The OS is burned into ROM or flash memory, and must use small amounts of RAM or programmable memory to keep track of its own work. An OS must work in a fundamentally different way under these conditions.

- Low memory usage—Small devices contain much less memory, of any type, than the simplest PC, thus the OS must be extremely lean and efficient. Preferably, the OS should provide only those services the device actually needs.

- Efficient power usage—Many of these devices run on battery power, thus the OS must operate in a way that conserves electricity.

To meet these needs, some hardware vendors developed proprietary OSs for their own devices, such as the popular Palm OS for the PalmPilot. To serve the market for small devices in general, Microsoft began developing special "embedded" OSs that meet the requirements listed above.

Thus far, Microsoft has released two embedded OSs, and a third is in beta testing at the time of this writing. The OSs feature a modular architecture that allows programmers to select the features of an OS that each device requires:

- Windows CE is designed for small consumer electronics, small communication equipment, industrial devices, and other relatively simple intelligent systems.

- Windows NT Embedded is for more sophisticated server-type hardware systems, such as telecommunication switching equipment and medical devices.

- Windows 2000 Embedded, in beta testing at this writing, is targeted toward client-type devices, such as Windows-based terminals, advanced set-top boxes, and retail point-of-sale kiosks.

Novell NetWare

Microsoft was a relative latecomer to networking. By the time Windows NT was released in 1993, Novell NetWare already had a decade of experience as a NOS, with a large installed base of loyal customers. Windows NT has gradually become a real competitor to NetWare; however, Novell products are still a major force in the networking industry, especially among very large corporations.

NetWare began in 1983 as "Sharenet," a way to share files between PCs. At a time when only mainframes and minicomputers were available, it was the first application to provide file and printing services to the growing PC desktop environment. NetWare evolved with the industry, moving away from dumb terminals toward connectivity for DOS, Windows, Macintosh, OS/2, and UNIX workstations.

NetWare has evolved from file and print sharing to become a richly featured NOS. Today, Novell is the world's fifth largest software vendor, with an installed base of 4.3 million servers, representing 81 percent of the Fortune 500 companies. This number increases continuously as Novell provides powerful networking solutions and services that benefit corporate and Web-based enterprises. Novell has built on this experience by expanding into Web services, management, communication, publishing, security, applications, and databases.

UNIX

UNIX is an open architecture OS that has been around since the early 1970s. Several versions of UNIX (both 32-bit and 64-bit) exist, each produced by a different vendor with some compiled for only that vendor's hardware. Some of the most common "flavors" are HP-UX of Hewlett-Packard, Sun Microsystems SunOS for Solaris systems, IRIX of Silicon Graphics Inc., and OpenServer/ UNIXWare/Gemini of Santa Cruz Operation (SCO).

Three components make up the UNIX OS:

- The kernel contains the core OS functions.

- The file system manages data stored on disks.

- The shell is the command-line user interface.

Just as Windows 3.11 was a separate application that provided a GUI for DOS, UNIX gets its GUI from separate applications. The best known of these is the X Window System, often called XWindows or simply X.

Unlike Windows NT and NetWare, UNIX is not composed of separate client and server components. Instead, networking capabilities are built into the kernel, thus UNIX can be used on both client and server platforms. As with all client/server processes, UNIX waits for client commands, and then executes the commands.

The main strength of any UNIX platform is the longevity of the OS. UNIX has been used in academia and industry since the 1970s; few products in the computer industry can boast such an accomplishment. The stability, functionality, and reliability of UNIX are beyond question.

UNIX is the OS the Internet was built on, and it is still the preferred OS for many Internet applications and servers. UNIX is the strategic platform for many vendors, including Sun Microsystems and Hewlett-Packard. It is also the dominant OS on mid-range systems and workstations that run engineering or scientific applications. Some workstation vendors, including Sun Microsystems, only offer UNIX on their platforms, and UNIX is used on many IBM mainframes.

Although UNIX has a solid future, its success has not been universal. The mid-range software market is characterized by competition between UNIX, which runs on a very wide range of hardware platforms, and the proprietary operating environments designed specifically for interactive multiuser applications developed by the leading system vendors. Some vendors only offer UNIX on their platforms (for example, Sun Microsystems with Solaris). Other vendors accept and support multiple operating environments: Windows on PCs; Windows NT, Linux, UNIX, or NetWare on LAN servers; UNIX on mid-range servers; and proprietary environments on mid-range systems and mainframes that need higher-than-average reliability and security.

Linux

Linux is an open-source (freeware) version of UNIX created as a class project by a Finnish graduate student named Linux Torvalds. By distributing the source code for the kernel (core program) over the Internet, and actively encouraging any and all to participate in its development, Linux has grown into a widely respected NOS.

One of the strengths cited by Linux devotees is that it is based entirely on new technology. While commercial versions of UNIX are all based on source code that may be decades old, Linux was entirely developed within this decade. And, because Linux is open-source software, an organization's programmers can modify it to meet their unique needs.

Linux offers all of the legendary stability of UNIX and regularly outperforms commercial OS packages on benchmark tests. As a result, more than one-fourth of all new network servers are now being shipped with Linux installed.

Another advantage of Linux is cost. Linux is freeware, thus distributors can charge only for the distribution media and any proprietary software and support included with the media. The market has fixed the price of most Linux distributions to a range of $30 to $50, and a one-time purchase allows a company to install the software on all of its computers. In contrast, an organization must purchase a separate license of Windows for each individual computer it owns. This factor alone can make Linux extremely attractive for a large company.

The most significant criticism of open-source software is lack of vendor support. Vendors of commercial NOSs justify their high prices, in part, by offering continued support for their products. Open-source software is supported by a "community" of programmers and users willing to provide assistance. However, open-source vendors typically include technical support, development tools, and documentation with their freeware distributions. This growing vendor accountability is one of the key reasons open-source software is entering the business mainstream.

Mac OS

Mac OS is Apple's OS for its Macintosh desktop computers and high-powered servers. Mac OS only runs on the Apple PowerPC processor, which was specifically designed to provide superior handling of images, color, and sound.

To take advantage of these hardware-based features, some high-end graphics and multimedia applications are only available for Mac OS, and those that run on both Macintosh and Windows generally offer more powerful multimedia features in their Macintosh versions. As a result, publishing, illustration, Web design, and advertising businesses generally choose Macintosh.

The latest version of Mac OS is OS X (OS Ten), which is based on one of the more popular flavors of UNIX. As such, it runs both Macintosh and UNIX applications. The core of OS X is open-source software, distributed under Apple's Open Source license.

Like Windows NT, OS X offers protected memory and preemptive multitasking. Like the new embedded OSs, OS X also uses a modular architecture for simplified updates and extensions of the OS.

With a much smaller market share than Windows, Mac OS includes a number of enhancements that simplify working with Windows disks and files. Mac OS also includes QuickTime, Apple's multimedia software that enables users to view full-screen video and edit video or music.

Apple's proprietary suite of networking software, called Apple-Talk, is also a standard feature of Mac OS. An application called AppleShare allows a Macintosh computer to perform as a file server on an AppleTalk network.

Activities

1. List at least five OSs that run on PCs or PC servers.

   _____

   _____

   _____

   _____

   _____

2. Contrast the functions/characteristics of an application program with an OS.

   _____

   _____

   _____

   _____

   _____

   _____

   _____

   _____

   _____

3. How is an embedded OS different from a typical computer OS?

   _____

   _____

   _____

   _____

   _____

   _____

   _____

   _____

Extended Activities

1. Using a research tool, such as an Internet search engine, list as many different "flavors" of UNIX OSs as you can find, and describe the hardware platform and applications that each type is typically used for.

   _____

   _____

   _____

2. Conduct research to find what other GUIs are available for UNIX-type OSs.

   _____

   _____

   _____

3. Visit the Web site of the Open Source Initiative at **http://www.opensource.org** to find out more about open-source software. Why is freeware becoming so attractive? How can anyone make money distributing software this way? Write a short paper that explains this growing trend in software development.

4. Conduct research to learn how virus protection programs work. Summarize your findings in a short report.

Summary

We began this course reviewing the essential components and functions of various types of computers. Each class of computers is defined by size, processing power, and bandwidth. It is important to note that each computer type serves a particular purpose. Servers act as local distributors of information. PCs are largely for single-user productivity or access to mainframes. Mainframes provide mass storage and high-end processing. PDAs provide simple storage and processing in a pocket-sized mobile device.

The internal components of these types of computers have a varying amount of capacity and power. However, all computers, from PDAs to mainframes, include the same basic components. A CPU processes information; the amount of work it can do depends on its clock speed and bandwidth. The I/O bus transfers data between input components, output devices, the CPU, memory, and other internal computer components. Like the CPU, there are a variety of I/O bus types, each with its own performance characteristics. Computer memory ranges from volatile RAM to various types of nonvolatile ROM.

To physically connect to a network, a computer must be equipped with a NIC. Each type of network cable connection requires a different type of NIC. The performance of a NIC depends on the performance of the computer's other components.

The computer hardware is controlled by the OS software and device drivers. An OS is a suite of software that manages applications, user interfaces, storage, and internal and external components. The OS provides many low-level services, such as reading and writing to disks, handling I/O, and assigning memory and processing time to multiple applications. Device drivers are like small OS modules that control internal and external accessories, such as disk drives, network connections, and printers.

Microsoft Windows is the dominant OS for desktop PCs. However, NOSs such as Novell NetWare, UNIX, and Linux are also common on larger systems, such as workstations, servers, midrange computers, and mainframes.

Application software is what a user sees and works with; applications are tools that help a user to be productive. The application software uses the underlying OS to perform low-level functions, such as file access and management. Some of the most common types of applications include word processors, spreadsheets, databases, games, and Web browsers. Some applications are designed for one user at a time, while others are made to support multiple simultaneous users on a network.

Network management and utility software is considered a distinct category of software, separate from user applications. This software is used by network and system administrators for managing and accessing network or computer OSs. Network management tools help keep a network healthy by monitoring data traffic flow, managing storage backup and recovery, providing remote network access, and preventing or eliminating viruses.

Unit 1 Quiz

1. List the four computer classifications, in order of processing power.

   _____

   _____

2. List four features of a mainframe.

   _____

   _____

3. What components are common to all computer systems?

   _____

   _____

4. What does I/O stand for?

   _____

5. Which is an example of a processor's clock speed?

   a. 400 MHz

   b. 64 bit

6. What is the difference between RAM and ROM?

   _____

   _____

7. A NIC is a device used for:

   a. Storage

   b. Processing

   c. Signaling

   d. Memory

8. If you buy a computer today, which of the following video display mode is it likely to support?

   a. VGA

   b. CGA

   c. SVGA

   d. EGA

9. Which of the following users is likely to need a video accelerator?

   a. A secretary performing data entry

   b. An engineer generating three-dimensional design renderings

   c. An analyst performing database queries

   d. An accountant producing large reports

10. Name the four features that distinguish different OSs.

    _____

    _____

11. Which of the following is managed by the OS?

    a. Keyboard input

    b. Screen display

    c. File I/O

    d. Peripheral control

    e. All of the above

12. List at least two OSs used on client/server networks.

    _____

    _____

13. What is the primary purpose of a device driver?

    _____

    _____

14. Who creates a device driver?

    a. OS vendor

    b. Device manufacturer

    c. Application publisher

    d. Open-source programming community

15. Which two of the following is not based on open-source software (choose two)?

    a. Windows NT

    b. Linux

    c. Mac OS X

    d. Windows 2000

Unit 2
Carrier Signals, Cable Types, and Network Topologies

In Unit 1, we discussed the types of devices that can communicate over a network. In this unit, we consider the physical qualities of the network itself.

We begin by discussing the nature of electronic communication and explain how information can be transmitted as analog or digital signals. We then explore the various physical layouts or topologies of data networks, and show how the pattern of signal flow depends on the topology of the network.

We then describe the characteristics of the three main types of physical transmission media used in networks: copper cable, fiber optic cable, and wireless communication (radio waves). We will learn how signals travel over each media, and their relative advantages and disadvantages.

As you work through this unit, it is important to remember that there is no "best" network topology or physical medium. A network designer's choice of topology and cabling (or lack of it) is determined by the type of work the network must do, and the type of physical environment it must work in.

Lessons

1. Communication and Signals
2. Network Topologies
3. Copper Cable
4. Fiber Optic Cable
5. Wireless Transmission
6. Overview of a Structured Cable Plant

Terms

amplitude—Amplitude is the height of a wave, or how far from the center it swings.

analog—A signal transmitted as a pattern of continually changing electromagnetic waves is referred to as an analog signal.

American National Standards Institute (ANSI)—ANSI is a U.S. voluntary organization that develops and publishes standards for data communications, programming languages, magnetic storage media, office systems, and encryption. ANSI represents the United States as a member of ISO and IEC.

asynchronous—Asynchronous operation means that bits are not transmitted on any strict timetable. Transmitting a start bit indicates the start of each character. After the final bit of the character is transmitted, a stop bit is sent, indicating the end of the character. The sending and receiving modems must stay in synchronization only for the length of time it takes to transmit the 8 bits. If their clocks are slightly out of synch, data transfer will still be successful.

backbone—A backbone is the portion of a network that carries the most significant traffic. It is also the part of the network that connects many smaller networks to form a larger network.

bandwidth—Bandwidth is a measure of the information-carrying capacity of a channel. In analog networks, bandwidth is the difference between the highest and lowest frequencies that can be transmitted across a communication link. Analog networks measure bandwidth in cycles per second (Hz). Digital networks measure bandwidth in Kbps, Mbps, and Gbps.

baseband—Baseband is a form of digital modulation in which one signal takes up the entire available bandwidth of the communication channel.

binary—Binary refers to the base 2 numbering system used by computers to represent information. Binary numbers consist of only two values: 1 and 0. In a binary number, each position is two times greater than the position to its right.

bit—A bit, also referred to as a binary digit, is a single value that makes up a binary number. A bit can be either 1 or 0. See binary.

BNC connector—BNC connectors are small devices used to connect computers to a thin coaxial cable bus (10Base2) or terminate the ends of a bus. There are several different types of BNC connectors. A BNC barrel connector joins two Thinnet cables. A BNC terminator is used to terminate the end of a cable. It acts as a resistive load that absorbs the signal that reaches one end of the bus. (Two terminators are needed on each bus.) BNC adapters connect different types of cable, such as Thinnet to Thicknet.

broadband—Broadband is a communication medium with enough bandwidth to carry multiple signals simultaneously. A broadband analog system assigns each signal to a different band of frequencies. A broadband digital system uses multiplexing to carry multiple signals.

carrier wave—A carrier wave is a consistent waveform that can be modulated to carry a signal. To receive a signal, a receiver must be tuned to the same carrier wavelength used by the transmitter.

channel—A portion of the total bandwidth of a physical transmission path, used to carry a single signal is referred to as a channel. Channels are also called links, lines, circuits, and paths. A physical connection, such as a cable, may support more than one channel.

cladding—Cladding is the clear plastic or glass layer that encloses the light-transmitting core of a fiber optic cable. The cladding has a lower refractive index than the core, and reflects the light signal back into the core as the light propagates down the fiber.

core—The innermost layer of a fiber optic cable, made of clear glass or plastic, is the core. It carries light signals down the fiber.

digital—A digital signal is transmitted as a pattern of binary bits. Information is represented as a series of 1s and 0s, high or low electrical voltages, or the absence or presence of light.

duplex—The process of transmitting data in two directions is referred to as duplex transmission. There are three modes of transmission: simplex, half-duplex, and full-duplex. In simplex transmission, a signal can only be transmitted in one direction. In half-duplex transmission, the signal can travel in both directions, but not simultaneously. Full-duplex transmission allows signals to travel in both directions simultaneously.

Electronic Industries Association (EIA)—EIA is a U.S. trade organization that publishes hardware-oriented standards for data communications.

encryption—Encryption is the process of scrambling data by changing it in a series of logical steps called an encryption algorithm. Most encryption algorithms use a numeric pattern or "key" to guide the scrambling process. Different keys and algorithms will each produce data scrambled or encrypted in different patterns. The recipient of a message uses the same algorithm and key to restore the original message.

Ethernet—The Ethernet protocol, originally developed in the 1970s by Xerox Corporation, in conjunction with Intel and DEC, is now the primary protocol for local area networking. The original Ethernet provides 10-Mbps throughput. Fast Ethernet (100 Mbps) and Gigabit Ethernet (1,000 Mbps) use the same basic technology, but at higher speeds.

frequency—Frequency is the number of times per second that a wave swings back and forth in a cycle from its beginning point to its ending point. It is the number of wave crests or cycles that passes a fixed point during a particular period of time.

half-duplex—See duplex.

hertz (Hz)—The frequency of an analog signal is measured in cycles per second or Hz. One Hz is 1 cycle per second; 1,000 cycles per second is 1 kHz; and 1 million cycles per second is 1 MHz.

hub—Also called a wiring concentrator, a simple hub is a repeater with multiple ports. A signal coming into one port is repeated out the other ports.

Institute of Electrical and Electronics Engineers (IEEE)—IEEE is a professional organization composed of engineers, scientists, and students. Founded in 1884, IEEE publishes computer and electronics standards, such as the 802 series that defines shared-media networks such as Ethernet and Token Ring.

International Electrotechnical Commission (IEC)—A voluntary organization, chartered by the United Nations, IEC defines standards for electrical and electronic technologies. ANSI represents the United States in the IEC.

International Standards Organization (ISO)—ISO is a voluntary organization, chartered by the United Nations, that defines international standards for all fields other than electricity and electronics (IEC handles that). ANSI represents the United States in the ISO.

International Telecommunication Union-Telecommunications Standardization Sector (ITU-T)—ITU-T is an intergovernmental organization that develops and adopts international telecommunication standards and treaties. ITU was founded in 1865 and became a United Nations agency in 1947.

light-emitting diode (LED)—An LED is a device that converts electrical signals into light pulses.

modem—The term "modem" is a contraction for modulator/demodulator. They are used to convert binary data into analog signals suitable for transmission across a telephone network.

modulation—Modulation is the process of modifying the form of a carrier wave (electrical signal) so that it can carry intelligent information on some sort of communications medium.

multiplexing—Multiplexing is a technology that allows multiple signals to travel over the same physical medium. Multiple signals are fed into a multiplexer and combined to form one output stream.

multistation access unit (MAU)—A MAU is a device used in Token Ring networks to provide connectivity between individual workstations. It is also called a Token Ring hub.

National Electrical Code (NEC)—The NEC is a set of safety standards and rules for the design and installation of electrical circuits, including network and telephone cabling. The NEC is developed by a committee of ANSI, and has been adopted as law by many states and cities. Versions of the NEC are dated by year; each local area may require compliance with a different version of the NEC.

repeater—A device that regenerates and boosts electrical or radio signals is referred to as a repeater. It can be used to lengthen a wire or a wireless transmission path.

RJ-45 connector—An RJ-45 connector is a snap-in connector for UTP cable, similar to the standard RJ-11 telephone cable connector.

simplex—See duplex.

synchronous—Synchronous communication is data communication controlled by a microprocessor clock, so that signals are permitted to start and stop at particular times. To use synchronous communication, the clock settings of the sending and receiving systems must match.

Telecommunications Industry Association (TIA)—TIA is a subgroup of EIA that focuses on electronic products for data communications.

Token Ring—Token Ring is a LAN protocol for ring topologies that operates at 4 and 16 Mbps.

Unshielded Twisted pair (UTP)—UTP is the most common type of network cabling, and is used extensively in telephone networks and many data communications applications. UTP is available in several grades, or categories, of increasing quality. See Category 5.

Lesson 1—Communication and Signals

A signal is any change in a measurable condition that is used to represent information. There is an almost endless number of ways we can send signals; however, they all require that we use some sort of energy to make a change that can be detected by someone or something. We can make sounds, wave flags, post signs, or use hand gestures. All of these can convey information, as long as both the sender and recipient agree on the meaning of the signal.

If we want to move data between computers, we must use a signaling method that machines can easily understand and that can span distances. Thus, data networks use three types of electromagnetic energy—electricity, light, and radio waves—to transmit signals. We will discuss each of these later in this unit.

Regardless of the type of energy used to carry a signal, all signals can be categorized according to one of three basic characteristics:

- Analog or digital

- One-way (simplex) or two-way (duplex)

- Timed (synchronous) or not timed (asynchronous)

In this lesson, we explain each of these characteristics and discuss what they mean for data networking.

Objectives

At the end of this lesson you should be able to:

- Describe the difference between baseband and broadband signaling

- Explain why a computer needs a modem to communicate over a telephone line

- Describe bandwidth and how it is measured

- Explain why standards are required for signaling, and name some of the most important organizations that make standards for network communication

 **Key Point**

Baseband (digital) signaling is predominantly used in data networks.

Analog and Digital Transmission

Analog and digital are the two ways we can use a flow of energy to carry data. As our various communication systems become computerized, more and more signals are being transmitted digitally. However, some key communication systems continue to use analog. If a data transmission must travel across many networks, such as a file downloaded from your favorite World Wide Web (Web) site to your home computer, the signal may be converted from digital to analog, and back again.

Analog Transmission

"Analog" means a signal is carried as a pattern of continually changing waves. For example, the sounds you hear are caused by waves through the air. Audio, video, and data signals are carried on electromagnetic waves. Analog transmission is commonly used in commercial radio and television broadcasting, cable television, and the telephone line that serves your home.

There are two basic qualities of an analog signal:

• Frequency refers to the number of times per second a wave swings back and forth in a cycle from its beginning point to its ending point. Think of frequency as the number of wave crests or cycles that passes a fixed point during a particular period of time. Therefore, frequency is measured in cycles per second or hertz (Hz). In sound waves, frequency determines the pitch of a sound. In visible light, frequency determines the color. The Frequency Diagram illustrates this quality of an analog signal.

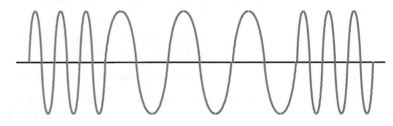

Frequency

The electromagnetic spectrum includes a wide range of frequencies, from infrared (low frequencies) through visible light, to ultraviolet, microwaves, and beyond (high frequencies).

- Amplitude refers to the height of a wave, or how far from the center a wave swings. Generally speaking, amplitude describes the power of a signal. On the Amplitude Diagram, the frequency does not change, but the amplitude does. If this diagram described a sound wave, the pitch would remain constant, while the loudness would change.

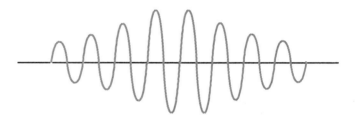

Amplitude

Modulation

We transmit analog signals by first establishing a constant, consistent wave form called a carrier wave. We then use the signal pattern to change the carrier wave's amplitude, frequency, or both. Another device, such as a radio receiver, can then extract the signal by detecting the way the carrier wave has been changed. This process of altering a carrier wave to represent information is called "modulation."

If we hold the frequency constant and vary the amplitude, this process is called amplitude modulation (AM). If we hold the amplitude constant and vary the frequency within a fixed range, the process is called frequency modulation (FM). You will encounter other forms of modulation as you continue your study of networking beyond this course.

Analog Bandwidth

Each frequency or range of frequencies can carry a separate signal. For example, radio and television stations all use radio waves to transmit information; however, each individual signal is carried over a different frequency.

The more frequencies a transmission medium can handle, the more channels of information it can carry. Each assigned slice of frequencies is called a "band." Therefore, the information-carrying capacity of a transmission path is called its "bandwidth." The bandwidth of an analog channel is expressed as the difference or span between its lowest and highest frequencies.

We generally use the term "broadband" to describe an analog communication medium that has a wide bandwidth. A single broadband connection, such as a television cable, can support many channels by assigning each one to a separate frequency. However, not all analog transmission is broadband. Some analog links, such as the telephone line to your home, may be capable of carrying only one channel. The term is also used to describe high-capacity digital connections. Later in this course, we will explain how a single digital link can carry multiple signals.

Digital (Baseband) Transmission

Instead of a pattern of continually changing waves, digital signals are transmitted in the form of binary bits: information represented as a series of 1s and 0s. The term "binary" refers to the fact that there are only two values for a bit: on or off, high or low. "On" bits are depicted as 1 and "off" bits are depicted as 0.

When bits are transmitted over wires, a 0 is represented by the absence of electricity or a low voltage. A 1 is represented by the presence of electricity or a higher voltage. A digital signal can travel in any direction down a wire, as shown on the Baseband Transmission Diagram.

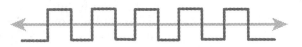

Baseband Transmission

Digital Signals Over Analog Links

We can also transmit digital data over an analog transmission system by representing binary bits as different patterns of analog waves. For example, a sudden change of amplitude or frequency could represent a "1." Either type of modulation (FM or AM) can be used to represent digital bits, as shown on the Analog Modulation Diagram.

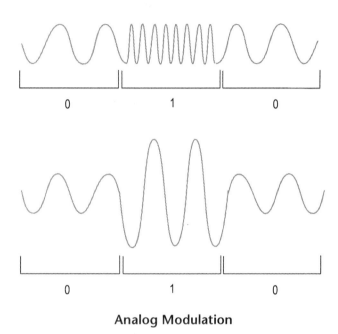

Analog Modulation

If you connect to the Internet over a standard telephone line, your modem converts (modulates) your computer's digital data patterns to the analog signals used on your telephone line. (The term "modem" is the shortened version of modulator-demodulator.) This process is shown on the Digital and Analog Signals Diagram.

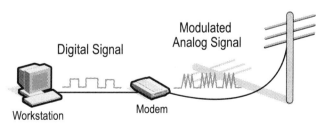

Digital and Analog Signals

65

Data networks, both small and large, use purely digital transmission. Baseband is relatively simple, less costly than broadband (analog), and yet still very fast. Thus, it is far more widely used than broadband. Although potentially much faster and able to span longer distances than baseband, broadband requires a modem at each end of a link, which increases the cost of every device attached to a local area network (LAN).

Digital Bandwidth

Unlike a broadband link, which can transmit multiple analog signals (each on a different frequency), a baseband link can usually only transmit a single signal at any particular moment. Thus, the bandwidth of a digital channel measures the number of bits it can carry per second. Digital bandwidth is commonly measured in kilobits (thousands of bits) per second (Kbps), megabits (millions of bits) per second (Mbps), and gigabits (billions of bits) per second (Gbps).

One-Way or Two-Way Transmission

Thus, we have categorized communication according to whether it uses digital or analog signals. A second characteristic of communication describes whether signals may flow in one or two directions simultaneously. In data networking, we use three terms to describe the way signals flow across a channel:

- Simplex—A signal may flow in only one direction. A commercial radio station uses simplex communication, because listeners cannot transmit radio signals back to the station.

- Half-duplex—Signals may flow in either direction, but not simultaneously. For example, a two-way radio allows only one user to speak at any one time.

- Full-duplex—Signals may flow in both directions simultaneously. A telephone is the best example of full-duplex communication. One wire brings a signal from the telephone company to your home, and a second wire carries a separate signal from your home back to the telephone company. Thus, you can both hear and speak simultaneously.

Signal Timing   We can also categorize communication according to the way it is organized or coordinated:

- Synchronous—The communicating parties or endpoints use time to organize communication. In a data network, two communicating computers use each clock "tick" to detect whether a digital bit is a 1 or 0. For example, as each time interval passes, a computer checks the network cable to see whether the voltage is high (binary 1) or low (binary 0). Because the timing determines the meaning of the signal, it is essential that the endpoints synchronize their clocks before sending signals.

- Asynchronous—Bits are not transmitted on any strict timetable. For example, a computer modem typically uses 8 bits to represent one character or letter. To indicate the start of each character, the sending modem transmits a "start" bit to alert the receiving end to the incoming signal. After the final bit of the character is transmitted, the sending modem transmits a "stop" bit to indicate the end of the character. This process is repeated for each character the modem transmits. Thus, the receiving modem must stay synchronized to the signal only for the length of time it takes to transmit 8 bits. If the sending and receiving clocks are slightly out of synchronization, these short data transfers will still be successful.

Signaling Standards

Imagine for a moment that you are alone in a telegraph office a century ago. Suddenly the telegraph sounder begins clacking a pattern of long and short signals. You know a message is coming in, but what does it mean?

If you are like most people today, you do not have the slightest idea what the signal means. However, if you are a trained telegraph operator, you understand Morse Code, which represents each letter of the alphabet by a different pattern of sounds. Beyond that, you can recognize that different parts of the signal identify the sender, recipient, and body of the message. You know that some special-purpose signals identify high-priority messages, or simply tell all listening telegraph operators when one of them steps out for lunch.

A network device, like a telegraph operator, is only aware of the changing patterns of a signal coming down the wire. If that signal is to carry information, the signal must follow some sort of rules that define the structure and content of a message. Most important, both the sender and receiver of a message must agree on what rules to use.

Data networks use many different types of rules for signaling. Some low-level rules define how to modulate a digital signal onto an analog wave form. Rules at higher levels define the communication between applications, or the content of electronic mail (e-mail) messages. These rules are called "protocols," and you will become familiar with many of them as you work your way through this course.

Signaling rules and protocols are developed by working groups of technical professionals. These associations put an enormous amount of effort into creating these technical standards and specifications, because they make network telecommunication possible. The groups that create and maintain the most important standards and protocols you will study in this course are described in the following sections.

ITU

The International Telecommunication Union (ITU) is an intergovernmental organization that develops international telecommunication standards. ITU standards, called "recommendations," make it possible for many types of electronic communications to occur across national borders. Because the advantages of standards-based interoperability are obvious to all members, ITU recommendations are generally adopted by vendors.

ITU is organized into three sectors, each one focusing on a major area of communications:

- ITU-R—Radiocommunication Sector

- ITU-D—Telecommunication Development Sector

- ITU-T or ITU-TSS—Telecommunication Standardization Sector

IEEE

The Institute of Electrical and Electronics Engineers (IEEE) is a world-wide society of technical professionals. In addition to promoting the development of electrical and electronic theory and methods, IEEE working committees develop and publish many important standards for communications, computing, and telecommunications.

One of the best known IEEE standards is the 802 series that defines the operation of LANs. For example, 801.3 defines Ethernet networks, while 802.5 defines Token Ring networks. Each standard describes one aspect of a system's operation, such as data transmission protocols, physical signaling, or the construction of cables or connectors. We will discuss both of these important networking standards later in this course.

EIA and TIA

The Electronic Industries Association (EIA) is a U.S. national trade organization that publishes hardware-oriented standards to guide its member companies. EIA consists of various product-oriented groups, such as the Telecommunications Industry Association (TIA) that focuses on electronic products for data communications.

EIA and TIA have taken the lead in providing industry-wide open standards for network wiring components and installation. Of particular relevance are the RS-232 standard for modem communication, and the Commercial Building Telecommunications Cabling Standard (EIA/TIA-568) (being renamed EIA/TIA SP-2840), which provides users and vendors precise guidelines for network wiring installation.

ANSI

The American National Standards Institute (ANSI) is a U.S. voluntary organization that develops and publishes standards for many types of industries, including data communications, programming languages, magnetic storage media, office systems, and encryption. An ANSI committee also develops the National Electrical Code (NEC), a set of U.S. safety specifications for electrical circuits.

ANSI members include large companies, government agencies, and professional organizations. Like ITU recommendations, ANSI standards are nonbinding, but widely adopted.

ISO

Just as ANSI membership is composed of other organizations, ANSI itself represents the United States as a member of the International Standards Organization (ISO) and International Electrotechnical Commission (IEC). Thus, ANSI standards are usually similar to ISO standards, differing only when unique aspects of North American systems need to be considered.

Different Signals, Different Media

Data networks transmit signals using three types of energy, and each one of these signals travels over a particular type of physical medium:

- Electrical current over copper wire

- Light pulses over plastic or glass fiber

- Radio waves through free space

Later in this unit, we will explain how signals travel over each of these physical media.

Activities

1. Modems convert digital signals from a telephone line to analog signals for a personal computer (PC). True or False

2. Baseband network technology is less expensive to implement than broadband network technology. True or False

3. Broadband cannot represent 1s and 0s because it uses analog transmission techniques. True or False

4. Baseband, unlike broadband, requires a modem at each end of a link. True or False

5. All analog transmission is broadband transmission. True or False

6. Indicate whether each of the following activities is synchronous or asynchronous:

    a. Viewing a broadcast television program

        _____

    b. Exchanging letters with a friend

        _____

    c. Meeting a client for lunch

        _____

Extended Activity

The following electrical signals are travelling along a cable. When the line is high, the signal represents a binary 1. When the signal is low, it represents a binary 0. Each of the eight signals below contains 7 bits of information. Write out the binary information (1s and 0s) in each signal.

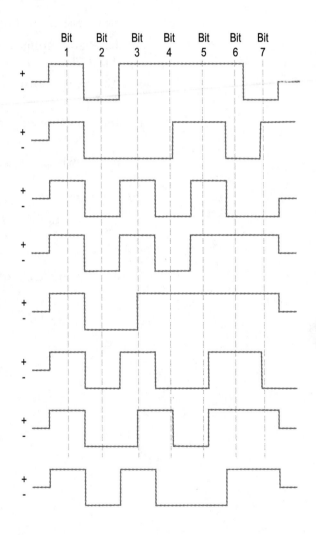

Lesson 2—Network Topologies

The physical structure of a network, or its "topology," describes the physical arrangement of wires, connectors, and other devices that connect a group of communicating nodes. A network's topology has a powerful effect on its operation and efficiency.

A network topology is like a system of roads and highways. Over time, different types of road systems have been developed to meet various types of transportation needs. For example, the winding, interconnected streets of a suburban neighborhood are designed for low-speed travel between individual homes. In contrast, straight, wide superhighways provide high-speed travel between entire cities.

In a similar way, different network topologies have been developed to meet various communication needs. This lesson introduces the main topologies used in data networks. A single network may be based on only one of these topologies or combine several of them.

Objectives

At the end of this lesson you should be able to:

* Draw the following topologies: bus, star, ring, and mesh

* Describe how a signal travels in a bus topology

* Explain the difference between physical and logical topologies

* Explain the difference between ring and star ring topologies

 **Key Point**

Most LANs use star topologies.

Types of Networks

Before we discuss topologies, let us first introduce the terms that describe networks with regard to their size. The size of a network is measured by the number of devices or nodes that need to communicate, and where these nodes are in relation to each other. There are several different types of networks:

- LANs can range from a few nodes in a home office, to several hundred nodes in a corporation. However, a LAN is typically confined to a single building.

- Campus networks consist of LANs connected across multiple buildings, using transmission links owned by the company that owns the network.

- Metropolitan area networks (MANS) are formed by connecting LANs in several locations across a city or small region. The links between LANs are typically leased from companies that provide telephone and data services.

- Wide area networks (WANs) are essentially the same as MANs, but span longer distances. A WAN may include sites in the same country or multiple countries.

Bus Topology

A bus topology is one of the simplest network designs and was the first topology used in LANs. A bus is a single electrical cable to which all devices in the network are connected (although the bus might be made up of many individual pieces of wire). This type of network structure is illustrated on the Bus Topology Diagram. The point where a device connects to the bus is called a "tap." Taps are made using different hardware and methods, depending on the type of cable used for the bus.

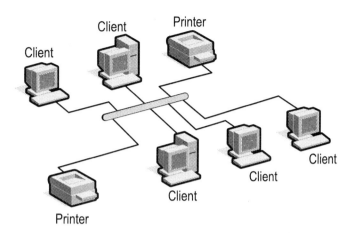

Bus Topology

When a node transmits data, the signal travels down the bus in both directions. Each node connected to the bus will receive the signal as it passes that connection point. However, a node will ignore any signal not specifically addressed to it. Because every node on the bus "hears" every message transmitted by any other node, a bus topology is considered a broadcast network.

When the signal reaches the end of the bus cable, a device called a "terminator" prevents the signal from reflecting back from the end of the wire. A terminator is an electrical resistor that essentially absorbs the signal energy. If a bus network is not terminated, or the terminator has the wrong level of resistance, each signal may travel across the bus several times instead of just once. This problem reduces network performance, because other nodes cannot transmit until the first signal dies down. (We will explain exactly how this works later in the course.)

A bus topology is simple and easy to understand. However, if the bus cable breaks, the entire network may be disabled. In addition, it can be difficult to change the number and position of nodes on a bus network.

Star Topology

A star topology network is the most common type of LAN topology today. A star topology consists of multiple computers attached to a central signal-distributing device called a "hub." Each computer or other device is attached to the hub by a separate cable, as illustrated on the Star Topology Diagram.

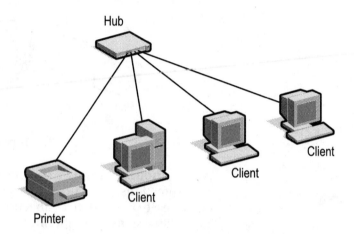

Star Topology

Like bus topology, a star topology is considered a broadcast network. When one computer transmits information to another computer, the signal first travels to the central hub device. The hub then copies the signal to all other computers attached to it. Thus, the hub performs the same function as the bus cable we just discussed. And, like a bus, the entire network may go down if the central hub fails.

However, star networks provide the following advantages over bus topologies:

- Some hubs have features that can detect defective cables and devices.

- Nodes are easily added and removed from a network.

- Network problems are easier to troubleshoot because suspect nodes can easily be disconnected from the hub.

Ring Topologies

A ring topology is another commonly used topology in computer networks. There are two common ring topologies used in networks: ring and star ring.

Ring

A "pure" ring topology consists of nodes connected in a series of point-to-point links, just as people join hands in a circle. Each node attached to the ring has one input and one output connection, so that each node is connected to two links.

In many rings, when a node receives a signal on its input connection, it immediately passes it to the output connection. Thus, data flows only in one direction, as illustrated on the Ring Topology Diagram. Like nodes on a star or bus network, a ring node only copies signals addressed to it. Each node can send messages by putting new bits onto the ring.

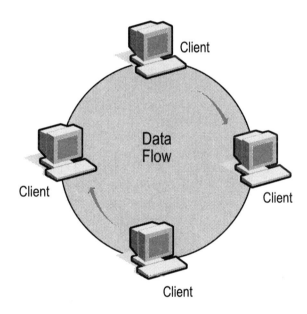

Ring Topology

If a ring node malfunctions or is shut down, it cannot repeat the signals it receives. In that case, the ring is broken, and data transfer stops until the failed node is restored or removed from the ring. The ring can also be broken if any cable between nodes is damaged or broken. To solve the problem of failed cables, some ring topologies incorporate a dual-ring structure. If one cable link fails, the other can immediately take over.

Star Ring

A star ring topology is built by combining ring and star topologies to obtain a reliable and serviceable configuration. A wire runs from each node to a central ring wiring hub, also called a multi-station access unit (MAU).

A star ring is a physical star configuration; however, information travels from node to node in a logical ring as the MAU copies each signal to each of its nodes in turn.

A star ring topology requires more wire than a pure ring or bus. However, the problems of a pure ring are solved because the MAU performs two important functions:

- It automatically detects when a node is not responding and bypasses it so that the ring can continue to operate, as shown on the MAU Bypassing a Node Diagram.

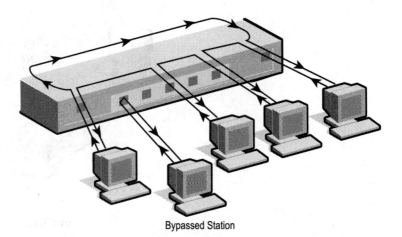

Bypassed Station

MAU Bypassing a Node

- It provides a "bridge" to other rings, sending information addressed to nodes on other rings across circuits to those rings, and accepting messages from other rings for its nodes. Rings joined in this manner effectively become a single ring. By connecting MAUs to each other, ring size is effectively unlimited, as shown on the Multiple MAUs in a Single Ring Diagram.

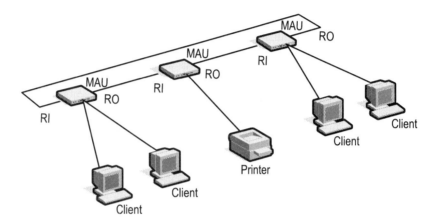

Multiple MAUs in a Single Ring

Each MAU receives a signal on its Ring In (RI) port. The MAU copies the signal to each of its nodes in turn, then sends the signal to its Ring Out (RO) port. The RO port of that MAU is attached to the RI port of the next MAU, thus the signal continues around the ring.

Wide Area Topologies

As we learned at the beginning of this lesson, a WAN or MAN is formed when two or more LANs are connected by point-to-point communication links. As the number of interconnected LANs increases, some networks develop a wide area star topology, in which all branch offices connect to one central headquarters location.

However, some organizations need each of their locations to be able to communicate directly with any other, without routing all communications through a central point. Two kinds of wide area topologies tend to develop to meet this need:

- Mesh
- Network cloud

Mesh

In a mesh topology, point-to-point links directly connect every site to every other site. Mesh networks are usually built over time as new sites are added to the overall network. The Mesh Network Topology Diagram provides an example of a mesh configuration.

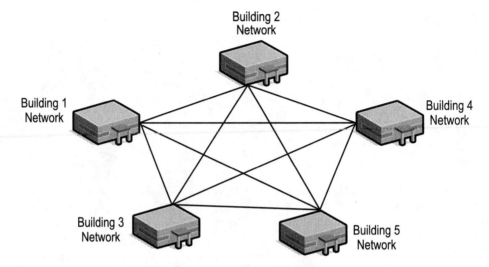

Mesh Network Topology

Mesh networks are fairly simple to understand. However, the number of point-to-point links increases sharply with the number of locations. For example, a three-site mesh network needs 3 links; however, four locations require 6 links, and five locations require 10 links. At that rate, it does not take long before the cost of a mesh network becomes too high.

Network Cloud

A network cloud, shown on the Network Cloud Diagram, is not really a topology. It is a representation of an unknown network structure, typically a transmission service offered by a networking service provider, such as a telephone company.

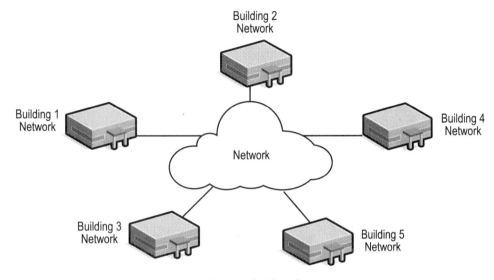

Network Cloud

The cloud symbol represents a private mesh network of switching devices that may span a city, region, or nation. The network is drawn as a cloud because users of the service do not have any knowledge about the internal workings of that network. Only the service provider understands the topologies and connections that make up the paths between the switching sites within the cloud. The public telephone system and the Internet are two well-known examples of cloud networks.

To use the services of a cloud network, a company subscribes to the service, connects its locations to the edge of the cloud, and trusts the network to handle the details of moving each message across to its destination.

Advantages of Cloud Networks

Cloud networks offer several key advantages over mesh networks:

- Cost—As we saw on the Mesh Network Topology Diagram, 10 point-to-point links are required to provide all-to-all connectivity between five locations. This number increases dramatically with the number of locations. By using a cloud network, only five point-to-point links are necessary to link five sites, plus network subscription fees. Each new location requires only one link to the cloud, and a proportional increase in network usage charges. Furthermore, a company must pay for a point-to-point connection even when it is not being used. Most cloud networks charge fees based on the amount of traffic they carry.

- Simplified network management—The cloud service provider, not the subscriber, is responsible for maintaining and upgrading the network's physical switching systems. For the subscribing organization, this can greatly reduce the costs of maintaining a WAN.

- Flexibility—It can be unwieldy to change the configuration of even a small mesh network. However, with only a few telephone calls and a few slight adjustments to each site's network, a network manager can increase the bandwidth or number of access points to the cloud. And, for an incremental fee, a cloud can usually provide temporary additional bandwidth on demand, without making special advance arrangements.

Network Backbone

A small network may consist of a single bus, single ring, or star based on a single central hub. However, as organizations grow, they often connect these simple topologies to form more complex networks. For example, the Three Workgroups Diagram shows how each of a company's departments has its own star-wired network. To provide communication across the entire organization, the company then connected the three workgroups.

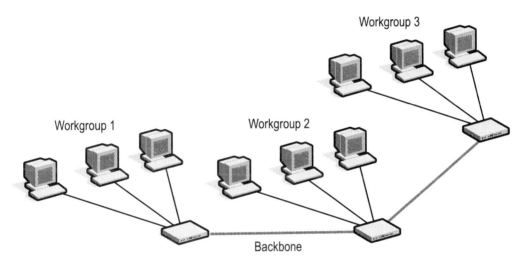

Three Workgroups

The three star networks are now linked by a topology called a backbone. A network backbone functions like a high-speed highway, providing direct communication between major segments of the network. Like a highway, a network backbone concentrates traffic that flows between the "side streets." Thus, a backbone must have a higher data-carrying capacity than the workgroup networks that connect individual computers.

Rings are often used as the backbone of large networks. A ring backbone often connects workgroups on different floors of a multistory building, buildings in an office campus, or locations in a MAN or WAN. This concept is illustrated on the Ring Backbone Diagram.

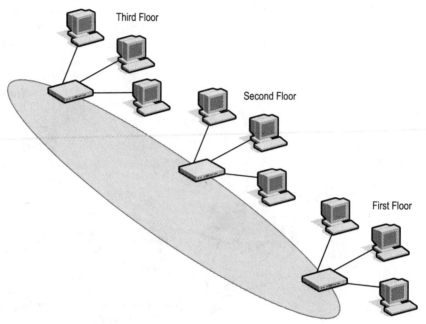

Ring Backbone

Unlike the MAU-centered star ring topologies used in LANs, ring backbones are often "true" rings that connect separate networks using point-to-point links. For example, imagine that a large corporation has locations in Los Angeles, Houston, New York, and Denver. It can link these four networks with a ring backbone, by connecting Los Angeles to Houston, Houston to New York, and so on, as shown on the Wide Area Ring Backbone Diagram.

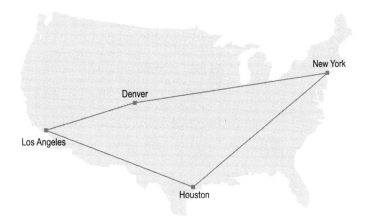

Wide Area Ring Backbone

Hybrid Topologies, Internetworks, and Enterprise Networks

The network topologies we have discussed, including bus, star, ring, backbone, mesh, and cloud, can be combined in many different ways to meet the needs of an organization. A network that mixes two or more of these structures is often called a "hybrid" topology.

Just as different topologies can be combined to form a single network, whole networks can also be linked to form a single large composite network. This sort of complex network, which often uses different topologies and network communication methods across a wide area, is called an "internetwork." The global Internet got its name because it is an internetwork made up of many individual private networks.

When all of an organization's networks are integrated into a single internetwork, we call this an "enterprise" network. For example, the Enterprise Network Diagram shows how different topologies and LANs are commonly linked in a single corporate WAN.

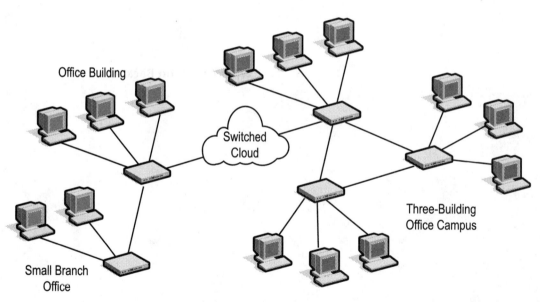

Enterprise Network

Logical and Physical Topologies

There are two ways in which data networking professionals refer to topologies:

- Logical topologies show where signals go. They eliminate some details to make the important relationships easier to see.

- Physical topologies show more details about a network's connectors, cabling, and wide area links.

Physical Star, Logical Bus

To understand this difference, think of bus and star topologies. As we learned earlier in this lesson, signals travel exactly the same way in both of these. However, for reasons described in the next lesson, hardly anyone is wiring new bus networks. New broadcast networks almost always use the more flexible star topology. Despite this fact, a broadcast network is usually diagrammed as a bus topology.

Therefore, this physical topology:

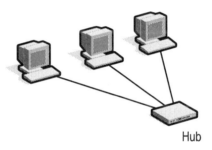

Hub

is equivalent to this logical topology:

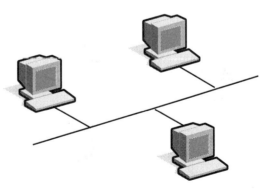

As you can see, the logical diagram does not show the hub that connects the group of computers. However, the drawing of the bus makes it easy to see that all of the devices directly share signals among themselves. Thus, when you see a bus diagram in this book or any other network text, remember that you are probably looking at a hub-centered star network.

Physical Star, Logical Ring

Ring topologies provide another good example of the difference between physical and logical diagrams. As we just learned, stations on a local area ring network are usually not connected directly to each other. Instead, they are all plugged to a central MAU. Thus, the physical diagram of a ring network looks almost identical to that of a broadcast network:

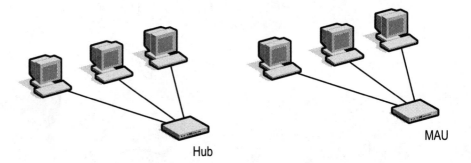

Hub

MAU

It is very easy to confuse these two networks. However, if we use logical diagrams, the difference between them is clear:

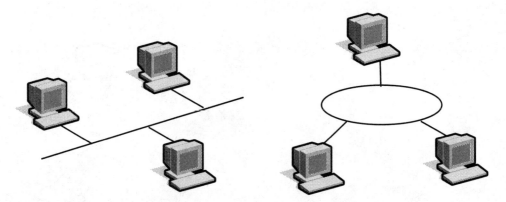

Thus, when you see a LAN represented as a ring, remember that the devices are probably all connected to a central MAU.

Activities

1. On a bus network, each node relays the signal to the node next in line. The recipient node removes the signal from the bus. True or False

2. On a ring network, a signal is relayed to each node in the ring in turn. True or False

3. What topology does the Internet use?

   _____

   _____

   _____

   _____

4. For each of the following situations, what network topology is the most appropriate? Choose from star, ring, mesh, and cloud. You may choose more than one option, if appropriate.

   a. In a small real estate office, four computers need to share a printer

   b. The builder of a five-building office campus wants to link each building to the others, using a minimum of underground cable. The buildings will be leased to various tenants, thus no one building can be assumed to be the central headquarters.

   c. A fast food chain has 150 restaurants in a three-state area and wants to connect all of them to the headquarters office.

   d. A bank has three branch locations in one city. All three must link to each other and to a central interbank clearing house.

5. Represent a bus by drawing a horizontal line approximately 4 to 5 inches long across the page. Draw four nodes connected to the line (bus), and label the Nodes A, B, C, and D.

   a. If Node B is transmitting data to Node C, circle the nodes that will receive the transmitted data.

6. Draw a four-port hub with four nodes attached. Label the Nodes A, B, C, and D.

    a. If Node B is transmitting data to Node D, circle the nodes that will receive the transmitted data.

7. Draw a logical ring network with five nodes attached. Label the Nodes (in order around the ring) A, B, C, D, and E, and draw an arrow depicting the direction of data flow from Nodes A to B, B to C, and so on.

8. If Node D transmits to Node C, how many times is the signal repeated?

9. Redraw the above ring network diagram as a physical topology, showing the nodes connected to a central MAU. Label the Nodes (in order) A, B, C, D, and E, and draw an arrow depicting the direction of data flow from Nodes A to B, B to C, and so on.

a. If Node D transmits to Node C, how many times is the signal repeated?

b. What topology requires less cable?

_____

_____

c. What topology is more vulnerable to a cable break?

_____

_____

Extended Activities

1. In this lesson, we explained that the number of connections in a mesh network increases dramatically as the number of points in the network increases. For the following number of individual networks, determine the number of circuits for a point-to-point solution versus a switched solution. Each node is connected to all other nodes; however, with bidirectional links, each link should be counted only once (not twice).

    The formula for calculating the number of links is N(N-1)/2, where N is the number of linked sites.

    For example, 5 links would be 5(5-1)/2 or 10; 10 links would be 10(10-1)/2 or 45.

Number of Individual Networks	Point-to-Point Solution	Switched Solution
5	10	5
6		
7		
8		
9		
10		

2. Would a pure ring or star ring topology be easier to maintain and troubleshoot? Explain.

    _____

    _____

    _____

    _____

Lesson 3—Copper Cable

Transmission media connect the various components of a network to one another. Each type of transmission medium strongly influences the type and quality of signals it can carry.

Copper is a popular transmission medium because it is an excellent conductor of electricity. It is commonly available, fairly inexpensive, and easy to work with. Copper is also prone to signal interference, which can limit its transmission speed. However, fairly simple techniques and cable designs have largely corrected this problem, making copper cable the most popular medium for connecting both telephone systems and LANs.

There are two types of copper cable used in LANs:

- Twisted pair cable is the most widely used medium.

- Coaxial cable is found in older installations.

Objectives

At the end of this lesson you should be able to:

- Describe the construction of coaxial and twisted pair cable

- Name the most popular type of copper cable and explain the reason for its popularity

- Explain the meaning of the terms "10Base5," "10Base2," and "10BaseT"

 **Key Point**

Twisted pair is the most common type of copper cable used in networks.

93

Coaxial Cable

Coaxial cable was one of the first types of cable used in LANs. It typically consists of a central copper or copper-coated conductor surrounded by flexible insulation, a shield of copper wire mesh, and an outer plastic jacket. The Coaxial Cable Diagram illustrates the construction of this type of transmission medium.

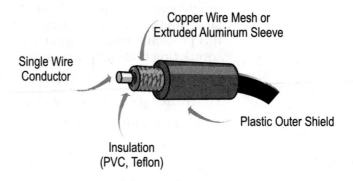

Copper Wire Mesh or
Extruded Aluminum Sleeve

Single Wire
Conductor

Plastic Outer Shield

Insulation
(PVC, Teflon)

Coaxial Cable

The shield serves as the second conductor (to complete the electrical circuit), and acts to dissipate electromagnetic interference (EMI) and radio frequency interference (RFI). This physical design makes coaxial cable fairly expensive and generally harder to install than other types of cables.

Coaxial cable was designed to support Ethernet networks using bus topologies. (Ethernet is a broadcast network protocol we will discuss in detail in Unit 5.) Each type of coaxial cable is identified by a number called the radio government (RG) standard. But when the first Ethernet networks were developed, each type of LAN specified a particular type of cable. Thus, coaxial cable is commonly identified by the name of the type of Ethernet LAN it implements, rather than its RG standard number. For example, it is more common to hear someone ask for "10Base2 coax" than "RG-58." The Coaxial Cable Types Table lists the two most common types of coaxial cable, their RG standard, and the maximum Ethernet bus length each can support.

Coaxial Cable Types

LAN Type	Cable Type	Maximum Distance (meters)
10Base2 (Thin Ethernet)	RG-58 A/U, RG-58 C/U	185
10Base5 (Thick Ethernet)	RG-8, RG-11	500

10Base5

10Base5 is the standard for using thick, RG-8-type coaxial cable to implement 10-Mbps baseband Ethernet networks using a bus topology. The "5" in the name represents 500 meters (m), which is the maximum length of a network bus using this cable. Thus, the term "10Base5" means "**10** Mbps, using **base**band signaling, and no longer than **500** m."

10Base5 cable is also called "Thicknet" or "Yellow Wire." This cable includes two layers of foil shielding and an additional copper mesh shield. In a 10Base5 network, a separate transceiver device connects a computer to the main bus cable to transmit outgoing signals and receive incoming signals. The transceiver connects to the computer's network interface card (NIC) by means of a separate transceiver cable called an "attachment unit interface (AUI)."

10Base2

10Base2 is the standard for using thin, RG-58-type coaxial cable to implement 10-Mbps baseband Ethernet using a bus topology. The number "2" in 10Base2 stands for approximately 200 m (to be precise, 185 m), which is the maximum length of this type of network bus.

10Base2 is also called "Thinnet," "ThinLAN," and "Cheapernet." 10Base2 uses twist-on T-connectors, called "BNC connectors," to attach to NICs (adapters) and other devices. In most 10Base2 implementations, the network adapter performs the transceiver functions. The first and final T-connectors in the series include a 50-ohm terminating resistor to eliminate reflected signals on the unterminated cable. The 10Base2 Adapter and Cable Diagram illustrates these two components.

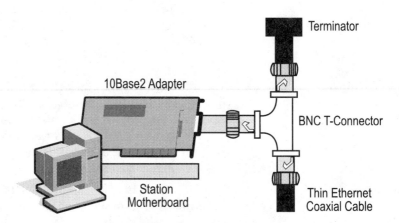

10Base2 Adapter and Cable

The 10Base2 Wiring Rules Table describes various parameters to consider when using this cable to wire an Ethernet system. The reason for some of these minimum and maximum values will become clear when we discuss the Ethernet protocol in Unit 5.

10Base2 Wiring Rules

10Base2 Parameter	Value
Maximum data rate	10 Mbps
Maximum repeaters between transceivers	4
Maximum stations per segment	30
Maximum stations	90
Minimum distance between stations	0.5 m
Maximum coaxial segment without a repeater	185 m
Maximum coaxial length with repeaters	925 m

Coaxial cable, including 10Base2 and 10Base5, has good EMI/RFI resistance provided by its shielding layer. However, coaxial cable is bulky and relatively difficult to install through wire ducts and other spaces within a building. In addition, a cable break anywhere along a bus can disable the entire network segment.

Most important, Ethernet networks over coaxial cable are limited to 10 Mbps. As network users and applications require more bandwidth, coaxial cable has been overtaken by twisted pair and fiber optic cable. Coaxial cable can still be found in older networks; however, it is not typically used in new installations.

Twisted Pair Cable

Twisted pair cable consists of two or more pairs of thin, stranded, insulated copper wires twisted around each other to cancel EMI/RFI. Twisted pair cable is available in two standard varieties: unshielded twisted pair (UTP) and shielded twisted pair (STP). Recently, a new type of twisted pair cable has been offered by some manufacturers: screened twisted pair (ScTP).

UTP Cable

UTP is the most popular LAN cabling because it is inexpensive, light, flexible, and easy to install. It relies on precisely twisted pairs of wire to minimize EMI/RFI, and is not shielded by an external conductor. The number of twists ranges from 2 to 12 per foot, depending on the type of cable. The UTP Cable Diagram illustrates this type of cable.

Twisted Pairs
of Copper Wires

Outer Plastic Sheath

UTP Cable

Although UTP is similar in appearance to standard telephone cable, it must meet higher criteria to perform as data-grade cable. In particular, it is important to avoid using untwisted lengths of telephone-type cable to carry LAN traffic.

97

In recent years, two compatible five-level standards have been established for rating UTP cable by EIA/TIA and the Underwriters' Laboratories (UL). The UL system uses the term "levels," and EIA/TIA uses the term "categories." Another slight difference is that the UL standard includes fire safety performance criteria similar to that specified by the NEC. Other than that, the EIA/TIA categories and UL levels are used interchangeably:

- Category 1—For analog and digital voice (telephone) and low-speed data applications
- Category 2—For voice, Integrated Services Digital Network (ISDN), and medium-speed data up to 4 Mbps. This cable is equivalent to IBM Cable Type 3, described later in this lesson.
- Category 3—For high-speed data and LAN traffic up to 16 Mbps
- Category 4—For long-distance LAN traffic up to 20 Mbps
- Category 5—For 100-Mbps LAN technologies such as 100-Mbps Ethernet
- Category 5e—Enhanced Category 5 provides for full duplex Fast Ethernet support

Higher category UTP cables are made from higher quality materials. Each higher category is also made with tighter cable twists for increased resistance to interference; in Category 5, those twists continue right up to the connector. Only Category 5 is currently recommended for data network installations.

It is possible to combine network sections that use different cable categories. However, it is better to use the same category throughout a network. Many analysts recommend installing only Category 5 cable to provide sufficient bandwidth capacity for future needs.

Special care must be taken when installing Category 5 cabling systems. Not only must the cable meet specifications, in addition, only the highest quality connectors must be used. When Category 5 cable is connected, no more than 0.5 inch (1.3 centimeters [cm]) of the twist must be unraveled, a sometimes difficult task that requires skilled installers. Care must also be taken not to exceed the bend radius of the cable or otherwise crimp it. This can cause a misalignment of the twisted pair and lead to transmission errors.

In addition, twisted pair cables must be terminated on connectors of the same category of cable or higher. For example, if Category 5 cable is terminated on Category 3 connectors, that part of the installation will usually perform at Category 3 data rates.

10BaseT Star Topology

The "T" in 10BaseT stands for twisted pair. Thus, this term represents a network running 10 Mbps, using baseband signaling, over twisted pair cable. 10BaseT adapters typically include the transceiver circuitry, and like 10Base2 adapters, do not require an external transceiver.

10BaseT uses a star topology. Each station is individually connected to a port on a multiport hub, which provides a central wiring point for each station connection or segment. The hub functions as a repeater and transceiver, receiving incoming signals from all stations, then broadcasting them to every station attached to the hub. In other words, if one computer transmits a signal, all stations attached to the same hub will receive that signal. (However, only the intended recipient will actually process the message.)

The 10BaseT Ethernet Configuration Diagram illustrates the most popular way to wire Ethernet LANs today. This configuration consists of an Ethernet hub using UTP cable to connect eight workstations.

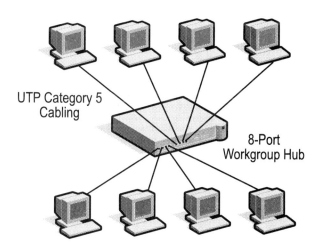

UTP Category 5 Cabling

8-Port Workgroup Hub

10BaseT Ethernet Configuration

Each end of the twisted pair cable is equipped with an RJ-45 connector, which is similar to a standard snap-in telephone connector, as illustrated on the RJ-45 Plug and Receptacle for UTP Diagram. All 10BaseT components, such as NICs and hub ports, use the same connectors, thus installation is fast and easy. A new device is connected by snapping a cable directly into the device NIC on one end and a hub port on the other end.

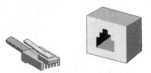

RJ-45 Plug and Receptacle for UTP

10BaseT is rapidly becoming one of the most popular wiring standards due to its lower cost and relative ease of installation. In addition, its star topology allows for efficient management, maintenance, fault isolation, and reconfiguration of a LAN.

A hub can be located in a central location, such as a wiring closet. In many offices, network cables run from the wiring closet, through the walls or ceiling, to each work area. Each cable is terminated at a wallplate near each workstation, thus attaching a new computer to the network is as simple as plugging in a telephone. A computer is connected to the wallplate, then the other end of the cable is connected to the hub in the wiring closet, as illustrated on the UTP Connections at Wallplate Diagram. Hubs can also be interconnected to enlarge a LAN.

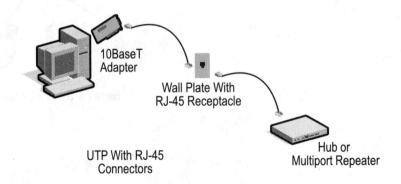

UTP Connections at Wallplate

Category 5 UTP cable is commonly used to wire 10BaseT networks. Category 3 cable is actually adequate for a 10-Mbps data rate, but network designers typically install Category 5 to ensure the network wiring can support future upgrades to faster data rates. This approach is wise, because the labor needed to install new cable is much more expensive than the slight increase in cable cost from Category 3 to Category 5.

Rules for installing 10BaseT are listed in the 10BaseT Wiring Rules Table.

10BaseT Wiring Rules

10BaseT Parameter	Value
Maximum data rate	10 Mbps
Maximum concentrators (hubs) in sequence	4
Maximum repeaters	4
Maximum segment length without a repeater	100 m

Similar wiring rules exist for higher speed technologies, such as Fast Ethernet (100BaseTX) and Gigabit Ethernet (1000BaseT).

STP Cable

STP cable consists of two or more twisted pairs of copper wire surrounded by flexible insulation, a foil shield, and an outer plastic sheath. In some types of multiwire STP cable, individual twisted pairs may be surrounded by their own foil shield. The foil shield helps dissipate EMI, particularly at data rates of 16 Mbps or higher. The STP Cable Diagram illustrates this type of cable.

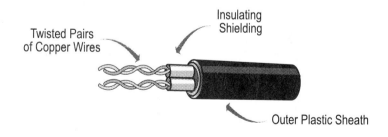

STP Cable

STP wiring was the original cable specified for ring topology networks, such as Token Ring and Fiber Distributed Data Interface (FDDI). (These ring network protocols are discussed later in this course.) STP provides considerably more resistance to EMI/RFI than UTP; however, it is also more bulky, less flexible, and more expensive to install.

IBM Cable Types

The IBM cabling system specifies several types of STP, fiber optic, and UTP cables. Types 1 and 3 are those most commonly referenced when discussing universal wiring plans. IBM has its own unique guidelines for cable installation:

- Type 1 consists of two STP pairs for data transmission and is the historic standard for Token Ring cable. Each pair is shielded with a foil shield and an outer sheath of plastic or corrugated metal. Type 1a cable is a newer, higher performance cable of the same general type.

- Type 2 includes six pairs of wire: two STP pairs for data and four UTP pairs for voice. This cable is used where both telephone lines and data lines terminate in the same wall outlet. It is also used to facilitate the wiring installation of telephone and data lines between closets.

- Type 3 consists of telephone-grade UTP cables. The original Type 3 cable specification was intended to be compatible with existing telephone-grade wiring, which would be equivalent to EIA/TIA Category 2 UTP, and which was recommended only for 4-Mbps rings. Currently, IBM recommends the use of data-grade UTP (equivalent to EIA/TIA Categories 3, 4, and 5) for both 4- and 16-Mbps installations, and increasingly only Categories 4 and 5 are recommended for new installations.

- Type 5 consists of two 100/140-micrometer (μm) optical fiber cables. IBM currently also recommends 62.5/125-μm multimode optical fiber for optical fiber installations (where 62.5 refers to the core diameter and 125 refers to the cladding diameter). Fiber optic cable is typically used with a pair of fiber optic repeaters to connect MAUs in Token Ring LANs. Optical fiber is discussed in detail later in this unit.

- Type 6 uses two twisted pairs for data transmission and is similar to Type 1, but is more flexible. Type 6 cable is used to connect workstations to wall outlets and for patch cords between Token Ring MAUs.

- Type 8 consists of two shielded pairs with a flat plastic housing designed for undercarpet use.

- Type 9 consists of a thinner, lower cost version of Type 1 cable, and supports shorter transmission distances than Type 1 cable.

ScTP

ScTP cable consists of four copper pairs shielded in an aluminum foil mesh with a polyvinyl chloride (PVC) jacket. The foil mesh provides significant EMI/RFI shielding and results in a cable that falls between UTP and STP in terms of cost, performance, and difficulty of installation. ScTP is also known as foil twisted pair (FTP) by some manufacturers. At the time of writing, the relative benefits of ScTP over Category 5 UTP are still being debated.

NEC

In addition to voluntary standards for signaling and hardware design, network installations are governed by several layers of legally enforceable regulations. The specific regulations that apply to a project depend on a network's design, physical implementation, and geographic location. However, most U.S. network installations must conform to the rules specified in the NEC.

The NEC is a set of safety standards and rules for the design and installation of electrical circuits, including network and telephone cabling. The NEC is developed by a committee of ANSI, and published every three years by the National Fire Protection Association. Its rules and standards are intended to prevent electrical fires and accidental electrocutions. The NEC has been adopted as law by many states and cities, and is usually enforced by the local building department. Any new network installation in such an area must pass an electrical inspection similar to that required for a building's power distribution wiring.

Activities

1. Twisted pair cable is used mostly for high bit rates over long distances. True or False

2. Twisted pair wires are twisted to make the cable stronger for ease of installation. True or False

3. 10Base2 uses a terminating plug at the ends of the bus. True or False

4. UTP cable is used extensively in data networks. True or False

5. What type of cabling does a star or ring topology typically use?

Extended Activities

1. Obtain samples of the following types of cable. Examine and discuss characteristics of each.

   a. Thicknet (10Base5) coaxial cable

   _____

   _____

   b. Thinnet (10Base2) coaxial cable

   _____

   _____

   c. UTP Category 3 cable

   _____

   _____

   d. UTP Category 5 (10BaseT) cable

   _____

   _____

2. Demonstrate star topology cabling, using a standard 10BaseT Ethernet hub and UTP cable.

3. Go to Web sites or manufacturers of network cable to find product information. Start with **http://www.belden.com** and **http://www.amp.com**.

Lesson 4—Fiber Optic Cable

A fiber optic cable is a thin strand of glass or plastic, coated with a protective plastic jacket. It is so thin that even the glass fibers bend easily. A beam of light can be trapped within a fiber, so that the optical cable essentially becomes a pipe that carries light around corners.

Fiber optic networks can support high data rates, theoretically as high as 50 Gbps. An optical fiber can carry a light signal for a long distance (typically up to 2 kilometers [km]) before the signal must be strengthened. Because light is not appreciably affected by electromagnetic fields, optical signals are immune to EMI/RFI. This makes fiber a good choice for "noisy" environments with many electrical motors, such as elevator shafts and factories. Because fiber does not corrode, it is well suited for high-humidity and underwater environments. Optical fiber is also a highly secure medium, because it is difficult to splice into a fiber optic cable without detection.

The primary disadvantage of fiber optic cable is its cost. Fiber optic cable and equipment are relatively expensive in terms of both materials cost and installation. However, industries that need the high capacity and secure features of fiber find it well worth the investment. For example, nearly all long-distance telecommunication lines are fiber optic.

This lesson describes some of the typical components of fiber optic systems and the characteristics of fiber optic transmission.

Objectives

At the end of this lesson you should be able to:

- Describe the composition of an optical fiber cable

- Explain how light travels down an optical fiber

- Name the main components of a fiber optic transmission system

 **Key Point**

Fiber optic cable is expensive and demanding to install; however, it offers many unique advantages.

Fiber Communication Systems

The basic model for a communication system includes a transmitter and receiver, connected by optical fiber cabling. The Fiber Optic Components Diagram illustrates a generic fiber optic communication system. In typical fiber optic systems, each device contains both a transmitter and receiver, combined in a single transceiver unit. Because fiber optic cable must be cut to present the light beam to a receiver, only point-to-point connections can be made; a bus cannot be constructed.

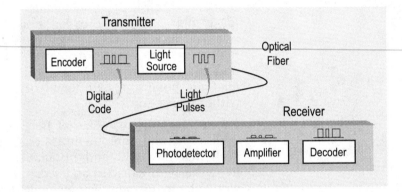

Fiber Optic Components

Transmitter

A transmitter includes the following components:

- Encoder that converts the input data signal into digital electrical pulses

- Light source that converts the digital electrical signal to light pulses

- Connector that couples the light source to the fiber through which the light rays travel

The transmitter accepts digital electrical signals from a computer. A diode converts the digital code into a pattern of light pulses (on and off) that are sent out to the receiver through the optical fiber.

There are two basic types of light sources for fiber optic systems:

- Light emitting diodes (LEDs) use less power and are considerably less expensive than lasers. LEDs can be used with multimode cable, and are the most common light source. (Multimode cable is discussed later in this lesson.) LEDs provide a bandwidth of approximately 250 megahertz (MHz).

- Laser diodes are used with single-mode fiber for long-distance transmission. (Single-mode cable is also discussed later in this lesson.) Laser light is more powerful because laser light waves are radiated in phase, which means the crests and troughs of all light waves are perfectly aligned with one another. This alignment or coherence creates a signal with much less attenuation and dispersion than noncoherent light. Laser diodes can provide much higher bandwidth (up to a theoretical maximum of 10 gigahertz [GHz]).

Warning: Never look into a fiber optic cable to see whether light is present. The infrared laser light used in fiber optic LANs is invisible; however, it can permanently damage your eyesight in an instant.

Receiver

A receiver converts the modulated light pulses back to electrical signals and decodes them. The receiver, contained within the destination computer system, includes:

- Photodetector that converts the light pulses into electric signals

- Amplifier, if needed

- Message decoder

Fiber Optic Cable Construction

Optical fiber cable consists of three parts, as shown on the Fiber Optic Cable Diagram.

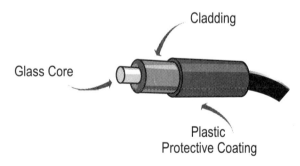

Fiber Optic Cable

- Core—A solid fiber of highly refractive clear glass or plastic that serves as the central conduit for light. The diameter and consistency of the core varies depending upon the specification of the fiber.

- Cladding—A layer of clear glass or plastic with a lower index of refraction. When light traveling down the core reaches the boundary between the core and cladding, the change in refractive index causes the light to completely refract or bend back into the core. The cladding of each fiber completely contains light signals within each core, preventing crosstalk. This effect is called "total internal reflection."

- Coating—A reinforced plastic outer jacket that protects the cable from damage.

Fiber Optic Dimensions

Fiber optic cable is very thin. The diameters of fiber optic cores and cladding are specified in μm. The thinnest fiber optic cable (single-mode) typically has a core diameter of 5 to 10 μm (0.005 to 0.010 millimeter [mm]). Thicker fiber optic cable (multimode) ranges from 50 to 100 μm in core diameter. In comparison, human hair is approximately 100 μm thick.

Fiber optic cable is specified in terms of its core and cladding diameter. For example, the most common type of fiber optic cable for LAN installations is 62.5/125-μm cable, where 62.5 refers to the core diameter and 125 refers to the cladding diameter.

The core diameter is also known as the aperture, because it determines the maximum angle from which the cable can accept light. Total internal reflection only occurs when light strikes the cladding at a shallow angle. If the angle is too steep, some or all of the light will penetrate the cladding itself, causing signal loss.

Each fiber optic core conducts light in one direction only. Therefore, to send and receive, devices are usually connected by two fiber optic strands. These may be single strand (simplex) cables, or duplex cables containing two fiber optic strands. Duplex cables are more commonly used than simplex cables.

Fiber cables can also consist of several bundles, as illustrated on the Multiple Bundle Fiber Optic Cable Diagram. These are used for high-capacity backbones for outdoor connections between campus buildings. Because light signals are completely contained within each fiber, no coating or shielding is necessary between fibers. However, reinforcing strands are usually added to increase the pulling strength of the cable.

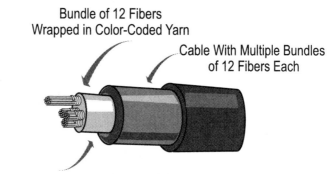

Bundle of 12 Fibers
Wrapped in Color-Coded Yarn

Cable With Multiple Bundles
of 12 Fibers Each

Fiber strands within bundles follow
the same color code sequence.

Multiple Bundle Fiber Optic Cable

Types of Fiber Optic Cable

Fiber optic cable is available in two general types:

• Multimode fiber is wide enough to carry more than one light signal. (Each signal is called a "mode.")

• Single-mode fiber is thin and can carry only one light signal.

Multimode Fiber

Each light signal or light ray that passes through a cable is called a "mode." Multimode fiber optic cable is wider than single-mode cable, thus it has enough room for more than one light ray. These light signals are separated by different angles of reflection as they travel down the core.

Because multimode signaling separates light signals by angle, not all light rays travel the same distance. Some light rays will travel nearly straight through the core, while others bounce off the cladding many times before reaching the far end of the fiber, as illustrated on the Multimode Fiber Diagram. With modes traveling different distances, but at the same speed, the spread of the signal increases over time, and can cause data errors due to the overlapping of light pulses. This problem is known as modal dispersion.

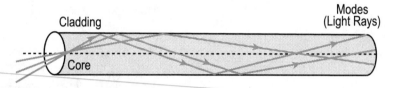

Multimode Fiber

The construction of a multimode fiber can either cause or fix this problem. There are two types of multimode fiber: step-index and graded-index fiber.

Step-Index Fiber

The standard type of optical fiber, called "step-index fiber", consists of only two transparent layers (core and cladding), and cannot compensate for the multimode signal dispersion effect. The fiber cable shown on the Fiber Optic Cable Diagram (shown earlier on page 107) is a step-index fiber.

Graded-Index Fiber

The core of a graded-index fiber cable has several transparent layers, each with a different refractive index. This planned inconsistency allows light modes to travel at different speeds through the core. The speed at which the modes travel depends upon the part of the core it is traveling through. Modes traveling down the center of the core do so at a slower speed than those refracting off the cladding. Thus, all modes reach the far end of the fiber more uniformly. The most commonly specified fiber optic cable is 62.5/125-µm multimode graded-index.

Single-Mode Fiber

Single-mode fibers have diameters sized to the wavelength they are designed to carry. A typical single-mode fiber core diameter is 8 μm. Only one mode will propagate through fiber with this core diameter. The narrower fiber diameter causes a light signal to travel in a straighter path, with less reflection and dispersion. However, the narrower core also makes single-mode fiber more difficult and expensive to install.

Single-mode fibers require laser diode transmitters. By using this coherent light source, single-mode fiber optic cable can support longer transmission distances than multimode fiber. Distances range from a few miles to as many as 20 miles.

Single-mode fibers are generally step-index fibers. Because only one mode travels along the fiber, the problem of diffusion does not occur in single-mode fibers. The Single-Mode Fiber Diagram illustrates this type of fiber.

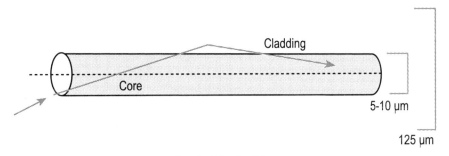

Single-Mode Fiber

Installing Fiber Optic Cable

Fiber optic cable is difficult to install correctly; therefore, it requires well-trained, careful installation technicians. This, combined with the time-consuming nature of each connection, make fiber optic cable the most expensive cable to install. Because of this need for training and experience, many organizations hire specialists to install fiber optic networks.

Connections and splices of fiber optic cable are particularly diffi-cult to make. Each end of the cable must be cut off at perfect right angles, the ends polished by hand or machine, and the cable pre-cisely aligned to the connector.

Like copper wire connectors, the snap-in connectors that termi-nate optical fibers provide a simple way to link one fiber to another, or a device. However, the nature of optical transmission means that fiber connectors must do their job at a higher level of precision. While it is fairly simple for copper connectors to make a secure electrical connection, fiber connectors must precisely align the ends of two very thin fibers.

There are many different types of fiber connectors and many of them are proprietary. The EIA/TIA-568 standard specifies two con-nector types, illustrated on the Fiber Optic Connectors Diagram:

- ST connectors are allowed in legacy installations.

- SC connectors are preferred.

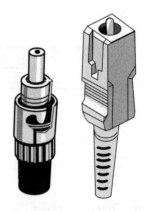

**Fiber Optic Connectors:
ST (left) and SC (right)**

Activities

1. Fiber optic cable is not sensitive to electrical noise.
   True or False

2. Single-mode fiber uses laser beams to generate a light signal.
   True or False

3. If light strikes the cladding at too steep an angle, the light will bounce too many times, causing the signal to travel too slowly. True or False

Extended Activities

1. Obtain samples of the following types of fiber optic cable. Examine and discuss the characteristics of each.

Note: Do not attempt to peel away the outer coating to reveal the fiber itself. The very thin glass fiber can easily penetrate bare skin.

   a. Single-mode fiber (10BaseF) and connectors

   _____

   _____

   b. Multimode fiber and connectors

   _____

   _____

2. Write a brief report that explains why laser light is different from the normal light we typically use. What quality of laser light allows it to travel so far without dispersing?

3. Visit **http://www.lightreading.com** and read some of the beginner tutorials on optical networking and fiber optic transmission. Summarize the most interesting tutorial for your class.

Lesson 5—Wireless Transmission

Radio waves are increasingly being used to carry voice and data signals through open space. Wireless transmission has traditionally been used where it is impossible or costly to install fixed cable, such as historical buildings or rough terrain. However, radio-based mobile communication, both voice and data, is growing explosively as consumers demand the flexibility and convenience of cell phones and wireless data networks.

The term "wireless" usually does not mean that a signal is carried using radio technology all the way. Most wireless transmission uses the cable-based telephone system as much as possible, only shifting to radio transmission when necessary.

Objectives

At the end of this lesson you should be able to:

- Describe how radio waves carry data

- Explain why the radio frequency (RF) spectrum is a finite resource

- Describe the advantages and drawbacks of satellite communication

 **Key Point**

Wireless networks use the RF spectrum below the range of visible light.

How Wireless Transmission Works

Wireless voice and data transmission works in basically the same way as your favorite radio station. The sending station transmits a consistent radio carrier wave at an assigned frequency and signal strength. To send a signal, the sending station uses the signal information to modulate the carrier wave. The modulated wave is amplified or strengthened, then sent to a transmitter on an antenna.

The antenna radiates the modulated wave outward through open space. Depending on the type of antenna in use, the modulated signal may radiate equally in all directions or focused into one area. The Wireless Transmission Diagram illustrates this type of technology.

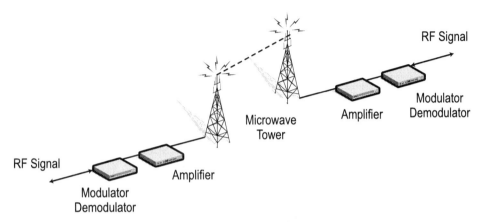

Wireless Transmission

As a radio wave travels, it can be blocked by large obstructions such as hills. Certain types of radio signals may reflect off large objects such as buildings. The wave also weakens or attenuates as it travels farther from its source, just as the sound of your voice (waves in the air) becomes faint over distance.

If a receiver's antenna is located within range of the transmitter (close enough so the signal has not completely faded), the second antenna will detect the modulated wave from the transmitter. Radio receiver hardware, tuned to the sender's carrier frequency, can then demodulate the transmitted waveform to restore the original signal information.

The Electromagnetic Spectrum

Radio waves are one part of the electromagnetic spectrum, which includes all types of radiated energy, such as radio waves, infrared waves (heat), visible light, and x-rays. This spectrum is illustrated on the Electromagnetic Spectrum Diagram.

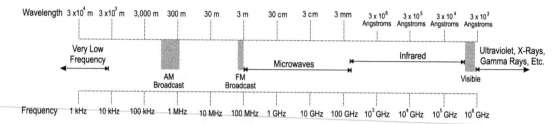

Electromagnetic Spectrum

At first glance, the electromagnetic spectrum seems very wide; however, not all of it is useful for sending signals through open air. The sun interferes with any messages sent in the visible light spectrum, and the atmosphere absorbs ultraviolet light. X-rays and gamma rays (and beyond) are so short that they simply pass through most receivers without being detected. Thus, to transmit signals, we must use wavelengths that are longer than visible light: infrared, microwaves, and radio. In general, we call these wavelengths the "RF spectrum."

We identify parts of the RF spectrum by either of the following measurements:

- Wavelength is the physical distance between the crests of a wave, as illustrated on the Wavelength Diagram. As we can see on the Electromagnetic Spectrum Diagram, these phenomena are arranged in order of their wavelengths. Some radio waves are as long as 30,000 m, while the wavelength of infrared energy ranges from 3 mm to 0.003 mm. Shorter wavelengths are measured in Angstroms: 1 Angstrom is one ten-millionth of a millimeter (10^{-9} m).

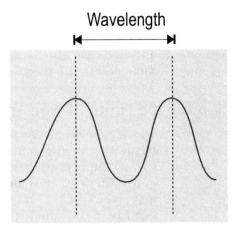

Wavelength

- Frequency measures the number of times per second that a wave moves from the highest point, through the lowest point, then back to the highest point again. This concept is illustrated on the Frequency Diagram. Frequency is measured in cycles per second or Hz. One Hz equals 1 cycle per second, 1 kiloHertz (kHz) equals 1,000 Hz, 1 MHz equals 1 million Hz, and 1 GHz equals 1 billion Hz.

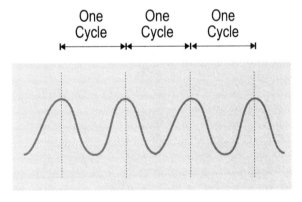

Frequency

Either of these measurements is equally good for identifying parts of the RF spectrum, because they are directly related to each other. As the wavelength of energy becomes shorter, so does its frequency. Thus, if one person says "the 100-GHz band," and another says "the 3-mm range," they are both talking about the same part of the spectrum.

Competition for the Finite RF Spectrum

The RF spectrum is a finite natural resource. Improvements in technology continue to expand the usable number of radio bands by making it possible to use tighter ranges of frequencies. However, each newly available frequency is still unique, thus two users may typically not transmit over the same frequency simultaneously in the same area.

To avoid interference, every type of radio transmission, from radar to navigation beacons to police scanners, must operate at assigned wavelengths and power levels. Therefore, the use of each frequency is carefully regulated by public agencies, and competition for the RF spectrum is fierce.

In the United States, the Federal Communications Commission (FCC) licenses the use of radio frequencies to prevent interference among potential users. International use of the RF spectrum is regulated by the ITU. With the growth of satellite communications, the ITU's role in frequency assignment has made it a very important player in worldwide communications.

Wireless Networking Applications

There is a staggering number of uses for radio transmission. However, wireless transmission in data networks tends to fall into the following categories:

- Point-to-point microwave systems
- Satellites
- Cellular systems and Personal Communications Services (PCS)
- Wireless LANs
- Short-range infrared transmission

As we discuss each of these wireless applications, remember that they are all based on the same principles that we have just discussed. In each case, a transmitter modulates a carrier wave and a receiver detects and demodulates that wave.

Point-to-Point Microwave Systems

Microwave systems normally use FM to beam directional signals between two dish-shaped antennae. These antennae are usually placed on top of high buildings or towers, and are connected by means of wire or cable to transmitting and receiving equipment. Microwave links are popular for connecting LANs in different buildings, especially in dense cities where it can be very expensive to lay new cable. However, microwave transmission can be degraded by water in the air (rain and fog), and is vulnerable to eavesdropping.

The major disadvantage of microwave is that the sending and receiving antennae must be in "line of sight" (aligned so one antenna can directly "see" the other). This means that they cannot be more than 20 to 25 miles apart, because the curve of the Earth will block the signal even if no hills are in the way. However, microwave links can be built over long distances, and around obstacles, by relaying the signal through a series of intermediate antennas, called "repeaters."

Satellites

A satellite is an orbiting device that receives a signal from a ground station, amplifies it, and rebroadcasts it to all Earth stations capable of seeing the satellite and receiving its transmissions. The satellite functions as a repeater, much like the repeaters used in terrestrial microwave communications. The Satellite Signal Path Diagram illustrates the path a signal takes through a satellite.

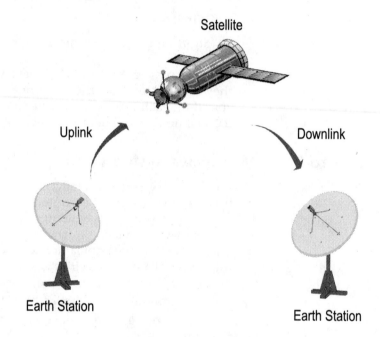

Satellite Signal Path

The four basic functions of a satellite include:

- Receiving a signal from an Earth station
- Changing the frequency of the received signal (uplink)
- Amplifying the received signal
- Retransmitting the signal to one or more Earth stations (downlink)

GEO Satellites

A geosynchronous (GEO) satellite circles the Earth at the same speed that the Earth rotates. As a result, the satellite remains stationed over the same point on the Earth's surface.

The advantage of GEO transmission is the vast amount of distance a single satellite is capable of covering. For example, the International Mobile Satellite system (INMARSAT) covers the entire Earth, except the poles, with four primary satellites. (Four additional satellites serve as backup.)

The big drawback to GEO transmission is the time it takes the signal to travel. The orbit of a GEO satellite is high, approximately 22,300 miles above the Earth for a satellite stationed above the equator. Thus, a signal transmitting to and from one of these satellites may travel more than 44,000 miles. This propagation delay causes a noticeable and annoying echo in telephone calls, and can disrupt some types of interactive data communication. However, this delay does not interfere with noninteractive transmissions, such as file transfers or video broadcast.

LEO Satellites

Low Earth Orbit (LEO) satellites solve the delay problem because they are positioned in a much lower orbit: 435 to 1,500 miles above the Earth. However, a satellite in a lower orbit does not remain stationary, it moves relative to surface locations. The lower a satellite's orbit, the faster it moves, and the smaller the area of the Earth it can cover.

Therefore, LEO systems require many satellites (40 to 70) that orbit in a carefully controlled pattern. The much larger cost of a fleet of satellites, and the added complexity of the control systems, greatly increases the cost of LEO satellites.

Cellular Systems and PCS

Like many wireless systems, cell phone systems route calls through the regular ground-based telephone switching network, only shifting to radio transmission for the last leg of the trip to the subscriber (replacing the copper local loop with a wireless link).

An array of cellular transceiver towers transmits signals to cell phone users and receives signals from them. Each transceiver tower is connected to the hard-wired telephone network and converts telephone signals to radio waves, and vice-versa.

The area covered by each tower is called a "cell." The number and placement of cells is critical to good performance, because cell phone transmitters, like other microwave antennae, require line-of-sight transmission. Physical obstructions, such as hills or large buildings, cause choppy calls and "dead spots" where cell phones simply do not work.

Despite the fact that cell phone performance is sometimes unreliable or unavailable, the demand for portable communication continues to rise. Mobile professionals, such as salespeople and construction contractors, now rely on cellular communication for much more than just voice calling. Increasingly, these "road warriors" use cell phone technology to send and receive e-mail, faxes, and other data.

PCS are wireless networks that use cellular transmission or LEO satellites to deliver both voice and data to small portable devices. Essentially, PCS describes cell phones that double as computers, or hand-held computers that double as telephones. As a result, PCS includes a wide range of smart devices, such as:

- Cellular telephones with text displays

- Personal Digital Assistants (PDAs), such as the PalmPilot

- Pagers

- Laptop computers with cellular modems

These human-used devices are the most visible aspect of PCS, but the technology is also used for monitoring and control of remote devices, such as meters, valves, or scientific monitoring systems. For example, a rancher can use cellular PCS to control a distant irrigation system, while a researcher can use it to monitor a mountaintop seismometer.

Wireless LANs

Wireless LANs are growing in popularity as workers and work teams become more flexible and mobile. Wireless LANs offer the benefit of relatively inexpensive installation and reconfiguration as users change their physical locations. In most cases, wireless LANs are intended to be an extension of an existing network and interoperate with a hard-wired LAN or LANs. However, wireless LANs can offer a cost-effective solution for office environments that are difficult or expensive to wire or rewire with traditional LAN cabling.

Historically, wireless LANs have been limited in popularity by problems with interference, security, low data rates of transmission, and higher installation cost.

Radio-based LANs include two categories:

- Licensed microwave LANs
- Nonlicensed spread-spectrum LANs

Licensed Microwave LANs

Microwave LANs use dedicated radio frequencies and can provide a relatively high data rate and the ability to transmit through walls and other partitions. However, the acceptance of this technology has been severely limited by the following drawbacks:

- In the United States, these systems must be licensed by the FCC. This requirement decreases the number of available RF spectrum assignments.
- It is relatively expensive.
- It has high power requirements.
- Some users are concerned about potential health risks associated with exposure to microwave radiation.
- Common devices, such as microwave ovens, can cause significant interference.

Nonlicensed Spread Spectrum LANs

While a microwave LAN transmits over a narrow assigned band of frequencies, spread spectrum techniques scatter a signal over a broad range of frequencies, using a low level of power for each individual frequency. The intent is to make each individual signal look like background noise, which allows a greater number of users to share a frequency band.

Currently, there are two approaches to spread spectrum transmission:

- Frequency hopping—Transmission switches rapidly between available frequencies. This works like two radio users who regularly change channels to avoid eavesdroppers.
- Direct sequence—This approach uses a coded pattern to spread a single signal over many separate frequencies.

In both of these methods, signal transmission is controlled by a code. In a frequency hopping system, the code determines the pattern and timing of the frequency hops. In a direct sequence system, the code determines what frequencies to use for spreading the signal.

123

The same transmitter uses a different code to communicate with each receiver, such as a cell phone. By knowing the code, each receiving station can extract its own signal from the apparent background noise. This approach prevents most interference, even though many users share the same band of frequencies. Because each transmitter/receiver pair uses a different code, each signal cannot be understood by any receiver that does not share that code.

In a typical spread spectrum wireless LAN, each computer is equipped with a wireless network adapter containing a transceiver, antenna, and software. A wireless access point unit, mounted on the wall or ceiling, passes signals between the mobile devices and a network hub. The Spread Spectrum Wireless LAN Diagram illustrates a spread spectrum segment connected to a 10BaseT hub.

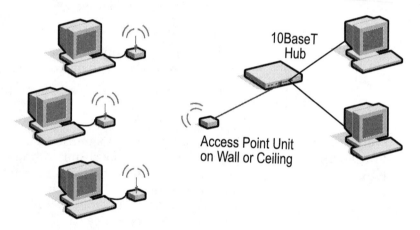

Spread Spectrum Wireless LAN

Spread spectrum systems can transmit through typical office building walls, allowing workgroups in different rooms to be in continuous communication. Typical working distances range from 35 to 200 feet inside a building, and up to 200 feet outside (or in open offices with no obstructions). This short transmission distance is the reason wireless LANs are not individually licensed.

One of the limitations of this technology has been relatively slow data transmission rates in the 1- to 2-Mbps range. However, current methods of wireless LAN transmission can achieve data rates up to 11 Mbps under optimum conditions.

Although original spread spectrum techniques developed for military applications are highly secure, spread spectrum techniques used in current wireless LAN implementations provide no inherent security.

Short-Range Infrared Transmission

Use of infrared wireless LAN systems has declined as a significant approach to providing a comprehensive LAN solution. Some of the drawbacks of infrared transmission for whole-office LANs include:

• Inability to transmit through opaque surfaces

• High cost and power requirements for infrared transceivers

• Potential eye damage due to high-power infrared transmissions

The only currently viable infrared technique is to provide short-range "point-and-shoot" connectivity for PDAs and peripheral devices. For example, a user can use an infrared link to download data to a PDA from a computer in the same room. Instead of exchanging business cards, two PDA users can "beam" their contact information to each other.

Wireless LAN Comparison

In recent years, several promising wireless LAN technologies have declined in importance, leaving spread spectrum techniques as the only currently viable approach for comprehensive wireless solutions. Within this category, it is important to carefully consider the features offered by different vendors to ensure they are appropriate for your specific requirements. Wireless LANs represent an area of rapid technological change that will likely continue.

The Wireless LANs Table presents a comparison between the two most popular wireless technologies: spread spectrum and infrared "point-and-shoot."

Wireless LANs

Wireless LAN Type	Advantage	Disadvantage
Radio: Spread spectrum	Transmission through walls Only comprehensive solution	Low data rate (1 to 2 Mbps)
Nonradio: Infrared point-and-shoot	Higher speed (up to 20 Mbps) Inexpensive	Short range, line-of-sight, point-to-point

Mobile Computing

Tremendous innovations are being made to provide mobile computer users with the ability to communicate with the rest of a LAN using long-distance wireless technologies. This is a very volatile area, and technologies are being developed based on satellite transmission, cellular (telephone) systems, special mobile radio, and other media. In many ways, these can be considered long-distance data communication technologies rather than LAN technologies. However, their success hinges on their ability to internetwork with the dominant "hard-wired" LAN protocols.

Activities

1. The wavelength of a 2-GHz signal is shorter than the wavelength of a 2-kHz signal. True or False

2. A radio transmitter uses a carrier wave with a 1-GHz frequency. What is the wavelength of that signal?

3. Radio signals travel at the speed of light (186,000 miles per second). How long does it take for a signal to travel up to a GEO satellite above the equator, then back to Earth? Assume the satellite adds no processing time of its own.

4. What are the drawbacks of infrared transmission in office networks? What is currently the most effective use of infrared transmission?

    _____

    _____

    _____

    _____

5. Why are spread spectrum wireless LANs not licensed by the FCC?

    _____

    _____

    _____

    _____

6. Why does a GEO satellite always remain over the same place on Earth?

    _____

    _____

    _____

    _____

Extended Activities

1. Visit the International Mobile Satellite Corporation at **http://www.inmarsat.org**. Make a list of the most common applications of GEO satellite communication.

   _____

   _____

2. Look for wireless LAN hardware in a few computer catalogs or Web sites. Compare the prices of wireless and hard-wired components, such as NICs (adapters) and hubs.

3. To get a better idea of the intense competition for the RF spectrum, visit the Web site of the U.S. Department of Commerce's National Telecommunications and Information Administration (**http://www.ntia.doc.gov/osmhome/allochrt.html**). They offer a free, downloadable chart that displays the RF spectrum assignments for the United States.

Lesson 6—Overview of a Structured Cable Plant

In many of today's office environments, the data network cabling has been installed incrementally, responding to changes in technology, networking needs, and company plans. Typically, this leaves a legacy of incompatible systems that may include telephone switching systems, mainframe or minicomputer systems, personal computer (PC)-based LANs, and other office communications equipment.

Because each system is installed according to its own set of wiring criteria using different types of cable, these systems are difficult to interconnect, and especially difficult to maintain and expand. This situation is typical of the unstructured wiring system, in which there is no single set of standards for interconnection. Although initial costs are comparatively low for unstructured wiring, the long-term difficulties and expense of integrating or replacing the incompatible wiring systems are considerable.

In recent years, a clear trend has emerged among network planners, to implement network cabling as a structured wiring system according to uniform standards. This involves a shift in perspective. Rather than seeing cabling simply as a way to connect devices, cabling is now seen as an important architectural entity: the cable plant, cabling system, or premises wiring. The intent is to install a wiring capability that not only provides interoperability for existing networking technologies, but also anticipates future growth by allowing for efficient reconfigurations.

Objectives

At the end of this lesson you should be able to:

- Name and describe the six subsystems of a structured wiring plan
- Describe the main connections between a building entrance and user's desktop
- Discuss the advantages of a standards-based approach to network wiring

 **Key Point**

In the telephone industry, an office building is known as the customer's premises; therefore, its wiring is known as the premises wiring.

Structured Wiring Systems

It is more efficient to install a structured wiring system when a building is constructed or remodeled, rather than pulling wires through existing walls, ceilings, and floors. As a practical issue, architects and building owners often need to install cable before they know what type of network a tenant will want. A structured wiring approach can solve this problem by providing guidelines for a universal wiring system that can be adapted to almost any network requirement.

The interest in universal wiring is supported by three technological trends:

- Convergence on three cable types

- Use of a hub-based distributed star physical topology

- Emergence of industry-wide standards

Cable Convergence

The ability to preinstall a cabling plant is based on the fact that all major LAN technologies can be supported by three types of cable:

- Shielded twisted pair (STP)

- Unshielded twisted pair (UTP)

- Optical fiber

Every significant LAN technology can be supported by either STP or UTP for the vast majority of short- to medium-length segments. Fiber optic cable can then be reserved for long backbone connections, or applications and locations that require greater immunity from interference.

Hub-Based Distributed Star Topology

Hubs are the key integrating devices of today's networks. They provide flexible expansion, and serve as centralized points for wiring interconnection, maintenance, and fault isolation. Hubs can be connected together by backbone segments to form a multiple-star physical topology, sometimes known as a distributed star. This concept is illustrated on the Distributed Star Topology Diagram. Because every hub manufacturer provides interfaces for all three cable types, a universal cabling system can be installed with confidence; any hub can be adapted to the existing cabling.

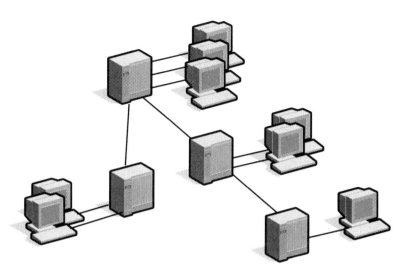

Distributed Star Topology

Industry-Wide Standards

Major vendors were among the first to realize the importance of structured wiring systems, providing proprietary pre-engineered wiring plans that ensured the proper functioning of their devices in an enterprise network. Telephone companies were among the leaders of this trend, based on their experience with telephone cable installations. Some of the major wiring systems are listed in the Proprietary Wiring Systems Table.

Proprietary Wiring Systems

Vendor	Structured Wiring Plan
AT&T	Systimax Premises Distribution System
DEC	DEConnect
IBM	IBM Cabling System
Northern Telecom	Integrated Building Distribution Network (IBDN)

The EIA/TIA-568 Standard

The Electronic Industries Association (EIA) and the Telecommunications Industry Association (TIA) have taken the lead in providing an industry-wide open standard for structured wiring. Of particular relevance is their Commercial Building Telecommunications Cabling Standard (EIA/TIA-568 [being renamed to EIA/TIA SP-2840]), which provides users and vendors precise guidelines for premises wiring. It includes:

- Sample topologies

- Distance limitations

- Cabling types for a given network speed

- Connector types to be used with a given cable type

- Minimum performance specifications for cables and connectors

Other important EIA/TIA standards include:

- Commercial Building Standard for Telecommunications Pathways and Spaces (EIA/TIA-569)

- Residential and Light Commercial Telecommunications Wiring Standard (EIA/TIA-570)

An open, standards-based structured wiring system offers benefits similar to that of standards-based networking protocols and architectures:

- Interoperability of devices regardless of vendor

- Long-term cost effectiveness based on installing enough cable for future needs, providing an upgrade path for new technologies, and reduced maintenance due to a consistent architecture and materials

Structured Wiring Subsystems

The structured wiring concept looks at the cable plant in terms of a typical office building. Structured wiring systems such as EIA/TIA-568 refer to premises wiring in terms of six modular subsystems:

- Building entrance
- Equipment room
- Vertical (backbone) cabling
- Wiring closets
- Horizontal wiring
- Work area

Each subsystem is characterized by typical types of devices and interconnections. The Structured Wiring Subsystems Diagram shows a simplified example of a building's wiring subsystems.

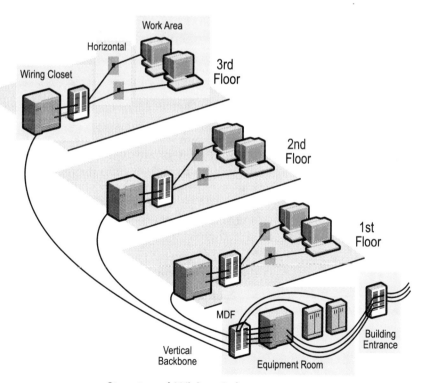

Structured Wiring Subsystems

Building Entrance

In a typical office building, there is one point of entry and exit for all telecommunication lines, including telephone, data backbones to other premises, and other wide area network (WAN) transmission facilities. This may occupy a separate closet or room, or share part of a common equipment room.

Within the building entrance, the telecommunication company's cables are terminated on a device that makes it simple to connect the customer's equipment to the transmission line. Any device that does this job is generally called the "demarcation point" or "demarc," because it marks the boundary between the facilities owned by the telecommunication company and equipment owned by the customer.

Cables used to provide T1 service (discussed in Unit 7) are terminated in a device called a "smart jack." A smart jack allows the telephone company to remotely test the electrical integrity of a transmission circuit from the switching office.

Other incoming telephone company cables, called "trunk cables," are generally terminated in a cross-connect device. Cross-connect devices allow large numbers of conducting wires to be mechanically interconnected in an organized fashion.

There are two types of cross-connect devices:

- Punch-down blocks

- Patch panels

Punch-Down Blocks

Punch-down blocks were developed to provide a connection point for telephone wires. They simplify wiring installation by providing a single termination point for cables entering a building or wiring closet. Each strand of twisted pair cable is semipermanently pressed into a channel on the punch-down block. The channel anchors the strand and penetrates the insulation to provide the electrical connection.

There are several types of punch-down blocks from various vendors; the two most common are:

- Siemens S66M1-50 termination block, commonly called a "66 block"

- AT&T 110/A Block, commonly called a "110 block"

From the punch-down block, patch cables can later be run to the ports of devices, such as hubs (for LAN cables) or a private branch exchange (PBX) (for voice cables).

The 66 Block Diagram shows how connectors are arranged on a punch-down block. In each horizontal row, the two left-hand contacts have a built-in electrical connection between them. Likewise, the two right-hand contacts also share a built-in connection. The center two contacts are not automatically connected to each other, but can be linked by punching a wire onto both contacts, or connecting them with a metal "bridging clip." When the two center contacts in the same row are connected, all of the other contacts on the same row are electrically connected to each other.

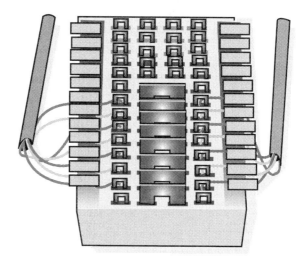

66 Block

The 66 Block Diagram shows how a punch-down block is typically used to connect customer-owned LAN wiring to the cables owned by the telephone company. Each incoming telecommunication company wire is connected to one of the outside connectors on the 66 block. To continue that connection into the LAN, the customer connects another wire, such as one strand of a Category 5 cable, to the opposite outside connector on the same row. Then the customer connects the two center contacts to connect the telephone company line to the LAN cable. This method of connecting cables is safer and more organized than simply twisting the ends of two wires together.

A 66 block contains 50 rows of contacts. This is enough to terminate an incoming 25-pair cable on one side, and connect each wire of that pair to a corresponding wire on the other side of the block.

In some cases, a network technician may terminate a 50-pair cable on a single 66 block, by using each outside pair of contacts to connect one incoming wire and one LAN wire. The two center contacts are not connected, so the opposite pair of contacts on the same row can be used to connect a different outside wire to another inside wire. This arrangement is called a "split 66 block," because the block is effectively split in two when the center pair of contacts is not connected.

Punch-down blocks are typically mounted to plywood panels attached to the wiring closet wall. Some punch-down blocks come with a series of RJ-45 outlets, so that individual wires can be punched down at one side, and connectorized patch cables can be attached at the other.

Patch Panels

Patch panels are designed for maximum ease of reconfiguration, by providing connectorized ports for the interconnection of devices. For example, a typical patch panel for UTP would have a series of RJ-45 outlets to accept RJ-45 cable terminations or patch cords. Patch panels are often mounted in equipment racks. The Cross-Connect Devices Diagram shows a punch-down block and patch panel configuration in a wiring closet.

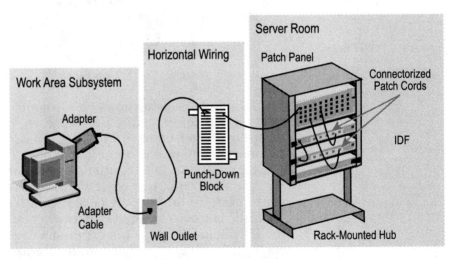

Cross-Connect Devices

Many cross-connect devices are pre-wired on one end with a 50-connector jack known as a telco connector, which is designed for a 25-pair cable. These are typically used for interconnecting cross-connect and network devices such as hubs or bridge/routers. The 25-pair cables come in a variety of configurations including:

- 50-connector interfaces at each end

- 50-connector interface at one end and 8 separate RJ-45 plugs at the other (an octopus)

- 50-connector interface at one end and a group of 8 RJ-45 outlets at the other (a harmonica)

Equipment Room

Larger office buildings may have a centralized equipment room to provide a controlled environment for devices such as the telephone system PBX, banks of modems, servers, and LAN hubs. In terms of structured LAN wiring, this room includes a main cross-connect, sometimes referred to as a main distribution frame (MDF). The MDF provides a central interconnection point for the network cabling.

Vertical (Backbone) Cabling

The backbone cabling is usually referred to as vertical cabling, because it often runs from an equipment room in the basement to a wiring closet on an upper floor. Vertical cabling interconnects equipment in the building entrance, equipment room, and wiring closets.

A separate backbone cable will often run from the MDF cross-connect to each wiring closet. In other cases, wiring closets may be directly connected to each other with backbone cable; these backbone cables are known as intercloset links.

Backbone cabling may be UTP, STP, or fiber optic cable. However, copper cabling is vulnerable to the high levels of electromagnetic interference/radio frequency interference (EMI/RFI) common in elevator shafts, typically the most convenient vertical wiring channel in a building. Therefore, many structured wiring installations use fiber optic cable for the vertical backbone, and less-expensive UTP in less "noisy" locations.

Wiring Closets

Wiring closets, typically at least one on each floor, house one or more hubs. The equipment in the wiring closet is known as intermediate distribution frame (IDF) equipment. The hubs are connected to stations located on each floor. Although the specific layout will vary from site to site, there will typically be one or more cross-connect devices that interconnect the rack-mounted hub to the backbone cable(s) and the horizontal cables that run to wall plates at each user work area. The short cables used to interconnect the hub and cross-connects are called patch cables.

Horizontal Wiring

Horizontal wiring connects the wiring closet on each floor to wall plates within each user's work area. According to EIA/TIA-568, the horizontal cabling subsystem includes the cable, wall outlets within each work area, and any patch cords that connect each cable to equipment within a wiring closet.

Horizontal cabling supports a variety of communications services, such as:

- Voice (telephone)
- Data communications
- LAN

Horizontal wiring is typically UTP or STP, because of the large quantities necessary to wire a workplace. However, horizontal cables are vulnerable to the same EMI/RFI that can disrupt backbone communications. When necessary, cabling must be diverted around sources of interference, or shielded. The EIA/TIA-569 standard specifies methods to protect horizontal cables from EMI.

Work Area

A work area subsystem consists of the cable and other devices (such as an Ethernet network interface card [NIC]) connecting the user station to the wall plate, but not the wall plate itself.

Work area wiring is typically UTP or STP. Copper work area cables usually have RJ-45 plugs at both ends, to insert into the adapter card port and wall plate outlet.

Under EIA/TIA-568, a work area must have a minimum of two telecommunications outlets:

- One outlet (typically for voice) connects to a four-pair UTP cable, Category 3 or higher.

- One outlet (typically for data) connects to any of the allowed cable types (UTP, STP, or fiber) described below.

Universal Wiring Subsystems

Not all premises wiring can be regarded as universal. The universal wiring system mainly consists of the horizontal wiring subsystem and the backbone cabling subsystem, including cross-connect panels in the wiring closets and equipment room. These are the parts of the cable plant that are vendor-independent and can be preinstalled prior to overall network design. The other parts of the equipment and cabling will vary by manufacturer and the type of LAN technology chosen.

Cabling Distances

The EIA/TIA-568 standard recommends typical maximum cabling distances according to the equipment subsystem and type of cable. Some of these are listed in the Cabling Distances Table.

Cabling Distances

Subsystem	Fiber Optic	UTP	STP
Backbone	2,000 m	800 m	700 m
Intercloset link	2,000 m	800 m	700 m
Horizontal Wiring Closet to wall plate Wall plate to adapter	 N/A N/A	 90 m 10 m	 90 m 10 m

However, these are flexible guidelines and must be compared to more specific limitations and parameters provided by manufacturers, the Institute of Electrical and Electronics Engineers (IEEE), and the American National Standards Institute (ANSI) Fiber Distributed Data Interface (FDDI) standards.

Cabling Types

The EIA/TIA-568 standard specifies the types of cable that may be used in various subsystems.

Vertical (Backbone) Cabling

- 100-ohm UTP, Category 3, 4, or 5 (Category 5 recommended), in 25-pair bundles.
- 150-ohm STP
- 62.5/125-micron (or millionths of a meter [µm]) multimode optical fiber cable (where 62.5 refers to the core diameter and 125 refers to the cladding diameter), in groups of 6 to 12 fibers per sheath. Multimode cable sheaths are colored beige.
- Single-mode optical fiber cable, in groups of 6 to 12 fibers per sheath. Single-mode cable sheaths are colored blue.

Horizontal Cabling

- Four-pair 100-ohm UTP, Category 3, 4, or 5 (Category 5 recommended)
- Two-pair 150-ohm STP
- Two-fiber, 62.5/125-µm multimode optical fiber cable

Activities

1. List the benefits derived from a standards-based approach to network wiring.

    _____

    _____

    _____

    _____

2. Draw a diagram illustrating a structured wiring system for a two-story building. Show all subsystems.

3. List and briefly describe the six subsystems of a structured wiring system.

_____

_____

_____

_____

_____

_____

Extended Activity

Using your favorite Internet search engine, locate information on the EIA/TIA-568 and EIA/TIA-569 standards. Choose one of the subsystems and discuss what you learned.

_____

_____

_____

_____

_____

_____

Summary

In Unit 2, we looked at the signals a network carries, network topologies that determine the flow of those signals, and physical transmission media used to build those topologies.

We learned that data can be carried by two types of signals: analog and digital. The term "broadband" describes an analog transmission system that can carry multiple simultaneous signals, each modulated on a different carrier frequency (channel). In contrast, "narrowband" analog transmission, like your home telephone line, may carry only one or two channels.

The term "baseband" describes digital transmission. Baseband transmission can only carry one channel of information at a time; however, it is fast and technically simpler to implement. Thus, baseband is commonly used in LANs, such as the popular 10BaseT standard for Ethernet networks.

While all data networks use baseband signaling, their physical layouts or topologies can vary widely. The topology of a network determines the direction and pattern of signal flow. When network professionals discuss a network design, they usually mean its logical topology, which shows how signals flow in the network. In contrast, a physical topology shows how individual devices are connected to each other.

The bus topology, using coaxial cable, was one of the first small network designs. The bus is a coaxial cable "spine." All nodes attach to that cable and communicate by sending information along the common bus. The bus topology has been largely replaced by the more flexible star configuration.

Star topology is currently the most popular way to wire a network. A signal-sharing device, called a "hub," forms the physical and logical center of the network. Each network node is connected to the hub by a separate twisted pair cable. Because each node is isolated on its own cable, a problem with one node does not necessarily affect the other computers attached to that hub.

The bus and star topologies are both broadcast networks. A hub serves the same logical function as a coaxial bus. All nodes connected to the hub (or bus) receive every signal transmitted; however, a node ignores any transmission not addressed to it.

In a ring network, the logical topology requires each node to receive each signal from its neighbor on one side, then relay the signal to its neighbor on the other side. Ring networks can use one of two physical topologies. In a "pure" ring, point-to-point connections link the nodes in a circle, like beads on a necklace. A break in one of the links, or a malfunction of one of the nodes, can take the entire network down.

In a star ring topology, all nodes are connected to a central MAU that distributes signals to each station in turn. If one node fails, the MAU can simply bypass it and maintain communication with the other nodes.

A mesh topology is a system of point-to-point links that connect each node to every other node. This topology is most often used to link separate locations in MANs or WANs. When the number of nodes in a mesh network grows, most network designers abandon the mesh topology in favor of a subscription to a switched "cloud" network owned by a telecommunications service provider (telephone company).

A backbone is any part of a network that connects other networks or network segments. A network backbone can use any of the topologies we have discussed in this unit. However, the data-carrying capacity (bandwidth) of the backbone must be much higher than the segments it connects, just as a major highway carries more traffic than a neighborhood road.

All of these topologies can be implemented by using any, or all, of three types of physical transmission media: copper cable, fiber optic cable, or radio waves. At the beginning of this unit, we stated that there is no one perfect transmission medium. The Media Characteristics Table makes this clear, by comparing the features of twisted pair, coaxial cable, fiber optic cable, microwave, and satellite transmission.

Media Characteristics

Character-istic	Twisted Pair	Coaxial Cable	Fiber Optic	Microwave	GEO Satellite	LEO Satellite
Capable of digital transmission	Good – distance sensitive	Better–less distance sensitive	Best – much less distance sensitive	Yes	Yes	Yes
Prone to attenuation	Most	Less	Least	Yes	Much less than ground-based microwave	Much less than ground-based microwave
Prone to electrical interference	Yes	Somewhat	No	Yes	Less than ground-based microwave	Less than ground-based microwave
Cost of installation	Moderate	Moderate	Moderately high	High	Very high	Extremely high
Cost of associated equipment	Low	Moderately high	High	High	High	High
Bandwidth	Low	Medium	High	High	High	High
International transmission	No	Yes	Yes	Yes	Yes	Yes
Appropriate for broad-cast video	No	Yes	Yes	Yes	Yes	Yes
Strengths	Inexpensive, easy to install	High band-width	Long-distance transmission, high security	Rugged terrain and mobile tele-phones	Very long-distance transmission	Mobile transmission without delay
Drawbacks	Limited to 45 Mbps	Limited to 45 Mbps, difficult to install	Expensive and difficult to install	Vulnerable to eaves-dropping, may be distorted by poor weather	Noticeable propaga-tion delay	Expensive and complex

Unit 2 Quiz

1. Which of the following is most typical of a broadband network?

    a. Digital to digital

    b. Multiple analog channels

    c. One-way transmission of digital information

    d. Single analog channel

2. When is UTP cable preferred over STP?

    a. When there is little electrical interference

    b. When cost is no object

    c. When going long distances

3. Which connector type is used with Thinnet coaxial cable?

    a. RJ-45

    b. RG-58

    c. BNC

4. What is the main advantage of star topology?

    a. Redundancy

    b. Ease of management

    c. Minimize cable requirements

5. Which of the following cable types can transmit data the longest distance?

    a. Thinnet

    b. UTP

    c. STP

    d. Fiber optic

6. Which of the following cable types uses a T-connector to connect each NIC to the cable?

    a. Thinnet

    b. UTP

    c. Thicknet

    d. Fiber optic

7. How are bits represented on fiber optic cable?

   a. Electrical signals

   b. Pulses (on/off) of light

   c. Changing wavelength

   d. None of the above

8. Which of the following are the two primary types of light sources in fiber optic cables?

   a. UTP and STP

   b. Laser diode and LED

   c. Multimode and single-mode

   d. EMI and RFI

9. Which of the following are the two types of fiber optic cables?

   a. UTP and STP

   b. Laser diode and Light Emitting Diode

   c. Multimode and single-mode

   d. EMI and RFI

10. Which of the following describes the purpose of cladding in a fiber optic cable?

    a. To reflect light as it passes through a cable

    b. To amplify the light signal

    c. To increase the propagation of light

    d. To decrease the angle of reflection

11. Which of the following would not be used in a typical star topology?

    a. UTP cabling

    b. Hub

    c. NICs

    d. Thinnet

12. Which of the following is a radio frequency wireless technology most often used for?

    a. Replace cabled LANs

    b. Point-to-point transmission

    c. Low data rate applications

    d. Replacement of Ethernet in LANs

13. Which of the following network topologies forms a closed loop?

    a. Bus topology

    b. Broadcast topology

    c. Loop topology

    d. Ring topology

14. Which of the following network topologies connects devices to a shared straight-line cable?

    a. Bus topology

    b. Ring topology

    c. Loop topology

    d. Star ring topology

15. A baseband signal refers to which of the following?

    a. Modulated analog signal

    b. Analog carrier wave

    c. Digital signal

    d. Radio signal

16. Which of the following describes the function of a broadband network?

    a. Transmits multiple analog signals on the same physical medium

    b. Transmits a single analog signal

    c. Transmits multiple digital signals on the same physical medium

    d. Transmits signals over a broad geographic area

17. In a typical 10BaseT network, which of the following is the maximum distance a signal can be sent over twisted pair?

    a. 100 m

    b. 1,000 m

    c. 10 km

    d. 200 m

18. What type of physical medium uses light to represent binary information?

    a. Fiber optic cable

    b. 10BaseT

    c. 10Base2

    d. Microwave

19. Which of the following is the most widely used LAN topology?

    a. Mesh

    b. Bus

    c. Star

    d. Ring and star ring

20. In a 10BaseT star topology, which of the following performs the logical function of a bus?

    a. MAU

    b. Hub

    c. Coaxial cable

    d. UTP

21. A bus topology uses which of the following to connect the computers?

    a. MAU

    b. Hub

    c. Coaxial cable

    d. Fiber optic cable

22. When the specific topology of a network is unknown, it is commonly called which of the following?

    a. Switch

    b. Cloud

    c. Mesh

    d. Web

23. Which of the following is the portion of a network that connects other segments or networks to each other?

    a. Trunk

    b. Spine

    c. Highway

    d. Backbone

24. When a company links all of its separate networks, the overall network is called which of the following?

    a. Campus

    b. Backbone

    c. Enterprise network

    d. Topology

25. Which of the following causes the propagation delay of a GEO satellite?

    a. Slow radio waves

    b. Long distance between the satellite and Earth

    c. Heavy traffic on satellite channels

    d. Conversion of digital data to analog radio waves

26. For office space, your startup company wants to rent a historic building that features carefully restored wallpaper, polished wood floors, and ornate plaster ceilings. Which of the following is the best choice of a physical medium for your LAN?

    a. Infrared LAN

    b. Spread spectrum radio LAN

    c. Coaxial cable

    d. Satellite

27. When a series of point-to-point circuits connect every node to every other, the network is called which of the following?

    a. Bus

    b. Cloud

    c. Mesh

    d. Ring

28. How many wire pairs can be terminated on a 66 block?

    a. 66

    b. 50 or 100

    c. 33

    d. 25 or 50

29. In a building entrance, the demarcation point is usually which of the following?

    a. A patch panel

    b. A cross-connect

    c. A smart jack

    d. Any of the above

30. Draw diagrams of a pure ring, bus, and star topology.

Unit 3
Computer Protocols and Services

In Unit 2, we explained that the sender and receiver of a signal must both follow rules that define the structure and meaning of a message. Just as humans must share a common language to communicate, computers that communicate across a network must also have a common language, as well as rules for the use of that language. Those languages and rules are called "protocols," and many different protocols are used in data networking.

This unit introduces you to the basic terms and concepts that underlie all computer communication protocols. You will learn how protocols work, and how different protocols work together to move data across a network. This knowledge will become the foundation of your understanding of how computer networks function.

Lessons

1. Protocols
2. Layers of Protocols and Services
3. Communicating Across a Network

Terms

client—A client is any program that requests a service or resource from another program (either on the same computer or a different one). This term is often used to refer to the computer that hosts the client program; however, a client program may also run on a computer that normally functions as a server. See server.

decapsulation—As a data transmission is passed up through the protocol stack of a receiving computer, each protocol layer first removes the header that was added by its peer process on the sending computer, then passes the remaining data to the protocol layer just above. This process is referred to as decapsulation.

device driver—A device driver is a program that controls hardware devices attached to a computer, such as a printer or hard disk drive.

encapsulation—As a data transmission is passed down through the protocol stack of the sending computer, each protocol layer adds its own header to the data it receives from the layer above. This is known as encapsulation. When a message is physically transmitted from a sending computer, it includes a header for each of the protocols that processed it.

header—A header is part of a message that contains information necessary to send the message from one node to another. The header normally contains a field specifying the length of the encapsulated message, together with at least one field providing information about the message. If, for example, the message is a segment of a larger message, the header might specify the relative position of the segment in the complete message and probably the total number of segments in the message.

operating system (OS)—An OS is the basic system software of a computer that provides low-level services to applications.

peer—Two programs or processes that use the same protocol to communicate, and perform approximately the same function for their respective nodes are called "peer processes." With peer processes, in general, neither process controls the other, and the same protocol is used for data flowing in either direction.

protocol—A protocol is a defined method of communication between computers or computer applications.

reassembly—Reassembly is the process of recombining a segmented transmission to restore the original message. See segmentation.

redirector—A redirector is a client software component that decides whether a request for a computer service or resource (for example, read a file) is for the local computer or another computer on the network. Each software vendor uses a different name for this function, such as "shell," "requestor," or "client."

segmentation—The process of dividing a long data transmission into smaller chunks that lower layer processes can handle is referred to as segmentation. See reassembly.

server—A server is any program that provides a service to a client program. This term is often used to refer to the computer that hosts a server program; however, a server program may also run on a computer that normally functions as a client. See client.

stack—A stack is a group of protocols that work together to provide data communication. In a stack, each protocol uses the services of the protocol below it, and provides services to the protocol above it.

Lesson 1—Protocols

Protocols are essential to data communication; however, protocols are also used by people. Thus, this lesson introduces the basic concepts of computer protocols by comparing them to some of the common protocols we use to communicate every day.

Objectives

At the end of this lesson you should be able to:

- Describe what protocols are and why they are necessary

- Explain the purpose of a protocol header

- Name and describe some of the human protocols we use to communicate with other people

 **Key Point**

Protocols are necessary to give meaning to signals.

What is a Protocol?

In the last unit, we asked you to imagine you are standing in a telegraph office a century ago, as the telegraph sounder begins chattering its pattern of short tones, long tones, and pauses. If you understand Morse Code, as presented in the International Morse Code Table, you can read the message as it comes across. If you do not understand this code, the telegraph signal is meaningless to you.

International Morse Code

Letter	Code	Letter	Code	Letter	Code	Numeral	Code
A	. —	J	. — — —	S	. . .	0	— — — — —
B	— . . .	K	— . —	T	—	1	. — — — —
C	— . — .	L	. — . .	U	. . —	2	. . — — —

International Morse Code (Continued)

Letter	Code	Letter	Code	Letter	Code	Numeral	Code
D	— . — .	M	— —	V	. . . —	3	. . . — —
E	.	N	— .	W	. — —	4	. . . . —
F	. . — .	O	— — —	X	— . . —	5	. . . . .
G	— — .	P	. — — ,	Y	— . — —	6	— . . . .
H	. . . .	Q	— — . —	Z	— — . .	7	— — . . .
I	. .	R	. — .			8	— — — . .
						9	— — — — .

There is nothing special about the way Morse Code assigns dots (short tones) and dashes (long tones) to letters of the alphabet. To save work for the telegraph operator, Samuel Morse assigned short codes to the most frequently used letters of the English alphabet; however, he could just as easily have assigned a dash to the letter E rather than a dot.

Now imagine that you have learned International Morse Code, but the distant telegraph operator uses dots where dashes would normally be, and vice versa. This time, when he taps out a message, you cannot understand it. (And neither can the other operators, thus his career will be short.)

Therefore, we can say that the system called "Morse Code" is what gives meaning to this signal. The telegraph signal contains information because both the sender (distant telegraph operator) and the receiver (you) are using the same rules to both create and interpret the signal.

A set of communication rules, such as Morse Code, is called a "protocol." Both the sender and receiver of a signal must use the same protocol. If they do not, the information the sender puts into the signal is lost, and no communication takes place.

Human Protocols

Protocols can go beyond the simple meaning of a signal to govern other aspects of an interaction. Because humans spend so much time and energy communicating with one another, we have developed a nearly endless number of protocols for all sorts of situations:

- Questions in class: A student raises a hand, waits to be acknowledged by the teacher, then asks a question.

- Telephone conversations: A receiver first says "hello" to signal the start of a conversation. The caller then states her name and the purpose of the call. Before ending the call, both parties confirm that they are finished, then say goodbye.

- Restaurant meals: Customers read a menu, wait for a server, give their choices to the server, then wait for the server to bring the food.

- Postal mail: A sender's name and address goes in the upper left corner of the envelope front or on the back flap. The recipient's name and address goes in the center of the envelope front. The stamp goes in the upper right corner of the envelope front.

- Written language: In European languages, letters are arranged from left to right on each line, and lines are arranged from the top to the bottom of a page. Arabic and Semitic languages arrange letters from right to left, but also arrange lines from top to bottom. Some Asian languages arrange letters in each line from top to bottom, then arrange lines from left to right.

These situations may not seem to apply to computer networking, but they emphasize the idea that common protocols allow clear communication and efficient interaction, and generally prevent chaos. For example, restaurant customers do not just walk into a kitchen and take the food they want. Telephone users do not simply hang up in the middle of a conversation (unless they want to send a different type of message altogether). Your letter will probably not reach its destination if the stamp is on the back of the envelope. And the rules of written language must be appropriate to the language being used; if English is printed from right to left, it is nearly impossible to read.

Computer Protocols

The human protocols just described were developed to make human communication smoother. Of course, two people with wildly different protocols can still manage to communicate, because they can eventually learn to adapt their protocols to each other's needs. This process can even be fun, which is why international travel is a stimulating experience.

However, computers do not have creative, problem-solving brains. They are not intelligent, only fast. Thus, their communication protocols must be very specific and unambiguous.

For example, assume the telegraph company has replaced its human operators with machines. These machines convert messages to Morse Code, transmit the code over the wire, receive messages that come from the wire, and convert Morse Code back to text again. They can do everything the human operators did except for one thing: they do not know when one message ends and another begins.

The human operators knew when a message was done, because they could understand the words represented by the dots and dashes. However, the machine can only understand the dots and dashes themselves; to the machine, there is no meaning beyond the signal itself.

A Simple Machine Protocol

To solve this problem, the machine programmers developed the very simple machine protocol illustrated on the Simple Machine Protocol Diagram. The protocol specifies that the first three characters of each message represent a decimal number that gives the length of the message that follows. Furthermore, the message length does not include the numbers themselves.

Simple Machine Protocol

Thus, to send the message "HELLO STUDENTS," which contains 14 characters (including the space), the sending program would first transmit the characters "O14" followed by "HELLO STUDENTS." The receiving program would interpret the first three characters as the length of the message, and then expect 14 more characters. When 14 characters have been received, the receiving program will expect three more numbers, to begin a new message.

This protocol works well, as long as the two computers follow the protocol exactly. If the receiving computer uses a different protocol (expecting the first two characters to represent the length of the message, instead of the first three), it would expect a message only one character long. When that one character is not followed by numbers to start the next message, the receiving computer would interpret the transmission as an error. Or, if the sending program transmits fewer characters than promised, that would also be an error.

Protocol Headers   When nonmessage data, such as message length, is added to the beginning of a message, we call that additional data a "protocol header." Headers function just like envelopes or packing labels to describe the content of a message, its length, the identity of its sender or recipient, the time of day it was sent, and any other information the communicating processes need to know about the message itself.

Activities

1. Use the Simple Machine Protocol (discussed in this lesson) to add a protocol header to the following command message:

    READ FILENAME.TXT

    This time, consider the header length part of the total length of the message. Also, count the space as a character.

    In the spaces below, write out the total message, starting with the header. Place one character or number in each space.

    What value (in decimal) does the header contain?

    Since this protocol represents numbers using the decimal system, what is the minimum number of header characters needed to specify a message 10,000 bytes long (not counting the comma)?

2. Assume four basic types of file commands, each one represented by a number:

    OPEN=   0
    READ=   1
    WRITE= 2
    CLOSE= 3

    Change the Simple Machine Protocol to use a number for the READ command instead of a word. Eliminate the space. Illustrate the new protocol header and message as you did above. (It is not necessary to fill every space in this grid.)

3. How many fields does this header now have?

    _____

4. Think of the postal system as a communication protocol. List as many rules as you can that govern the delivery of a letter.

    _____

    _____

5. The public postal system is not the only protocol that can be used to deliver a letter. Compare the postal protocol you just analyzed to the protocol of an express delivery service such as United Parcel Service, Airborne, or FedEx. Name some of the key differences in these protocols.

_____

_____

_____

_____

Extended Activities

1. View the "raw" text of an e-mail message. (Methods will vary. In Microsoft Outlook, display a message, then choose the Options tab.)

   What items of information does the message header contain? List as many as you can recognize.

   _____

   _____

   _____

   _____

   _____

2. A protocol is a set of agreed-upon rules for carrying out some form of activity. Analyze and describe a communication protocol used in everyday life. Your protocol rules should describe the roles of each "endpoint," and specify the types of information one or the other must provide. You may choose your own protocol or pick one of the following:

   a. Asking a question during a classroom lecture

   b. Making a telephone call to a family home or other group residence

   c. Ordering fast food over a drive-up speaker

   d. Hitchhiking

   e. Returning a defective product to a store customer service desk

Lesson 2—Layers of Protocols and Services

When two computers communicate over a network, several different processes may take part in the message transmission. At first, this might seem like an inefficient way to communicate. However, in this lesson we will see that there are real advantages to using several protocols to transmit a message, rather than one protocol that does it all. To understand how this works, let us see how a familiar type of communication (a letter) may use multiple protocols to reach its destination.

Objectives

At the end of this lesson you should be able to:

- Explain why a network uses several protocols that each perform part of a job, instead of just one protocol that does it all

- Describe how each layer in a protocol stack interacts with other layers

- Explain what a peer process is

- Explain what a protocol stack is

- Explain the processes of encapsulation and decapsulation

 **Key Point**

It takes several layers of protocols to move information across a network.

A Layered Communication System

John is the busy Chief Executive Officer (CEO) of a big corporation, and he wants to send a letter to the head of the company's Manufacturing division. The company uses English for internal communication, thus he will use the English language protocol for his letter. He also chooses to use the simplest of all word processing applications (and the most widely compatible), a pen and paper. He writes this letter:

> Send me this month's production figures right away.
> Thanks,
> The CEO

John is such a high-powered executive that he does not even know or care who the head of Manufacturing currently is. He just wants the latest manufacturing statistics, so he places a sticky note over the message. On that note he writes:

To: Head of Manufacturing

John hands the letter, with its sticky note, to his secretary. She checks her company directory and finds that the Manufacturing department is in Cincinnati. She politely does not write anything on John's letter or its sticky note. Instead, she places the letter and note in an envelope, and writes on the envelope:

Manufacturing Department
123 Any Street
Cincinnati, Ohio

She now hands this envelope to the mail room clerk. It is the mail room's job to get each letter to its destination, using the most appropriate method. Messages within the same city are sent by bicycle courier. Letters to the company's London office go out by the public postal service, and letters to Cincinnati are sent by FedEx, thus the mail clerk places John's envelope into a FedEx envelope and hands it to the delivery driver.

During this process, each person added a separate protocol header to the combined transmission. By the time the message leaves John's building, the one-line message from John now carries three layers of protocol headers:

• "To: Head of Manufacturing" on the sticky note

• The address on the inner envelope

• The FedEx envelope

The FedEx process is now in charge of the message. It uses its protocol header information (on its envelope) to transport the message to the company's Cincinnati office. When the envelope reaches 123 Any Street, the entire process is reversed:

• The mail room removes the FedEx envelope, reads the inner envelope, and delivers it to the Manufacturing department.

• The Manufacturing department secretary removes the inner envelope, reads the sticky note, and delivers the letter to the Head of Manufacturing.

• The Head of Manufacturing removes the sticky note and reads the letter.

Why Layers?

This process seems rather inefficient. After all, why doesn't John just mail the letter himself? This layered approach actually increases the efficiency of each person's job, because changes to one layer do not affect the others.

Assume John decides to use the public postal system to send his letter. He addresses the letter himself and adds a stamp. However, when he goes to the mailbox, he finds that the postal workers are on strike. He wastes time and money as he repackages his letter for a different delivery service. By allowing the mail room to handle his transmission, he avoids this problem. The mail room can keep track of current delivery conditions and use the best one for each message.

By arranging processes in layers, it is also easier to update information. For example, if we remove the secretary from this chain of processes, then all of the executives must now maintain their own corporate address directories. Each time an address changes, the company must provide address updates to many people. By assigning the address book function to one secretary who serves many executives, updates are faster and all of the executives know that their letters will incorporate the most recent address information.

Each layer may use a different language or protocol. In our example, John wrote his letter in English. However, he could have just as easily written it in German or French. As long as his secretary can read his sticky note address, the letter will reach its destination. Likewise, the secretary may use a different language to communicate with the mail room.

When each layer has full responsibility for one part of the process, that layer can do its job as it sees fit. As long as the secretary gets the right address on each letter, nobody cares whether she stores her address book in her computer, a notebook, or file cards. Likewise, the FedEx workers use their own methods to move packages through their private shipping system. That does not matter to John the CEO, because his letter will reach its destination. However, if John was responsible for giving detailed instructions to each FedEx driver, then they would all have to share the same language and knowledge of the delivery system. Most important, John would have a lot less time to do his own job.

As you can see, John's job is a lot easier and more productive when he delegates these communication details to other functional layers of his organization. He can concentrate on running the company, and let the mail room and delivery service concentrate on moving messages. Changes to lower layers do not affect John, and changes to his job do not affect the lower layers.

Layers of Computer Protocols

Computer networking is conceptually very similar to the example we have just discussed. However, instead of different people working together to communicate a message, a computer network uses different network communication programs to perform different parts of the job. Each of these programs moves a message along its way by following the rules of a particular protocol. As each program handles its particular communication process, it adds its own protocol header to the transmission; just as different people each added a new envelope or shipping label to John's message.

Each communication program is tightly associated with a particular protocol. The communication program provides a service. To perform that service, it obeys the rules and language of a particular protocol. Thus, we often say "process," "protocol," or "layer" to refer to a communication program that implements a protocol.

Layers of Services In computer networking terms, each of these programs or protocols functions as a logical layer of the communication process. Each layer provides services to the layer just above it, and uses the services of the layer just below it. Thus, in our example, the secretary provided addressing services to John the CEO, and used the services of the mail room. The mail room provided services to the secretary, and used the services of FedEx.

Upper layer protocols typically provide services to the user. Those programs depend on lower layer protocols to address messages, break them into manageable pieces, and convert those chunks of data into signals to be transmitted over a physical medium such as a network cable. Thus, only the highest layer of protocols provides services to the user. The lower layer protocols provide services to each other.

Because each layer provides services only to the layer above it and uses services only of the layer below it, a change to a single layer will affect only the layer above. Layering breaks a single large process into separate functions, each isolated from the another. This makes computer programs easier to write and change.

For example, we have learned that computer networks can communicate over three types of physical media: copper cable, fiber optic cable, and radio waves. To send a signal over one of these media, a computer must have a particular type of network interface card (NIC), and a device driver for that NIC. The NIC device driver functions at the lowest layer of the communication process, receiving messages from the layers above, then transmitting them onto a physical medium. If engineers suddenly invent a completely new type of physical transmission medium, then a computer user could communicate over that medium by simply installing a new NIC and device driver. All of the upper layer programs would remain untouched, just as John the CEO does not know whether his letter travels by means of the postal service, FedEx, or some brand-new delivery service.

Layering does extract a performance penalty. There is some overhead associated with moving data through multiple layers of programs. However, the advantage of easily maintained programs is generally worth the performance price.

Peer Processes

In networking, processes in the same layer, on both the sending and receiving computers, are called "peer processes." In our letter-writing example, the two mail rooms are peer processes. The two upper managers (John and the Head of Manufacturing) are also peers, as are both of their secretaries.

Thus, John wrote a letter in English to his peer, the Head of Manufacturing. To get the letter to his peer, John "passed" the letter to the layer below him (the secretary). The service of this layer was to address the letter to a final destination "across the network," then pass the letter down to the next layer, the mail room.

Just as each protocol depends on the layers above and below it, it also depends on cooperation with its peer protocols. This hand-in-hand effort is called a "peer process," as illustrated on the Peer Processes Diagram. In a network system that uses layered protocols and services, a process passes data to a lower process and receives data from an upper process. However, the process actually communicates only with its peer process.

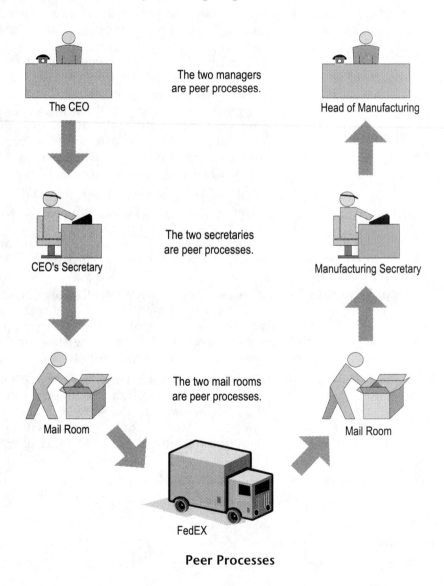

Peer Processes

For example, the secretary took a letter from John, addressed it, and passed it to the mail room. However, she did not read the letter from John, and she may not have understood it if she had tried. That is because John may have written his letter in a language his secretary does not understand. He is free to do this, as long as he provides the correct instructions to her.

However, John's secretary can also communicate with the secretary at the destination location by placing additional information in the protocol header (the envelope) that she adds to the message. Assume she wants to keep her address book up to date. Thus, along with the address, she adds a note to the envelope that says, "Update address if needed." The other secretary receives this message when the envelope is delivered to her. If the destination address has changed, she can then send an update message to the first secretary.

Thus, peer processes communicate across a network by using a peer protocol, and adding information to the protocol header. In the example above, two secretaries communicated by the simple protocol of adding notes to an envelope. When you send electronic mail (e-mail) to a friend, your e-mail application uses the same network communication protocol to send the message as your friend's e-mail application uses to retrieve it. Your e-mail program and your friend's e-mail program are functioning as peer processes.

Differences between Protocol Layers

Cooperating layers of protocols are called "protocol stacks" or "protocol suites." In a protocol stack, the services offered by each layer progress from abstract, higher level services in the top layers, to more concrete, transmission-oriented services in the bottom layers. Some of the main ways processes on the top of a protocol stack differ from those at the bottom include:

* Meaning versus signaling
* Logical versus physical
* End-to-end versus point-to-point

Meaning vs. Signaling

The upper layers are concerned with the format and meaning of a message and communicating that meaning between peers (the sender and receiver). The lower layers are concerned with the physical method of transmitting a signal that represents a stream of binary bits. Thus, the highest layer protocol deals with complete data structures or objects ready to be used by an application program or displayed to a user. The lowest layer protocol is concerned only with the type of signal that comes over a physical connection.

Logical vs. Physical

Upper protocols use abstract or symbolic terms to represent the recipient of a message. Lower protocols use more specific identifications, such as a street address. If you think back to our letter-writing analogy, John the CEO simply addressed his letter to the "Head of Manufacturing." He did not need to know who that person is or where that person was located. The lower layers provided progressively more specific addresses that were necessary to move the message to the physical destination.

End-to-End vs. Point-to-Point

Binary data bits (pulses of electricity, light, or radio energy) cannot travel without a physical connection (a cable or radio channel). Therefore, a bottom-layer protocol can only support communications between devices that are somehow physically connected. In contrast, upper layer processes do not need to be physically connected, because they communicate with peers that may be many physical links away.

To understand this difference, think of a food vendor at a sports stadium. He needs to deliver a hot dog to his customer who is 10 seats away. He passes the hot dog to the nearest person, who passes it to the next, and so on until it reaches the intended recipient. In this case, the vendor and customer are communicating end-to-end, even though they are not physically connected. However, that end-to-end process is carried out over multiple point-to-point links, as each person sitting between the vendor and customer passes the hot dog one seat farther down.

How Layers Work Together

As we have seen thus far, a protocol provides services to the layer above it, and uses the services of the layer below it. Whenever different layers of protocols work together, they use the following basic techniques:

- Encapsulation and protocol headers
- Segmentation
- Decapsulation
- Reassembly

Encapsulation and Protocol Headers

In the letter-writing example, each of the "layers" below the CEO placed its own envelope around the envelope it received from above. None of those layers removed the envelope added by the previous layer. Thus, the message was wrapped in several layers of envelopes as it was transmitted.

Virtually all modern communication systems use this approach, called "encapsulation." As data moves down the protocol stack, each layer that receives data from above "repackages" it by adding its own protocol header to the transmission, as shown on the Encapsulation Diagram. Some protocols also add data to the end of a message; this data is called a "trailer."

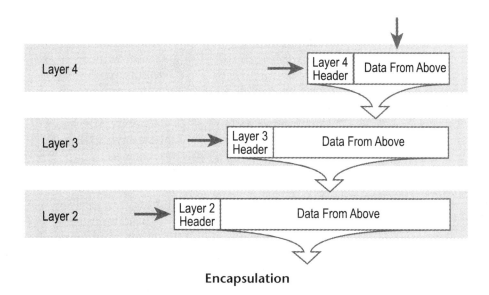

Encapsulation

Each protocol header contains several items of data that are useful to a peer process at the other end of the communication. Each of these items is called a "field." Each protocol specifies the order and length (in bits) of its header fields. The number, length, and content of header fields vary among different protocols. For example, one protocol header may assign 8 bits to describe the length of the encapsulated data, 32 bits to carry the address of the sender, and 32 bits to carry the address of the recipient. Another protocol may include fields that describe the priority of a message or the type of data it contains.

Segmentation

Suppose an upper layer process has a long message to send to its peer process. If the message is too long, the lower layers cannot carry it, just as a delivery service has rules that limit the maximum size of a shipping box.

If you must transport a shipment that is too large for one container, you can divide it into several small boxes. To tell the recipient the total number and order of the boxes, you can add sequencing information to each box, such as "1 of 5," "2 of 5," and so on.

In the same way, some protocols can divide a long message into shorter segments or fragments. The protocol header includes fields that specify the relative position of each piece in the complete message, and the total number of pieces in the message. All segments are then passed to the layer below.

A possible alternative approach is to insert this sequencing information into the message itself, indicating that there are multiple parts and where each part fits in the whole message. However, that would require lower layers to open each envelope and look at the original message to determine the order in which the individual letter parts must be passed to the higher layers on the other end. This makes the highest layers involved in the operation of the lower layers, which defeats the many advantages of a layered communication architecture.

Decapsulation

As the message is passed down the protocol layers on the sending computer, it has been encapsulated within several protocol headers. When that message reaches the destination computer, the encapsulation process is reversed. Starting with the bottom layer, each process removes its own header (opens its own envelope) and passes the encapsulated data up to the layer above. This process is called "decapsulation."

Each program only removes the header added by its peer process. It does not disturb the encapsulated data in any way, but simply passes it to the layer just above, as shown on the Decapsulation Diagram. By the time the data reaches the highest layer, only the original message is left. The highest level program never sees the lower layer protocol headers that wrapped the message during transmission.

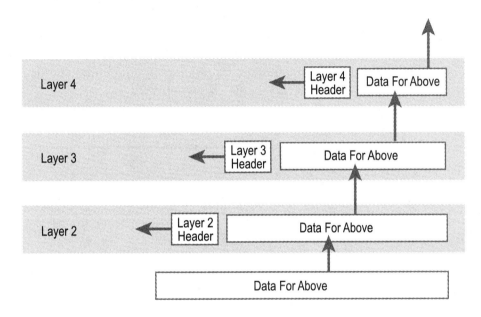

Decapsulation

Reassembly

If the original message was segmented into a series of smaller transmissions, one of the processes on the receiving end places the segments in order before decapsulating them. It then reassembles the segments into their correct order, then passes the restored message up to the layer above.

Activities

1. In order to communicate, peer entities must use the same protocol. True or False

2. Programs and processes provide services. True or False

3. Peer processes operate at the same layer. True or False

4. Each layer provides services to all of the layers above it. True or False

5. Programs at the lowest layers provide the most sophisticated services directly to the user. True or False

6. When a process receives data from the layer above, what does it do with that data?

   _____

   _____

   _____

   _____

7. If a protocol receives data from above that is too long for it to handle, what does it do?

   _____

   _____

   _____

   _____

8. If a protocol receives data from below, what does it do?

   _____

   _____

   _____

   _____

Extended Activities

1. Layering of services is common in everyday life, because specialization is an efficient way to perform many jobs. For example, there are several layers of services that operate in a fast-food restaurant, manufacturing plant, or bureaucracy. Each service layer does part of the job, then performs a "hand-off" operation to move the work to the next layer. Describe three everyday examples of a layered organization.

   _____

   _____

2. Explain the relationship between services, programs, processes, and protocols.

   _____

   _____

   _____

   _____

Lesson 3—Communicating Across a Network

In this lesson we explain the basic principles of how information makes its way from one computer to another computer across a network. We will go into the specific details of this process in the rest of this course. But for now, we will use the concepts discussed thus far to give you a general idea of how a local area network (LAN) handles a routine task such as transmitting an application's request for data on another computer.

Objectives

At the end of this lesson you should be able to:

- Explain the role of the client redirector software

- Describe the steps that occur when a computer requests a resource from another computer over the network

- Explain the difference between requesting local and remote data

 **Key Point**

Client redirection software is responsible for directing messages over the network.

Making a Local Request for Data

Assume you are working with a database application on your desktop computer, and you command that application to display a particular set of records. If those records are physically stored on the hard disk in your computer (the "local" hard drive), your command begins a chain of actions necessary to get that job done.

The application asks the operating system (OS) to retrieve the data from your hard drive. The OS then communicates with the hard drive device driver to read the data from the drive and move it into memory for the application to use. Of course, everything except your application command is invisible to you.

What if the database records are stored on a hard drive in a computer on the other side of the building, over the network? How can your application get its data in that case?

Configuring the Client Computer

Before you can request a resource across the network, you must first be able to communicate on the network. To do this, the following items must be installed on your computer (in addition to your desktop OS):

- A NIC transmits and receives signals on the physical network medium (cable or radio channel).

- A NIC device driver allows the OS to communicate with the installed NIC.

- The network communication software, or protocol stack, provides the layered communication protocols that handle the details of network communications.

- Network redirection software is shipped with your desktop OS; however, it must be installed and configured like any other application. OS vendors use different names to describe their redirectors, such as "requestor," "shell" (UNIX), "Client for Microsoft Networks" (Microsoft Windows), or "Client for NetWare" (Novell NetWare). A client redirector must be compatible with the networking software used by its servers and peers. Thus, if the network's servers are using Windows NT Server software, the client workstations must use Client for Microsoft Networks.

Once the redirector software is installed, it waits for an application to make a request for a file or service. If the request is for a local resource, the redirector passes the request to the local OS. If the request is for a resource on a network server (or peer computer), the redirector uses the client's network communication software and NIC to send the request out over the network to the appropriate computer. This process is shown on the Communicating Across a Network Diagram.

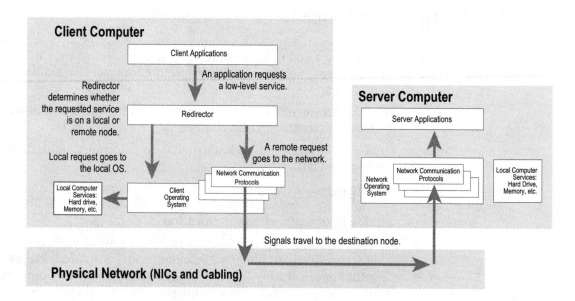

Communicating Across a Network

Requesting Data from a Drive Across a Network

Assume your computer is connected to the network and your client software is set up and configured. Here is what happens when you tell your database application to display records stored on another computer:

1. When you command the application to open the records, you select a target drive on a different network computer. This computer could be a file server or peer computer. However, you may only access files on a peer computer if the user of that computer has configured that drive or data to be shared by the rest of the network.

2. The application asks the OS to retrieve the data. However, this time your computer's redirection software intercepts the request that would normally go straight to the OS.

3. The redirector recognizes that the request is directed at a remote disk drive. The redirector passes the request to the network communication software.

4. Each layer of the protocol stack handles a different part of the job of preparing the request to be transmitted. For example, one layer addresses the request to the specific destination computer, while another layer checks to see whether the network cable is ready to accept a new transmission. Each layer adds its own protocol header to the request.

5. The lowest layer protocol passes the completed request to the NIC. This requires the help of the OS, but here the OS is providing a different service from the original "read data" request.

6. The completed request is sent from the central processing unit (CPU) of the computer, across the local bus, to the NIC.

7. The NIC creates a physical signal (electrical, optical, or radio) that represents the binary data in the request. It then transmits that signal onto the transmission medium of the network (cable or radio channel).

8. The destination computer's NIC recognizes that the signal is addressed to itself. It copies the bits off the network, while other computers ignore the signal. It then passes the request to the local computer's network communication protocol stack.

9. The request is passed up the destination protocol stack and is decapsulated as it moves from one layer to the next. When the message reaches the top of the stack, the highest layer passes the request to the database server application.

10. The database server application then works with its local OS to read the data from its hard drive.

When the database server application transmits the data back to the client that requested it, this process is reversed. The data is passed down and encapsulated through the server's network protocol stack, transmitted over the physical network, received by the destination computer, decapsulated by the destination protocol stack, and delivered to the client application.

Activities

1. The client redirection software replaces the client OS. True or False

2. Match each of these components with its function:

   a. Provides low-level computer services

   b. Performs a specific task for a user

   c. Routes local requests to the OS and remote requests to the network

   d. Adds headers that contain addressing and control information

   e. Converts binary data to a physical signal

   f. Carries a physical signal

   Redirector

   OS

   NIC

   Application

   Network transmission medium

   Protocol stack

3. The following client components are needed to communicate over a network: user application, OS, NIC, NIC device driver, client redirector, and network communication protocol stack. Arrange these components in a logical stack that shows how a request flows down from a user application.

<table>
<tr><td>User application</td></tr>
<tr><td></td></tr>
<tr><td></td></tr>
<tr><td></td></tr>
<tr><td></td></tr>
<tr><td></td></tr>
</table>

Extended Activity

Use members of your class to model the network components shown on the Communicating Across a Network Diagram. For example, one person will play the role of a client application, another takes the role of the client redirector, and so on. For simplicity, use only one person to represent the entire network protocol stack.

Practice client/server communication by passing messages from layer to layer, encapsulating each message within envelopes or paper wrappers. (The physical network does not encapsulate messages, but merely transports them.) To move each message across this network, what sort of information does each layer need in its protocol header?

Now make the exercise more interesting by modeling three applications on the client and three on the server. Each application on the client may communicate with any of the three applications on the server. Is more protocol information now necessary to deliver each message to the correct recipient? Do all protocols need more header information, or only some?

Summary

In this unit, we learned one of the most basic principles of data communication: that computers use multiple processes and protocols to transmit information across a network. These protocols work together like an assembly line, forming a "stack" of logical layers. Each layer uses the services of the layer below, and provides a service to the layer above.

Upper layer protocols direct data from one application to another, while lower protocols direct data to a particular destination machine. The lowest protocols are concerned only with transmitting and receiving signals on the network's physical transmission medium.

On a logical layer above the network protocol stack, a client application called a "redirector" plays a vital role. When client applications request resources, such as data or storage services, the redirector intercepts these requests that would otherwise go straight to the OS. The redirector then determines whether each requested resource is available on the local computer, or on a computer across the network. If the resource is local, the redirector passes the request to the local OS. If the resource is remote, the redirector passes the request to the network protocol stack for transmission across the network.

Unit 3 Quiz

1. What purpose do protocols serve in computer networking?

    a. Decide who gets information first

    b. Decide how computers perform internal processing

    c. Provide rules for communication

    d. Provide commands for users to control the computer

2. Which scenario does not appear to have a protocol in effect?

    a. A translator helping ambassadors from different countries communicate

    b. Taking a walk in the park

    c. A host at a fine restaurant asking a patron to wear a tie

    d. Inviting guests to a party

3. Which statement best describes the relationship between processes, services, and protocols?

    a. Services allow protocols to get where they are going.

    b. A process provides a service by using a protocol.

    c. All processes use the same protocols.

    d. All of the above

4. In a firefighting bucket brigade, a line of people work together to move water-filled buckets from a water source to a burning building. In the line, each person accepts a full bucket from the person to the right, then passes it to the person to the left. What type of communication is used to move the bucket from one person to the next?

    a. End-to-end

    b. Point-to-point

    c. Client/server

    d. Master/slave

5. In the same bucket brigade, the person at one end of the line fills buckets with water, while the person at the other end throws the water onto the fire. What type of communication is occurring between those two people?

   a. End-to-end

   b. Point-to-point

   c. Master/slave

   d. None of the above

6. What is another word for a layered group of cooperating protocols?

   a. Pile

   b. Heap

   c. Stack

   d. Program

7. What does a receiving layer do to information that has been passed up from a layer below?

   a. Unaddress

   b. Recapitulate

   c. Decapsulate

   d. Encapsulate

8. When a process in one computer operates at the same layer as a process in another computer, it is considered a:

   a. Client

   b. Peer

   c. Server

   d. None of the above

9. Data added to a message, that provides information about the message, is called which of the following?

   a. Protocol header

   b. Protocol translator

   c. Protocol stack

   d. Character provider

10. Decapsulation means that each layer does which of the following?

    a. Removes its protocol header and passes the remaining data up the stack

    b. Adds its protocol header and passes the whole message up the stack

    c. Breaks a message into smaller segments then passes those segments up the stack

    d. None of the above

11. Communication programs are arranged in layers to do which of the following?

    a. Allow programs and processes to provide specialized services

    b. Provide error-free service to the application

    c. Tell the sender the address of the receiver

    d. None of the above

12. When a process receives data that is too long for it to transmit, it does which of the following?

    a. Sends the data back to the sending layer

    b. Transmits only as much as it can

    c. Ignores the data

    d. Divides the data into shorter segments

13. In a client computer, what program is responsible for determining whether a requested resource is local or located across the network?

    a. Application that needs the resource

    b. Network interface card driver

    c. Client redirection software

    d. Desktop OS

14. Which of the following describes how computer processes communicate?

    a. Peer-to-peer

    b. Client/server

    c. Master/slave

    d. All of the above

15. A program can provide a service to a user or another program. True or False

16. Layering protocols and services does not affect performance. True or False

Unit 4
The OSI Model

Building on the concept of layered protocols, this unit introduces the very important Open Systems Interconnection (OSI) model. The OSI model began as a reference model, that is, an abstract model for data communications. The OSI model is used to provide a logical structure to the course, and serves as a reference throughout the remainder of the units.

Lessons

1. Introduction to the OSI Model
2. The Physical Layer
3. The Data Link Layer
4. The Network Layer
5. The Transport Layer
6. The Session Layer
7. The Presentation Layer
8. The Application Layer

Terms

address—An address is a unique value that identifies the source or the destination of data being transmitted across a communication link. A single item of data may have different addresses that identify a station's place in a network, the computer hardware itself, and the address of a software process.

American Standard Code for Information Interchange (ASCII)—ASCII is one of the most widely used codes for representing keyboard characters on a computer system. ASCII uses 7 bits to represent 128 elements. For example, when the character "A" is pressed on the keyboard, the ASCII binary representation is 100 0001. The other major encoding system is EBCDIC. See Extended Binary Coded Decimal Interchange Code (EBCDIC).

authentication—Authentication is the process of accurately identifying a computer user, usually done through passwords.

capacity—The term "capacity" refers to using the data-carrying capability of a component or communication link. It is the number of bits the component or link can process in a period of time.

compiler—A compiler is an application that converts code written in a programming language (source code) into machine-level instructions (an executable program).

compression—The process of reducing the number of bits required to represent data, without altering the information conveyed by the data, is referred to as compression. The primary reason for using compression techniques is to optimize the use of a communication channel.

connection-oriented—A connection-oriented data communication mode is one in which the sending and receiving computers stay in contact for the duration of a session, while packets or frames are being sent back and forth.

connectionless—Connectionless transmission treats each packet or datagram as a separate entity that contains the source and destination addresses. Connectionless services can drop or deliver packets out of sequence.

de facto—De facto standards are standards that are not developed by an official standards-making organization, and are usually created by a single vendor or group of vendors. Nevertheless, they are widely accepted and used, usually to allow interoperation with a popular system.

decryption—The process of unscrambling encrypted data to restore the original meaningful message is referred to as decryption.

encoding—Encoding is the process of translating binary data (1s and 0s) into signals to be transmitted across a physical link. The most common signaling forms are electrical signals, light signals, and radio signals. Encoding also describes the process of using binary values to represent symbols or keyboard characters. Two of the most common encoding systems for keyboard characters are ASCII and EBCDIC.

encryption—Encryption is the process of scrambling data so it cannot be read by anyone except the intended recipient.

Extended Binary Coded Decimal Interchange Code (EBCDIC)—EBCDIC is the IBM standard for binary encoding of characters. It is one of the two most widely used codes to represent characters, such as keyboard characters. (ASCII is the other.) See American Standard Code for Information Interchange (ASCII).

File Transfer Protocol (FTP)—FTP is an Application Layer protocol used in TCP/IP networks. FTP is commonly used to transfer files between hosts on the Internet.

flow control—Flow control is the process of controlling the volume of data sent between two computer systems. Practically every data communication protocol contains some form of flow control to keep the sending computer from sending too much data to the receiving node.

frame—A frame is a unit of information processed by the Data Link Layer. Each frame contains the hardware address (NIC address) of its destination node. Control frames are used to set up and manage a communications link. Information frames contain packets from the Network Layer above. The format of each frame depends on the Data Link Layer protocol in use (for example, Ethernet or Token Ring).

handshake—An exchange of signals and data that prepares two devices to communicate with each other is referred to as a handshake.

Hypertext Markup Language (HTML)—HTML is a text-based language used to generically format text for Web pages. HTML tags different parts of a document more in terms of their function than their appearance. A Web browser reads an HTML document and displays it as indicated by the HTML formatting tags and the browser's default settings.

Hypertext Transfer Protocol (HTTP)—HTTP is the Application Layer protocol used to request and transmit HTML documents. HTTP is the underlying protocol of the Web.

International Standards Organization (ISO)—ISO is a voluntary organization, chartered by the United Nations, that defines international standards for all fields other than electricity and electronics. (IEC handles electricity and electronics standards.) ANSI represents the United States in ISO.

Internet Protocol (IP)—IP is a Network Layer protocol responsible for getting a packet (datagram) through a network. It is the "IP" in "TCP/IP."

Internetwork Packet Exchange (IPX)—IPX is Novell NetWare's proprietary Network Layer protocol.

multiplexing—Multiplexing is the technology that allows multiple signals to travel over the same physical medium. Multiple signals are fed into a multiplexer and combined to form one output stream.

Network File System (NFS)—NFS is a file management system commonly used in UNIX-based computer systems.

network interface card (NIC)—A NIC is a workstation or PC component (usually a hardware card) that allows the workstation or PC to communicate with a network. A NIC address is another term for hardware address or MAC address. A NIC address is a unique value built into a NIC.

Network News Transfer Protocol (NNTP)—NNTP is a protocol used to post and retrieve USENET news group messages.

packet—A unit of information processed by the Network Layer is referred to as a packet. The packet header contains the logical (network) address of the destination node. Intermediate nodes forward a packet until it reaches its destination. A packet can contain an entire message generated by higher OSI layers or a segment of a much larger message. A packet is sometimes called a "datagram."

port—There are two primary ways the term "port" is used in networking. Port can refer to a physical port in a device, such as a port on a switch or MUX. Port can also refer to a software port, a number typically used to identify a software process within a computer.

proprietary—A proprietary network solution is one that is designed and implemented using equipment and protocols specific to one vendor. Purchasing equipment from one vendor typically creates proprietary networks. The opposite of a proprietary network is an "open" network, which is based on industry standards.

regulation—Technical or operational rules that protect health, safety, national security, or environmental cleanliness are referred to as regulations. Because they deal with such important human needs, regulations are backed by the force of law.

Sequenced Packet Exchange (SPX)—SPX is Novell NetWare's proprietary Transport Layer protocol.

Simple Mail Transfer Protocol (SMTP)—SMTP is a protocol and set of processes that use the protocol to transfer e-mail messages between user mailboxes.

standard—Standards are the technical specifications and working methods necessary for different vendors' equipment to interoperate. Standards enhance efficiency and usability; however, they generally do not protect life or limb.

Systems Network Architecture (SNA)—SNA is IBM's architecture for computer networking. It was designed for transaction processing in mission-critical applications, often involving a large number of "dumb" terminals communicating with a mainframe. Typical transactions perform inquiries and update information in a database. For example, a commercial bank might have a number of 3270-type display units and printers in each of hundreds of branch offices that are used to access a central database in the home office.

Telnet—Telnet is an Application Layer protocol that provides a remote login capability to another computer on a network.

Transmission Control Protocol (TCP)—TCP is a Transport Level protocol that provides reliable, full-duplex communication between two software processes on different computers. TCP normally uses IP to transmit information across the underlying network.

UNIX-to-UNIX Copy Program (UUCP)—UUCP is a protocol used for communication between consenting UNIX systems.

virtual circuit—A virtual circuit is a communication path that appears to be a single circuit to the sending and receiving devices, even though the data may take varying routes between the source and destination nodes.

World Wide Web (Web)—The Web is the global collection of HTML documents (Web pages) made available for public access by means of the Internet. To retrieve Web pages, a user must have a browser application.

X.25—X.25 is a connectionless packet-switching network, public or private, typically built upon leased lines from public telephone networks. In the United States, X.25 is offered by most carriers. The X.25 interface lies at OSI Layer 3, rather than Layer 1. X.25 defines its own three-layer protocol stack, and provides data rates only up to 56 Kbps.

Lesson 1—Introduction to the OSI Model

The first networking protocols were developed by computer manufacturers. Each manufacturer developed its own protocols for its own platforms. Some manufacturers even had multiple protocols, because protocols were developed independently for different computer platforms. IBM, for example, had more than a dozen protocols back in the 1960s.

However, as you have learned, computers and programs must use a common protocol to communicate. If many different protocols for data communication exist, it is difficult to link computers into common networks.

Thus, to correct the chaos of multiple protocols, computer vendors developed communication standards, both official and de facto. One of the most important of these is the OSI model.

The OSI model is not a protocol, but a reference model, or an abstract structure that describes the functions and interactions of various data communication protocols. It provides a conceptual structure that helps us discuss and compare network functions, just as other classification systems help biologists or chemists talk about their fields.

As a networking professional, there are two good reasons you must have a solid understanding of the OSI model:

- The OSI model is widely used in networking literature. Data communication texts structure their presentations by the OSI model.

- Many software and hardware vendors use the OSI model as a guide for the development and documentation of products. When you understand the OSI model, you can quickly learn many different types of networking protocols, products, and services.

Thus, the OSI model provides a logical structure to the rest of this course, and we will refer to it often.

Objectives

At the end of this lesson you should be able to:

- Explain why the OSI model was created

- Name the layers of the OSI reference model

- Describe what an open standard is and why it benefits both vendors and customers

Key Point

The layers of the OSI model provide a framework for understanding networking.

The OSI Open Standard

The OSI model was created by the International Standards Organization (ISO). ISO is composed of members from national standards organizations of many countries, including the American National Standards Institute (ANSI), the principal nongovernment U.S. standards organization. The standard was intended to allow the interconnection of networks without regard to the underlying hardware, as long as the communication software used adheres to the standard. In other words, the OSI model defines a neutral set of rules for data communication. Products that follow those rules can usually work together, even if they are made by different manufacturers.

The OSI model is an open standard. The term "open" means the standard's specifications are publicly available. Compliance with the standard is also voluntary; new products are not required to adhere to the standard. However, many manufacturers have found that standards-based products are more competitive. Customers want the flexibility of hardware and software that is "interoperable" with other manufacturers' products, and do not want to be locked into a single vendor's proprietary solutions.

The OSI standard was patterned after, and is similar to, the IBM layered networking scheme called "Systems Network Architecture (SNA)." IBM introduced SNA in the early 1970s to provide a consistent standard for its product platforms. However, the OSI model is simpler and more elegant than SNA.

The OSI Stack

The OSI reference model describes a theoretical protocol stack, shown on the OSI Model Diagram. The model consists of seven layers of services and protocols, from the concrete Physical Layer, which contains protocols that transmit bits over physical media, to the abstract Application Layer, where programs such as electronic mail (e-mail) reside.

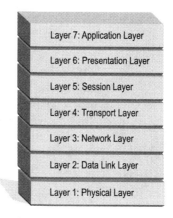

OSI Model

The OSI model, consisting of seven layers, falls logically into two parts. Layers 1 through 4, the "lower" layers, are concerned with transmitting raw data between computers. Layers 5 through 7, the "higher" layers, are concerned with communication between applications.

Each layer of the OSI model describes the services that a protocol provides, but it does not specify exactly how a protocol must do that. Thus, several different protocols provide the functions of OSI Layer 3 (the Network Layer), and a developer can create a new one at any time.

We will now study each of the layers, from the lowest to the highest, to learn about the services and protocols at each level.

Activities

1. Manufacturers and developers are legally required to create products that conform to the OSI model. True or False

2. Why have the OSI model? What precisely does it do for networking?

   _____

   _____

   _____

3. Draw a seven-layer stack of small rectangles that represent the OSI model layers. To the left of each rectangle, write the number of the layer. Inside each rectangle (box), print the name of the OSI model layer represented by the box. Draw a dotted line between the "higher" layers and the layers concerned primarily with communication of raw data.

Extended Activities

1. Could networks exist without a model? Discuss the ramifications.

   _____

   _____

   _____

2. Create a mnemonic device (or memory tool) to help you remember the names and order of the layers of the OSI model. Create one from the top to bottom layer, and one from the bottom to top layer.

3. Find charts that list the character sets of the Extended Binary Coded Decimal Interchange Code (EBCDIC) and the American Standard Code for Information Interchange (ASCII). Compare these encoding systems and note their similarities and differences. Spell your first name using both numerical systems.

Lesson 2—The Physical Layer

As we learned in the last unit, each protocol provides a service to the layer just above it in the protocol stack, and uses the services of the layer below. Because the Physical Layer (Layer 1) is the lowest layer of the OSI model, it does not use the services of any other layer. However, it provides Layer 2 the service of transmitting a signal, across a physical communication medium, that represents binary bits.

Objectives

At the end of this lesson you should be able to:

- Describe the function of Physical Layer protocols

- Explain why each physical medium requires its own Physical Layer protocol

- Explain the difference between Manchester encoding and Differential Manchester encoding

 **Key Point**

The Physical Layer deals with transmitting and receiving bits across a physical medium.

Hardware Devices

As we have learned, the physical medium can be a copper cable (coaxial or twisted pair), fiber optic cable, or radio channel. Thus, the Physical Layer includes the following types of hardware devices that send and receive signals over each type of physical medium:

- Network interface cards (NICs)

- Fiber optic transceivers

- Radio transceivers

- Modems

197

A Stream of Bits

Physical Layer processes are concerned only with transmitting and receiving physical signals that represent data bits. They do this without any knowledge of the meaning or structure of the data itself, just as a conveyor belt has no understanding of the packages it carries.

A Physical Layer process is only aware of the transmission medium itself, and is not aware of any communicating device that may be sending or receiving transmissions over that medium. Thus, when a Layer 1 process receives a signal, it is only aware that it is coming from a cable or radio channel. If the process is sending a signal, it is only aware that it is placing the signal onto the wire, or modulating a radio wave. It is not aware that any other device at the other end of that physical connection is either the source or destination of a signal.

Physical Layer processes use different transmission protocols, depending on the nature of the physical communication link (copper, fiber, or radio). Physical transmission protocols are concerned with issues such as:

- How bits (1s and 0s) are represented. For example, a bit may be a flash of light over a fiber optic cable, high voltage on a copper cable, or change of frequency or amplitude on a radio channel.

- How to tell when each bit, or a whole transmission, starts and ends. Synchronous protocols use coordinated clocks to detect the start and end of a message. Asynchronous protocols use special signals to mark each message.

- Whether bits can flow in one direction only or in both directions simultaneously.

Minimal Error Detection

A data error can be defined as an incorrect pattern of bits. However, Physical Layer processes are only aware of individual bit signals, they cannot detect errors in data transmission.

Some Physical Layer processes can detect basic faults, such as an open connection, and alert higher layers to the problem. However, most error detection, and all error correction, are the responsibility of higher layers.

Example: Manchester Encoding

A simple example of a Physical Layer protocol is the Manchester encoding technique used on copper-cabled local area networks (LANs). This is a synchronous protocol, because it is based on the "ticks" of an electronic timer. Each binary bit is allocated a fixed slice of time. At the middle of that time slice, if the voltage changes from low to high, this is interpreted as a binary 1. If the voltage drops from high to low at the middle of the bit time, this is a 0. The Manchester Encoding Diagram shows how a binary number is represented using this signaling technique. The device that receives this signal, such as a NIC, only pays attention to voltage changes that occur in the middle of a 1-bit time segment. Thus, to represent a series of 1s, the signal must first drop to low voltage at the beginning of a bit time, so it is ready to change from low to high again to represent another binary 1.

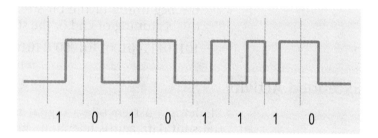

Manchester Encoding

A variation of this method, called Differential Manchester encoding, avoids this skipping signal. It counts each voltage change at a clock tick, from high to low or low to high, as a binary 1. A binary 0 is represented by no voltage change at the clock tick. The Differential Manchester Encoding Diagram displays an example of this encoding scheme.

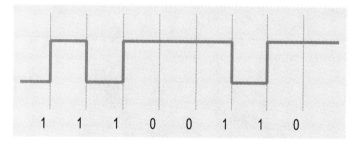

Differential Manchester Encoding

Activities

1. The Physical Layer always uses a cable. True or False

2. The Physical Layer knows what characters the Data Link Layer has sent for transmission. True or False

3. Each of the following binary numbers is the equivalent of the decimal number just below:

   00110100   00110000   00110101   00110110
      52   48   53   54

   When the numbers are written out like this, it is relatively easy to see the difference between them (especially when white space is inserted!). However, now the binary numbers are part of a bit stream at the Physical Layer. Inspect this bit stream, and determine in what order the four numbers now appear. You cannot assume that one of the numbers starts at the beginning of the bit stream. "Noise" bits may appear at the beginning or end of the stream.

   10110111001001101000011010100110110001100001100011000100

Extended Activity

Modems must encode a digital signal onto an analog carrier to transmit data across telephone lines. Using the World Wide Web (Web), research what modulation and encoding techniques modems use.

_____

_____

_____

_____

Lesson 3—The Data Link Layer

The Data Link Layer is the second layer in the OSI reference model. It uses the signaling services of the Physical Layer below it. To Layer 3 above, it provides the service of addressing a message to a device located across a single physical transmission path. The physical path that connects two nodes is called a "link."

Objectives

At the end of this lesson you should be able to:

- Describe what a link is
- Name the main services of the Data Link Layer
- Explain the relationship between packets and frames
- Describe how each frame is addressed to its destination

 **Key Point**

The Data Link Layer deals with frames over a single physical link. A Data Link Layer address is the unique address built into a NIC.

Frames Across a Link

While the Physical Layer streams bits one at a time onto a link, the Data Link Layer addresses groups of bits to a particular node that is attached somewhere on that physical link. Each group of bits the Data Link Layer transmits is called a "frame." Frames are typically generated by the NIC of the sending computer.

Packets Within Frames

The Network Layer handles data in units called "packets." Thus, the Network Layer passes a packet to the Data Link Layer, which encapsulates the packet by placing a header and trailer around it, just as we encapsulate a letter within an envelope. The encapsulated data (header, packet, and trailer) forms the frame. As it encapsulates the packet passed down from the Network Layer, the Data Link Layer is not aware of the meaning of that data.

Frame Addressing

The frame header includes the unique NIC addresses of the sending and receiving nodes. Thus, each frame is addressed to an individual computing machine. The frame trailer contains error-checking information that allows the receiving Data Link Layer process to determine whether the frame has been damaged during transit.

The Data Link Layer passes each frame down to the Physical Layer for transmission across the link as a stream of bits. The receiving Data Link Layer process receives the bit stream from the Physical Layer and determines where each frame begins and ends. It then removes the frame header and trailer, then passes the packet up to the Network Layer.

Data Link Layer Services

The Data Link Layer provides the following services to the Network Layer:

On the Transmitting Node

- Accepts data packets of arbitrary length from the Network Layer.

- Accepts the address of an adjacent node to which it is to transmit the data. An adjacent node is one connected to the sending node by a Physical Layer link.

- Controls access to a shared Physical Layer medium, such as a broadcast network.

- Adds sequence information to the frames. If they get out of sequence during error recovery, they can be put back into the right sequence by the receiving peer process.

- Adds error detection and correction codes to the frames so the receiving peer process can tell when an error has occurred. (Remember that the Physical Layer cannot detect data errors.)

- Adds handshaking information to the data frames so it can cooperate with the peer process to correct problems, such as a frame that is completely lost.

- Handshakes with its peer to ensure that the complete packet is received correctly.

- Uses the services of the Physical Layer to transmit frames.

- During transmission, does not send frames to the Physical Layer at a faster rate than the receiving Data Link Layer process can handle them.

On the Receiving Node

- Receives bits passed up from the Physical Layer and interprets groups of bits as frames.

- Checks each frame for errors. If errors are found, it takes corrective measures, such as requesting a retransmission from the transmitting peer process.

- Handles problems, such as missing frames, through handshaking with its peer process.

- Puts the frames back in the correct sequence to reconstruct the packet.

- Passes each decapsulated packet up to the Network Layer.

The Data Link Layer and Physical Layer Diagram shows how the Data Link Layer passes frames to the Physical Layer, which transports the frames as a stream of bits.

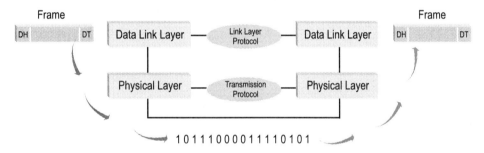

Data Link Layer and Physical Layer

Error Detection and Correction: FCS

All protocols, except the Physical Layer, add header information to the data they transmit. However, the Data Link Layer also adds a trailer. The trailer typically contains a data field, called the Frame Check Sequence (FCS), that is used by the receiving Data Link Layer process to determine whether each frame has been transmitted without errors.

The sending Data Link Layer process creates the FCS by running the frame's data through a special calculation. The result of this calculation is a binary number that becomes that frame's FCS. When the destination Data Link process receives the frame, it runs the same calculation against the data. If the calculation produces the same binary number, it is likely the frame was not damaged in transit.

The FCS can only detect the most basic types of errors, such as a bit that has changed from a 1 to a 0. Thus, the Data Link Layer does not have complete responsibility for error detection. Other types of error correction can occur in higher layers.

Data Link Layer Protocols

There are many different Data Link Layer protocols. Some of the most common are:

- High-Level Data Link Control (HDLC), an ISO standard, and subsets of HDLC, such as:

  - Synchronous Data Link Control (SDLC), an IBM protocol

  - Link Access Procedure for D Channel (LAPD), used in Integrated Services Digital Networks (ISDNs)

- LAN protocols, such as Ethernet, Token Ring, and Fiber Distributed Data Interface (FDDI). (We will explain each of these LAN protocols in detail later in the course.)

- Wide area network (WAN) protocols, such as frame relay and ISDN.

As we learned in the last unit, two peer processes must use the same protocol to communicate. For example, communication at the Data Link Layer is not possible if the node at one end of a link uses the Ethernet protocol, while the node at the other end uses the frame relay protocol.

One Link, One Frame

As we know, the Physical Layer is only "aware" of the transmission medium itself. The Data Link Layer is a little smarter, because it knows there is another node on the other end of a physical link. However, a Data Link Layer process can only communicate with one peer node at a time, over one physical link.

Of course, many devices may be connected by the same physical link. As we have seen, all nodes connected to the same bus or hub form a single broadcast network. Each node's Physical Layer process receives every signal transmitted by every other node. However, the Data Link Layer does not keep track of all those devices. It simply follows the instructions of the Network Layer, and addresses each packet and frame to the destination the Network Layer provides. Meanwhile, only the destination node's Data Link Layer process decapsulates the frame and passes the packet up to its Network Layer. The Data Link Layer processes on other nodes recognize that the frame is not addressed to them, and they discard the frame.

Each frame carries a packet of data across a single physical link. A new frame is built for the trip across each link, just as we use a different ticket to board an airplane, then a bus, then a train. However, the Network Layer packet stays intact as each frame is built and removed around it.

Thus, we often say that the Data Link Layer is concerned with transmitting data to the "next node" in the network. The next node may be the data's final destination, or it could be an intermediate routing device that can forward the data to its final destination by encapsulating it within a new frame and sending it over a different physical link.

As you can see in the Frames and Links Diagram, the sending computer and receiving computer are not physically connected. Thus, any data sent from the sending computer to the receiving computer must travel over two physical links, from the sending computer to the routing device, then from the routing device to the receiving computer.

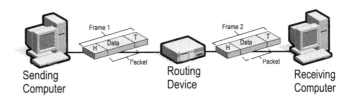

Frames and Links

If data must travel between two computers not directly connected, higher layers of the OSI model coordinate the data's journey across multiple physical links. In the next lesson, we explain how the Network Layer serves as a travel agent that plans the itinerary of each data packet.

Activities

1. Most OSI model protocol layers add headers to the data they transmit. The Data Link Layer also adds a trailer. What is the purpose of the trailer?

2. In the following diagram, "W/S" means Web Server, while "W/B" means Web Browser. "R" stands for routing device. A single physical link ("L") connects each pair of devices.

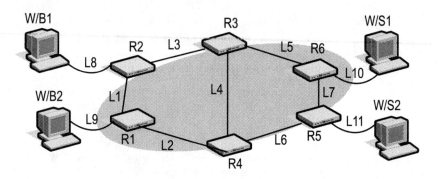

a. List all of the possible link paths, in order, between Web Browser 1 and Web Server 1.

b. List all of the possible link paths between Web Browser 1 and Web Server 2.

3. How many different frames must be built to carry data between Web Browser 2 and Web Server 2, assuming the data travels over the shortest path?

    _____

    _____

4. List the link paths between Web Browser 2 and Web Server 1.

    _____

    _____

Extended Activity

Contrast the services of the Data Link Layer with those of the Physical Layer.

_____

_____

_____

_____

_____

_____

Lesson 4—The Network Layer

The Network Layer is Layer 3 in the OSI reference model. It is responsible for transmitting data packets between source and destination nodes that may not be connected by the same physical link.

If the source and destination nodes are not directly connected, the message must pass through a third node, called an "intermediate node." The Network Layer's job is to use intermediate nodes, when necessary, to transmit a packet to its destination.

Objectives

At the end of this lesson you should be able to:

- Explain how a packet address differs from a frame address

- Describe how the Network Layer transmits a packet over multiple links

- Explain the difference between circuit-switched and packet-switched networks

- Explain the difference between connectionless and connection-oriented networks

 **Key Point**

The Network Layer deals with packets. Network Layer addresses are symbolic computer addresses.

Packets Across Networks

As we have just seen, a process in the Data Link Layer communicates with only one other peer process across a single communication link. However, a process in the Network Layer communicates with multiple peer processes across all communication links to which that node is attached.

The Network Layer accepts data passed down from the layer above (Transport Layer) and encapsulates it by adding a Network Layer header to the data. The header contains protocol information used by peer Network Layer processes as they forward the packet to its final destination. The Network Layer then passes the packet down to the layer below, the Data Link Layer. The Packets and Network Layer Diagram illustrates the relationship between these layers.

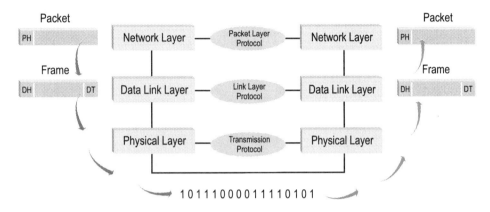

Packets and Network Layer

Network Layer Addresses vs. Data Link Layer Addresses

The addresses in a Network Layer header identify source and destination computers; however, a network address is fundamentally different from a Data Link Layer address.

A Data Link Layer address (NIC address) identifies a particular piece of hardware, because it uses the unique identification number built into each NIC at the factory. A Data Link Layer address is like a name or fingerprint, which identifies a unique individual.

In contrast, Network Layer addresses are symbolic or "logical" addresses assigned to computers through software. A Network Layer address identifies a computer's role in the network or relationship to other computers. Different computers may be assigned the same Network Layer address over time; however, each of those computers will always have its own unique NIC address.

If you think back to our Unit 3 analogy of sending a letter from the Chief Executive Officer (CEO), the job title "Head of Manufacturing" is like a Network Layer address. Different people may perform that job over time, thus whoever happens to sit at that desk will receive mail addressed to that job title. However, the unique identity of each person is like a Data Link Layer address.

Packet Routing

By using more than one type of address to identify each item of data, the Network Layer in an intermediate node can forward packets between two nodes not directly connected. To see how this works, refer to the Network Layer and Packet Routing Diagram.

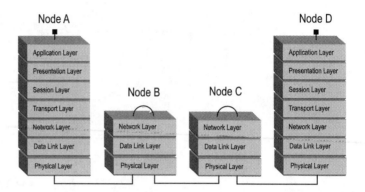

Network Layer and Packet Routing

Imagine that Node A has a packet to send to Node D. The nodes are not on the same physical link, so Node A's Data Link Layer process cannot deliver the packet directly. However, Node A's Network Layer software knows that Node B is the "next hop" on the way to Node D. Thus, it addresses the packet to the network address of Node D, then passes the packet down to its Data Link Layer with instructions to transmit it to Node B. Thus, the Data Link Layer frame that leaves Node A is addressed to Node B (using Node B's NIC address); however, the packet it carries is addressed to Node D (using Node D's network address).

Node B's Data Link Layer process recognizes that the frame is addressed to Node B. It decapsulates the packet and passes it up to its Network Layer process. However, that software recognizes that the packet is addressed to Node D. Node B's Network Layer knows it must forward the packet, but Node B and Node D are also not directly connected. Thus, Node B transmits the packet to Node C, which its Network Layer software knows is closest to Node D.

Once again, Node C's Network Layer recognizes that it must forward the packet. However, because Nodes C and D are directly connected, it transmits the packet and frame directly to the destination.

Basic Data Transmission Methods

One of the most important services of the Network Layer is to relay data between disconnected nodes. The Network Layer provides other important services, but before we discuss them, we first need to explain a few basic concepts about data transmission.

In Unit 2, we learned the difference between a network that connects all of its nodes with point-to-point links, and one that uses a switched service to provide all-to-all connectivity. Switched networks include two subcategories:

- Circuit-switched networks

- Packet-switched networks

Circuit Switching

Telephone service is an example of a circuit-switched network. A telephone call sets up a temporary path, called a "virtual circuit," through the public telephone switching network. A portion of network capacity is set aside for each call, and all signals for that call are sent over the same physical path until the call is finished. If a caller hangs up and immediately calls the same destination, the network may establish a different pathway for the new call. However, once again, that path is reserved for that call until it is finished.

In either case, however, both ends of the circuit are unaware of the switching necessary to set up that circuit. As we can see on the Virtual Circuit Diagram, the two nodes only know that they are communicating across the switched network. The details of the physical path are invisible.

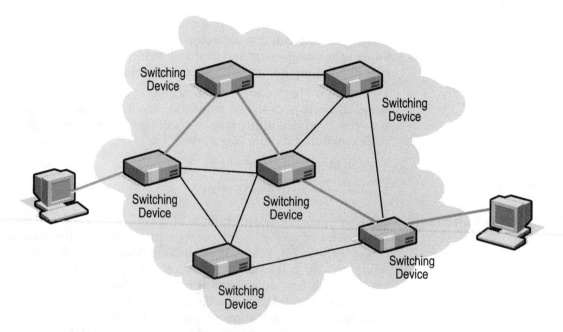

Virtual Circuit

A circuit-switched network is dependent on a completed connection. When you place a telephone call, the connection is not complete until someone at the other end of the line answers. In this way, circuit switching is like being able to reserve a lane on the highway when you visit a friend. Before you can travel, you first make sure your friend is home and that the highway has a free lane. If both of these conditions are true, you will be guaranteed an exclusive lane to drive on, and assigned a particular route to travel.

On the negative side, when traffic is light on a virtual circuit, its unused capacity is wasted. For example, long-distance telephone charges add up until you end a call, even during periods when you are not talking.

Packet Switching

Packet-switched networks, on the other hand, work more like the real highway system. If you want to visit your friend, you do not need to reserve an entire highway lane between you and your destination. All you really need is enough space for your vehicle. Other vehicles can share the same lane, and everyone will get where they are headed. It is a very flexible approach, because lots of data packets can share the same physical transmission link. This type of network is illustrated on the Packet-Switched Network Diagram.

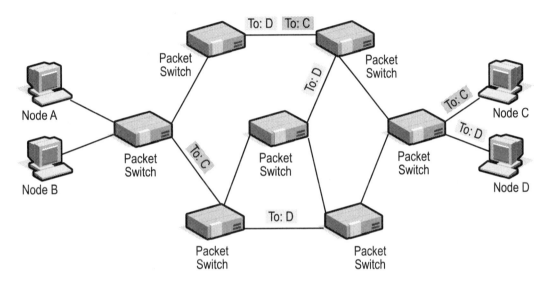

Packet-Switched Network

Packet-switched networks also include two subcategories:

- Connection-oriented
- Connectionless

Connection-Oriented Networks

Connection-oriented packet networks combine the features of packet switching and circuit switching. They break a transmission into packets, but then send all of those packets, in sequence, over the same virtual circuit through the network. And, like circuit-switched networks, a complete connection between source and destination must be established before any packets can begin to move.

Routing is established only once, when the virtual circuit is set up. For example, after you establish a telephone connection, you do not need to keep dialing the telephone number.

However, if a node in the virtual circuit fails, the circuit is broken and must be reestablished through some other route before data transfer can resume. (When a telephone line goes down, it must be fixed, unless the telephone company has another line across which it can route the call.)

Because the same virtual circuit is used for all packets in a transmission, and intermediate nodes know in advance where to send each packet, individual packets need not contain addresses. Thus, connection-oriented networks can carry data efficiently.

Because a virtual circuit is dedicated to each connection, packets are transmitted in sequence and arrive in order at the receiving end. The process of setting up the virtual circuit usually also reserves enough bandwidth for the transmission. Thus, service is predictable and will not vary much due to other traffic in the network. This makes connection-oriented transmission good for time-sensitive applications, such as voice or video.

Connectionless Networks

In contrast, connectionless packet networks send data packets over any available path. Packets may change paths during the same transmission, and may even be sent over multiple parallel paths. As packets reach the destination node, it puts them back into their original sequence.

Because packets may follow different paths, each packet must contain the full Network Layer address of the destination node. Each intermediate node that handles a packet uses that address to decide where to transfer the packet next. This approach increases the "overhead" data that each packet must carry, and requires each node to do more processing on each packet. However, if a node goes down, the network can immediately reroute messages along an alternate route.

Because physical links are shared by the packets of many transmissions, service is degraded by high levels of traffic, just as highway travel slows down at rush hour. However, this shared approach allows data links to be more fully utilized.

On a connectionless network, packets can easily get out of sequence as they travel different paths. Thus, real-time applications, such as audio or video, do not perform well using this type of transmission. However, applications that move data in chunks, such as file transfers, World Wide Web (Web) page requests, and e-mail transmissions, perform quite well with connectionless transmission. Because of this, the Internet is the biggest example of a connectionless packet-switched network.

Network Layer Services

The Network Layer provides the following services to the Transport Layer:

- It maintains a unified addressing scheme that assigns each node in the network a unique logical (symbolic) address. Each Network Layer address is not unique everywhere in the world, but only within a single network. If a packet's source and destination are in different networks, the Network Layer may have to resolve different addressing conventions and duplicated node addresses used in different types and versions of networks.

- The Network Layer handles packets to and from node types that may use different Data Link Layer protocols.

- In circuit-switched networks, it establishes and maintains the virtual circuit.

- In connectionless packet networks, the Network Layer of an intermediate node independently forwards packets from one neighbor to the next. This process is repeated until the packet reaches its final destination.

- In connection-oriented packet networks, a Network Layer process of an intermediate node routes a packet to the next node in the established connection.

Network Layer Protocols

Common protocols used by the Network Layer include:

- X.25 is a connection-oriented, packet-switching protocol defined by the International Telecommunication Union-Telecommunications Standardization Sector (ITU-T). X.25 was widely used for public data networks, especially in Europe; however, it has been largely replaced by faster protocols based on the same basic approach.

- Internet Protocol (IP), derived from X.25, is the primary Layer 3 protocol used across the Internet.

- Internetwork Packet Exchange (IPX) is Novell NetWare's Network Layer protocol. It was derived from the Xerox Network System (XNS) protocol suite, which was used in early LANs.

Activities

In the following network configuration, "W/S" means Web Server, while "W/B" means Web Browser. "R" stands for an intermediate routing device. A single physical link ("L") connects each pair of devices.

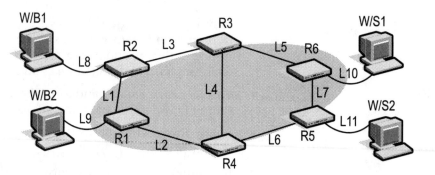

For each of the questions below, provide a type of address: network address (logical address) or NIC address (Data Link Layer address).

1. Web Browser 1 sends a packet to Web Server 1. As the packet leaves Web Browser 1, what destination node address does the packet header contain, and what type of address (network or NIC) is it?

   _____

   _____

2. The packet from Web Browser 1 to Web Server 1 is encapsulated within a different frame each time it crosses a physical link. As the frame moves from R2 to R3, what destination address does the packet header contain?

   _____

   _____

3. What destination address does the frame header contain as the frame moves between routing devices R3 and R6?

   _____

   _____

4. Virtual circuits are used in what types of networks?

   _____

   _____

5. The Internet is the best example of what type of network?

   _____

   _____

6. Indicate whether each of the following characteristics is provided by:
   - Circuit-switched networks
   - Packet-switched, connection-oriented networks
   - Packet- switched, connectionless networks

   a. Unused transmission capacity is wasted.

   b. A Virtual circuit is established.

   c. Performance is consistent and guaranteed.

   d. A Predictable rate of data flow exists.

   e. Data flows over multiple simultaneous paths.

   f. Data packets contain little or no addressing information.

   g. Unused transmission capacity is used for other traffic.

   h. Performance depends on the overall traffic load.

   i. Data arrives in the order it was sent.

Extended Activity

In class, discuss the similarities and differences between delivering a letter by means of the postal service and delivering data across a network. In particular, consider how a letter is forwarded if the original recipient moves without providing a new address to the postal service. What "layer" is responsible for moving the message to its destination?

Lesson 5—The Transport Layer

Thus far in this unit, we have seen that each layer in the OSI model describes a destination in increasingly finer detail. The Physical Layer simply puts the signal onto a transmission medium, with no concept of where it goes. The Data Link Layer addresses a data frame to a hardware device on the other end of a physical link. The Network Layer addresses a data packet to the logical description of a computer that may be located several links away from the source.

However, computers run multiple applications simultaneously. Thus, once the data arrives at the correct computer, it must also be delivered to the correct software process within that computer. If you suspect this requires yet another layer of addressing information, you are correct. The Transport Layer (Layer 4) addresses data to a particular process running on a destination computer.

Objectives

At the end of this lesson you should be able to:

- Describe how applications transmit information to other applications

- Describe how "ports" are used to transmit information to the correct applications

- Name common Transport Layer protocols

 **Key Point**

The Transport Layer carries messages between processes. Transport Layer addresses are process addresses called "port numbers."

End-to-End Communication

The Transport Layer is the lowest "end-to-end" layer of the OSI model, that is, the lowest layer in which peer software processes at either end of a connection carry on a conversation. Processes in the Transport Layer act as if their nodes are adjacent. They rely on lower layers to handle the details of passing data through intermediate nodes and transmitting it across the network, as shown on the Messages and Transport Layer Diagram.

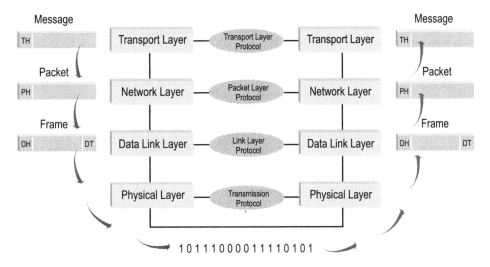

Messages and Transport Layer

The Transport Layer has been termed a "keystone" in the layer hierarchy, because it frequently resides at the border between the delivery mechanism, such as a public IP network, and the upper software layers of the enterprise network.

Transport Layer Services

The Transport Layer provides reliable, cost-effective data transmission, despite a possibly unreliable network underneath it, and it insulates the higher levels from all concerns about the transportation of data.

Basic services provided by the Transport Layer include:

- Addressing
- Connection management
- Flow control and buffering
- Multiplexing and parallelization
- Reliable and sequenced delivery
- Service quality management

Addressing

The Transport Layer delivers data to a specific process within a node. The Transport Layer must also keep track of multiple "connections" between different pairs of processes, because many processes on the same node may be communicating simultaneously. For example, the same user may be accessing a Web server on one computer, downloading a file from another, and checking e-mail on a third. Conversely, a single Web server may host a Web server application, e-mail application, and file repository.

Each node is identified by its network address. Each process is identified by a number called a "port number." When establishing a connection, the sending Transport Layer process passes to the Network Layer both the network address of the target host and the port number of the target application process.

The network address becomes part of the Network Layer header. The port number is placed in the data's Transport Layer header. For convenience, frequently used processes are assigned "well-known" port numbers that are published among the technical community. For example, Hypertext Transfer Protocol (HTTP) for Web access is accessed by means of Port 80.

Connection Management	The Transport Layer is responsible for establishing and releasing connections between processes. When a connection is established, both peer processes are aware of the communication taking place between them. Essentially, they first agree to communicate, then cooperate to exchange data. In contrast, lower layers are only aware of one packet, frame, or bit at a time.

On each node, the Transport Layer allocates resources, such as memory, that the task will require. During data transfer, the Transport Layer processes on both hosts communicate to verify that data is being received without errors or loss. If the established connection fails because of network problems, both computers will detect the failure and report it to the appropriate higher layer application. When the communication is complete, the peer processes terminate the connection to free up resources for other processes.

Flow Control and Buffering

Each node on a network is capable of receiving data at a certain rate, which is determined by the computing capacity of its computer and other factors. Each node also has a certain amount of processor memory available to store data. If data arrives too fast for the receiving node to process it, or more data arrives than the node can store, the excess data is simply lost, like water spilling over a full bucket.

The Transport Layer is responsible for ensuring that the receiving node has enough memory buffers to store the incoming data, and that data is not transmitted faster than the receiving node can accept it.

Multiplexing and Parallelization

Because more than one process may be communicating on the same node, the Transport Layer must keep track of multiple connections. To provide efficient service to the layers above, Transport Layer processes must also work with one or more transmission channels using two techniques:

- Multiplexing—When the transmission channel provides faster service than the upper layers need, the Transport Layer will multiplex transmissions across a single channel to make more effective use of the channel's bandwidth. Multiplexing simply means that the Transport Layer interleaves the packets from two or more processes, as shown on the Multiplexing Diagram. The Transport Layer process at the receiving end then sorts the packets, recreating the original messages based on addressing and sequencing data stored in the Transport Layer headers.

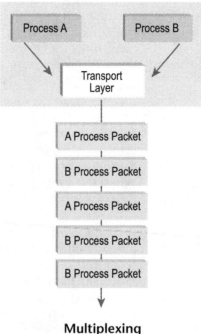

Multiplexing

- Parallelization—When the upper layers require faster service than a single channel can provide, the Transport Layer can send data flowing over multiple channels (if available), multiplying the effective throughput rate for the higher layers. This assumes that the Transport Layer process is running on a machine capable of multitasking, so that the lower layer processes which support the actual data transfer across the channels can operate in parallel. Multitasking capability is a function of the operating system (OS) used on each node.

Reliable and Sequenced Delivery

The Transport Layer also has responsibility for the reliability of the communication service provided to the upper layers. It must be able to recover from a wide variety of problems, such as:

- Corrupted (damaged) packets
- Lost or delayed packets
- Duplicate packets
- Packets delivered out of sequence

If packets are damaged, lost, or delayed for too long, the receiving Transport Layer corrects the error by asking the sending Transport Layer to retransmit the problem data. Of course, if a delayed message is retransmitted, and the original message also gets through, the receiving node will receive duplicate messages. Thus, in addition to error-detection data, a Transport Layer header also includes sequencing information that identifies each segment of data and its place in the overall transmission. This allows the receiving Transport Layer to discard duplicate messages.

Service Quality Management

In data networking, "quality of service" describes the characteristics of a transmission link, such as throughput, setup time, or accuracy. For example, a geosynchronous (GEO) satellite link has good speed and accuracy, but a long delay to set up the transmission.

The OSI reference model lets the Transport Layer's users (the layers above it) specify the quality of service (QOS) they require. They do this by providing parameters along with each request to establish a communication channel or deliver a packet. Different parameters are defined for both circuit-switched (connection-oriented) and packet-switched (connectionless) service.

For example, an interactive application that needs good response time might specify high QOS parameter values for connection establishment delay, throughput, transit delay, and connection priority. That same application might also specify a lower QOS value for residual error rate, because the impact of errors on the user is relatively low. (The receiving node just requests a retransmission.) On the other hand, a file transfer application that moves large volumes of data at night can accept slower response and connection establishment, but must have error-free transmission. That application would provide a different set of QOS parameters based on its needs.

Transport Layer Protocols

The following protocols are found at the Transport Layer:

- Transmission Control Protocol (TCP) was developed for the Internet. TCP works in conjunction with IP, in the widely used TCP/IP protocol stack.

- Sequenced Packet Exchange (SPX) is Novell NetWare's Transport Layer protocol. It works in conjuction with IPX.

Activities

1.   What is a port number, and how does the Transport Layer use it?

   _____

   _____

2.   Describe what can happen on a network that does not have a method of flow control.

   _____

   _____

3.   What is the difference between multiplexing and parallelization?

   _____

   _____

4.   A port number only identifies a software process. How does a Transport Layer message get to the computer that hosts that process?

   _____

   _____

Extended Activities

Demonstrate Transport Layer functionality by having class members role play a simple two-node network. To each node (group), assign a computer name, Network Layer address, and Data Link Layer address. Then assign one person to represent each one of the following components on each node:

•   Three software processes, each identified by a port number

•   One Transport Layer process

•   One Network Layer process

•   One Data Link Layer process

•   One Physical Layer process

Connect your two "nodes" with a single person who represents the network's transmission medium.

1. Have one process send a short message to a process on the other node. Encapsulate and decapsulate the message as the players pass it down one protocol stack and up the other. Make sure that each layer of encapsulation uses the correct address for that layer.

2. When your group is good at passing one message, make the game more challenging by having one process send a long message to the other, broken into several small segments. Now add sequencing information to your Transport Layer header, so the receiving node can reassemble the fragments.

3. After two processes set up a connection and begin transferring data, complicate the game by introducing and correcting transmission errors. For example, pretend a power failure occurs on the receiving node, so it cannot acknowledge messages from the sending node. Or, have the Physical Layer occasionally lose a message. What layer is responsible for detecting these problems and notifying the upper layers?

4. Finally, set up multiple simultaneous connections between processes, or add another node, and see how many interactions your network can keep track of. Who has the most challenging job in this exercise?

Lesson 6—The Session Layer

In this lesson, we begin to discuss the top three layers of the OSI model. Important differences exist between the four lower layers we have studied so far, and the remaining three layers.

As we have seen, the job of the lower layers is to provide reliable communication of data across a network. The job of the upper layers, taken collectively, is to provide user-oriented services through a set of widely available standard applications, and specialized applications written for the users by programmers. The Session Layer, and the Presentation Layer above it, provide reusable services for the applications that reside in the Application Layer.

The Session Layer is so named because it facilitates a step-by-step interaction or session between two entities. For example, an interactive user session begins with a user logging on to the computer, and ends with the user logging off.

Objectives

At the end of this lesson you should be able to:

- Describe the services of the Session Layer
- Explain the relationship between sessions and connections
- Describe the process of token passing

 **Key Point**

The Session Layer is where a conversation starts and stops, and the rules of the conversation are agreed upon.

Electronic Conversations

A session between processes is like a conversation between people. Certain conventions in conversation help avoid confusion and allow for orderly and complete transfer of information between the parties. The conventions include:

- The parties first agree to talk to one another.
- They (usually) do not talk simultaneously.

- They divide the conversation into parts. ("Let me describe it to you, and you can tell me what you think.")

- They end the conversation in an orderly fashion. ("I will talk to you later." "Okay. Bye.")

Similarly, the Session Layer provides higher layers with services that can be used to conduct sessions, including:

- Establishing a session (separately from a connection)

- Conducting dialogs that prevent both parties from transmitting data simultaneously

- Managing activities by dividing the session into parts

- Ending a session gracefully

Establishing, Conducting, and Ending a Session

A session controls the way information flows between entities over a connection that has been established by the Transport Layer. There are two possible relationships between sessions and connections:

- One or more sessions can take place during a single connection. Several sessions can take place without reestablishing the connection over and over. This is analogous to passing a telephone around during a family call. Multiple conversation sessions begin and end during a single call connection. (However, the Session Layer does not combine several sessions onto a single connection. That is the job of the Transport Layer.)

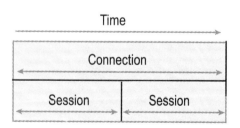

- A session can require several connections to complete. In other words, a connection can be interrupted and reestablished without disturbing the session. This is equivalent to a telephone connection that is disconnected before you are finished talking. Because your conversation was not complete when the call disconnected, you must reestablish the connection (call the person back) to finish the session.

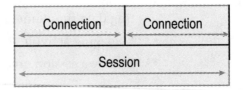

An important component of Session Layer services is that of "orderly release" of the connection. The lower layers support only an abrupt termination of the connection. However, in a conversation, it is more polite and efficient to confirm that the other party is finished talking before you hang up the telephone. In other words, we end the conversation (session) before we hang up (end the connection). The Session Layer takes care of this for dialogs between nodes.

Dialogs

The Transport Layer allows simultaneous communication in both directions across a channel (full-duplex); however, a meaningful conversation requires a dialog, in which only one party speaks at a time.

Token Passing

The Session Layer provides a service that allows the application to conduct a dialog: when one node is "talking," the other is "listening." This is managed by a system called "token passing." As we can see on the Token Passing Diagram, only the node that has the token may talk. When that node is finished talking, it passes the token to the other node. The nodes pass the token back and forth to control the dialog.

Node A has Token.

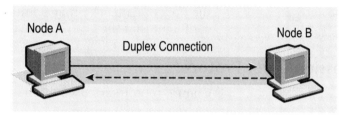

Node B has Token.

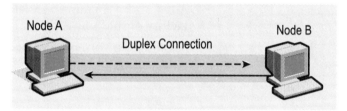

Token Passing

Activity Management

In a dialog, it is also necessary to identify where data starts and ends as it flows between the nodes participating in a conversation. For example, if a file transfer application is transferring several files, the receiving node must be told where one file ends and the next starts. Markers, called "delimiters," can be inserted into the data stream by the sender, but then the recipient has to scan the stream for them, and that effort requires computing cycles. Data that looks like delimiters can also confuse the recipient.

Activity management solves these problems by dividing the data stream into "activities." For the file transfer example, each file becomes an activity. The Session Layer signals the start and end of activities by inserting control information into the Session Layer header.

Sync Points

Within activities, the Session Layer supports "sync points." In a human dialog, sync points amount roughly to asking "Did you get that?" They allow you to make sure that the other person understands what you have said, or has written it down, before you continue talking.

Sync points perform a similar function for programs. A sync point tells the recipient, "Process everything I have sent you before we go on." Using the file transfer application as an example, a sync point might mean, "Write all the data I have sent you to disk before you take any more." Then, if something happens to disturb the flow of data after that point, both ends of the connection are confident that they can start over from the last sync point.

Session Layer Protocols

Common protocols used by the Session Layer include:

- ISO 8327, defined for use by programs being written to conform to the OSI model

- Advanced Program-to-Program Communications (APPC), a facility of IBM's SNA

- Session Control Protocol of Digital Equipment Corporation's (DEC's) Digital Network Architecture (DNA)

Activities

1. Illustrate, using arrows pointing between "caller" and "called party," the steps in a telephone session between two people. Show all the steps and "protocols," including beginning and ending the call. The Session Layer interacts with the _____ and _____ Layers.

2. Assume you are in the middle of downloading a file when your Internet service provider (ISP) drops your connection. You quickly reestablish the connection, then begin the download again. However, instead of starting over from the start of the file, your download resumes where it left off. What Session Layer feature makes this possible?

Extended Activity

Network Basic Input/Output System (NetBIOS) is a common protocol that operates at both the Session and Transport Layers. IBM developed NetBIOS Extended User Interface (NetBEUI) in 1985 as a transport protocol for LANs. In relation to the OSI model, NetBEUI operates at both the Network and Transport Layers. NetBIOS and NetBEUI are integrated in the LAN environment to provide an efficient communication system. Research these protocols and summarize your findings.

_____

_____

_____

_____

Lesson 7—The Presentation Layer

Just as different human languages use different symbols to represent the same ideas, computers can use different symbols and methods to represent information. The primary job of the OSI Presentation Layer, (Layer 6), is to deal with the format of stored computer information. Thus, the Presentation Layer would be better named the "representation" layer. It is concerned with all of the problems of the representation of data that are transmitted between nodes of a network.

Objectives

At the end of this lesson you should be able to:

- Name and describe the basic services of the Presentation Layer

- Describe common ways to represent information on a computer

- Understand how to make information travelling across a network secure

- Explain the reason for compressing information

 **Key Point**

The Presentation Layer is the process concerned with how data is presented on the computer and represented inside the computer.

Computer Numbering

Before we discuss these Presentation Layer services, we must first explain how computers handle data. To human users of computer applications, words, numbers, and images are all different. However, the computer hardware treats all of those different types of data as numbers. Each letter of the alphabet is represented by a number. Each color in a picture is a number. And, as we will see, different types of numbers can be represented in different ways.

The Binary Numbering System

Binary numbering is the underlying language of all computers. The binary numbering system is a positional numbering system, just like the decimal system. However, there are two important differences between decimal and binary:

Binary is Base 2—The decimal system is a base 10 system. That means that each position of the decimal system is 10 times greater than the position to its right. Thus, a 1 in the "tens" place is 10 times greater than a 1 in the "ones" place, and a 1 in the "hundreds" place is 10 times greater than a 1 in the "tens" place.

The binary system is a base 2 system, which means that each position is two times greater than the position immediately to its right. For example, the values of the first eight places of the binary system are as follows:

Place:	128	64	32	16	8	4	2	1

Binary Uses Two Values: 1 and 0—While the decimal system uses 10 different values (0 to 9) in each position, the binary system uses only two: 1 and 0. We represent the number 10 in binary as follows:

Place:	128	64	32	16	8	4	2	1
Value:	0	0	0	0	1	0	1	0

Machines can represent these two values in a variety of ways, such as:

• Positive or negative magnetic charges

• High or low electrical voltage, frequency, or current

• Absence or presence of holes in a card or paper tape

• Absence or presence of pits in the surface of a compact disc (CD)

Each 1 or 0 is called a "bit," which is short for "binary digit." A bit is the smallest unit of information a computer can process. Most computers store binary information in "bytes," which are groups of 8 bits. The 8 bits can represent up to 256 different values, from binary 00000000 (decimal 0) to binary 11111111 (decimal 255).

In a binary data transfer, the stream of bits flowing between two computers is not altered during transmission. Data communication facilities, such as modems, do not evaluate or manipulate the bits as they are being transferred. Binary information is sometimes called "raw data."

The Hexadecimal Numbering System

Humans have a hard time reading long strings of binary bytes, thus we use the hexadecimal number system, a base 16 numbering system, to condense binary bytes into a compact form for printing or analysis.

The hexadecimal numbering system is used to condense binary bytes into a compact form for printing or analysis. Because it is a base 16 system, it uses 16 different values: the numbers 0 through 9, plus the letters A through F. (A represents 10, B represents 11, and so on.) Each "nibble" (4 bits) of an 8-bit byte is represented by one of these 16 values. The binary representation of a byte, and the decimal and hexadecimal equivalents for the decimal numbers 0 through 31 are presented in the Binary and Hexadecimal Representations Table.

Binary and Hexadecimal Representations

Decimal Number	Binary Equivalent	Hex Equivalent	Decimal Number	Binary Equivalent	Hex Equivalent
0	0000 0000	00	16	0001 0000	10
1	0000 0001	01	17	0001 0001	11
2	0000 0010	02	18	0001 0010	12
3	0000 0011	03	19	0001 0011	13
4	0000 0100	04	20	0001 0100	14
5	0000 0101	05	21	0001 0101	15
6	0000 0110	06	22	0001 0110	16

Binary and Hexadecimal Representations (Continued)

Decimal Number	Binary Equivalent	Hex Equivalent	Decimal Number	Binary Equivalent	Hex Equivalent
7	0000 0111	07	23	0001 0111	17
8	0000 1000	08	24	0001 1000	18
9	0000 1001	09	25	0001 1001	19
10	0000 1010	0A	26	0001 1010	1A
11	0000 1011	0B	27	0001 1011	1B
12	0000 1100	0C	28	0001 1100	1C
13	0000 1101	0D	29	0001 1101	1D
14	0000 1110	0E	30	0001 1110	1E
15	0000 1111	0F	31	0001 1111	1F

Presentation Layer Services

The Presentation Layer provides three main services:

- Data representation—The Presentation Layer resolves differences between different types of encoding systems. For example, it handles communication between an IBM mainframe that uses Extended Binary Coded Decimal Interchange Code (EBCDIC) character coding, and an IBM or compatible personal computer (PC) that uses the American Standard Code for Information Interchange (ASCII) character code. An encoding system represents each alphabetical character with a binary number; different systems use different numbers to represent the same letter or punctuation mark.

- Data security—The Presentation Layer encrypts and decrypts data so that anyone who covertly accesses the communication channel cannot obtain confidential information, alter information as it is being transferred, or insert false messages into the stream. It authenticates the source of information and confirms that a party to a communication session is indeed the party represented.

- Data compression—The Presentation Layer also represents transmitted data in a compact fashion to make optimal use of the communication channel. It does this by compressing data passed to it by the Application Layer, and decompressing the data before passing it back at the receiving end.

Data Representation

Data is represented in different ways on different computers. A computer cannot process data in a form used by another computer if the forms are different. The primary ways in which data vary are:

- Byte ordering within integers—The first (left-most) byte of an integer can be either most significant or least significant. For IBM mainframes, and the Apple Macintosh and Sun Microsystems Scalable Performance Architecture (SPARC) models, bytes within integers are ordered in an intuitive manner, with the most significant hexadecimal digits to the left, so that the binary number 1 would appear as "00000001" in processor memory. In machines such as the IBM PC, and others based on Intel microprocessors, and in DEC products, the least significant bit is first, thus 1 would be "10000000."

- Character coding—EBCDIC and ASCII are common codes; however, others exist as well.

- Format of floating point numbers—A floating point number consists of a mantissa field, exponent field, and sign. For example, the number 3^{-1} is a floating point number, where 3 is the mantissa and $^{-1}$ is the sign and exponent. Each is represented with some number of bits in a certain order within a word (single precision) or double-length word (double precision). The number of bits for each varies from computer to computer.

The way in which data is represented in certain compilers also varies, even for compilers that compile the same programming language. For example, a Boolean value (variable that takes two values, "true" and "false") might be stored as 1 byte on one computer, but occupy a word (2 bytes) on another.

Representation Example: ASN.1—Differences in data representation could, of course, be handled by the application program, and in many networks they are. However, the Presentation Layer of the OSI model provides a generalized way of dealing with these differences called "Abstract Syntax Notation 1, (ASN.1)." With ASN.1, the burden of data translation is removed from the application programmer's shoulders.

ASN.1 provides a standardized format for data transfer between nodes, as illustrated on the Abstract Syntax Notation Diagram. Each node is only concerned with translating to and from ASN.1, and does not need to know anything about the format in which data is stored elsewhere on the network.

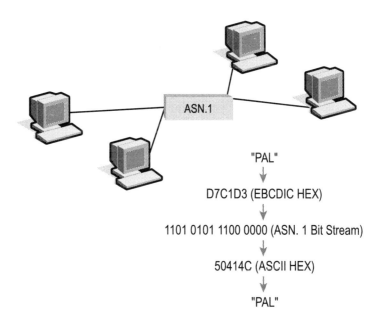

Abstract Syntax Notation

ASN.1 data transmission proceeds as follows:

1. When the application code is written, the programmer includes a definition of the program data structures.

2. When the application program needs to communicate, it provides the ASN.1 definition along with the actual data structure to the Presentation Layer process.

3. The Presentation Layer process converts the data from native format (for example, EBCDIC) to ASN.1 format, and returns the structure into a self-defining bit stream. That is, each data element in the bit stream is preceded with a code that defines its type and, if necessary, its length. The format of this bit stream is called "transfer syntax."

4. The data, in transfer syntax, is transmitted by means of the lower layers.

5. The Presentation Layer process at the receiving end uses the corresponding ASN.1 definition (its name is included in the bit stream) to convert the bit stream back into an application data structure in the proper format for the application at that end.

Data Security

The security of data within the network falls within the province of the Presentation Layer, which must guard against three main types of threats:

- Unauthorized use of the network, including false identification. False identification means pretending to be someone else, either by logging on to the network as that person or sending messages falsely attributed to another user of the network.

- Stealing data from the network, such as wiretapping.

- Inserting false messages into the data stream, or removing messages from the stream.

The first threat is related to user authentication, which often is the responsibility of the logon process of the OS. OSs have a variety of ways to detect attempts to defeat their user authentication. For example, most systems will not allow more than a few attempts at entering a password. This makes it more difficult to break passwords by repetitive experimentation.

When user authentication is the responsibility of the application, the application must provide user authentication safeguards similar to those the OSs provide. These safeguards lie within the province of the application, rather than the OS or network.

Theft of data and insertion of false messages are network issues. The threat of both can be minimized by encrypting messages at their source, and decrypting them at their destination. The application header data that authenticates and sequences messages must be encrypted, as well as the data itself, to prevent false messages or deletion of messages.

There are many good methods of data encryption. In general, they all use a series of mathematical operations, called "encryption algorithms," to either reorder the bits, bytes, or words of a message (transposition method), or substitute one or more encryption bytes or words for the "plaintext" bytes or words of the message (substitution method). A numeric value or "key" is used to guide the encryption algorithm. This means that if the same message is encrypted with two different keys, it will yield two different blocks of encrypted text, called "ciphertext," even if the same algorithm was used both times.

At the receiving end, the same encryption key is used to unscramble or decrypt the received ciphertext. There are two main methods of encryption:

- Single-key or symmetric encryption uses the same key to both encrypt and decrypt a message. Therefore, both the sender and recipient must have the same key before they can exchange coded messages. Symmetric encryption systems include Data Encryption Standard (DES), triple DES (3DES), RC5, International Data Encryption Algorithm (IDEA), and other algorithms that are extremely fast. Their strength lies in the length of the key and the difficulty of analyzing the encrypted data.

  Because DES is a standard, and it is quite computer-intensive to encode and decode data using the DES algorithm, the DES process has been built into a specific computer chip. As shown on the DES Encryption Diagram, the DES chip accepts a 64-bit block of plaintext and the key; it then outputs the ciphertext that represents that block of data. The same chip can be used to reverse the process by inputting the ciphertext and key to produce the plaintext.

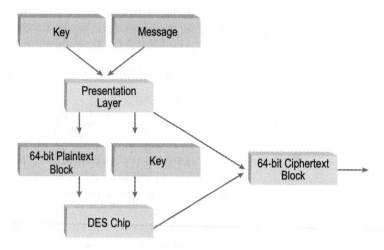

DES Encryption

- Public-key encryption uses a pair of encryption keys for each party that needs to receive encrypted information. Each key in the pair acts as a one-way channel. One key (either one) is used to encrypt the data; the other is used to decrypt the data. Data encrypted with one key cannot be decrypted with the same key, only with its corresponding "partner" key. To use public-key encryption, a person or organization freely distributes its public encryption key and safeguards the corresponding private key. Anyone may use the public key to encrypt messages to a recipient, who uses the private key to decrypt them. Public-key encryption is very central processing unit (CPU)-intensive. It is typically used for small amounts of data where strong security is required, such as Internet e-commerce applications.

Data Compression

Data transmitted between nodes of a network can be quite repetitive. Financial data and bitmapped images, for example, often contain long sequences of zeros. Many messages contain far more printable characters than unprintable characters, and more blanks, vowels, and numeric characters than consonants and signs.

The number of bits actually transmitted between nodes in a network ultimately governs the cost of operating the network and the network's capacity to do useful work. Thus, it is often desirable to "compress" data before transmitting it. Data compression reduces the number of bytes that must be transmitted by translating the data into a more efficient form that requires less storage.

If data is compressed by the sender, it must be expanded by the recipient; thus, a variety of data compression protocols have been defined. For example, a technique called "run length encoding" represents a set of repeated bits by a count of the bits followed by the encoded bit, as illustrated on the Run Length Encoding Diagram. In this example, the "+" character is used to mark the start of a length-encoded field. Thus, the characters "+70" represent a series of seven zeroes.

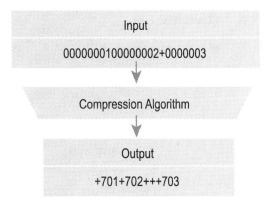

Run Length Encoding

If the "+" character actually appears in the input message, the recipient could mistake it for the start of a compressed field. This problem is avoided by coding each "+" in the source message as "++."

Run length encoding takes advantage of data that has repetitive adjacent elements. A number of other techniques take advantage of other characteristics of data. The decision as to which technique to use depends on the specific application and characteristics of the data.

Activities

1. Authentication is always performed by the Presentation Layer. True or False

2. _____and _____ are two character coding standards commonly used to represent data.

3. _____ is the act of reordering data for security purposes.

4. _____ is performed on data to reduce the number of bytes carried by a communication link.

5. The process of translating secured data so that it can be understood by a user program is called _____.

6. The three services of the Presentation Layer are _____.

Extended Activities

1. What is the decimal equivalent of the following binary numbers?

   a. 1000 1111

   b. 1101 1001

   c. 1010 1010

   d. 0101 0101

   e. 1111 1111

2. What is the binary equivalent of the following decimal numbers?

   a. 2

   b. 64

   c. 69

   d. 222

   e. 319

3. What is the hexadecimal equivalent of the following binary numbers?

    a. 1000 1111

    b. 1101 1001

    c. 1010 1010

    d. 0101 0101

    e. 1111 1111

4. What is the hexadecimal equivalent of the following decimal numbers?

    a. 2

    b. 64

    c. 69

    d. 222

    e. 319

5. What is the binary equivalent of the following hexadecimal numbers?

    a. A3

    b. FF

    c. 0A

    d. 01

    e. FF 89

6. What is the decimal equivalent of the following hexadecimal numbers?

    a. A3

    b. FF

    c. 0A

    d. 01

    e. FF 89

Lesson 8—The Application Layer

The Application Layer, the highest layer in the OSI protocol stack, contains the programs that invoke the services of the network to get useful work done. Some of these applications are written specifically for one network, while others are widely used standard applications. When these applications need to communicate with peers over the network, they can use their own protocols, plus the services of the lower layers.

If the Application Layer contained only custom user programs with their own custom protocols, we would not need to say much about this layer. In fact, in the original OSI model, the Application Layer was not "feature-rich." However, over the years, requirements for services that needed to be provided at this layer, that is, services that did not fit logically into the lower layers, were identified, and a number of Application Layer facilities were specified for OSI.

Therefore, Application Layer programs fall into two classes:

- User applications provide standard services directly to the user. Each of these applications has its own standard protocol at the Application Layer level. Chief among these applications is e-mail.

- Application services provide services to other applications, but not directly to the user. The purpose of these facilities is to keep application programmers from having to reinvent the wheel when they write network applications. Chief among these services is virtual filestores.

Objectives

At the end of this lesson you should be able to:

- Explain the difference between a user application and an application service

- Name some of the most common Application Layer programs and describe what they do

- Describe a typical interaction between a Web browser and Web server

 **Key Point**

The Application Layer includes some programs that interact directly with users, and some that provide services to user applications.

Common Application Layer Programs

Application Layer services are often different from user applications we typically work with. A user application may provide an easy-to-use interface to an unseen process that operates in the Application Layer. Because the user application uses the services of the Application Layer, the user application logically functions above the OSI protocol stack.

However, user application programs may also use their own protocols to communicate across a network, without using the services of the Application Layer. In that case, the OSI Application Layer process simply passes that information from the user application to the Presentation Layer, without modifying or encapsulating the information.

The Application Layer includes many programs and processes. The most commonly used examples are:

- E-mail
- USENET newsgroups
- File transfer and access
- Virtual terminals
- Web browsers and servers

E-Mail

E-mail is perhaps the most visible application on many networks. Its primary benefit is very fast delivery of messages. If the sender and recipient are on the same network, an e-mail message can be delivered almost instantaneously.

One of the most widely used e-mail protocols is Simple Mail Transfer Protocol (SMTP). SMTP defines a protocol, and set of processes that use the protocol, to transfer e-mail messages between users' mailboxes on e-mail servers. Unlike other communication protocols that use binary codes in structured fields, SMTP uses plain English headers. It does not define the programs used to store and retrieve mail messages. Although a basic mail "reader" program is included with virtually every OS, many different mail readers have been developed to provide a user-friendly front end to SMTP.

USENET Newsgroups

USENET is a widely used bulletin-board discussion system that predates the Internet, although its traffic is now carried over the Internet. A newsgroup is a file of e-mail messages relating to a certain topic. Some organizations set up public newsgroups to serve as online users' groups. However, others install news server software on their private servers, to create privately operated newsgroups.

The thousands of public USENET discussion groups are hierarchically organized, branching from seven fundamental categories (comp, misc, news, rec, sci, soc, and talk). For example, one USENET newsgroup, called "comp.databases," focuses on databases.

We access USENET through a special news reading program. The program initially notifies you of the groups available and lets you choose the groups to which you wish to subscribe. The news reader then notifies you of new messages in your subscription groups and keeps track of which messages in those groups you have read.

Each USENET site, or news server, maintains a copy of each of the newsgroups to which there are subscribers at that site. New messages for each group are copied from site to site by simply sending them as e-mail messages. For example, if someone posts a new message, that message is first put into the copy of the group at the subscriber's site. The message is forwarded from site to site until, in a short while, it has spread around the world.

USENET can be considered to be a layer on top of e-mail, because it uses SMTP to forward postings between servers. SMTP was designed to accommodate both news and e-mail. However, news reader applications use the Network News Transfer Protocol (NNTP) to post and retrieve messages from news servers.

File Transfer and Access

Two data manipulation capabilities are universally required by network users:

- File transfer is the ability to copy a file from one node to another. File transfer is straightforward: the user issues commands specifying the source and destination, and the file transfer facility creates a copy of the file on the target node, leaving the original intact. In some cases, the data might need to be transformed if the source and destination nodes run different OSs. In the OSI model, this is handled by the Presentation Layer. However, individual applications can also take care of any transformation between nodes.

  The File Transfer Protocol (FTP) process is widely used to transfer files between two computers. UNIX systems also provide a widely used program called UNIX-to-UNIX Copy Program (UUCP). UUCP uses its own special purpose protocol to copy files from one UNIX system to another.

- File sharing, or remote file access, allows more than one user to access a file that resides on another node. File sharing is more complex than file transfer, because it is necessary to maintain only one copy of the file. When a remote node accesses a file to change it, the file, or at least the relevant portion of the file, must be locked. Locking prevents multiple programs from changing the same data simultaneously, because each node could undo the changes made by the other nodes. It is difficult to provide file sharing while preserving the integrity of the files and addressing possible network interruptions.

  A virtual filestore is a file system that uses file sharing protocols. Virtual filestores allow the user of a node, as well as application programs that run on the node, to view the shared file as an extension of the file system on that node. The shared file looks and behaves as if it were local, except for differences in the data access speed. However, transfer of data across a network is always much slower than transfer of data from a local disk.

  A virtual filestore is a file system that implements file sharing as described above in such a way that, to both the user and application programs, the remote file appears to be resident on the node. Sun Microsystems' Network File System (NFS) is a commonly used virtual filestore system.

Virtual Terminals

A terminal is essentially a display monitor and keyboard used for input to and output from a mainframe computer. It is often called a "dumb" terminal because it has little or no software of its own, and is the slave to the master mainframe. Commonly used terminals included the IBM 3270 and the DEC VT-100.

However, no standard existed for terminal equipment. Terminals made by different companies require different control codes in the input streams that are sent to them in order to produce a desired result. (Even different models from the same vendor can require different codes.) Thus, an application program must generate different control codes for each type of terminal it must use.

As networks developed, many different terminals were in use. To avoid incompatibilities between applications and terminals, the concept of the virtual terminal was developed. Virtual terminal protocols provide an abstract definition of a "generic" terminal that combines all of the common features of most real terminals, but leaves out any vendor-specific features.

Application programs are written to generate control codes for the virtual terminal. A software driver is then written for each type of actual terminal hardware, to translate the standard virtual terminal codes into the codes required by that hardware. If the application needs to take advantage of any unique hardware on a given terminal, it must "escape" the virtual terminal protocol to issue the special commands. However, it then risks becoming incompatible with other terminal types.

The most commonly used virtual terminal is the Telnet program. The IBM 3270 protocol has also become a de facto virtual terminal protocol.

However, a virtual terminal protocol is not the same as a terminal emulator program. A terminal emulator program is an application that allows a computer, typically a PC, to emulate a terminal by mimicking the protocol of the terminal. For example, a program called "tn3270" makes an Intel-based PC appear to the network to be a specific model of an IBM 3270-display device. Confusion between terminal emulators and virtual terminal protocols arises because terminal emulators can emulate virtual terminals. For example, programs are available for the PC and Macintosh that make them appear to be Telnet terminals. As a result, the term "Telnet" is used loosely to mean the emulator program rather than the protocol.

Web Browsers and Servers

The mid-1990s marked the dawn of a new era for the Internet: the Web. What once was the domain of command-line tools and UNIX servers became the world of the Web browser. Due in large part to the graphical user interface (GUI) of desktop computers, the ease of use and popularity of the Internet has increased dramatically. Web browsers have become one of the most popular applications in use today.

A Web browser, such as Netscape Communicator or Microsoft Internet Explorer, is a client application that allows a user to retrieve documents from a remote host computer called an "HTTP server" or Web server. As shown on the Web Browser and Server Diagram, the browser application uses HTTP (an Application Layer protocol) to request a Web page from a Web server. The Web browser's main job is to display Hypertext Markup Language (HTML) documents retrieved from HTTP servers. HTML is a text-based formatting language used to generically format text. The Web browser reads the document and displays it as indicated by both the HTML formatting code and the user's display preferences stored in the browser. Because the instructions for displaying HTML documents are built into the browser, Web page documents are generally fairly small in size.

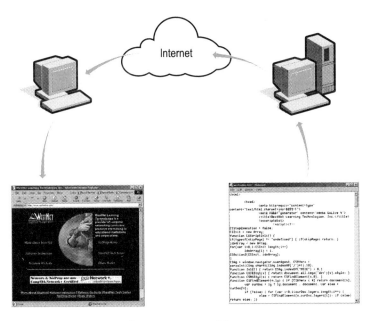

Web Browser and Server

The Web server's job is to respond to browser requests by transmitting Web pages. HTTP server applications can handle millions of requests per hour (if the hardware is powerful enough), because each connection is "stateless." This means that every time a client browser wants to retrieve a document, it sends a separate request to the server. To the server, each request is a unique event, unrelated to any other request. Thus, if a user spends several hours reading a particular Web page, the server has no knowledge of it.

In a typical session between a Web browser and server, the following actions take place:

1. The Web browser sends a connection request to the HTTP server.

2. The HTTP server accepts the request and notifies the browser of the successful connection.

3. The browser transmits the document request to the server.

4. The server retrieves the document and transmits its contents to the browser.

5. The browser receives the incoming document data and displays it for the user.

6. After the server has transmitted the entire document, it breaks the connection with the browser.

Note that in this example there are actually two processes at work. The application protocol (HTTP) transfers information (HTML) between the Web server and Web browser. The browser application provides the user interface, and displays the retrieved HTML document.

Activities

1. The Application Layer always provides services directly to the user. True or False

2. Choose the functions and items that relate to the following applications:

    a. E-mail

    b. Share files

    c. Copy documents

    d. Transfer files

    e. Implement USENET

    f. Virtual terminal/emulator

    g. Retrieve HTML documents

    FTP _____

    Web browser _____

    Telnet _____

    UUCP _____

    NFS _____

    SMTP _____

3. Describe what the term "stateless" means, as it applies to the connection between the Web browser and Web server.

    _____

    _____

    _____

Extended Activities

1. Divide into focus groups. From the following list, choose (by lot or assignment) an application program/service for your focus group to research. Give a brief, informal overview to the other focus groups on what your research yielded.

    a. Domain Name System—(DNS)

    b. NNTP

    c. SMTP

    d. Telnet—virtual terminal

    e. APACHE—Web server application

    f. Server Message Blocks (SMB)—Server messaging application (for example, file services)

    g. Samba—UNIX platform application

2. In this lesson, we explained that HTTP is a stateless protocol. However, many Web sites offer "stateful" interaction, such as recognizing returning users, maintaining shopping carts, and tracking a multistep ordering process. Research the Web technique called "cookies," and explain how they allow stateful interactions over HTTP.

Summary

In Unit 4 we examined how the seven layers of the OSI model work together to reliably move information from a source computer to a destination computer across a network.

The Physical Layer generates and receives the signals that represent bits moving over a single physical transmission medium. That medium may be a copper cable, optical fiber, or radio channel. This layer is not aware of any other nodes that can be reached by that medium.

The Data Link Layer exchanges data frames with a single peer process across a single physical link. This layer can detect and recover from simple data errors. Each Data Link Layer frame contains a data packet passed down from the Network Layer above.

The Network Layer is aware of several peer processes, one for each data link, and takes responsibility for moving packets between links to send them on their way to their final destination. The Network Layer address is concerned with getting a single packet from one end of a network to the final destination.

The Transport Layer is aware of the entire network, and is the first end-to-end layer. A Transport Layer process is concerned with transmitting a complete message from a process on one node to the peer process at the destination node.

The job of the uppermost three OSI layers (Session, Presentation, and Application) is to provide services to user applications. By providing a suite of protocols and standardized services to accomplish tasks that would have to be recoded over and over again, these upper layers allow user applications to more easily share data and communicate with one another. Together, Layers 5 through 7 provide capabilities for:

- Handling differences in data representation between computers

- Handling differences in physical characteristics of terminals on a network

- Ensuring data is not stolen or compromised during network transfer and the network is not used to gain unauthorized access to data

- Making the most efficient use of network resources

- Managing dialogs and activities by the application and synchronization of application activities

- Sharing data between nodes on a network

In addition to these application services, a number of common network applications are part of the Application Layer (Layer 7):

- E-mail
- USENET newsgroups
- File sharing and transfer
- Virtual terminals
- Web browsers and servers

The OSI Summary Diagram summarizes the process of encapsulation and decapsulation, which is the most important concept of this unit. As data is passed down through the protocol stack, each layer encapsulates it by adding its protocol header. Note that the Data Link Layer is the only layer that truly encapsulates the data by adding both a header and trailer when constructing a frame.

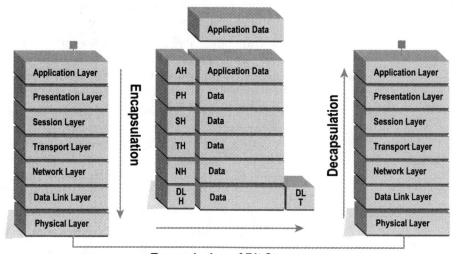

Transmission of Bit Stream

OSI Summary

At the receiving end of the communication link, each layer removes its header (decapsulation) and passes the data portion up to the next layer. Peer layer communication occurs because corresponding layers process only the data contained in their specific protocol header.

Unit 4 Quiz

1. Which OSI model layers are concerned primarily with applications?

   a. All seven

   b. The top three

   c. The lower four

2. Which layers are primarily concerned with moving raw data?

   a. All seven

   b. The top three

   c. The lower four

3. A purpose of the OSI model is to provide which of the following?

   a. A standard for the software/networking industry

   b. A standard for the hardware/networking industry

   c. A reference for network users and administrators

   d. All of the above

4. Which activities occur at the Application Layer?

   a. File transfer and access

   b. E-mail

   c. Web browser

   d. All of the above

5. The OSI model Presentation Layer does which of the following?

   a. Manages the way computers read information

   b. Is where information can be scrambled

   c. Is concerned with the order of bytes and integers

   d. All of the above

6. Compressed data is a function of which of the following layers?

   a. Application Layer

   b. Data Link Layer

   c. Session Layer

   d. Presentation Layer

7. The Session Layer is concerned with which of the following?

    a.   Managing dialog

    b.   Beginning dialog

    c.   Ending dialog

    d.   All of the above

8. Which of the following is the primary purpose of a Transport Layer protocol?

    a.   Transmit bits across a physical link

    b.   Transmit frames across a physical link

    c.   Transmit packets across a network

    d.   Transmit messages from process to process

9. The Transport Layer is not concerned with which of the following?

    a.   Addressing

    b.   Connection management

    c.   Flow control

    d.   Buffering

    e.   None of the above

10. Which layer uses port numbers for communication?

    a.   Session Layer

    b.   Transport Layer

    c.   Data Link Layer

    d.   Application Layer

11. Which of the following is an example of a Transport Layer protocol?

    a.   Ethernet

    b.   IP

    c.   TCP

    d.   RS-232

12. As the Transport Layer is to a message, the Network Layer is to a:

    a. Server

    b. WAN

    c. Ethernet

    d. Packet

13. Which of the following is an example of a Network Layer protocol?

    a. Ethernet

    b. IP

    c. TCP

    d. RS-232

14. Which of the following is the primary purpose of a Network Layer protocol?

    a. Transmit bits across a physical link

    b. Transmit messages between processes

    c. Transmit frames across a physical link

    d. Transmit packets across a network

15. Which of the following is the primary purpose of a Data Link Layer protocol?

    a. Transmit bits across a physical link

    b. Transmit messages between processes

    c. Transmit frames across a physical link

    d. Transmit packets across a network

16. The Network Layer is to packets as the Data Link Layer is to:

    a. Frames

    b. Signals

    c. Bits

    d. Protocol suites

17. Which of the following hardware devices builds a frame?

    a. Media adapter unit

    b. Node port

    c. Light emitting diode (LED)

    d. NIC

18. Which of the following is the primary purpose of a Physical Layer protocol?

    a. Transmit bits across a physical link

    b. Transmit frames across a physical link

    c. Detect duplicate packets

    d. Transmit packets across a network

19. Which of the following will not occur at the Physical Layer?

    a. Transmission of bits

    b. Two-way traffic

    c. Modulation

    d. Rerouting of information

20. Frame headers and packet headers contain addresses.
    True or False

21. Name the seven OSI model layers in order, from the top down.

    _____

    _____

    _____

22. Briefly summarize, in your own words, what each OSI model layer does.

Unit 5
LANs

In the first half of this course, we learned many fundamental concepts and theories about networking. After focusing on the Open Systems Interconnection (OSI) model, we now know the basic vocabulary networking professionals use to talk about data communication systems.

In this unit, and the rest of this course, we will use those concepts to explain the specific technologies and protocols used in most local area networks (LANs). Specifically, this unit will teach you about the popular LAN protocols of Ethernet and Token Ring, and the increasingly important technology of wireless networking. As with earlier units, we will start low in the OSI protocol stack, then work our way up to higher layers of LAN networking protocols and software.

Lessons

1. LAN Data Link Protocols
2. Ethernet
3. Token Ring and FDDI
4. Wireless LANs
5. LAN Software Architectures
6. Information Flow Between Client and Server

Terms

100VG-AnyLAN—100VF-AnyLAN is a 100-Mbps LAN technology standard that directly competes with 100BaseT Ethernet. The IEEE 802.12 committee is currently investigating this standard. The access method used by this standard is different from the CSMA/CD method used by 10-Mbps Ethernet and Fast Ethernet. However, the MAC frame format stays the same. The new access method is called "demand priority."

Bluetooth—"Bluetooth" is an open standard (IEEE 802.15.1, under development) for short-distance wireless personal area networking between handheld computers, peripheral devices, and other smart electronic appliances. It uses frequency hopping spread spectrum radio transmission in the 2.4-GHz range.

daisy chain—A daisy chain is a type of bus topology created by connecting each device to the next device with a separate cable. Node A connects to Node B, Node B to Node C, and so on in a line. In an AppleTalk network, the daisy-chain topology is created using PhoneNet connectors and twisted pair wiring (regular telephone wire). A daisy-chain configuration must be terminated at both ends using terminating resistors.

Data Link Control (DLC)—DLC is a generic term that refers to a protocol, such as Token Ring or Ethernet, used to transfer data across a single physical link.

datagram—The term "datagram" is another word for a Network Layer packet.

internetwork—A complex network that may combine smaller networks in different physical locations, based on different types of network architectures is referred to as an internetwork.

Internetwork Packet Exchange (IPX)—IPX is Novell NetWare's proprietary Network Layer protocol.

NetBIOS Extended User Interface (NetBEUI)—NetBEUI is a Network and Transport Layer protocol designed to work within a single physical LAN. (It does not provide packet routing between networks.) NetBEUI is typically integrated with NetBIOS.

NetWare Core Protocol (NCP)—NCP is the proprietary protocol used by the NetWare OS to transmit information between clients and servers. NCP messages are transmitted by means of IPX, NetWare's Network Layer protocol.

Network Basic Input/Output System (NetBIOS)—NetBIOS is a software system originally developed by Sytek and IBM to allow a NOS to communicate with computer hardware. NetBIOS has been adopted by Microsoft Windows NT and Novell NetWare, and has become the de facto standard for application interface to all types of LANs. Thus, many LANs are described as "NetBIOS compatible."

Moving Pictures Experts Group, Layer-3 (MP3)—MP3 stands for MPEG Layer-3, which is an extension of the Motion Picture Experts Group (MPEG) standards for compressed digital video. MP3 is the most popular compression format for digital audio files, and is commonly used to distribute music over the Internet.

personal area network (PAN)—A PAN is a short-distance wireless network that connects a user's personal electronic devices, such as a cell phone, PDA, and headphones. It is also called a WPAN. See Bluetooth.

piconet—A piconet is a Bluetooth PAN that links up to eight devices. Each piconet is controlled by one master device, and up to seven slave devices at any one time. Any device may be a member of more than one piconet, changing its membership as a user moves from one area to another. See Bluetooth.

Point-to-Point Tunneling Protocol (PPTP)—PPTP was developed by Microsoft for VPNs using Microsoft Windows 95/98 and Windows NT. PPTP can support tunneling of IP, IPX, NetBios, and NetBEUI protocols inside IP packets.

redirector—A redirector is client software component that decides whether a request for a computer service or resource (for example, read a file) is for the local computer or another computer on the network. Each software vendor uses a different name for this function, such as "shell," "requestor," or "client."

RS-232—RS-232 cables are used for connecting a computer to a modem. The RS-232 specification details the electrical and mechanical interface between the computer and modem.

Sequenced Packet Exchange (SPX)—SPX is Novell NetWare's proprietary Transport Layer protocol.

Server Message Block (SMB)—SMB is an Application/Presentation Layer protocol used between clients and servers on a LAN. Functions requiring LAN support, such as retrieving files from a file server, are translated into SMB commands before they are sent to the remote device. Applications use SMB "calls" to perform file operations across a network.

Systems Network Architecture (SNA)—SNA is IBM's architecture for computer networking. It was designed for transaction processing in mission-critical applications, usually involving a large number of terminals communicating with a mainframe. It was the first data communications protocol that sent and received an entire terminal screen of information.

Transmission Control Protocol (TCP)—TCP is a Transport Layer protocol used to send messages reliably across a network. It is usually paired with IP to form TCP/IP.

User Datagram Protocol (UDP)—UDP is a Transport Layer protocol (an alternative to TCP) that provides a simple, connectionless datagram delivery service, without error checking, for certain specialized application services that do not require the full services of TCP.

Xerox Network System (XNS)—XNS is the protocol suite developed by PARC for their first versions of Ethernet networks. Several of the major LAN vendors (notably Novell and Banyan) have based portions of their network architectures on the XNS model.

Lesson 1— LAN Data Link Protocols

When networking professionals say "LAN protocol," they usually mean the protocols that operate at the OSI Data Link Layer. These protocols determine the basic operation of a network, because they control how data flows between nodes. In this lesson, we will learn why it was necessary to develop specific protocols for LANs, and understand the technical problems that any LAN protocol must address.

Objectives

At the end of this lesson you should be able to:

- Describe what "medium access control" means, and why it is important

- Describe the two main approaches to medium access control

- Name the corporations and organizations that played key roles in the development of today's LAN protocols

 **Key Point**

LAN protocols differ in the method of medium access control they use.

A Short History of the LAN

To better understand today's LANs, it is important to take a look back at the way networks worked before personal computers (PCs) and the client/server model existed.

When Mainframes Ruled the Earth

When data communications began in the 1960s, the mainframe/terminal network was the predominant network architecture. Most computing was done in batch mode, and companies needed an efficient way to transmit files between computer sites. Thus, the emphasis was on communication over long distances, between cities and often over much greater distances, but at relatively slow data transfer rates.

In the 1970s, interactive terminals began to proliferate; however, most data communications still took place over long distances. For example, IBM's Systems Network Architecture (SNA) was designed for transaction processing in mission-critical applications, often involving services provided to customers. SNA networks usually consisted of a large number of interactive terminals typically querying and updating a centralized database on a mainframe. A commercial bank might have had a number of 3270-type terminals and printers in each of hundreds of branch offices, all of which were used to access a central database in the home office.

Much of this communication was done over point-to-point links. In point-to-point communication, each node always knows who is at the other end of a link. Thus, it is fairly simple to organize transmission between two devices.

Enter the PC

In 1972, at Xerox's Palo Alto Research Center (PARC), small computers began to be configured as "personal" computers. Their users began sharing resources, such as printers, within a local area, across communication links that used the RS-232 protocol.

RS-232 was developed to connect two computers or devices directly to each other. For example, RS-232 is still commonly used to connect computers to modems. However, as we have learned, a mesh of point-to-point links is an inefficient and confusing way to link more than a few computers. Thus, if many small computers were to have any-to-any communication, they needed some way to share a common transmission medium, just as people share the public transportation system.

New Data Link Protocols

Several companies began working on this problem at the same time, taking two main approaches. IBM developed the Token Ring protocol, which carries data like a mass transit system shuttles riders. Xerox, Intel, and Digital Equipment Corporation (DEC) worked together to create Ethernet, which allows data to compete for transmission capacity like cars on a highway.

As these new LAN protocols were developed, they tended to form two sublayers of the OSI Data Link Layer:

• Logical Link Control (LLC)

• Medium Access Control (MAC)

LLC Sublayer

OSI's Data Link protocol for point-to-point communications is High-Level Data Link Control (HDLC). The early LAN developers saw the need to provide the same services to the Network Layer for LANs that HDLC provides for point-to-point links. To satisfy that need, they created the LLC sublayer.

LLC accepts packets from the Network Layer, divides them as necessary into frames, and then hands them off to the MAC sublayer for transmission, while handshaking with its peer process to ensure error-free delivery.

MAC Sublayer

When many nodes share a common transmission medium, there must be some set of rules that determine when a node can transmit data. The problem is similar to a crowd of people in the same room who all have something important to say.

When a node transmits on a bus network, every other node on the same medium receives the transmission. When two nodes transmit simultaneously, a collision or garbled transmission results. Because it is possible that two nodes might wish to transmit simultaneously, some means must be available to prevent collisions or handle them properly when they occur.

On a ring network, only one node transmits over each point-to-point link of the ring, thus the problem of garbled transmissions does not exist. But how does a node get to transmit its own data when the ring is busy? That is the problem of medium access control in a ring architecture.

The MAC sublayer contains various types of rules that solve these problems. As we can see in the IEEE 802 Suite Diagram, there are many different protocols in the MAC sublayer. (We have shown only the main ones.) However, each protocol uses one of two general approaches to the problem of medium access:

• Let nodes compete for access, and deal with collisions as they occur. Ethernet uses this approach. A node transmits as soon as it has something to say. Collisions occur; however, the network ensures that no data is lost or damaged when collisions happen.

- Require nodes to take turns transmitting, and prevent collisions. For example, the network can schedule time for each node that wants to transmit. Token-passing protocols use this approach, which prevents collisions and ensures that each node is regularly guaranteed the opportunity to access the LAN.

We will discuss each of these approaches in detail in later lessons. As we will see, each approach has both advantages and disadvantages.

The IEEE 802 Suite of LAN Protocols

In the mid-1980s, the new LAN protocols were brought into the standards-making process of the Institute of Electrical and Electronics Engineers (IEEE), where they have been continually refined and documented by working groups of network professionals. The IEEE 802 standards committee produced the 802 suite of LAN standards, illustrated on the IEEE 802 Suite Diagram, which has been adopted by the International Standards Organization (ISO) as OSI standard 8802.

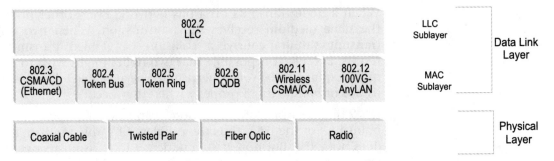

IEEE 802 Suite

The IEEE 802 suite of LAN protocols includes:

- 802.1—Abstract definitions of interactions between LAN services.

- 802.2 LLC—Standards for Data Link frame addressing and error checking.

- 802.3 Carrier sense multiple access with collision detection (CSMA/CD)—A MAC standard used in Ethernet networks. (Ethernet and CSMA/CD are explained in detail in the next lesson.) Further extensions to 802.3 describe the Ethernet cabling standards 10Base2, 10Base5, 10BaseT, and 100BaseT.

- 802.4 Token Bus—A MAC standard that uses token passing on a bus topology. (Token passing is explained in detail in a later lesson.)

- 802.5 Token Ring—A MAC standard that uses token passing on a pure ring or star ring topology.

- 802.6 Distributed Queue Dual Bus (DQDB)—A MAC protocol for switched metropolitan area networks (MANs).

- 802.11 Wireless LANs—The Physical Layer and MAC protocols for radio communication, using carrier sense multiple access with collision avoidance (CSMA/CA). (Wireless LANs are explained in detail in a later lesson.)

- 802.12 100VG-AnyLAN—A 100-megabits-per-second (Mbps) standard that uses demand priority media access as its MAC method. It is currently overshadowed by its direct competitor, Ethernet (802.3), thus we will not discuss it in this course.

Activities

1. Match each of the LAN protocols with its IEEE standard number.

   a. Ethernet

   b. Token Ring

   c. Token Bus

   d. Wireless

2. Describe the two main approaches to medium access control.

   _____

   _____

   _____

   _____

Extended Activity

Research the 100VG-AnyLAN standard (802.12). It promises to deliver high data rates while preventing collisions. If that is true, why is Ethernet still the dominant LAN protocol?

Lesson 2—Ethernet

Ethernet, originally developed in the 1970s by Xerox Corporation in conjunction with Intel and DEC, is now the most widely implemented LAN technology. More than 75 percent of all LANs are Ethernet LANs. This lesson introduces the basics of Ethernet technology and describes the most common Ethernet configurations.

Ethernet is popular because it is fast, inexpensive, and reasonably simple to implement. Ethernet was designed to minimize wiring by connecting computers to a common coaxial bus cable. The original version of Ethernet operated at a burst rate of 10 Mbps. Today's versions use twisted pair cable in a star topology, and can run at throughputs of 10 Mbps, 100 Mbps, or 1 gigabit per second (Gbps), depending on the type of network interface cards (NICs) and cabling used.

Standard Ethernet equipment (NICs, hubs, and cabling) is inexpensive and widely available from many vendors. Most Ethernet LANs use easily installed twisted pair cabling to connect computers and peripherals to hubs.

Objectives

At the end of this lesson you should be able to:

- Describe a collision

- Explain how Ethernet controls each node's access to the physical medium

- Describe common Ethernet configurations

 **Key Point**

Any Ethernet node may attempt to transmit when the medium is idle.

Ethernet Medium Access Control

Ethernet is a Data Link and Physical Layer specification for medium access control. In other words, the Ethernet specification defines how multiple network nodes can use the same shared medium to transmit signals to each other.

The shared medium is the cable (bus) or hub that connects a series of network nodes. With a bus architecture, when a node transmits, every other node on the bus receives the transmission, as illustrated on the Single Transmission Diagram.

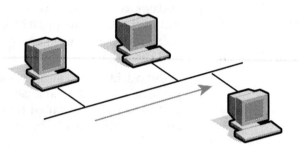

Single Transmission

However, a bus or hub can carry only one signal at a time. If two nodes transmit at the same instant, the two signals will overlap (that is, collide) and garble each other, as illustrated on the Simultaneous Transmissions Diagram.

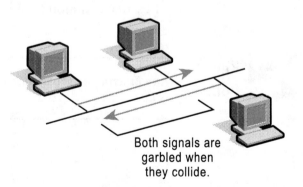

Both signals are
garbled when
they collide.

Simultaneous Transmissions

On a network, many nodes might want to transmit simultaneously. Therefore, a network must have some way to either prevent collisions or handle them properly when they occur. Ethernet allows collisions to occur; however, it provides a fairly simple way to correct any errors they cause.

CSMA/CD

Ethernet's approach to medium access is similar to an informal telephone conference call. When a person has an idea to share, he first listens to determine whether anyone else is speaking. If nobody is speaking, he begins to speak. When that speaker finishes talking, another speaker may take a turn.

Of course, it is common for two or more people to begin speaking at the same time. When this "collision" occurs, all speakers immediately stop talking, and quickly decide who will speak next.

In the Ethernet specification, this approach is called CSMA/CD. This term spells out the major principles of Ethernet medium access control:

- Carrier sense—Each node monitors the bus to determine whether any other node is transmitting.

- Multiple access—More than one node may attempt to transmit at the same time.

- Collision detection—Each node can detect signal collisions by determining whether its own transmission has been garbled.

When a node is ready to transmit a frame, it performs the following steps:

1. Sense the carrier signal on the bus to determine whether any other node is transmitting. If transmission is detected, continue listening until the channel is idle.

2. When no signal is detected, start transmitting the frame.

3. While transmitting, also listen to the bus. Compare the received frame to what was transmitted. As long as they are the same, continue transmitting. If what is received is not what was transmitted, assume a collision. Stop transmitting. (Other similar protocols do not require the node to stop transmitting until the end of its message. In this case, a great deal of time is lost when any of the colliding nodes is transmitting a long message.)

4. Warn all other stations that a collision has been detected by transmitting a special signal called a "jam sequence."

5. Wait a random time interval, then start over with Step 1.

An important aspect of the CSMA/CD algorithm is the random-length time interval (a few milliseconds) that a node waits before trying to retransmit a frame after a collision occurs. This usually prevents a second collision, because the probability of both nodes waiting the same length of time is very small. Therefore, the random wait time ensures that nodes do not keep "butting heads" after a collision, which would prevent any node from being able to access the bus.

Advantages of Ethernet

There are several advantages of Ethernet:

- Ethernet is the prevalent network standard, with hundreds of thousands of nodes installed.

- The protocol is straightforward, especially with respect to error handling. Cabling is simple and taps are passive. Nodes can be installed and removed without bringing a network down.

- The CSMA/CD approach is logically simple.

- Performance can be very good on a lightly used network, when fewer nodes compete for medium access.

Disadvantages of Ethernet

Ethernet also has several disadvantages:

- More collisions occur on a heavily used network, and time is lost with each collision as nodes stop, wait, and retransmit. Therefore, the performance of an Ethernet network decreases as traffic increases.

- Ethernet requires a minimum frame size (64 bytes), which can reduce its efficiency. A minimum-sized frame is necessary because it takes time for an electrical signal to travel from one point on the bus to another. In a large network, if two nodes, Nodes A and B, are at opposite ends of the bus and both start transmitting at the same moment, Node A might transmit the last bit of its message before the first bit has had time to get to Node B, and vice versa. The Too-Short Ethernet Frame Diagram illustrates this problem. Neither node would detect a collision, yet the signal would be garbled for some or all the nodes in between. Ethernet solves this problem by requiring both a minimum frame length and maximum network segment length. This ensures all nodes can detect all collisions.

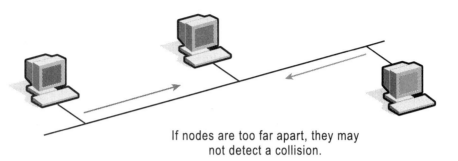

If nodes are too far apart, they may
not detect a collision.

Too-Short Ethernet Frame

Ethernet Configurations

The most straightforward Ethernet configuration is shown on the
Ethernet Hub Configuration Diagram. This star configuration
uses unshielded twisted pair (UTP) to connect an Ethernet hub to
workstations, peripherals, and servers. All nodes attached to the
hub share the same 10-Mbps bandwidth.

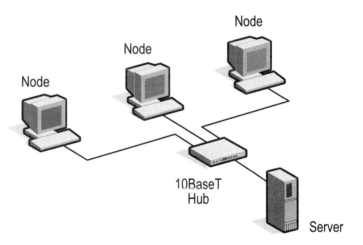

Ethernet Hub Configuration

However, 10-Mbps Ethernet networks may not provide enough bandwidth for an organization. As network applications are implemented using high-resolution graphics, video, and other rich media data types, pressure is growing for increased bandwidth. Two additional Ethernet standards, Fast Ethernet and Gigabit Ethernet, can allow an organization to provide higher data rates while continuing to use familiar and proven Ethernet technology.

Fast Ethernet

The Fast Ethernet standard (IEEE 802.3u) can send Ethernet frames at 100 Mbps over Category 5 UTP (100BaseTx) or fiber optic cabling (100BaseT). The frame format of Fast Ethernet is identical to that of 10-Mbps Ethernet, thus a network can move up to the higher data rate if it can meet the following requirements:

- If UTP cabling is used, it must be Category 5 or higher.

- All NICs and hubs must support the 100-Mbps data rate.

In addition, a network may need to adjust its UTP wiring layout to meet the shorter maximum distances allowed in the 100BaseTx standard. To provide such a high data rate, the longest length of UTP may only be 100 meters (m).

Smart network administrators plan for future upgrades to Fast Ethernet by using Category 5 cabling in all new installations, and by equipping all computers with NICs that support both 10- and 100-Mbps data rates. The slight extra cost of these components is more than offset by a simpler network conversion.

Gigabit Ethernet

Gigabit Ethernet (IEEE 802.3z) provides throughput of 1,000 Mbps (1 Gbps). Like earlier versions, Gigabit Ethernet uses the frame format specified in the IEEE 802.3 standard, as well as the familiar CSMA/CD medium access control method.

The Gigabit Ethernet standard includes three specifications for optical fiber cabling and two specifications for copper:

- 1000BaseSX ("S" for short wavelength) defines optical transceivers or Physical Layer devices for multimode fiber cabling using laser light at a wavelength of 770 to 860 nanometers (nm). This wavelength range is commonly referred to as 850 nm. 1000BaseSX transceivers are less costly than those found in products implementing the long wavelength specification described below.

- 1000BaseLX ("L" for long wavelength) defines optical transceivers or Physical Layer devices for either multimode or single-mode fiber, using laser wavelengths of 1,270 to 1,355 nm (commonly referred to as 1,350 nm).

- 1000BaseLH ("LH" for long haul) is a multivendor specification that defines optical transceivers for Physical Layer devices that support distances greater than the 1000BaseLX specification. Each vendor has a set of transceivers designed to cover different distances. Although it is not an IEEE standard, many vendors are working to interoperate with IEEE 1000BaseLX equipment.

- 1000BaseCX ("C" for copper) defines transceivers or Physical Layer devices for shielded copper cabling. 1000BaseCX is intended for short-haul copper connections (25 m or less) within wiring closets.

- 1000BaseTX ("T" for twisted pair) will specify Gigabit Ethernet over four-pair Category 5 UTP copper cabling for distances up to 100 m. This standards development effort is still in progress.

Activities

1. Collisions are normal on CSMA/CD LANs and not usually the result of errors. True or False

2. The majority of 10-Mbps Ethernet LANs use fiber optic technology. True or False

3. Briefly describe the CSMA/CD Ethernet access method.

   _____

   _____

4. If a network is currently wired with Category 5 UTP, it can upgrade to Gigabit Ethernet by replacing its hubs and NICs. True or False

5. Why does the Ethernet standard specify a minimum frame size?

   _____

   _____

6. What are IEEE 802.3u and 802.3z?

   _____

Extended Activities

1. How did Ethernet get its name? Visit Charles Spurgeon's Ethernet World Wide Web (Web) site to find out at **http://wwwhost.ots.utexas.edu/ethernet/**.

   _____

   _____

2. When was the original Ethernet design foreseen?

   _____

   _____

3. Does a desktop computer really need 1,000 Mbps? Explain.

   _____

   _____

Lesson 3—Token Ring and FDDI

In the last lesson, we saw that Ethernet's approach to medium access is similar to an informal conversation. Each node simply begins transmitting as soon as the bus is idle, then takes corrective steps in case of a collision. In contrast, a Token Ring network avoids collisions altogether. It does this by using a system similar to a formal meeting, in which a "speaking stick" is passed from one person to the next. A person may speak only when holding the stick. If a person is holding the stick but has nothing to say, she passes the stick on to someone else.

Objectives

At the end of this lesson you should be able to:

- Explain the basics of Token Ring medium access and operation

- Describe how Token Ring medium access differs from Ethernet

- Describe common Token Ring configurations

- Explain key differences between Token Ring and Fiber Distributed Data Interface (FDDI) (pronounced "fiddee") networks

 **Key Point**

A Token Ring node may transmit only when it has a free token.

Token Ring Medium Access Control

In our formal meeting scenario, a 3-byte "token" functions like a speaking stick in a Token Ring network. The token circulates continuously around the ring, and a node may not transmit a frame until it receives the token. Each node's NIC contains a repeater that receives bits from one of the two links and transmits them on the other. It receives frames simply by copying bits as they go by. Specifically, token passing works as follows:

- A 3-byte token circulates continuously around the ring, even when the network is idle. Only a single token can circulate on the ring at any given time, although multiple information frames can appear at various transmission points on the ring when using Early Token Release (ETR).

277

- A node may transmit a frame when it receives a free token. It inserts its data into the frame, sets a bit in the Access Control field to mark it as a data frame (it is no longer a token), then transmits the frame onto the ring. If a node has more data to send, it must stop transmitting after 10 milliseconds and wait for a token to come around again. If ETR is being used, the station will issue a new token immediately; otherwise, it will issue a new token when the data frame it sent is returned. Additionally, a token has priority and reservation (R) bits that are used for certain traffic requirements.

- When each node receives the data frame, the node repeats it to the next node on the ring.

- When a node receives a frame addressed to it, it copies the data frame. It then sets the "A" and "C" bits in the frame to indicate the address has been recognized and the frame has been copied. It then repeats the frame to the next node.

- When the frame returns to the node that originally transmitted it, the node reads the "A" and "C" bits to see that the frame was successfully received. The original sending node then strips the data frame from the ring. If it had previously released a new token because of ETR, the node's job is finished. If ETR was not enabled (as in the case of a 4-Mbps ring), it would then issue a new token.

Types of Token-Passing Networks

There are three main types of token-passing technologies:

- IBM Token Ring (IEEE 802.5) is a LAN protocol that delivers 4- or 16-Mbps throughput over UTP cabling.

- FDDI is a high-speed ring protocol based on fiber optic transmission. FDDI is often used for network backbones, because it provides throughput of up to 100 Mbps.

- Copper Distributed Data Interface (CDDI) implements the basic approach of FDDI, using copper wiring instead of optical fiber.

This lesson introduces the basic features of a Token Ring network, and briefly covers FDDI.

Advantages of Token Ring

There are several advantages of Token Ring:

- Built-in acknowledgement—When the node that sent the message gets the frame back, it knows the message has traversed the ring and should have been received by the addressee.

- Simple engineering—Ring networks use point-to-point digital transmission. Standard twisted pair cabling is cheap and easy to install, and it is easy to detect and correct cable failures.

- Deterministic response—The token circulates around the network at a steady, predictable rate. This consistent network speed makes Token Ring a good choice for real-time applications, such as computer-aided manufacturing.

- Prioritized traffic—The token contains three priority bits that indicate whether a busy token can be used by a node with higher priority data to transmit. If the priority of the token is higher than the frame to be transmitted, the token is passed on.

- No minimum frame size—Because ring networks prevent collisions, frames may be as small as necessary. This improves the efficiency of network transmission.

- Excellent performance under heavy load—On a heavily used network, nodes must usually wait longer to transmit. However, the lack of collisions means ring networks perform better than Ethernet in high-traffic conditions.

- Easily extended ring size—Small rings can be interconnected by their multistation access units (MAUs) into what is effectively one large ring.

Disadvantages of Token Ring

Token Ring also has several disadvantages:

- Necessary monitor function—Ring networks are susceptible to certain types of errors. For example, an entire network can be idled if a failed node leaves a frame endlessly circulating or fails to transmit a free token. Therefore, each Token Ring LAN must contain a node that, in addition to its normal functions, serves as a monitor. This node monitors traffic on the ring to detect failure modes and take corrective action, such as inserting a free token when necessary. Of course, this requires electing a new monitor when the monitor node fails.

- No improvement with light traffic—The deterministic nature of ring networks makes them perform well under heavy loads; unfortunately, it also means that they cannot run faster under light loads. If a network is idle except for two nodes, those nodes must still wait for the token to come around.

Token Ring Configurations

Two main types of Token Ring configurations are found in networks today. The Simple Token Ring Diagram illustrates how several ring segments are connected by means of MAUs. MAUs can be linked to form large rings, by connecting the ring-out (RO) port of one MAU to the ring-in (RI) port of the next.

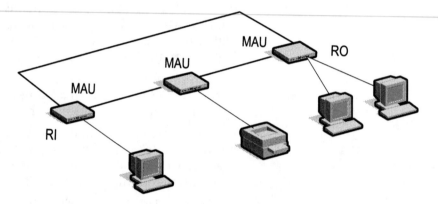

Simple Token Ring

The Token Ring and IBM Host Connectivity Diagram illustrates three traditional Token Ring configurations used to access an IBM host. Token Ring nodes can access host resources by means of front-end processors or cluster controllers, or through LAN gateway devices such as an IBM 3172.

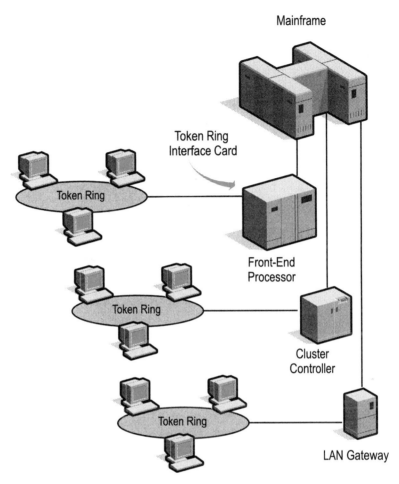

Mainframe

Token Ring
Interface Card

Token Ring

Front-End
Processor

Token Ring

Cluster
Controller

Token Ring

LAN Gateway

Token Ring and IBM Host Connectivity

FDDI

Because fiber optic cable supports both higher transmission speeds and greater distances than copper wire, it is easy to see how we can speed up a network by replacing twisted pair cable with optical fiber. FDDI does this; however, it uses more than just a faster medium to achieve high speed and throughput.

FDDI is a token-passing ring protocol based on the Token Ring standard. A FDDI ring can be combined with Token Rings or Ethernet buses to provide a high-throughput "backbone" for a network, as illustrated on the FDDI Diagram.

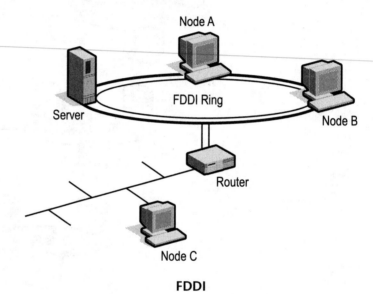

FDDI

Although FDDI is similar to Token Ring, three important differences make the technology and protocols of FDDI more complicated:

- Dual channels
- ETR and multiple messages
- Synchronous traffic

Dual Channels

The FDDI standard specifies dual channels running in opposite directions. (In contrast, a Token Ring can have only one physical link between adjacent nodes.) This double-ring design provides much greater reliability and recoverability, a highly desirable goal for a standard aimed at network backbones. The dual-channel architecture is implemented as follows:

- A node can communicate on one or two of the channels. (The standard does not require communication on both channels, thus lower cost, single-channel machines can be built.) The two types of FDDI stations are Dual Attachment Station (DAS) and Single Attachment Station (SAS).

- If the node communicates on both channels and one channel fails, the node will often still be able to communicate on the other channel.

- When a break occurs in both channels on the ring because of a node failure or damaged link, nodes on either side of the break connect the two channels, effectively turning them into one longer ring. This allows operation to continue until the problem is resolved.

- Each DAS on a double-ring network, whether it communicates on one or both channels, must still connect to both channels and provide shunt circuits to handle recovery.

ETR and Multiple Messages

It takes time for a token to make its way around a ring, because each node's repeater must copy each bit from its input to its output. In a Token Ring network, this time is wasted, because a single token serves the entire ring. The token must travel all the way around and be freed by the originating node before any other node can transmit.

However, a FDDI backbone ring may contain as many as 1,000 nodes and up to 200 kilometers of optical fiber. There can be a long delay from the time a node transmits the final bit of a message until it receives the first bit of the returning token. Therefore, the FDDI standard uses a Token Rotation Timer (TRT) to control token operations.

When a FDDI node has finished transmitting a message and is not receiving, it immediately transmits a free token. This creates a new token where there was none before. The token can then be used by the next node on the ring that needs to transmit, and the transmission will occur simultaneously with the transmission of other messages that may be making their way around the ring. In other words, both 16-Mbps Token Ring and FDDI use ETR.

Synchronous Traffic

A portion of a FDDI ring's data transmission capacity can be allocated to "synchronous" traffic, such as voice traffic. This essentially layers one or more high-speed communication channels onto the ring.

For example, imagine a FDDI ring that serves as the backbone for a large network. If network traffic is lower at night than during the day, a significant portion of the backbone capacity goes unused during those hours. Thus, the FDDI standard allows a portion of its 100-Mbps bandwidth to be dedicated to other types of traffic, such as telephone calls or multimedia applications.

Activities

1. When a station on a Token Ring network is in possession of the token, it means the station can transmit data.
    True or False

2. When a Token Ring network is "idle," it means there is no token circulating on the ring. True or False

3. CDDI is essentially the same as FDDI; however, it uses copper wiring. True or False

4. Token Ring operation is called "deterministic" because a station is guaranteed it can transmit equitably, because of the token-passing algorithm. Briefly describe how Token Ring works.

    _____

    _____

    _____

    _____

5. Ethernet operation is described as "nondeterministic," because there is no guarantee it will be able to send its data. Briefly contrast Ethernet and Token Ring operations.

    _____

    _____

    _____

    _____

6. List one advantage and one disadvantage of Token Ring.

    _____

    _____

7. What is the length (in bytes) of a token?

    _____

8. Draw a simple Token Ring network using four MAUs connected to form a larger ring.

9. List at least one significant difference between FDDI and Token Ring.

   _____

   _____

10. What is the difference between a DAS and SAS?

    _____

    _____

Extended Activities

1. Using the Web as a research tool, find information on at least two vendors that sell FDDI products. List some of the technical specifications you encountered.

   _____

   _____

   _____

   _____

   _____

   _____

2. Using your favorite Web search engine, try to find information relating to how Gigabit Ethernet might be displacing FDDI in certain backbone configurations. What are the trends?

_____

_____

_____

_____

Lesson 4—Wireless LANs

Over the past few years a new trend in local area networking has developed. This new technology is typically called "wireless local area networks (WLANs)," but some people use the term "local area wireless networks (LAWNs)." WLANs use radio signals to carry signals instead of wires. As more and more people accept the convenience of cell phones, it is likely that people will also see the benefit of linking portable computers through wireless networks.

Objectives

At the end of this lesson you should be able to:

- Explain the difference between CSMA/CD and CSMA/CA

- Describe the "hidden node" problem, and show how CSMA/CA solves it

- Explain the difference between wireless LANs based on the 802.11a and 802.11b standards

 **Key Point**

All wireless networks share a few narrow slices of the radio frequency spectrum.

Wireless Protocols

Wireless LANs interface with the rest of a LAN system in one of two ways:

- At the Physical Layer using existing Data Link Layer protocols

- At the Data Link Layer using proprietary protocols

Wireless at the Physical Layer

Wireless technologies that simply provide a new Physical Layer channel can be implemented in relatively simple devices that use standard Data Link Layer protocols such as Ethernet. This approach has the following benefits:

- High interoperability with existing LAN equipment, because all devices use the same MAC sublayer protocol

- Higher speed

- Lower cost

- Lower power requirements
- Smaller device size

Wireless at the Data Link Layer

The Data Link Layer wireless technique requires proprietary protocols and hardware for both the Data Link and Physical Layers. This technique produces more sophisticated (and costly) devices than implementing wireless technology as a purely Physical Layer technique.

CSMA/CA

A radio channel, like a network bus, is a shared transmission medium on which only one node may transmit at any time. Therefore, wireless networks need some form of medium access control, just as wired networks do.

On a hard-wired Ethernet network, nodes detect collisions by simultaneously transmitting data and monitoring the shared medium. However, in a radio network, nodes cannot speak and listen at the same time. Therefore, 802.11-based wireless LANs use a MAC method called "CSMA/CA."

CSMA/CA is very similar to the CSMA/CD approach used by Ethernet, with a few key differences. A typical CSMA/CA sequence follows:

1. When a station is ready to transmit, it first senses the channel.

2. If the channel is busy, the station waits a random time, then senses the channel again.

3. If the channel is idle, the station transmits a Ready to Send message that contains the destination address and length of the coming transmission. The length information tells other stations how long they must wait before they will be allowed to transmit.

4. If the destination station also senses that the channel is idle, it responds with a Clear to Send message.

5. When the sending station receives the Clear to Send message, it begins transmitting its data.

6. When the destination station receives the transmission, it transmits an acknowledgement (ACK) frame to the sender (after following the above steps).

7. If the sending station does not receive the ACK frame, it assumes a collision has occurred, and repeats the sending sequence to retransmit the frame.

On hard-wired networks, the process of requesting a channel and acknowledging a transmission is usually handled by upper layer protocols, such as the Transmission Control Protocol (TCP). Performing this job at the Physical Layer adds additional overhead that reduces the efficiency of wireless LANs. However, it allows them to correct radio-specific problems, such as the one illustrated on the Hidden Node Problem Diagram.

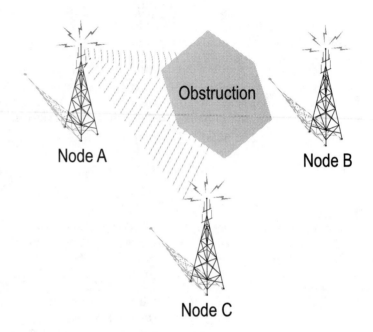

Hidden Node Problem

On the diagram, Nodes A and C can communicate, as can Nodes B and C. However, Nodes A and B are separated by an obstacle, such as a hill, that blocks their signals to each other. Therefore, if Node A is trying to transmit to Node C, Node B is unable to detect that the channel is busy, and may attempt to transmit to Node C at the same time. Thus, by explicitly requesting permission to transmit, and acknowledging each received message, wireless nodes can minimize collisions even when many nodes are "invisible" to each other.

802.11 Wireless Standards

The IEEE Project 802.11 committee drafted a standard for LAN interoperability based on a minimum bandwidth of 1 Mbps. This consists of a new wireless MAC sublayer protocol that can interface with a variety of Physical Layer protocols corresponding to vendor approaches to the technology.

In Europe, the European Telecommunications Standards Institute (ETSI) and the Conference European des Postes et des Telecommunications (CEPT) are responsible for broad-scale standardization. The European version of the IEEE 802.11 standard is ETSI Res 9.

Spread spectrum systems that comply with 802.11 can operate in three nonlicensed frequency bands, commonly called the Industrial, Scientific, and Medical (ISM) bands:

- 902 to 928 megahertz (MHz)
- 2.4 to 2.483 gigahertz (GHz)
- 5.725 to 5.875 GHz

High-frequency carrier signals can carry data faster than low-frequency signals, because each cycle of a radio wave can be modulated in various ways to represent one or more digital bits. In other words, the more cycles per second a signal provides, the more data it can carry. Therefore, of the three ISM bands, most new wireless LAN development is occurring in the 2.4- and 5.7-GHz ranges.

The IEEE 802.11 standard defines the basic technology of wireless networking. However, that approach could only deliver 1- to 2-Mbps throughput. Thus, the IEEE 802.11 committee and other working groups have continued working to develop better standards and protocols that will enhance the growth and development of this new technology. These new 802 wireless standards include:

- 802.11b—This direct sequence spread spectrum system can deliver a maximum raw throughput of 11 Mbps. This technology, currently used in most wireless office LANs, operates within the 2.4-GHz range.

- 802.11a—This approach uses frequency hopping spread spectrum radio, and multiple parallel channels, to deliver a raw data rate up to 54 Mbps. In the United States, this new technology operates in several portions of the 5.7-GHz range. (Channel hopping occurs within the assigned band of frequencies.) However, there is more competition for this part of the spectrum in Europe and Asia, thus fewer channels will be available for 802.11a there.

Because both of these standards operate at the Physical Layer, they can support existing Data Link Layer protocols such as Ethernet and Token Ring. However, because 802.11a and 802.11b each use a different part of the spectrum and different method of spread spectrum transmission, they are incompatible with each other.

Wireless LAN Configurations

Wireless LANs can be configured in many different ways; we will discuss three of the most common approaches.

All Wireless LAN

The first configuration, shown on the All Wireless LAN Diagram, shows a typical LAN configuration, only in this configuration there are no wires. The physical medium, such as Ethernet cabling, is replaced with wireless antennas.

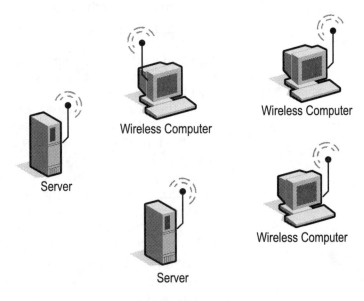

All Wireless LAN

**Wireless Links
Between LANs**

The LAN-to-LAN Wireless Links Diagram shows another wireless LAN configuration. In this diagram, two hard-wired Ethernet LANs are interconnected by a wireless link. The distance between the two wireless antennas in this configuration varies depending on the wireless technology used.

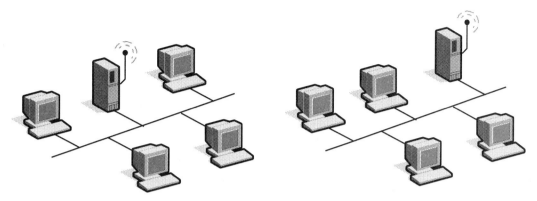

LAN-to-LAN Wireless Links

Mobile Nodes   The third configuration, shown on the Mobile Nodes Diagram, links a few mobile nodes to a hard-wired LAN. This configuration provides quick network access to laptop computers equipped with wireless NICs, and is especially popular with workers who use laptops in meetings. The wireless laptop computers can communicate with each other directly, and all mobile devices can access hard-wired LAN services such as printers and electronic mail (e-mail).

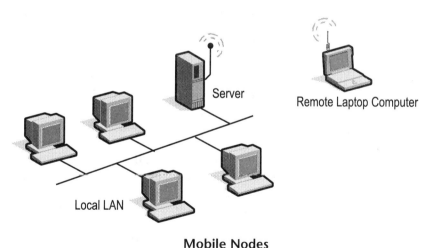

Mobile Nodes

WPANs and Bluetooth

As smart handheld devices become more common, a process is underway to develop a standard that can link them into short-distance wireless personal area networks (WPANs). In March 1999, the WPAN Study Group became IEEE 802.15, the WPAN Working Group, with the goal of creating a wireless communication standard for personal area networks (PANs). In July 1999, the Bluetooth Special Interest Group, part of the WPAN Working Group, released the Bluetooth 1.0 specification for a small, low-cost, low-power WPAN.

The Bluetooth specification (802.15.1) essentially promises to remove the wires that currently connect devices such as headphones, computer mice, and keyboards. Furthermore, the technology has the potential to provide seamless connectivity between devices that are near each other, even temporarily. For example, a traveler might check e-mail by simply moving a Personal Digital Assistant (PDA) near an airport kiosk that provides Internet access.

Bluetooth defines a low power level that covers a short distance, such as a single room, and a higher power level that can cover a medium range, such as a home or office. A Bluetooth PAN or "piconet" includes one master device, which controls the frequency hopping pattern for its small area. The master can link to up to seven slave devices at one time. However, each device may be a member of multiple piconets, moving from one to another as a user changes position.

Bluetooth uses frequency hopping spread spectrum radio in the 2.4-GHz range. Because 802.11b wireless LANs use the same frequency band, some interference between the technologies is likely, because a Bluetooth PAN will occasionally hop to one of the frequencies being used by the 802.11b LAN. The effect of this interference becomes stronger the closer two interfering devices are to each other. A device that contains both an 802.11b NIC and Bluetooth transceiver could notice poor performance on both systems if they are being used at the same time. For example, if a user listens to a Moving Pictures Experts Group, Layer-3 (MP3) file on Bluetooth headphones, while using the same computer to transfer a file over the wireless LAN, then both operations will suffer. To correct this problem, other IEEE working groups are currently developing techniques to reduce interference between Bluetooth devices and wireless LANs.

Activities

1. What is the main difference between CSMA/CD and CSMA/CA?

   _____

   _____

   _____

   _____

2. How does CSMA/CA solve the hidden node problem?

   _____

   _____

   _____

   _____

3. Why is more development necessary before Bluetooth devices can be used within an 802.11b wireless LAN?

   _____

   _____

4. What is the difference between the 802.11a and 802.11b wireless LAN standards?

   _____

   _____

Extended Activity

Visit the Bluetooth Web site at **http://www.bluetooth.com**. What sort of user services might this technology make possible?

_____

_____

_____

_____

Lesson 5—LAN Software Architectures

In the first part of this unit, we discussed how networks differ at the Physical and Data Link Layers, through approaches such as Ethernet, Token Ring, and wireless LANs. In this lesson, we will examine the various software technologies that operate at Layer 3 and above. We will introduce the key elements and protocols of the most important network operating systems (NOSs), and compare the layered protocols of each NOS to the OSI model. In general, you will find that each PC LAN architecture maps fairly closely to the OSI model as shown here. However, you will also discover some notable departures from this system.

Objectives

At the end of this lesson you should be able to:

- Explain the role of Network Basic Input/Output System (NetBIOS) and NetBIOS Extended User Interface (NetBEUI) (pronounced "net-Boo-ee")

- Describe the difference between the medium access control methods of Ethernet and AppleTalk

- Compare the TCP/Internet Protocol (IP) protocol stack to the OSI model

Key Point

Most LAN architectures conform largely to the OSI reference model. All major LAN architectures support TCP/IP.

NOSs and LAN Architectures

As we learned in an earlier unit, a NOS manages the interface between a network's underlying transport capabilities and the applications resident on a server. On the PC LANs and OSI Model Diagram, the NOS itself operates at a high level in the OSI model. However, each major NOS also includes protocols that operate between the Session Layer and Data Link Layer. We call this combined suite of NOS and underlying protocols a "LAN architecture."

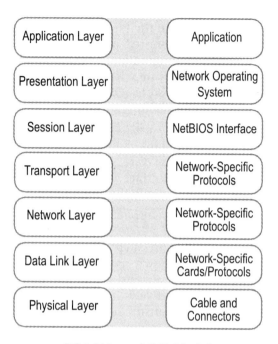

Application Layer	Application
Presentation Layer	Network Operating System
Session Layer	NetBIOS Interface
Transport Layer	Network-Specific Protocols
Network Layer	Network-Specific Protocols
Data Link Layer	Network-Specific Cards/Protocols
Physical Layer	Cable and Connectors

PC LANs and OSI Model

These suites of software are sometimes referred to as "internet-working protocols," because the upper layers of the OSI model provide communication between separate LANs. For example, Layer 3 protocols are responsible for routing data from one network to another. Communication between different LAN architectures is provided by higher layers. One of the most common examples of this practice is the use of the worldwide Internet as a common ground to link separate LANs.

We will discuss the Internet later in this course, but in this lesson you will see that most of the major LAN software architectures support common protocols, such as TCP/IP. Those protocols can be used to establish communication between networks that operate in very different ways.

NetBIOS and NetBEUI

On the PC LANs and OSI Model Diagram, the Session Layer is represented by a protocol we have not discussed yet. NetBIOS was originally developed by Sytek and IBM to allow a NOS to communicate with computer hardware. Thus, just as a desktop operating system (OS) calls its local computer's Basic Input/Output System (BIOS) for services such as reading a file, a NOS can call NetBIOS for network services such as transmitting a file to a remote node.

NetBIOS has been adopted by Microsoft Windows NT and Novell NetWare, and has become the de facto standard for application interface to all types of LANs. Thus, many LANs are described as "NetBIOS compatible."

An application makes its request for network services in the form of a Network Control Block (NCB). Each NCB includes information such as the destination node. Although NetBIOS is often shown as operating at the Session Layer, it also provides some Transport Layer services. Thus, it can control continuous sessions between two computers, as well as provide connectionless packet transmission. However, it does not support routing of data to destinations in another network, and must use the services of TCP to do that job. NetBIOS also does not specify its own standard format for the data it transmits.

IBM later developed NetBEUI, which functions at the OSI Network and Transport Layers. NetBEUI defines a standard format for data frames to be passed down to the Data Link Layer. It also does not route messages to other networks. However, for data transmitted within the same network, NetBEUI can increase network efficiency. Because it does the job of both the Transport and Network Layers, it reduces the amount of network overhead.

Novell NetWare

Novell, incorporated in 1983, has experienced phenomenal success. Originally developed as a file server OS, NetWare has gone through several revisions, each one strengthening and broadening the product. The current version, NetWare 5.1, has become a top choice for Internet-enabled businesses.

Today, NetWare provides a full suite of networking functions and services, including communications, database, Internet services, and message store-and-forward. With NetWare, customers can start small and build to massive networks, based on their networking requirements. Novell's distributed, multitasking NOS is designed to provide and coordinate all network services, including file directory services, print services, software protection services, network security, and messaging.

NetWare Protocol Layers

NetWare's architecture readily maps to the OSI model, as shown on the OSI Model and NetWare Diagram. At the Physical and Data Link Layers, NetWare supports the 802.2 Logical Link Layer, Ethernet, and Token Ring, as well as a number of other network architectures.

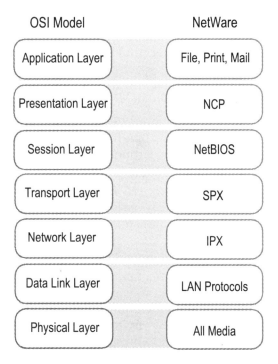

OSI Model and NetWare

The Network and Transport Layer functions are handled by Novell's Network and Transport Layer protocols, Internetwork Packet Exchange (IPX) and Sequenced Packet Exchange (SPX), respectively.

At the Session Layer, NetWare supports the NetBIOS interface. The Presentation and Application Layers provide NetWare value-added services, various user applications, and NetWare Core Protocol (NCP) services. PCs and workstations use NCP to communicate with the OS to obtain network services for their local applications.

AppleTalk

AppleTalk is Apple Computer's proprietary LAN software for Macintosh computers. Consistent with the simple Macintosh interface, an AppleTalk network was designed to be very easy to set up.

Originally, an AppleTalk network used a proprietary Physical Layer technology called "LocalTalk." Users plugged a low-price LocalTalk connection box into the Macintosh printer port, then attached a 2-m cable to the connection box on the next Macintosh or peripheral device in the network. Each Macintosh was shipped with the hardware and software required to participate in the network.

Shift to Open Standards

However easy an AppleTalk network was to build, users argued that it had major flaws. Its data transfer rate was only 230.4-kilobits per second (Kbps), and the network could only support 32 Macintoshes. Customers were also required to use shielded twisted pair (STP) wiring in a daisy-chain topology.

In June 1989, Apple's determination to be taken seriously resulted in AppleTalk Phase II. AppleTalk Phase II represented a complete turnaround from Apple's usual proprietary stance.

The LocalTalk Physical Layer offered alternatives, such as the PhoneNET system, which used unused telephone wires as cabling. Fiber optic connections were also developed, and wiring concentrators for both types of cable made star topologies possible.

In addition to the improved LocalTalk, AppleTalk Phase II also operated over Ethernet and Token Ring networks (by means of EtherTalk and TokenTalk software, respectively), supported coaxial cable as well as STP, and supported products that facilitate the integration of Macintoshes into digital, IBM, TCP/IP, UNIX, and OSI environments. The OSI Model and AppleTalk Phase II Diagram illustrates how this software maps to the reference model.

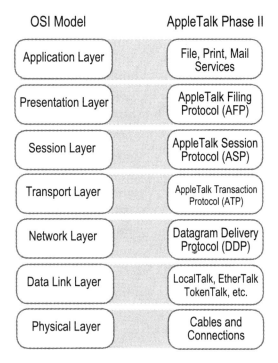

OSI Model and AppleTalk Phase II

AppleTalk Phase II Protocol Layers

At the Data Link Layer, AppleTalk uses the AppleTalk Link Access Protocol (ALAP). Media access control is CSMA/CA. Unlike CSMA/CA used in wireless networks, ALAP does not specifically request permission to transmit. Instead, a node that is ready to transmit waits until the medium has been silent for a minimum time, plus an additional random time. If a collision occurs, all nodes stop, then back off for a random time, as in Ethernet.

One of the major benefits of AppleTalk networks is dynamic node addressing, which continues to be supported in AppleTalk Phase II. This feature assigns node addresses dynamically when a machine is powered on. Unlike Ethernet, which uses hard-coded NIC addresses as frame addresses, ALAP assigns a station a random node number when it is booted up.

At the Network Layer, the Datagram Delivery Protocol (DDP) supports communication between two sockets (software ports), which are the addressable entities within a node. DDP also handles routing of data between two or more interconnected AppleTalk networks. Conversion of socket addresses to node addresses is the responsibility of the AppleTalk Address Resolution Protocol (AARP).

At the Transport Layer, AppleTalk supports four different protocols. The Routing Table Maintenance Protocol (RTMP) maintains information about the current configuration of the network. The AppleTalk Echo Protocol (AEP) is used for maintenance. The Name Binding Protocol (NBP) provides translations between character-oriented names and network addresses. Reliable application-to-application transmissions are the responsibility of the AppleTalk Transaction Protocol (ATP).

Four protocols are also supported at the Session Layer. The AppleTalk Session Protocol (ASP) opens, maintains, and closes sessions between sockets. The AppleTalk Data Stream Protocol (ADSP) ensures reliable service between sockets. The Zone Information Protocol (ZIP) maintains a "map" of the zones within the network. The Printer Access Protocol (PAP) handles requests for access to Apple LaserWriter printers.

At the Presentation and Application Layers, the AppleTalk Filing Protocol (AFP) provides access to remote files, and the PostScript protocol supports desktop publishing.

Cross-Platform Communication

Software is available to let a Macintosh emulate an IBM 327x terminal to access data on an IBM mainframe. The MacAPPC application also lets Macintosh computers exchange information with systems that support IBM's Advanced Program-to-Program Communications (APPC) on a peer-to-peer basis.

The AppleTalk Internet Router lets Macintoshes communicate with systems on the Internet, and MacX25 is available for communications over an X.25 packet-switched network. Apple also provides programs that developers can use to create Macintosh applications for communication with DEC systems and TCP/IP environments.

Microsoft Windows NT

Microsoft's Windows NT is a 32-bit OS that was designed to support client applications easily and transparently in a distributed network environment. Networking is built into Windows NT, including both client and server capabilities. This allows any Windows NT computer to participate in a network in either capacity.

Windows NT supports a variety of network protocols, including TCP/IP, NetBIOS/NetBEUI, NWLink (for IPX/SPX compatibility), AppleTalk, Point-to-Point Tunneling Protocol (PPTP), and Data Link Control (DLC) (for mainframe connectivity). Thus, with no additional software required, Windows NT can interoperate with the following networks:

- Microsoft networks
- Novell NetWare
- TCP/IP, including UNIX hosts
- AppleTalk (Windows NT Server only)
- Remote access clients

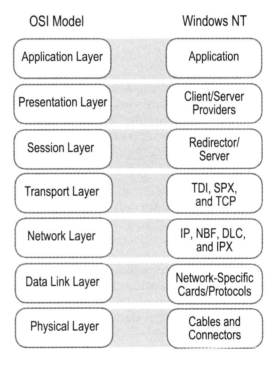

OSI Model and Windows NT

At this writing, Microsoft has announced plans to release two new desktop OSs at the end of 2001. The Windows XP OS will be the first one that offers one version for business applications as well as one version specifically designed for home users. Most programs that work on Windows 95/98/Me and NT will work on upcoming versions of Windows XP.

The OSI Model and Windows NT Diagram shows how Windows NT relates to the OSI reference model. At the Physical and Data Link levels, Windows NT supports various NICs and protocols, such as Ethernet and Token Ring. The low-level device drivers that run on the NICs interface with the Network Layer protocols through the Network Driver Interface Specification (NDIS). NDIS provides linkage between the Physical Layer protocols and several Network Layer protocols including:

- NetBEUI Format (NBF)
- DLC
- IPX
- IP

At the Transport Layer, Windows NT supports TCP and SPX. The Transport Device Interfaces (TDI) layer provides an interface between multiple transport protocols, such as TCP, and multiple networking environments.

At the Session Layer, client redirectors for Windows NT and NetWare can be loaded on the same workstation. The client/server provider, at the Presentation Layer, allows multiple applications to access the underlying protocol stack.

Windows NT provides support for both client/server applications and peer-to-peer processing through preemptive multitasking, and shared and protected memory support. This allows Windows NT to be used in small businesses that do not require large LAN services.

UNIX and TCP/IP

Networking in UNIX is accomplished using interprocess communication (IPC) between applications and the networking protocol stacks. The UNIX Networking Diagram shows a typical UNIX protocol stack.

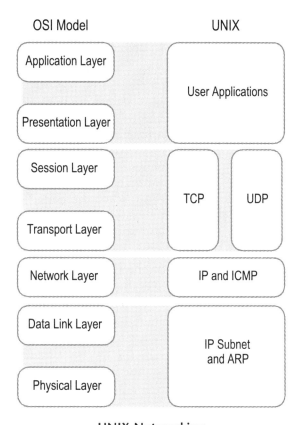

UNIX Networking

As we can see on the diagram, the UNIX protocol stack essentially compresses the OSI model. UNIX uses one process to perform some tasks that the OSI model splits into two layers. The reason for this is simple: UNIX was developed before the OSI model. Most UNIX systems provide multiple protocol suites, including TCP/IP, SNA, Xerox Network System (XNS), and NetBIOS. However, the "standard" protocol layers shown above include:

- IP Subnet and Address Resolution Protocol (ARP)—The IP subnet functions of IP, also called the "network interface," use the services of a variety of lower level protocols, such as the IEEE 802.2 LLC. ARP is used to convert an IP network address to a Data Link hardware address (NIC address).

- IP and Internet Control Message Protocol (ICMP)—IP is responsible for connectionless, unreliable, best effort packet delivery service to the upper layers. ICMP, an integral part of IP, delivers messages used by IP to control the network.

  When we say IP is "unreliable," that means it makes no attempt at error correction or recovery. No checks for correctness of data are performed at this level. If a message is garbled due to a transmission error, IP will simply pass the garbled information up to the next layer. If it encounters an error condition that it can detect, but from which it cannot recover, IP will simply throw the datagram away. However, IP will not throw data away capriciously. If it encounters an error, it will not discard the packet until it has made a thorough attempt to recover by retrying the transmission. Because of this, we also say IP is a "best effort" service.

- TCP—The TCP layer is responsible for providing connection-oriented, end-to-end, error-free message delivery. Because it uses the IP layer's unreliable delivery service, its major responsibilities are error correction and connection management.

- User Datagram Protocol (UDP) — An alternative to TCP, UDP provides a less reliable, connectionless, datagram delivery service for certain specialized application services that do not require the full services of TCP.

- Typical user applications and application services include the following:

  - rlogin allows remote login from one TCP/IP system to another.

  - Simple Mail Transfer Protocol (SMTP) provides electronic messaging for the mail service and Network News.

  - Telnet is the TCP/IP standard protocol for connection of remote terminals.

  - File Transfer Protocol (FTP) provides for the transfer of files between systems. FTP uses Telnet to establish a control connection.

  - Domain Name System (DNS) converts a hierarchical Internet domain name, such as Sales.mycompany.com, to an IP address, such as 144.49.4.70.

  - Network File System (NFS) is the de facto standard for file sharing.

Common Ground: TCP/IP

The acronym TCP/IP represents the common working combination of the Transmission Control Protocol and Internet Protocol. However, the term is often used to denote much more than just the protocols themselves. The TCP/IP "world" can be considered to include other components, such as the entire suite of protocols, software, and applications that are standard parts of most UNIX-based and PC-based OSs.

TCP/IP is normally used as the protocol stack in UNIX networking implementations. As we have just seen however, those protocols are also supported by all major NOSs. Now that the Internet has become an essential business tool, many corporate networks find it convenient to use TCP/IP as their Transport and Network Layer protocols. Thus, while various networks may use NetWare, Windows NT, or AppleTalk, it is likely each of those OSs is also configured to use TCP and IP.

Activities

1. For each protocol below, name the original LAN architecture or NOS.

   a. IPX

   b. TCP

   c. DDP

   d. NDIS

   e. IP

   f. SPX

   g. ALAP

2. AppleTalk and Ethernet use similar, but different, methods of medium access control. Name the MAC method used by each and describe how they differ.

   _____

   _____

   _____

   _____

3. All of the LAN architectures discussed in this lesson, except one, run over any Physical Layer technology. What LAN architecture originally specified its Physical Layer, and what type of hardware did it require?

   _____

   _____

Extended Activities

Using a Web search engine resource, try to find out what the installed customer base is for Windows NT and NetWare.

_____

_____

_____

_____

Lesson 6—Information Flow Between Client and Server

In this unit, we have discussed some of the many hardware and software elements that make up a LAN. This lesson shows how those devices and protocols work together to perform a common task, such as allowing a client to read a file stored on a server attached to the same physical network.

Objectives

At the end of this lesson you should be able to:

- Describe how the format of information changes as it flows between client and server

- Explain the purpose of the Server Message Block (SMB) protocol

 **Key Point**

The SMB protocol uses Request/Reply pairs to communicate between clients and servers.

Protocols and Layers

This example assumes a Windows 98 client is communicating with a server running Windows NT version 4, using the following protocols commonly found in Windows-based networks:

- SMB
- NetBIOS
- TCP
- IP
- Ethernet

SMB

SMB is an Application/Presentation Layer protocol used between clients and servers on a LAN. Functions requiring LAN support, such as retrieving files from a file server, are translated into SMB commands before they are sent to the remote device. Applications use SMB "calls" to perform file operations across a network. All Windows OSs can run SMB as a client, server, or both.

As we can see on the SMB Diagram, SMB can use either NetBIOS or NetBEUI to communicate across a LAN. NetBIOS uses underlying protocols, such as TCP/IP or SPX/IPX, to deliver SMB messages, while NetBEUI uses its own frame format to deliver messages directly.

OSI Model

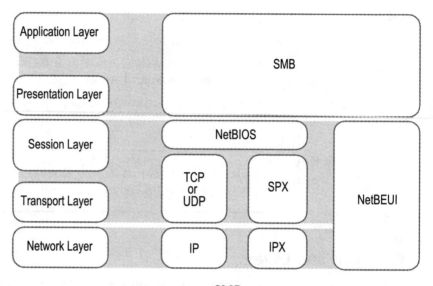

SMB

Information Flow and Format

In this example, the client reads a file that is stored on the server. To do this on a Windows NT network, six messages must be exchanged:

1. Client asks server to open the file.

2. Server informs client that the file is open.

3. Client asks server to read the file.

4. Server reads the file and transmits the contents to the client.

5. Client asks server to close the file.

6. Server informs client that the file is closed.

Client Asks Server to Open the File

The File Open Request from Client Diagram illustrates the SMB/NetBIOS/TCP/IP/Ethernet protocol stack located inside the client and server computers. The application program interfaces to the network through a series of processes, beginning with a call to SMB. SMB on the client side initiates a request to the server SMB process for file operations. When that request reaches the server side, the server's SMB process will be responsible for opening, reading, and closing a file.

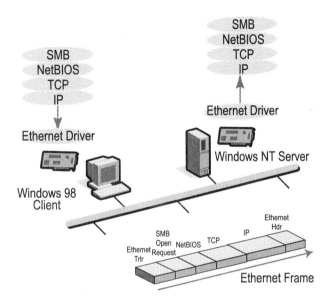

File Open Request From Client

The protocols "underneath" the SMB protocol are used for transmitting the SMB requests and responses back and forth across the network. For example, as the Network Layer protocol, IP is responsible for transmitting the request across the network. In this example, the packet does not need to go through any intermediate nodes. However, IP is still required to direct the packet to the network address of the server. The Ethernet header is responsible for transmitting the frame and frame contents to the correct NIC, which is located inside the server.

Notice the correlation between the processes in the client and server, and the frame, packet, and message and application headers. These headers are built on the sending computer station and "decapsulated" by the corresponding process on the receiving station. By the time the SMB request gets processed by the SMB software on the server, the other headers have been stripped off by the appropriate processes on the receiving node.

Server Informs Client That the File is Open

The Open Reply from Server Diagram illustrates the response from the Windows NT file server. The reply confirms that the file is on the server and has been opened by the server application.

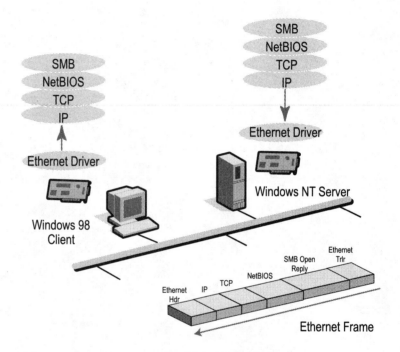

Open Reply From Server

Notice that the frame is essentially the same as in the previous diagram. The difference is that the frame is carrying the SMB response from the server. There will also be a difference in the destination addresses of the frame, packet, and message. The destination addresses will now indicate the NIC, IP process, and TCP process on the client because the response is going back to the client.

This diagram shows an Ethernet bus topology. However, remember that network professionals use a bus diagram to represent any shared-medium broadcast network. Thus, when you see a bus drawing, remember that the network probably uses a hub-centered star topology. In either case, a real broadcast network would contain many nodes, not just the two nodes shown on the diagram.

When several nodes share the same transmission medium (hub, bus, or radio channel), each node will receive the frame transmitted between client and server, and vice versa. However, only the node with a NIC address that matches the address in the Ethernet frame header will process the information inside the frame.

Thus, to return to the Open Reply from Server Diagram, the Windows 98 client will receive the frame at its Ethernet NIC. The NIC address will match the destination address located inside the Ethernet header. The client's NIC will then remove the packet from inside the frame and pass the packet to the IP process running in the client's central processing unit (CPU).

The client's IP process will process the IP packet, first checking to make sure the destination address of the packet matches the machine's IP address. If there is a match, the IP process will pass the contents of the packet (message) to the TCP process. Information will continue to move up the protocol stack, losing protocol headers, until it arrives at the SMB process. The reply destination is SMB, which generated the initial file open request.

Client Asks Server to Read the File

Now that the file is open, the client makes a separate request to the server, asking it to read from the open file and return that information to the client. This request is shown on the Client Read Request Diagram.

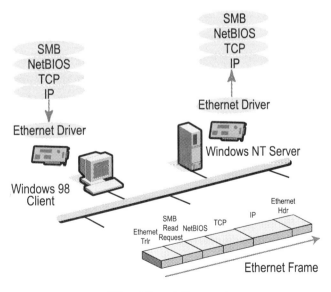

Client Read Request

The same processes generate protocol headers for the read request. Each header is added as the request is moved down the protocol stack until the frame exits the Windows 98 client by means of the NIC. When the request reaches the server, it is decapsulated and processed just as the open request was.

Server Reads the File and Transmits the Contents to the Client

The Server Read Reply Diagram illustrates the response from the server after it reads the file. If the file is small, only one packet may be needed to transfer the data from the server to the client. In this example, a small file is sent from the server to the client, carried within a single packet.

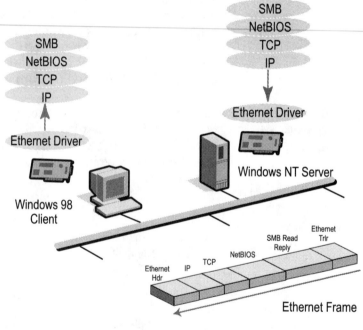

Server Read Reply

A large file would require a series of packets, each one identified with sequencing information. The packets would have to be reassembled on the client by the Transport Layer, before the file is passed up to the SMB process.

For example, assume the file is 3 kilobytes (KB) in size and the default packet size is 1 KB. It would take three packets to transmit the file across the network. Each packet is encapsulated within a separate frame, thus it would also take three frames to move the file across the network. At the receiving node, the client's Ethernet NIC would receive and decapsulate each frame, then pass the three packets up to the IP process. The IP process would pass each message segment to the TCP process, which would reassemble the segments into the original message. TCP would then pass the message (file) up to SMB, which would process the file.

Client Asks Server to Close the File

When the client first asked the server to open the file, the server probably locked the file to prevent other users from changing it. Thus, after the client has received the data it needs, the file must be closed so that other users can have access to the file. This close request, sent from the client to the server, is shown on the Client Close Request Diagram.

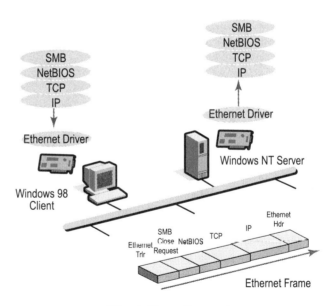

Client Close Request

Server Informs Client That the File is Closed

The final frame, from the server back to the client, is illustrated on the Server Close Reply Diagram. The message confirms that the file is closed and the transaction is complete.

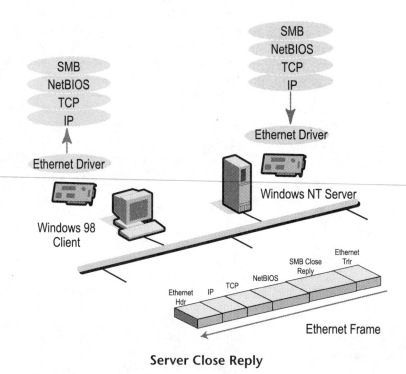

Server Close Reply

This completes one transaction between client and server. During this same period, the server could have been processing requests from many other clients as well. In an environment in which many clients share a server, the server is responsible for tracking each client's progress and making sure each client task is processed in order of priority.

Activities

Consider the following network:

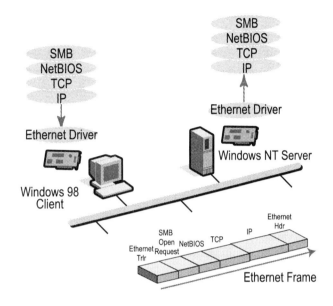

1. Briefly describe the services shown in the above protocol stack.

    _____

    _____

    _____

    _____

    _____

    _____

2. Using short lines with directional arrows, describe the information flow between the client and server for a complete file read operation (including open and close). The sequence is started for you.

    ClientServer

    Client needs to read a file

    SMB open file request from client —>

    <—Open file reply

Extended Activities

Break into six focus groups, one for each of the client/server file operation diagrams presented in this lesson. (Adjust focus groups according to class size.)

1. Each group will discuss among themselves the functions the various layers are performing on the client side and server side.

2. If the client and server are located on the same physical network, is IP required? Explain.

_____

_____

_____

_____

3. If the network in this example used NetBEUI instead of Net-BIOS, how would the encapsulation process be changed?

_____

_____

_____

_____

Summary

Unit 5 covered the technologies that define the main types of LANs. These basic protocols fall into two categories: Data Link protocols, and LAN software architectures from Layer 3 and up.

Data Link protocols determine how signals and data flow between nodes on the same physical network. One of the most important aspects of any Data Link technology is its method of medium access control. In this unit, we saw that Ethernet's MAC technique allows nodes to compete for access to the shared medium. Token-passing networks, such as Token Ring and FDDI, give each node a periodic opportunity to transmit.

Ethernet, the dominant Data Link protocol, comes in several versions and speeds. Basic Ethernet, the most common version, provides 10-Mbps throughput over UTP. Fast Ethernet delivers 100 Mbps over UTP, and Gigabit Ethernet offers 1,000 Mbps (1 Gbps) over STP or optical fiber. Ethernet networks are most commonly configured in a star network topology.

LAN software architectures are entire suites of layered protocols from major vendors such as Microsoft, Novell, and Apple. Each of these suites defines and uses its own proprietary protocols. However, each one typically supports some of the protocols of the others, and all support de facto standards, such as TCP/IP and NetBIOS. These shared protocols can be used to provide communication between networks based on different LAN architectures.

We also looked at two ways communication flows throughout a LAN: peer-to-peer and client/server. Peer-to-peer communication is when the nodes attached to the network are basically equal, and any node can initiate communication with any other node on the network. With client/server networking, a server is present in the network for processing client requests. Information is typically generated by the client in the form of a request to the server. The server responds with a reply to each specific request of the client.

To see how all of these layers and protocols work together, we looked at a brief example of information flow between a client and server. We reviewed how protocol headers are generated by a client computer as information is moved from an application, through communication processes, and down to the NIC. The NIC generates a frame that encapsulates the packet, message, and request. The frame is then transmitted across the communication channel. At the receiving end, information in each protocol header is used to send the request up through the protocol layers to the receiving application. Each protocol header is processed and removed (decapsulated) by the client's peer process on the receiving side.

Unit 5 Quiz

1. Which of the following is not a LAN communication process?

   a. Peer-to-peer

   b. Client-to-server

   c. Client-to-peer

   d. Server-to-client

2. Ethernet operates at all speeds except which of the following?

   a. 16 Kbps

   b. 10 Mbps

   c. 1 Gbps

   d. 100 Mbps

3. Which of the following is the most popular LAN Data Link Layer technology?

   a. Token Ring

   b. FDDI

   c. SNA

   d. Ethernet

4. An Ethernet LAN that uses coaxial cabling as the physical medium is called which of the following?

   a. Star

   b. Star/ring

   c. Bus

   d. Ring

5. An Ethernet LAN that uses UTP cabling and a hub as the physical medium is referred to as which of the following?

   a. Star

   b. Star/ring

   c. Bus

   d. Ring

6. The CD in CSMA/CD refers to the ability of an Ethernet node to do which of the following?

    a. Access the physical medium

    b. Detect frame collisions

    c. Detect node failures

    d. Sense an electrical signal

7. The CS in CSMA/CD refers to the ability of an Ethernet node to do which of the following?

    a. Access the physical medium

    b. Detect frame collisions

    c. Detect node failures

    d. Sense an electrical signal

8. Which of the following are differences between peer-to-peer and client/server traffic?

    a. Both are identical.

    b. Clients initiate the request in a client/server network.

    c. Peer-to-peer networks require a stand-alone hub.

    d. Peer-to-peer networks require a NIC.

9. Which of the following is not a NOS?

    a. NetWare

    b. Windows NT

    c. AppleTalk

    d. TCP/IP

10. Which of the following protocols is responsible for moving packets across a TCP/IP network?

    a. TCP

    b. IP

    c. SMB

    d. NetBIOS

11. Which layer of software is responsible for storing a file on a remote server?

    a.   TCP

    b.   IP

    c.   SMB

    d.   NetBIOS

12. Which of the following is true?

    a.   IP encapsulates Ethernet.

    b.   Ethernet encapsulates IP.

    c.   TCP encapsulates IP.

    d.   SMB encapsulates Ethernet.

13. Which of the following headers is used to create a packet?

    a.   Ethernet

    b.   IP

    c.   TCP

    d.   SMB

14. Wireless networks based on the 802.11b standard use what type of transmission?

    a.   Frequency hopping spread spectrum

    b.   Synchronous

    c.   Direct sequence spread spectrum

    d.   Manchester encoding

15. Why does an 802-compliant wireless network use CSMA/CA?

    a.   To increase the data rate

    b.   To reduce collisions

    c.   To strengthen the signal

    d.   To increase the bandwidth

16. Wireless LANs are allowed to use any of the following frequency bands. Which band can provide the highest data rate?

    a. 902 to 928 MHz

    b. 2.4 to 2.483 GHz

    c. 5.725 to 5.875 GHz

    d. The data rate is the same on any band.

17. Collisions are normal on CSMA/CD LANs and not usually the result of errors. True or False

18. The majority of 10-Mbps Ethernet LANs use fiber optic technology. True or False

19. Redirection software on the client determines whether requests are being made for local or remote system resources. True or False

20. To be accessible, a server must be on the same LAN as the client. True or False

21. If a client has been enabled to communicate with a server, the client cannot participate in peer-to-peer exchanges. True or False

22. UNIX functions as a NOS. True or False

23. Name at least three LAN architectures (NOSs).

    _____

    _____

    _____

Unit 6
Network Components

Thus far, we have discussed the simplest, smallest broadcast networks, in which each computer is connected to every other through a ring topology, bus, or central hub. In these single-segment networks, every device receives every frame transmitted by any other device. Each device processes frames that are addressed to it, and ignores frames that are not.

For this system to work, only one device is allowed to transmit at any time. (Simultaneous signals will garble each other.) As we have seen, different Data Link Layer protocols, such as Ethernet and Token Ring, enforce this rule in different ways.

Single-segment networks provide good service to many small and mid-sized businesses. However, as an organization grows, two main factors force changes in the structure of a network:

- When too many devices compete for the same limited transmission capacity, network performance becomes sluggish. (Imagine a highway at rush hour.) When traffic is heavy, users may have difficulty accessing some resources, such as electronic mail (e-mail).

- When a business adds a new office location, the new local area network (LAN) must be connected to the old one over a wide area or metropolitan-area telecommunications link. However, it is impractical to treat widely separated LANs as a single broadcast network, because wide area connections are slower and much more expensive than private LAN facilities.

To solve both of these problems, network designers break a single broadcast network into separate segments. Internetworking devices, such as repeaters, hubs, switches, bridges, routers, and gateways, function as the connectors between the individual segments. These devices manage data traffic as it flows within and between networks, in some cases over great distances. They can also increase the effective transmission capacity of a network and enhance its security.

The operation of most of these components can be configured and optimized by a network administrator. For simple devices, network management is conducted with switches on the device itself. More complex "managed" devices are configured and controlled by software, from a separate management console that plugs into one of the device ports, or by management commands sent through the network itself.

Each internetworking device operates at a particular layer of the Open Systems Interconnection (OSI) model. As we introduce each device, we will start with Layer 1 (the Physical Layer) and work upward.

Lessons

1. Repeaters and Hubs
2. Bridges
3. Switches
4. Routers
5. Gateways

Terms

Address Resolution Protocol (ARP)—ARP is a protocol that allows a host to use a logical (network) address to obtain the hardware (NIC or MAC) address for a remote station. ARP is used only across a single physical network, and is limited to networks that support hardware broadcasts.

architecture—The design and method of construction of a particular entity is referred to as its architecture. Different computer network architectures were developed for particular purposes. Examples of network architectures include IBM's SNA and Apple's AppleTalk.

broadcast domain—A broadcast domain is the area of a network that will receive broadcast packets. Routers and Layer 3 switches create network segments that are separate broadcast domains, because they do not forward broadcast packets from one segment to another.

broadcast frame—A broadcast frame is a frame addressed to all nodes on a network. The frame address is a special number that tells all nodes that receive the frame to process it.

broadcast storm—Due to differences between nodes and bridges in different parts of a network, a broadcast frame can sometimes be misinterpreted. This leads to another broadcast frame by the bridge that misinterpreted it. The second broadcast frame is again misinterpreted, and so on. The result is a "storm" of broadcast frames that can severely degrade network performance. Sometimes storms can persist and eventually bring down an entire network.

collapsed backbone—A collapsed backbone is a network topology that uses a multiport device, such as a switch or router, to carry traffic between network segments or subnets. This is in contrast to the original backbone that, in the case of Ethernet, consisted of a single common bus cable to which nodes were connected.

collision domain—The portion of a network where all nodes receive every frame transmitted is referred to as collision domain. A bus, hub, or group of interconnected hubs forms a single collision domain.

default gateway—A default gateway is a router that provides access to all hosts on remote networks. Typically, a network administrator configures a default gateway for each node on a network.

firewall—A firewall is a controlled access point between sections of the same network, designed to confine problems to one section. It is also a controlled access between a private network and public network, such as the Internet, usually implemented with a router and special firewall software.

gateway—The term "gateway" can have two definitions in the context of networking. 1. A gateway can be a protocol converter. This type of gateway converts data between two distinct types of protocol architectures, often at the higher layers of the OSI model. 2. A gateway can also be a router used to connect a private network to a public network, typically the Internet.

High-Level Data Link Control (HDLC)—HDLC is a Data Link Layer protocol for point-to-point and point-to-multipoint communication. The HDLC protocol suite represents a wide variety of link layer protocols, such as SDLC, LAPB, LAPD, frame relay, and PPP.

Internet—The term Internet, capitalized, refers to the global internetwork of TCP/IP networks.

latency—Latency is the transmission delay created as a device processes a frame or packet. It is the duration from the time a device reads the first byte of a frame or packet, until the time it forwards that byte.

NetBIOS Extended User Interface (NetBEUI)—NetBEUI is a Network and Transport Layer protocol designed to work within a single physical LAN. (It does not provide packet routing between networks.) NetBEUI is typically integrated with NetBIOS.

Network Basic Input/Output System (NetBIOS)—NetBIOS is a software system originally developed by Sytek and IBM to allow an NDS to communicate with computer hardware. NetBIOS has been adopted by Microsoft Windows NT and Novell NetWare, and has become the de facto standard for application interface to all types of LANs. Thus, many LANs are described as "NetBIOS-compatible."

segment—A physical portion of a network is referred to as a segment. A network is composed of one or more physical segments.

subnet—A subnet is a subdivision of a network, in which users are grouped logically based on their network address. Subnets are formed by routers, thus each subnet is a separate broadcast domain.

Synchronous Data Link Control (SDLC)—See High-Level Data Link Control (HDLC).

Systems Network Architecture (SNA)—SNA is IBM's architecture for computer networking. SNA was designed for transaction processing in mission-critical applications, often involving a large number of "dumb" terminals communicating with a mainframe. Typical transactions perform inquiries and update information in a database. For example, a commercial bank might have a number of 3270-type display units and printers in each of hundreds of branch offices that are used to access a central database in the home office.

unroutable protocol—An unroutable protocol is a network protocol that does not support routing at OSI Layer 3, such as NetBIOS or DEC-LAT. This type of protocol does not create packets, thus Layer 3 devices, such as routers, cannot be used.

Lesson 1—Repeaters and Hubs

Repeaters and hubs are Physical Layer devices. Like a piece of wire, they transmit bits, but do not evaluate them. However, unlike a wire, these devices are not electrically passive; they add power to the signal as they actively retransmit it. Even though these devices are simple, they are important tools for organizing a physical network layout. This lesson looks at the primary features of both repeaters and hubs.

Objectives

At the end of this lesson you should be able to:

- Describe what repeaters and hubs do

- Explain how repeaters and hubs are similar, and how they are different

- Explain what a collision domain is

- Name the main types of hubs

 **Key Point**

Repeaters operate on bits and extend the length of a physical medium. Hubs provide a central point of connectivity for networking devices.

Repeaters

A repeater is the simplest type of internetworking device. Repeaters receive a signal (bits) on a LAN segment and regenerate the bit pattern to boost the signal and extend the physical length of the segment.

Because a repeater operates at the Physical Layer of the OSI model, as illustrated on the Repeater and OSI Diagram, the job of a repeater is to repeat bits. If a "1" bit is received on the input port of a repeater, a "1" bit is regenerated at the output of the repeater. Similarly, if a "0" bit is received on the input port of a repeater, a "0" bit is regenerated at the output of the repeater. Thus, a repeater is considered a "nondiscriminating" device, because all incoming signals are passed on to each connected segment. These devices are also transparent to the sending and receiving (end) devices. Because a repeater reproduces exactly what it receives, bit by bit, it also reproduces errors. However, it is very fast and causes very little delay.

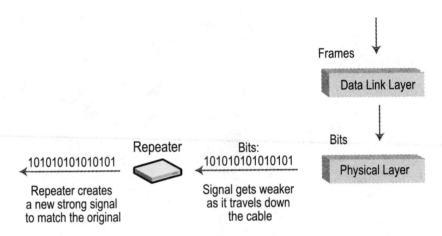

Repeater and OSI Model

A repeater connects one segment of a LAN to another, possibly connecting different types of media, as shown on the Repeater and Physical Media Diagram. For example, an Ethernet repeater can connect Thinnet cables to twisted pair cables or Thicknet cables. However, a repeater cannot be used to connect two different LAN protocols, such as Ethernet and Token Ring.

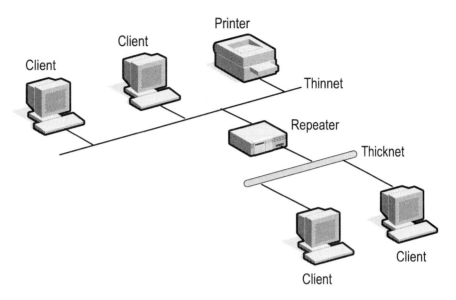

Repeater and Physical Media

As internetworking devices for Ethernet LANs, repeaters are feasible only for relatively small LANs (less than 100 nodes) confined to a small geographic area, such as one or two floors of an office building. A repeater should not be used to connect heavily used LANs, because all data passes through a repeater. Therefore, if you connect multiple LAN segments using a repeater, you may experience performance problems, because repeaters do not filter out any data passing through them.

Repeaters are not normally used to add more devices to a network, only to extend the distance a workstation or group of workstations can be located from other parts of a network. To increase the number of devices connected to a network, we use a device called a "hub."

Hubs

A hub, sometimes called a "wiring concentrator," logically functions as a shared bus or multiport repeater. All devices connected to a hub receive frames transmitted by any other device on that hub.

The most common type of hub is an Ethernet 10BaseT hub used to connect computers attached to an Ethernet network. The simplest type of Ethernet hub is a stand-alone hub purchased for small organizations, as illustrated on the Ethernet Star Diagram. Eight and 12-port stand-alone hubs are common. A separate cable connects the network interface card (NIC) of each individual node (clients, servers, or peripherals) to one port of the hub.

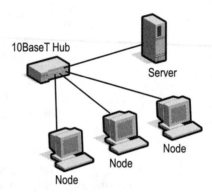

Ethernet Star

Token Ring MAUs

The Token Ring Hub/MAU Diagram presents a special type of hub used in Token Ring networks, the multistation access unit (MAU). Each MAU connects to an adjacent MAU through special ports. The ring-out (RO) port of one MAU connects to the ring-in (RI) port of the next MAU to form large rings. In most cases, network management of a MAU is limited to simply checking the state of front-panel light emitting diodes (LEDs).

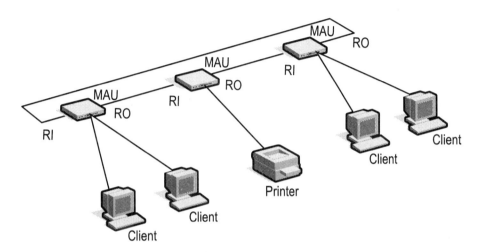

Token Ring Hub/MAU

Token Ring Repeaters

Token Ring repeaters, sometimes called "lobe repeaters," may be used in pairs to extend the main ring path to MAUs in distant locations, or used alone to extend the cable length to a single workstation. Fiber optic Token Ring repeaters are used primarily to interconnect remote MAUs, and convert the twisted pair RI and RO port connections to fiber optic connections. The Token Ring Repeaters Diagram illustrates this type of repeater.

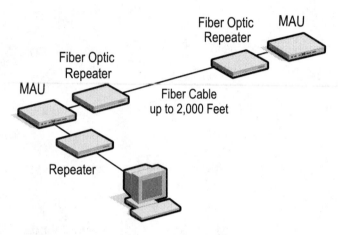

Token Ring Repeaters

Ethernet Collision Domains

A collision domain is a portion of a network where all nodes receive every frame transmitted by all other nodes, and compete for access to the shared medium. For example, in a small, one-hub 10-megabits-per-second (Mbps) Ethernet network, every node in the network receives every frame transmitted by any other node. Thus, all nodes attached to the hub share the same 10-Mbps bandwidth. The Ethernet Collision Domain Diagram illustrates this principle.

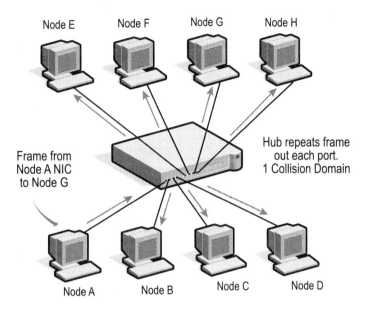

Ethernet Collision Domain

In this diagram, Node A wants to send information to Node G. A frame is sent from Node A to the hub. The hub, which is essentially a multiport repeater, repeats the frame out every port. Each node attached to the hub receives the frame. However, only the node that has a NIC address (in this case, Node G) that matches the frame address will process the frame and pass its contents to the next highest layer.

Hub-to-Hub Connectivity

After an Ethernet hub fills to capacity, additional computers cannot be connected to the hub. As a network grows and more nodes are needed, hubs can be added to provide more physical ports to connect additional devices. The Ethernet Hub-to-Hub Diagram illustrates this principle.

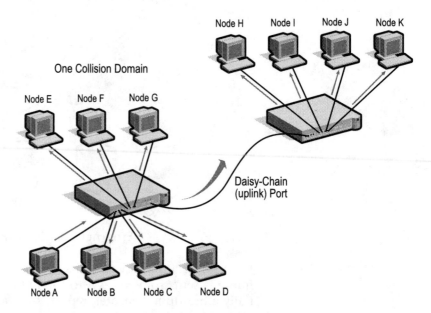

Ethernet Hub-to-Hub

In this diagram, Node H is removed from the first hub and a connection is made to another hub. Many hubs provide the ability to use one of the hub ports for either device connectivity or hub connectivity. A switch is normally mounted under this port for switching between computer connectivity and hub connectivity. (Another method used to connect hubs built without a switch is to use an Ethernet crossover cable.) The switch is put in one position for attaching a computer, and the opposite position when attaching to another hub.

As noted on the diagram, the port that was used to attach to Node H is now used to attach to the hub. Node H now resides on the second Ethernet hub. Once again this configuration represents a single collision domain. If a frame is generated from Node A to the hub, the hub will repeat the frame out each port. This includes the uplink port that attaches to the second hub. The second hub will then take this frame and repeat it out each of its ports as well.

As networks grow, more and more hubs may be added to increase the number of nodes attached to a network. At some point, servers must be added to provide options not available in a strictly peer-to-peer network. However, when hubs are interconnected, all of their nodes are still in the same collision domain. Regardless of where the information is going to or coming from, each node receives the frame transmission.

As traffic increases in the network, there will be a point where performance is unacceptable. In other words, the 10-Mbps bandwidth shared by all devices in this broadcast network will no longer be adequate. To correct this problem, other devices can be used to divide the network into separate collision domains. We will learn about these devices in upcoming lessons.

Stackable Hubs

A stackable hub consists of modules stacked on top of one another and connected by short cables, as shown on the Stackable Hub Diagram. These hubs are typically stacked in a rack and located in a communications closet.

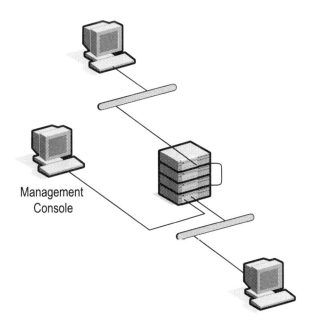

Management
Console

Stackable Hub

Although they are physically composed of separate modules, a stack of hubs appears to the network as a single logical device. Stackable hubs have flexible port densities due to their modular nature. Each stackable hub can have 12 or 24 ports in each module, and typically stack up to a total of 128 ports or more. Stackable hubs are ideal for a small office, and are often called "departmental" hubs. Network management capabilities exist with these types of devices, thus they can be configured with software from an administrator's workstation.

Chassis Hubs

A chassis hub is the largest hub configuration available, providing between 48 and 144 ports. Chassis hubs offer a variety of module and physical connection options, as illustrated on the Chassis Hub Diagram. Fiber, routers, gateways, bridges, and repeaters can all be mixed and matched within a chassis hub.

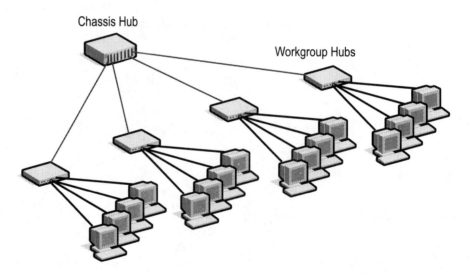

Chassis Hub

A chassis hub is efficient, because multiple modules share a single case, backplane, central processing unit (CPU), cooling system, and power supply. Chassis hubs are most appropriate for a larger business or enterprise environment where 100 to more than 1,000 users will be connected. A chassis hub typically offers the lowest cost per port when a large network needs a high-port-count device.

Activities

1. The job of a repeater is to filter out the bits that would cause errors to be repeated. True or False

2. A repeater is used to extend the length of a cable segment to any length the user requires. True or False

3. A repeater is a logically passive device. True or False

4. A repeater can be used to connect Ethernet and Token Ring segments. True or False

5. Repeaters and hubs operate at the Physical Layer of the OSI model. True or False

6. A Token Ring MAU and Ethernet hub perform similar functions. True or False

7. A managed hub is one with front-panel LEDs. True or False

8. Draw an Ethernet network consisting of a single 12-port hub, 10 clients, and 2 servers.

9. An additional four clients must be added to the network. Draw another diagram showing how to add another 12-port hub to the network, and how the additional clients will be added.How many collision domains are in the network you just drew in Activity 9?

10. Draw a diagram showing how two Token Ring MAUs are connected using RI and RO ports.

11. Draw a diagram of a stackable hub with four stacked hubs and a management console.

Extended Activities

Use any computing vendor's World Wide Web (Web) site or catalog to find information on various hub and repeater products to answer the following questions.

1. What are the price ranges for hubs?

   _____

   _____

2. What is the port count on the various hubs?

   _____

   _____

3. What are typical prices of rack-mounted and stackable hubs?

   _____

   _____

4. Compare the costs of nonmanaged hubs and managed hubs.

   _____

   _____

Lesson 2—Bridges

Bridges operate at the Data Link Layer of the OSI model, and are sometimes called "Layer 2 devices" or "Link Layer devices." These devices are used to increase the overall performance of a network by isolating traffic within network segments. Bridges are also used to provide connectivity across a wide area. Although the popularity of bridges has diminished because of the widespread use of switches (discussed in the next lesson), they are still commonly found in today's computer networks.

Objectives

At the end of this lesson you should be able to:

- Describe what a bridge does

- Explain how a bridge creates separate collision domains

- Name at least two reasons to use a bridge

 **Key Point**

Bridges use frame addresses to make bridging decisions.

Bridge Functionality

The operation of a bridge requires both hardware and software. A bridge listens to all traffic on its connected network segments, examines the destination NIC address of each incoming frame, and uses an internal table of ports and destination addresses to decide whether to forward a frame to the rest of the network.

A bridge provides three important functions:

- Forwarding—If the frame's destination address is on a different segment than its source, the bridge sends the frame only to the port connected to that segment.

- Filtering—If the incoming frame is destined for a device on the same port where the frame was generated, the bridge does not forward the frame to any other ports. All nodes on the originating segment have already received the frame.

- Learning—The bridge automatically builds and maintains its own bridge table, by noting the source addresses of incoming frames. If a frame is addressed to a destination not yet recorded in the table, the bridge broadcasts the frame to all ports.

The Bridge Table Diagram illustrates how a bridge uses its bridge table to determine where to forward a frame. When an incoming frame arrives with a destination address of ADR1, the bridge checks its table and finds that the destination is on the segment attached to Port 3. If a frame is received with a destination address of ADR3, the bridge forwards the frame to Port 1, which is connected to the segment that contains the destination address.

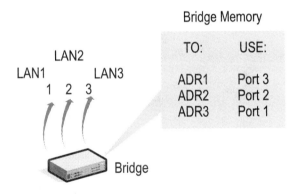

Bridge Table

A frame may also have a special type of destination address, called a "broadcast address." This address simply means "send to all nodes," thus when a bridge receives a frame with a broadcast address, it also transmits the frame to all ports.

Bridges operate on frame headers and have no regard for the content of the frame, as shown on the OSI and Bridges Diagram. Bridges are completely transparent to the Network Layer and above, because data from those layers is encapsulated within the frame header and trailer. For example, a bridge could link LANs with nodes that use different upper layer protocols.

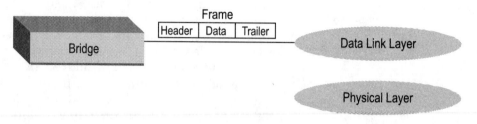

OSI and Bridges

Traffic Isolation

When traffic on a LAN starts to cause performance problems, bridges can reduce the load by dividing the network into separate segments. This works because the filtering action of a Layer 2 device creates separate collision domains within the same network. The nodes within each collision domain share the full bandwidth of the network among just themselves, not the entire network.

This approach works best when most LAN traffic is local, in other words, when nodes within a department tend to communicate with one another much more than they do with nodes in other departments. For example, if a server node provides a virtual filestore for a department, much of the traffic in that department tends to be between that department's nodes and the server.

If a bridge is used to divide a LAN into two segments, the traffic on each segment will be approximately one-half what it was before. A relatively small proportion of network traffic will need to flow across the bridge, as illustrated on the Bridges and Traffic Isolation Diagram. The technique, called "traffic isolation," is an important tool for controlling network utilization. It can also be used to control traffic between segments and the network backbone.

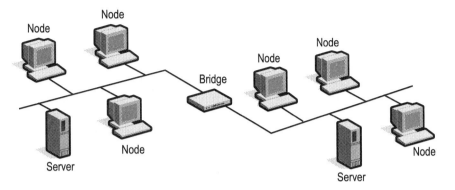

Bridges and Traffic Isolation

As an enterprise network grows, it will tend to be dispersed over a wide geographic area. Thus, another important use of bridges is to connect LANs remotely, as illustrated on the Wide Area Bridges Diagram. Wide area network (WAN) bridges, also called "half bridges," work together in pairs as shown. One port of each half bridge is connected to a leased point-to-point line. The halfbridges cooperate to send frames across the point-to-point link using a protocol such as Synchronous Data Link Control (SDLC) or High-Level Data Link Control (HDLC). The point-to-point link, usually 56 kilobits per second (Kbps), is much slower than either Token Ring or Ethernet, thus traffic between the two LAN segments must be relatively light. The filtering capability of the bridge ensures that only traffic between locations crosses the WAN link.

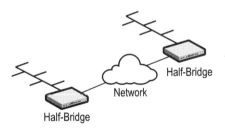

Wide Area Bridges

Types of Bridges

Bridges come in many shapes and sizes. The simplest bridges are adapter cards (NICs) in a personal computer (PC) that attach to small LAN segments. The most elaborate bridges convert frames from one type to another, and/or deliver frames over long distances at very high speeds.

Bridges offer many advantages and are still commonly found in computer networks. However, they can form traffic bottlenecks, because they can only forward traffic between one pair of ports at a time. Also, their operation is software-intensive and fairly slow. Thus, bridges are largely being replaced by a faster and more efficient Layer 2 device, the switch.

Activities

1. Bridges can be used to connect LAN segments located in the same building, as well as LAN segments 1,000 miles apart. True or False

2. A bridge is typically used for traffic isolation; however, a hub can serve the same purpose. True or False

3. A bridge operates at the _____ Layer of the OSI model.

4. Bridges _____ and _____ Medium Access Control (MAC) frames.

5. _____ occurs when a bridge does not forward a frame.

6. If a bridge receives a frame with a broadcast address, what does it do?

7. Two _____ _____ function as one wide area bridge.

   For Activities 8 and 9 consider the following configuration:

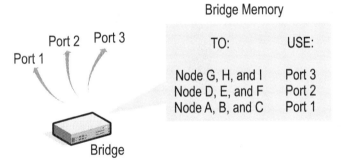

8. Node C has not yet sent any traffic. Node A sends a frame to Node C. At what port(s) will Node A's traffic appear on the bridge?

   _____

9. Node B sends traffic to Node E. At what port(s) will Node B's traffic appear on the bridge?

   _____

10. Why does it sometimes make sense to group servers with departmental workstations (workgroups), instead of on a corporate backbone?

_____

_____

_____

_____

Extended Activities

There are essentially two types of bridging:

- Transparent (learning)
- Source route bridging

1. Research and compare the two types of bridging. Summarize your findings.

_____

_____

_____

_____

2. Research the Spanning Tree Algorithm? What type of bridge does it apply to?

_____

_____

3. The term "latency" means the delay caused by software or hardware processing. Would bridges have higher latency than hubs? Explain.

_____

_____

_____

_____

Lesson 3—Switches

Switches are Data Link Layer (Layer 2) devices used to increase performance in LANs. In many networks, switches have replaced hubs and bridges to increase end-user performance. This lesson introduces the operation of switches and explains how they are implemented in networks.

Objectives

At the end of this lesson you should be able to:

• Describe how a switch works

• Explain the difference between a switch and a bridge

• Explain how a switch effectively increases network bandwidth

 **Key Point**

A switch uses frame addresses to make switching decisions, and provides faster performance than standard hubs.

Switch Functionality

A switch is a device that consists of many high-speed ports connecting either LAN segments (segment switching) or individual devices on a port-by-port basis (port switching). Many types of switches exist, each supporting different speeds and LAN types, such as Ethernet, Token Ring, and Fiber Distributed Data Interface (FDDI).

Like a bridge, a switch isolates traffic and creates separate collision domains by forwarding, filtering, and learning. It works by evaluating the destination Medium Access Control (MAC) address (NIC address) in each frame, and switching individual frames to the correct port. The forwarding decision does not consider other information encapsulated in the frame. Like a bridge, a switch also transmits broadcast frames (frames with a broadcast address) to all ports.

When a switch first turns on, it broadcasts individual frames just like a standard passive hub does. Over time, the switch builds a table that associates frame addresses with port numbers by watching incoming frames for new source addresses and adding those addresses to the switch memory table, as shown on the Switch Memory Diagram.

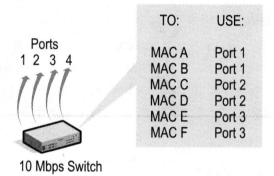

Switch Memory

Unlike a bridge, a switch does more of its job in high-speed hardware, providing performance closer to single-LAN performance than bridged-LAN performance.

Also unlike a bridge, which shares the LAN bandwidth among all of its ports, a switch dedicates the entire LAN media bandwidth, such as 10-Mbps Ethernet, to each port-to-port frame transmission. In this way, a switch multiplies the amount of effective network bandwidth. This is illustrated on the Ethernet Switch Diagram.

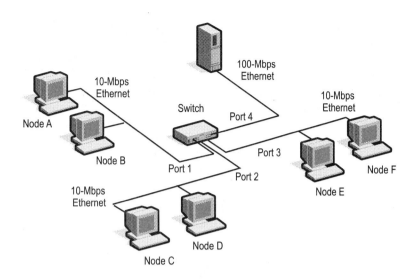

Ethernet Switch

When a switch connects several LAN segments, as shown on the Ethernet Switch Diagram, it is considered a segment-switching device. A switch port may also be connected to an individual device. In that case, we say that the switch is performing device switching or port switching. Technically, we can say a switch is always performing port switching, because its job is to forward frames from one port to another. However, the term "port switching" is widely used in the industry to describe the practice of connecting a single node to a switch port.

When a frame is sent by Node A destined for Node E, the switch routes the frame between Port 1 and Port 3. In this case, Port 2 and Port 4 are also free to simultaneously send frames at a full 10-Mbps rate. If Node A sends a frame to Node B, the switch will contain the frame to the individual segment, which contains both Node A and Node B. Switches, therefore, maximize overall network bandwidth by creating temporary logical connections between nodes, or virtual circuits, on a per-frame basis.

If a frame enters the switch with a destination address of the NIC in Node A, the switch will route this frame to Port 1. If a frame enters the switch with a destination address of the NIC in Node E, the switch will route the frame to Port 3.

Switches may switch frames between multiple segments simultaneously. For example, if the switch on the Frame Switching Diagram receives a frame from Node E destined for Node G, and simultaneously receives a frame from Node A destined for Node D, it could switch these two frames simultaneously. In this case, the normal LAN bandwidth is doubled.

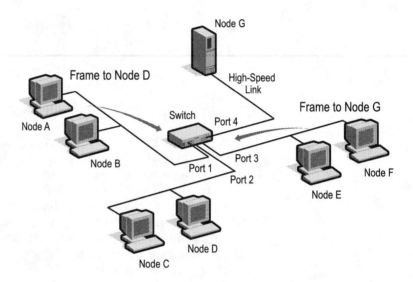

Frame Switching

Whenever a switch receives a frame destined for a device with a destination address that is not resident in the switch's memory, the switch will send the frame out to all ports just as a hub would do. If the switch receives a frame with a broadcast (or multicast) address, it will also send the frame out to all ports (or to all ports belonging to the multicast group).

Some switches operate on both frames and packets, and are called "Layer 3 (or Level 3) switches." These devices are essentially high-speed routers (described in the next lesson). However, the majority of switches found in networks are Layer 2 switches that operate on frames.

Traffic Isolation with Switches

Because a switch filters traffic according to frame addresses, it can isolate network traffic within separate segments or collision domains. However, a switch can also improve overall network performance, because it allocates the entire network bandwidth to each temporary port-to-port connection. In contrast, a bridge shares the network bandwidth among all of its connections.

The Ethernet Switch Diagram illustrates a common Ethernet configuration, in which an Ethernet-switched LAN is connected to a hub-centered LAN by means of a pair of half bridges. Note the difference in the bandwidth available from the 10BaseT hub versus the potential bandwidth of the three devices connected to the Ethernet switch. The hub shares 10 Mbps among all of its devices, while the switch allocates 10 Mbps to each of its devices. Thus, the effective bandwidth of the switch is 30 Mbps.

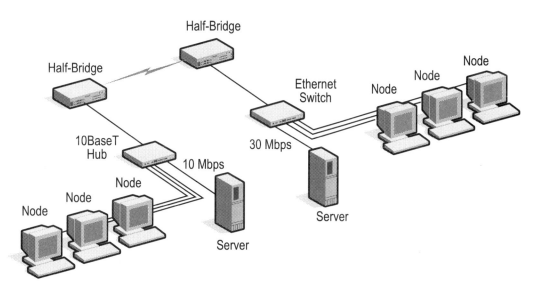

Multiplying Bandwidth and an Ethernet Switch

Activities

1. A switch normally operates at the _____ Layer of the OSI model.

2. Briefly describe the difference between device switching and segment switching.

3. What will a switch do with a frame destined for a node that does not yet have its address in the memory table?

4. What will a switch do with a frame that has a broadcast address for its destination?

5. Draw a diagram illustrating a five-port hub. Number the Ports 1 through 5, and show a connection to Nodes A through E. (Node A is on Port 1 and Node E is on Port 5.)

If Node A is transmitting to Node E, list all port numbers where Node A's data will appear.

_____

_____

6. Using the same diagram in Activity 4, fill in the switch memory table with the appropriate port number.

To Node	Use

7. Draw the same diagram as above, substituting a five-port switch for the hub. If Node A is transmitting to Node E, list all port numbers where Node A's data will appear.

Extended Activities

1. Go to a Web site such as **http://www.3Com.com** and research information on switches. Classify the switch information found (e.g., small office/home office or enterprise). Present your findings.

    _____

    _____

    _____

2. Use a Web search engine and find information on Layer 3 switching. What is it? What benefits does this technology offer? Is the technology proprietary?

    _____

    _____

    _____

Lesson 4—Routers

A router operates at the Network Layer of the OSI reference model, distinguishing between Network Layer protocols and making intelligent packet-forwarding decisions based on each packet's network address. As Network Layer devices, routers are protocol-dependent. They can interconnect networks that have the same network communication architecture, but possibly different lower level architectures. In contrast, Layer 2 devices (bridges and switches) are considered protocol-independent, because they can connect networks that use different Layer 3 protocols.

Objectives

At the end of this lesson you should be able to:

- Explain how routers work

- Describe how a router is different from a bridge or a switch

- Explain the difference between a collision domain and a broadcast domain

- Name the key advantages and disadvantages of routers

 **Key Point**

Routers use packet addresses to route information between networks.

Router Functionality

Routers are typically more complex and software-intensive than repeaters, bridges, or switches. They are general-purpose devices that can segment a network into separate logical subnetworks, and provide security, control, and redundancy between individual subnetworks. Each port of a router connects to a different network or subnet.

For traffic isolation purposes, a router can usually be used instead of a bridge or switch. However, in order to be "routable," architectures must have a Network Layer process, as illustrated on the Router and OSI Model Diagram.

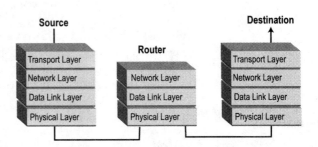

Router and OSI Model

"Unroutable" protocols include the Digital Equipment Corporation's (DEC's) Local Area Transport (DEC-LAT) terminal communications protocol, IBM's Systems Network Architecture (SNA), and Network Basic Input/Output System (NetBIOS)/NetBIOS Extended User Interface (NETBEUI). These protocols must be segmented with Layer 2 devices (bridges or switches) instead of routers.

Routers provide physical and logical separation of networks. This is done by evaluating the destination address of the packet, which indicates where the destination node is on the network. A Network Layer address (packet address) identifies both the destination network and destination node, just as a person's name identifies both a family and an individual.

Thus if the packet address indicates the destination node is in the same network (or subnetwork) as the source node, the router will isolate traffic within that network or subnet. If the packet is destined for another network or subnet, the router will send the packet out the physical port that is connected to that network, as illustrated on the Subnets and Routing Diagram.

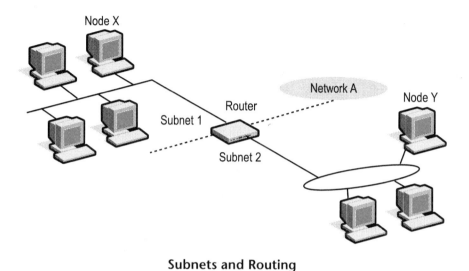

Subnets and Routing

A routing table is stored in the router's memory to associate each network address with a physical port number. Routers use specialized routing protocols to maintain and exchange the internetwork path information stored in their internal routing tables. Depending on the protocol in use, these tables can allow routers to flexibly choose routing paths based on distance, speed, quality of service (QoS), or other factors.

Multiprotocol Routing

Routers can interconnect LANs that use different Data Link Layer protocols, as long as both networks use the same higher level communication architectures. For example, a router can connect one network that uses NetWare over Ethernet to another network that uses NetWare over Token Ring.

If two interconnected LANs use different communication architectures (for example, SNA and Transmission Control Protocol/ Internet Protocol [TCP/IP]), then two routers can be used, one for each architecture. Each router can use the same set of Data Link Layer protocols. Communications between TCP/IP nodes will go through one router, while communications between SNA nodes go through the other.

To avoid the expense and additional administration of having two routers with separate LAN ports, multiprotocol routers have been developed. These devices do not perform protocol conversion above the Data Link Layer, however. They simply bundle the function of two routers into a single box. Multiprotocol routers require a single port on each LAN to which they are connected.

How Routers Move Packets Between Networks

When the IP process on the source node is preparing a packet, it places the destination and source addresses in the packet header. It then compares the destination address to its own address to determine whether the destination is on the same network (or subnet) as itself.

If it is, IP sends the packet directly to the destination machine using whatever protocol is appropriate to the Data Link Layer (for example, Ethernet or Token Ring). If the destination is not on the same network, IP examines its routing table to see whether any specific route to the destination has been set.

If IP finds a preset route, called a "static" route, it sends the packet to a specified router. Essentially, a static route configuration tells the IP process, "If you see an address that begins with xxx., send it to Router Y for further routing." The specified router may, in turn, forward the packet to other routers on other networks until the packet reaches its destination.

If IP does not find a static route, it forwards the packet to its default gateway for further routing and delivery. IP's default instructions essentially say, "If you do not have a static route defined for a network address, send it to Router X and let it worry about it."

Routers Rebuild Frames

As an IP packet traverses a network, it stays intact. However, routers remove and add frame headers and trailers as the data moves from one type of Data Link Layer protocol to another. For example, consider the network shown on the Routers and Data Links Diagram. Two Ethernet LANs are connected to a FDDI backbone with routers.

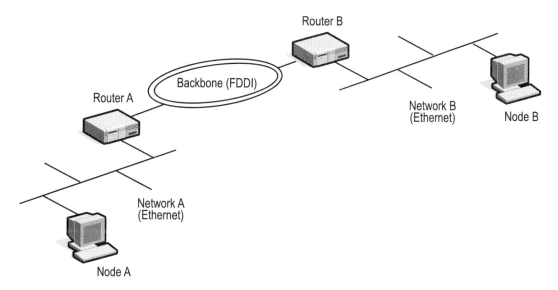

Routers and Data Links

If Node A sends data to Node B, the Node A IP process recognizes that the data is addressed to a distant network and must be forwarded by a router. Thus Node A encapsulates the IP packet (addressed to Node B) within an Ethernet frame addressed to its default router, Router A. Node A then transmits that frame, over the Ethernet network, to Router A.

Router A processes the frame because it is addressed to it. When it inspects the packet header, it sees that the packet is addressed to Network B. Thus Router A encapsulates the packet in a FDDI frame addressed to Router B, then transmits that frame over the FDDI ring.

Router B processes the frame because it is addressed to it. When it inspects the packet header, it sees that the packet is addressed to Node B. Thus Router B encapsulates the packet in an Ethernet frame addressed to Node B, then transmits the frame over the Ethernet network.

By the time Node B receives the data packet sent from Node A, the packet has been encapsulated within three different frames, using two different Data Link Layer protocols. However, during all the changes of frame format, from Ethernet to FDDI and back again, the IP packet was never changed.

Internet Routers

The Internet, as its name implies, is a network of networks. Individual networks, such as those of Internet service providers (ISPs) and telephone carriers, are linked by routers and point-to-point links.

A packet moves across the Internet by being relayed from one network to the next until it reaches its destination. The routers that link those networks handle all the packet forwarding themselves. Individual users do not have to tell their messages what path to travel across the Internet, and could not even if they wanted to.

A router examines the IP network address of each packet, then uses its internal routing table to forward the packet to the routing port associated with the best path to the packet's destination. If the packet is addressed to a network that is not connected to the router, the router will forward the packet to another router that is closer to the final destination. Each router, in turn, evaluates each packet, then either delivers the packet or forwards it to another router.

Broadcast Domains

Earlier in this unit, we introduced the concept of a collision domain, which is a segment of a network in which devices compete for access to the shared transmission medium. Equally important is the idea of a broadcast domain, which is an area of a network in which broadcast frames are transmitted.

Broadcast traffic or background traffic consists of frames that carry the network's "administrative overhead." Broadcast frames are sent out for several reasons. For example, if a node has a packet to send and knows the destination network address but not the NIC address, it will broadcast a message asking for the node with the matching packet address to reply with its NIC address. In a TCP/IP network, this process is performed by the Address Resolution Protocol (ARP). Servers, routers, and printers also broadcast periodic messages, called "service advertisements," that announce their presence to other network devices.

These nonproductive (or semiproductive) transmissions typically represent 5 to 20 percent of overall network traffic. Thus, excessive broadcast traffic can significantly decrease the available bandwidth in a LAN.

Broadcast frames have a special destination address of all 0s. This special address tells all computers that receive the frame to process it. When a bridge or switch sees a frame addressed to a specific NIC address, it makes a switching decision. However, when a Layer 2 device sees a frame with a broadcast address, it has no choice but to send the frame out every port. Thus, broadcast traffic is received by all devices physically connected to each other or to a Layer 2 device. This area of the network is called a "broadcast domain" and is illustrated on the Ethernet Broadcast Domain Diagram.

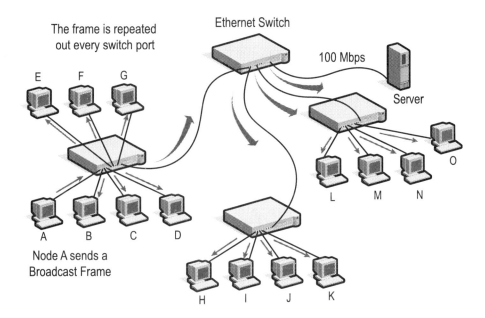

Ethernet Broadcast Domain

In other words, a switch or bridge can segment a single large LAN collision domain into several smaller collision domains. However, the individual collision domains created by the switch are still members of the same broadcast domain, because a switch transmits broadcast traffic out all ports. This means that broadcast traffic originating in one collision domain is still forwarded to all other collision domains.

One way around this particular broadcast traffic issue (when using switches) is to program each switch and tell it where to send broadcast frames. This technique is referred to as creating "virtual LANs" or VLANs. The *Introduction to Local Area Networks* course discusses VLANs in more depth.

Routers for Broadcast Containment

To create separate broadcast domains, it is necessary to segment the network at Layer 3. A router effectively contains both regular network traffic and broadcast traffic within each network segment, and only directs intersegment traffic between network segments. This approach can improve the effective throughput of the entire network.

Router Advantages and Disadvantages

Routers offer several advantages over bridges and switches:

- Like a switch, a router provides users with seamless communication between individual LAN segments. Unlike a switch, a router forms the logical boundary between entire networks or groups of network segments.

- Routers provide efficient WAN access, because they do not forward broadcast traffic.

- A router can provide a firewall service, because it forwards only traffic specifically addressed to go across the router. Routers keep potentially disastrous events, such as broadcast storms, local to the area in which they occur, preventing them from spreading across the corporate network.

- The enhanced intelligence of a router allows it to support redundant network paths, and select the best forwarding path based on several factors in addition to the destination network address. This increased intelligence can also result in enhanced data security, improved bandwidth utilization, and more control over network operations.

- Routers can flexibly integrate different Data Link Layer technologies, such as Ethernet, Fast Ethernet, Token Ring, and FDDI. They can also consolidate legacy IBM mainframe networks with PC-based networks.

However, routers also have several disadvantages:

- The additional software processing performed by a router can increase packet latency, reducing the router's performance when compared to simpler switch architecture.

- To be "routable," an architecture must have a Network Layer. Not all architectures do, and those protocols must be bridged. "Unroutable" protocols include the DEC-LAT terminal communications protocol, IBM's SNA, and NetBIOS/NetBEUI.

Activities

1. Routers can connect networks with different Layer 2 architectures. True or False

2. A router operates at the _____ Layer of the OSI model.

3. Consider a router connected to the following networks:

   The router has three links (L1, L2, and L3) connected. It has received the following path information by exchanging routing information with routers in other networks:

   Network A—L2

   Network B—L1

   Network C—L1

   Network D—L2

   Network E—L3

   Illustrate what the router's routing table would contain.

4. Identify the number of collision domains and broadcast domains in each of the following three configurations:

   a. Stackable Hub on page 337

   _____

   b. Routers and Data Links Diagram on page 361

   _____

   c. Frame Switching Diagram on page 352

   _____

Extended Activities

1. Go to Web sites of router vendors, such as **http://www.3Com.com**, **http://www.cisco.com**, and others, to find information on the latest router products.

2. Draw a diagram that contains three collision domains and one broadcast domain.

Lesson 5—Gateways

As we have seen, bridges and routers can be used in networks that run more than one Data Link Layer protocol. However, they cannot interconnect nodes that use different LAN architectures. For example, TCP/IP nodes can communicate with other TCP/IP nodes, but not with AppleTalk nodes or SNA-based nodes. Devices called "gateways" provide connectivity between networks that use different architectures.

Objectives

At the end of this lesson you should be able to:

- Describe what a gateway does

- Recognize when a gateway is necessary

- Explain the difference between a protocol converter and an Internet gateway

 **Key Point**

Gateways translate traffic between two networking architectures.

Types of Gateways

There are as many types of possible gateways as there are combinations of communication architectures and application-level protocols. One type of gateway, called a "protocol converter," changes a protocol from that of one communication architecture to that of another. An example of a protocol converter is a node that can connect a TCP/IP network to an SNA network, as shown on the Protocol Converter Gateway Diagram.

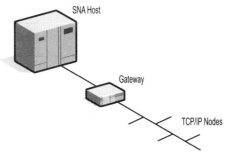

Protocol Converter Gateway

A gateway handles differences in multiple layers of protocols. It may operate at all protocol levels, while remaining transparent to the processes in those layers at each end of the connection.

To illustrate the need for a gateway, assume that we must connect a network that uses the SNA communication architecture to a network that uses TCP/IP. The TCP/IP and SNA Conversion Diagram compares both the TCP/IP and SNA protocol stacks with the OSI model.

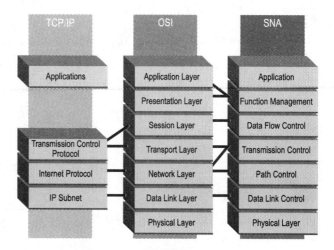

TCP/IP and SNA Conversion

As we can see, neither of these architectures matches each other or the OSI. Two problems are apparent:

- The protocols in each stack do not correspond exactly and cannot be independently converted. Instead, their conversion must be handled as an integrated task. For example, when converting from IP to the SNA Path Control protocol, elements of IP must also be reflected in the SNA Transmission Control protocol.

- Layers are missing. For example, the conversion program must handle the Function Management protocol even though that layer does not exist on the TCP/IP side.

If a frame must travel from the TCP/IP network to the SNA network, a gateway must convert the TCP/IP protocol headers to the equivalent SNA protocol headers. This is a very software-intensive process.

Gateways and Remote Access

The term "gateway" is also used to describe a router, typically an Internet router that serves as a "remote gateway" between a private network and the public Internet. These router gateways provide access to remote networks; however, they do not convert stacks of protocols.

Activities

1. A gateway performs the exact same functions as a router. True or False

2. Gateways might convert all seven layers of the OSI model. True or False

3. A gateway must use the same Data Link Layer protocol when converting between architectures. True or False

4. A gateway is a type of protocol converter. True or False

5. It will typically take less time for information to go through a gateway than a repeater. True or False

Extended Activity

Gateways convert data between entire LAN architectures. Is this an efficient way to connect two networks that only use different protocols at Layer 2? Explain.

_____

_____

_____

_____

Summary

Unit 6 introduced the devices commonly found in computer networks. Repeaters, hubs, switches, bridges, routers, and gateways essentially form the junctions or intersections of a network. These devices provide direction, capacity, and management of data traffic as it flows within networks and between networks, in some cases over great distances.

We started by looking at hubs and repeaters, which operate at the Physical Layer of the OSI model. A repeater is used to boost the electrical signal to improve the reachability of computers and network segments. The majority of hubs function as multiport repeaters. A hub provides a central junction box for multiple cables connected to computers or nodes. We refer to this class of hub as a simple or stand-alone hub, typically connecting only a few nodes. All devices connected to a hub belong to a single collision domain.

We also examined stackable hubs. Stackable or departmental hubs can be stacked on top of each other for larger network population requirements, typically from 24 to 72 node ports. With most stackable hubs, we also find network management software. Chassis hubs can provide the largest number of ports. They also provide a variety of modules with varying cable connection types, as well as other network components. A large common backplane, shared power supply, and cooling system are all characteristic of chassis/enterprise hubs.

A bridge is a Layer 2 device primarily used to isolate traffic to local LAN segments, and forward remote traffic across a wide area link. Bridges operate on frames and base their decisions on the destination address of a frame. Each segment attached to a bridge is a separate collision domain.

Switches are similar to bridges because they are also Data Link Layer devices that filter and forward traffic based on frame addresses. Each segment attached to a switch is a separate collision domain. However, switches dedicate the entire LAN bandwidth to each port-to-port connection. Because a switch can create multiple connections simultaneously, switches effectively multiply the total bandwidth of a LAN. Switches also operate faster than bridges, because more of their functions are performed in fast hardware, unlike the software-intensive bridge.

A router is a Layer 3 device that operates on packets and the contents of packet headers. Routers are software-intensive devices that are more complex than repeaters, bridges, and switches; however, they provide greater functionality. A router isolates traffic within entire networks or subnetworks. Unlike switches and bridges, a router does not forward broadcast frames. Thus, each segment attached to a router functions as a separate broadcast domain. Routers exchange network path information with each other, and can independently determine the best route to each packet's destination. This automatic forwarding is the basic feature of the Internet.

A gateway is typically the most complex device used in computer networks. Gateways convert entire protocol stacks to provide communication between different networking architectures.

As the functionality of an internetworking device increases, its complexity also increases. The cost of the device, and the time it takes to move information, increase as well. In other words, a repeater is less complex than a router, thus data travels faster through a repeater than through a router. However, a router provides much greater functionality than a repeater, at a correspondingly higher price. The Device and OSI Model Diagram illustrates how devices discussed in this unit relate to the OSI model. Note that a switch also understands bits, and a router also understands bits and frames.

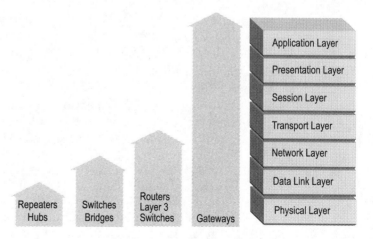

Device and OSI Model

Unit 6 Quiz

1. Token Ring MAUs are interchangeable with Ethernet hubs. True or False

2. Hubs and repeaters operate at which layer of the OSI model?

   a. Physical Layer

   b. Network Layer

   c. Transport Layer

3. Which of the following is a function of hubs and repeaters?

   a. Provide for cable extension

   b. Repeat digital signals

   c. Interconnect different cable types

   d. All of the above

4. Why shouldn't hubs and repeaters be used to interconnect entire LANs?

   a. They are too expensive.

   b. They are too powerful.

   c. They do not manage traffic efficiently enough.

   d. They cannot connect different physical media.

5. At which OSI layer do switches reside?

   a. Data Link Layer

   b. Physical Layer

   c. Transport Layer

   d. Network Layer

6. Can switches switch two frames simultaneously?

   a. Yes

   b. No

7. Which of the following devices isolate traffic in an Ethernet network?

   a. Bridge

   b. Switch

   c. Router

   d. All of the above

8. Performance will likely increase in an Ethernet network when which of the following occurs?

    a. Switches are replaced by hubs.

    b. Routers are replaced by hubs.

    c. Switches are replaced by bridges.

    d. Hubs are replaced by switches.

9. At which OSI layer do bridges operate?

    a. Data Link Layer

    b. Transport Layer

    c. Physical Layer

    d. Network Layer

10. What is a broadcast frame?

    a. A frame addressed to "all nodes"

    b. A frame addressed to one node, but received by all nodes on the same hub

    c. A frame transmitted over a wireless LAN

    d. A frame transmitted over a cable television Internet connection

11. What do bridges require that hubs and repeaters do not?

    a. Software

    b. Address tables

    c. Two segments

    d. All of the above

12. Bridges are needed in which of the following situations?

    a. Too much traffic on the LAN

    b. Remote connection of two LANs over a WAN link

    c. Broadcast storms

    d. All of the above

    e. A and B only

13. At which OSI layer do routers operate?

    a.   Data Link Layer

    b.   Network Layer

    c.   Transport Layer

    d.   Physical Layer

14. What distinguishes routers from bridges?

    a.   Routers operate on packets.

    b.   Routers are for the Internet only.

    c.   Routers are faster.

    d.   Routers are always more expensive.

15. Which of the following scenarios requires a gateway?

    a.   Connecting an IP network to an AppleTalk network

    b.   Connecting an IP network to an IP network

    c.   Connecting three IP networks

    d.   Connecting a twisted pair network to a fiber optic network

16. Consider a 10BaseT network that has four workgroup hubs. Each hub connects eight nodes. Each of the workgroup hubs is connected to each other. The network administrator decides to connect each of the four hubs to a central switch instead of to each other. What is the effect of this change?

    a.   Each of the hubs has 10-Mbps bandwidth.

    b.   Each of the hubs has 2.5-Mbps bandwidth.

    c.   Each of the nodes has 10-Mbps bandwidth.

    d.   Each of the nodes has 1/32 of the 10-Mbps bandwidth.

17. The term "gateway" also means which of the following?

    a.   A router that subdivides a network

    b.   A bridge that connects a LAN to a wide area link

    c.   A router that connects a LAN to the Internet

    d.   A Web server

18. Consider a network that has three workgroup hubs, with each hub connected to six nodes. Each of the three hubs is connected to one port of a switch. How many collision domains and broadcast domains are in this network?

    a. One collision domain, one broadcast domain

    b. Three collision domains, one broadcast domain

    c. Three broadcast domains, one collision domain

    d. Three collision domains, three broadcast domains

19. Consider a network that has three workgroup hubs, with each hub connected to six nodes. Each of the three hubs is connected to one port of a router. How many collision domains and broadcast domains are in this network?

    a. One collision domain, one broadcast domain

    b. Three collision domains, one broadcast domain

    c. Three broadcast domains, one collision domain

    d. Three collision domains, three broadcast domains

20. List one advantage of stackable hubs.

    _____

21. List two advantages of chassis hubs.

    _____

    _____

    _____

    _____

Unit 7
WANs

This unit introduces the technologies used to connect two or more local area networks (LANs) over an extended distance. The resulting network is either a metropolitan area network (MAN) or wide area network (WAN). The difference between MANs and WANs is the distance between the connected LANs. A MAN covers a metropolitan area, using local public telecommunication services. A WAN spans multiple sites over a wider geographic area, typically using both local and long-distance carrier facilities.

However, the same transmission technologies can be used to create both MANs and WANs. Thus, we will use the term "WAN" to include both types of network.

This unit introduces the two main classes of technologies used for WAN connectivity: point-to-point services and switched services.

We will also describe the devices needed to implement each type of service. In general, LANs are interconnected using routers. A router is installed between a LAN and point-to-point connection, or between a LAN and public-switched network. The router's job is to keep all data off the expensive WAN link except traffic destined for a distant site. This is why routers are often called "gateways." Each type of transmission service also requires hardware specific to that technology.

As we will see, there is no single right way to establish a WAN. When choosing a WAN technology, or combination of technologies, a network professional must consider the cost and performance of each service, plus many other factors. The final lesson in this unit introduces some of the most important factors to consider when choosing products and services to build a WAN or MAN.

Lessons

1. Point-to-Point WAN Services

2. Switched WAN Services

3. Choosing WAN Products and Services

Terms

Asynchronous Transfer Mode (ATM)—An ATM is a connection-oriented cell relay technology based on small (53-byte) cells. An ATM network consists of ATM switches that form multiple virtual circuits to carry groups of cells from source to destination. ATM can provide high-speed transport services for audio, data, and video.

cell—A cell is a unit of data similar to a frame. It is very small (53 bytes for ATM) and fixed in length. Cells are typically associated with ATM technology.

central office (CO)—A CO is a telephone company facility where local loops are terminated. The function of a CO is to connect individual telephones through a series of switches. COs are tied together in a hierarchy for efficiency in switching. Other terms for a CO are "local exchange," "wiring center," and "end office."

channel service unit (CSU)—A CSU is a device that connects to the end of a T1 or T3 line, between the line and a DSU. The CSU maintains an electrical connection on the line and functions as a repeater, regenerating and amplifying both incoming and outgoing signals. A CSU is usually combined with a DSU in a device called a "CSU/DSU."

connection-oriented—A connection-oriented data communication mode is one in which the sending and receiving computers stay in contact for the duration of a session, while packets or frames are being sent back and forth.

connectionless—Connectionless transmission treats each packet or datagram as a separate entity that contains the source and destination addresses. Connectionless services can drop or deliver packets out of sequence.

data service unit (DSU)—A DSU is a device that converts a binary signal from the format used on a LAN to that used by a T1 line. It resolves differences in the way each system represents binary numbers. It sits between a CSU and a T1 MUX, and is usually combined with a CSU in a device called a "CSU/DSU."

digital access cross-connect switch (DACS)—A DACS is a connection system that establishes semipermanent (not switched) paths for voice or data signals. All physical wires are attached to the DACS once, then electronic connections between them are made by entering instructions.

Digital Subscriber Line (DSL)—DSL is a modem technology that converts existing twisted pair telephone lines into high-speed data lines that can also carry separate telephone communications. Variants of DSL include ADSL, RADSL, ADSL Lite, IDSL, and VDSL.

encryption—The is the process of scrambling data so it cannot be read by anyone except the intended recipient is referred to as encryption.

facilities—The term "facilities" refers to the physical media that are necessary to provide a telecommunication service. For example, twisted pairs of copper wire, or fiber optic cables, are facilities. Private facilities are owned and used by a private organization. Public facilities are leased from a telecommunication carrier, such as a local telephone company or long-distance service provider.

fractional T1 (FT1)—FT1 is a telephone company service that provides data rates from 64 Kbps to 1.544 Mbps, by allowing a user to purchase one or more channels of a T1 link. If the customer needs less bandwidth than 1.544 Mbps, FT1 is a low-cost alternative to purchasing a full T1.

frame relay—Frame relay is a packet-forwarding WAN protocol that normally operates at speeds of 56 Kbps to 1.5 Mbps.

Integrated Services Digital Network (ISDN)—ISDN is a WAN technology used to move voice and data over the telecommunication network. ISDN operates at speeds of 144 Kbps to 1.5 Mbps.

interexchange carrier (IXC)—An IXC is a long-distance company that provides telephone and data services between LATAs.

Local Access and Transport Area (LATA)—LATAs are the geographic calling areas within which an RBOC may provide local and long distance services. LATA boundaries, for the most part, fall within states and do not cross state lines. Although, one state may have several LATAs.

Local Exchange Carrier (LEC)—A LEC is a company that makes telephone connections to subscribers' homes and businesses, provides telephone services, and collects fees for those services. The terms LEC, ILEC, and RBOC are equivalent.

local loop—A local loop is the pair of copper wires that connects a customer's telephone to the LEC's CO switching system.

modem—The term "modem" is a contraction for modulator/demodulator. Modems are used to convert binary data into analog signals suitable for transmission across a telephone network.

multiplexer (MUX)—A MUX is a device that transmits multiple signals over the same physical medium. Multiple signals are fed into a MUX and combined to form one output stream.

RS-232—RS-232 cables are used for connecting a computer to a modem. The RS-232 specification details the electrical and mechanical interface between the computer and modem.

Synchronous Optical Network (SONET)—SONET is an optical transmission standard that defines a signal hierarchy. The basic building block is the STS-1 51.84-Mbps signal, chosen to accommodate a T3 signal. The STS designation refers to the interface for electrical signals. The optical signal standards are correspondingly designated OC-1, OC-2, and so on.

T1—T1 is one of the T-carrier telecommunication standards for multiplexing digitized voice signals. A T1 channel operates at 1.544 Mbps. Each T1 channel (64 Kbps) was designed to carry a digitized representation of an analog signal (a telephone call) that has a bandwidth of 4,000 Hz. Originally, 64 Kbps was required to digitize a 4,000-Hz voice signal. Current technology has reduced that requirement to 32 Kbps or less; however, a T-carrier channel is still 64 Kbps.

T1 multiplexer (MUX)—A T1 MUX is a device that breaks an outgoing bit stream into T1 time slices, and reassembles incoming time slices into a continuous bit stream. It sits between a LAN and a DSU (or DSU side of a CSU/DSU).

time-division multiplexing (TDM)—TDM is a technology that allows multiple signals to travel over the same physical medium by guaranteeing each signal a fixed amount of bandwidth on a rotating basis.

virtual circuit—A virtual circuit is a communication path that appears to be a single circuit to the sending and receiving devices, even though the data may take varying routes between the source and destination nodes.

virtual private network (VPN)—VPNs use end-to-end network encryption to establish a secure connection from machine to machine. Each VPN is an encrypted data stream that travels over a public network, such as the Internet.

X.25—X.25 is a connection-oriented packet-switching network, public or private, typically built upon leased lines from public telephone networks. In the United States, X.25 is offered by most carriers. The X.25 interface lies at OSI Layer 3, rather than Layer 1. X.25 defines its own three-layer protocol stack and provides data rates only up to 56 Kbps.

Lesson 1—Point-to-Point WAN Services

A point-to-point link is a physical connection between two separated LANs or stations. An organization can create a point-to-point link by simply installing its own physical link (cable, fiber, or radio) between its sites. This approach is commonly used to connect buildings within an office park or campus; however, it is prohibitively expensive over a metropolitan area or wider region.

Thus, when companies need to connect two or more sites over a wide area, they typically use the previously installed facilities of the public-switched telephone network (PSTN). These links come in a variety of data rates, at costs that correspond to their speed and capability. This lesson introduces the most common point-to-point options found in WANs.

Objectives

At the end of this lesson you should be able to:

*   Name and describe the most common WAN point-to-point technologies

*   Explain the structure of the Digital Signal Hierarchy

*   Describe the main differences between T1 and fractional T1 (FT1) service

 **Key Point**

A point-to-point link directly connects two sites, using either analog or digital technology.

Common Point-to-Point Services

Point-to-point links come in a wide variety of data rates and costs, as summarized in the Point-to-Point Link Options Table.

Point-to-Point Link Options

Service	Link Speed	Equipment Needs
Dial-Up Analog	300 bps to 56 Kbps	Modem
Leased Analog	300 bps to 56 Kbps	Modem
DSL	Varies, up to 1.544 Mbps	DSL Modem
ISDN	128 Kbps to 1.544 Mbps	Terminal Adapter
FT1 (DS0)	64 Kbps to 1.544 Mbps	DSU and CSU
T1	1.544 Mbps	DSU, CSU, and MUX
E1	2.048 Mbps	DSU, CSU, and MUX
T3	44.736 Mbps	DSU, CSU, and MUX
E3	34.368 Mbps	DSU, CSU, and MUX
SONET	51 Mbps to 13.21 Gbps	MUX

POTS Analog Connections

Plain Old Telephone Service (POTS) was originally designed for analog voice transmission, not binary data. Although most of the U.S. telephone network is now digital, most of its local loops, that is, the wires that connect homes to the telephone company, are still analog.

Modems

We can transmit computer data over analog local loops, by using a modem to convert (modulate) data signals to analog signals. The term "modem" is a contraction of modulator/demodulator.

Modems are used in pairs, one at each end of a telephone line, as shown on the Modems and Dial-Up Networking Diagram. Each modem attaches to a computer or terminal by means of an RS-232 cable, the input/output (I/O) bus, or Universal Serial Bus (USB).

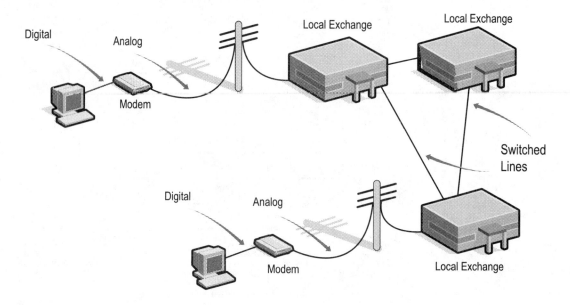

Modems and Dial-Up Networking

To transmit a message, the modem accepts digital data from the computer or terminal on the RS-232 interface. It modulates the telephone line by generating a signal with an audible frequency. The receiving modem demodulates the signal, generating digital data that is transmitted to the terminal or computer. Because the signal falls within the range of 300 to 3,400 Hertz (Hz), it can be transmitted across a telephone network as if it were a voice conversation.

Modems at either end of a connection must use the same modulation/demodulation protocol. A variety of standards have been published by the International Telecommunication Union - Telecommunications Standardization Sector (ITU-T) and International Standards Organization (ISO), so that modems from different manufacturers can be used together.

The simplest modem protocol represents 0s and 1s by switching the audible tone off and on, respectively. This technique can transmit data at a maximum of 1,200 bits per second (bps). More complex protocols can increase the effective data rate to 56 kilobits per second (Kbps). However, that speed is only possible if the local loop is in very good condition. Because that is not usually the case, it is rare for an analog modem to actually deliver 56 Kbps.

Dial-Up Lines

A dial-up line is a temporary point-to-point circuit between two nodes, set up across the switched telephone network. For example, remote workers who need access to a corporate LAN often use a dial-up connection to the company's modem. The Modems Dial-Up Networking Diagram illustrates dial-up connections.

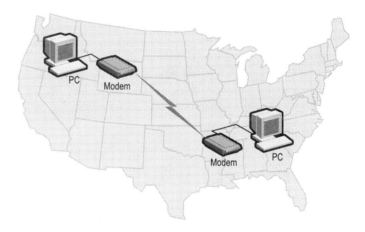

Modems Dial-Up Networking

Dial-up lines have the following characteristics:

- 2.4- to 56-Kbps transfer rates
- Any-to-any connectivity (one circuit at a time)
- Compatible modems at each end
- Transmission only after call initialization occurs
- Inexpensive

Leased Lines

Leased lines are also set up through the telephone network; however, these circuits are set up on a permanent basis. Leased lines are most appropriately used when traffic requirements are steady and uninterrupted service is important.

Advantages of leased lines over private lines include:

- Security of information

- Constant quality of service (QoS)

- Control of circuit

Disadvantages of leased lines are:

- Expense

- Increased equipment needs and costs associated with increased connections

Modems and analog lines are used by most home users and many small businesses. However, the top speed of a modem is limited to approximately 56 Kbps, which is barely adequate for most Internet access, painfully slow for large file transfers, and totally inadequate for video services.

DSL

Digital Subscriber Line (DSL) is a Physical Layer technology that provides high-speed service over the local loop. Telephone companies are using DSL to provide high-speed Internet access to homes and businesses, in competition with cable television operators.

A DSL line is a dial-up analog connection with a special DSL modem on each end of a twisted pair telephone line: one DSL modem at the subscriber's end, and one at the telephone company central office (CO). (A CO is also called a local exchange.) The DSL Connectivity Diagram illustrates this type of setup. A DSL connection creates three information channels:

- Downstream digital channel (carrying data from the CO to the customer).

- Upstream digital channel (carrying data from the customer to the CO).

- Analog POTS channel, separate from the two digital channels. Analog telephone service is uninterrupted even if DSL fails.

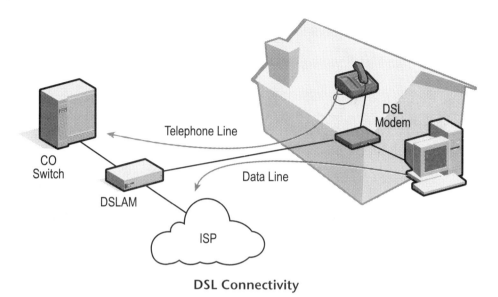

DSL Connectivity

DSL has the potential to deliver data at 160 times the speed of the 56-Kbps modems currently used for Internet access over POTS lines. The speed of a particular DSL installation depends on the type of DSL in use, thickness and condition of the copper wire, and user's distance from the telephone company's CO. Generally speaking, higher speeds are possible at shorter distances; however, performance is lower as the distance between the user and CO increases. (Beyond a maximum distance, DSL is not available at all.)

The various types of DSL include the following:

- Asymmetric DSL (ADSL)—ADSL provides downstream transmission rates of 1.544 megabits per second (Mbps) across up to 18,000 feet of twisted copper pair wire. ADSL is "asymmetric" because its downstream data rates are much faster than its upstream data rates. Asymmetric solutions are attractive because they match Internet user patterns. For example, to send a 100-kilobyte (KB) graphic image downstream, a World Wide Web (Web) user sends as few as 10 keystrokes upstream.

- ADSL Lite—This is a slightly slower version of ADSL that requires simpler equipment.

- Rate Adaptive DSL (RADSL)—RADSL overcomes the varying conditions and lengths of copper cable. RADSL has the same maximum data rates as ADSL; however, both downstream and upstream rates are adjusted to the physical wire conditions at the time of transmission. Therefore, RADSL can be very fast under good conditions; however, less fast under poor conditions.

- High Bit Rate DSL (HDSL)—HDSL offers both upstream and downstream speeds up to 1.544 Mbps, without the POTS line, over two wire pairs.

- Symmetrical DSL, or Single Line DSL (SDSL)—SDSL offers both upstream and downstream speeds of 384 to 784 Kbps, over one wire pair, including a POTS line.

- Integrated Services Digital Network (ISDN) DSL (IDSL)—This new hybrid technology uses ISDN technology to deliver 128 Kbps. Unlike ISDN, which supports both voice and data, IDSL is a dedicated data communication service only.

- Very High Bit Rate DSL (VDSL)—Although currently not commercially available, VDSL promises downstream rates of approximately 13 Mbps across up to 4,500 feet of wire, and higher rates across shorter distances. To achieve these data rates, VDSL will require fiber optic connections instead of copper pairs.

T-Carriers and E-Carriers

The T1 line (E1 in Europe) is a purely digital service. It is the basic unit of the U.S. digital telephone transmission system, and is the most popular type of dedicated leased line. T1 was originally designed for digital voice communications between telephone company COs (local exchanges). However, it has become a data transmission workhorse as well, because T1 is a Physical Layer technology. Several higher layer WAN protocols can use the basic transmission services of a T1 line.

Businesses with multiple locations now use T1 lines to connect their separate computer networks into single integrated systems. Companies with high volumes of Internet traffic often use T1 to connect their office networks to their Internet service providers (ISPs).

T1 Bandwidth

T1 was originally developed to carry 24 digitized telephone calls over four copper wires, using time-division multiplexing (TDM). TDM transmits multiple signals over the same transmission link, by guaranteeing each signal a fixed time slot to use the transmission medium. A T1 line essentially allows up to 24 different signals to take turns using the transmission line.

Sixty-four Kbps is needed to digitize one voice conversation, thus 1,536 Kbps of bandwidth is needed to accommodate 24 conversations. To keep the multiplexed signals separated, and help sort them out on each end, approximately 8 Kbps of bandwidth is added to carry control information, just as a train sets aside a seat for the conductor to keep everything organized.

Thus, a "full" T1 line provides a total bandwidth of 1.544 Mbps (although only 1.536 Mbps is usable by customers). That 1.544 Mbps is divided into 24 channels of 64 Kbps each (56 Kbps is usable). An E1 line works the same way; however, it carries 32 channels of 64 Kbps each, for a total bandwidth of 2.048 Mbps.

The T1 level of bandwidth was originally called "Digital Signal Level 1," or DS1. Thus, T1 and DS1 are equivalent terms. Each 64-Kbps channel is called DS0. The multiple channels of a T1 or E1 line provide flexible communication options. For example, a company can order a full T1, then use some of its channels for telephone calls and some for data.

DS Hierarchy

Just as 24 channels are multiplexed to form a single T1 line, multiple T1 lines are multiplexed to form higher capacity digital transmission lines. This method forms a complete Digital Signal (DS) hierarchy, as shown in the DS Hierarchy Table.

DS Hierarchy

DS Level	T-Carrier Level	Bandwidth	Number of Voice Channels
DS0	One channel	64 Kbps	1
N/A	FT1	n x 64 Kbps	1 to 24
DS1	T1	1.544 Mbps	24
DS2*	T2	6 Mbps	96
DS3	T3	45 Mbps	672
DS4*	T4	274 Mbps	4,032

*Rarely used.

T-carriers, such as T1 and T3, are used to connect LANs over extended distances. The Sample T1 Configuration Diagram shows how a T1 or T3 circuit could be used to connect two sites that each include a telephone system and data network. The same physical circuit can serve both types of systems, because each channel of a T1 or T3 line can carry either voice traffic or data traffic.

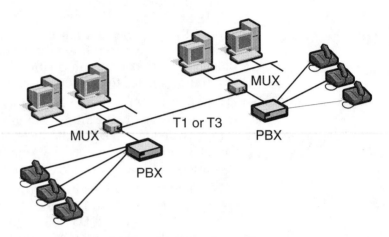

Sample T1 Configuration

FT1

Leasing a T1 line means paying for the entire 1.544-Mbps bandwidth 24 hours a day, whether it is used or not. FT1 lets you lease one or more 64-Kbps DS0 channels. You might, for example, lease only 6 of the 24 circuits to obtain an aggregate bandwidth of 384 Kbps.

FT1 is useful whenever the cost of a dedicated T1 is prohibitive. FT1 is not as efficient or flexible as switched services, however, because you are still paying to have the fraction of bandwidth you have leased available on a 24-hour basis.

Other than bandwidth, the main difference between T1 and FT1 service is control over the physical endpoints. Because we are not leasing an entire T1 circuit, we are sharing the T1 with other customers. Therefore, we cannot dictate the location of the other end of the circuit.

To understand this difference, think of the difference between chartering a bus and buying a single ticket. Buying a T1 is like hiring the whole bus. When you rent the whole vehicle, the bus will pick you up at your door and take you all the way to your destination. In contrast, buying an FT1 is like buying a ticket on a bus.

Many others will share the ride with you, thus everyone must get on and off the bus at a bus station.

In the case of an FT1, the "bus station" is a telephone company CO. There, the remote end of each FT1 circuit terminates in a device called a "digital access cross-connect switch (DACS)." In the DACS, the telephone company has a network of T1 interconnects, where FT1 channels get on and off the T1.

Due to the one-end nature of FT1, a separate FT1 circuit must be leased between each network site and its nearest CO. In contrast, we need only lease one T1 circuit between each pair of nodes. For this reason, as the size of the fraction increases, FT1 eventually becomes more expensive than a full T1.

T1 and FT1 circuits are useful WAN options because they offer adaptable bandwidth at essentially fixed costs within a metropolitan area. T1-capable routers and bridges typically support one or more T1 circuits, and automatically make connections with other routers or bridges in the network.

Customer Premise Equipment for T-Carriers

As we have seen, each type of physical transmission medium requires a particular type of equipment to generate and receive signals. For example, on a LAN, each computer needs a network interface card (NIC). To transmit digital data over an analog telephone line, a computer needs a modem. And, to connect a network to a T1 line, three devices are needed:

- T1 Multiplexer (MUX) breaks the outgoing digital bit stream into T1 time slices. (Each time slice represents one DS0 channel.) It also converts an incoming multiplexed signal back into a continuous bit stream.

- Data Service Unit (DSU) converts the outgoing multiplexed signal into the signaling format used by the T1 line. It also converts incoming signals to the signaling format used by the customer's network. The DSU essentially reconciles differences in the way each transmission system represents a binary 1 or 0.

- Channel Service Unit (CSU) maintains the electrical circuit between the customer and telecommunication company, and detects basic transmission errors, including loss of signal. The CSU essentially functions as a repeater, regenerating and boosting both incoming and outgoing signals. When the telecommunication company sends special testing signals over the T1, the CSU also repeats those signals back to the telecommunication company CO, in a process called "loopback."

391

The T1 Connecting Equipment Diagram shows each of these functions as a separate device, and they can be purchased that way. However, the CSU and DSU are usually combined into a single device called a "CSU/DSU," or a T1 Service Unit (TSU). Both of these may also be included as part of a T1 MUX, or all three may be built into another WAN device such as a router. If you look back at the Sample T1 Configuration Diagram, the component marked "MUX" would represent all three of these functions combined in one box.

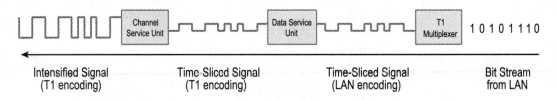

| Intensified Signal (T1 encoding) | Time-Sliced Signal (T1 encoding) | Time-Sliced Signal (LAN encoding) | Bit Stream from LAN |

T1 Connecting Equipment

ISDN

ISDN is a circuit-switched digital service that offers all the capabilities of a voice telephone line, as well as data features. Although ISDN has been around for a while, it is finally taking off as customers increase their demand for fast access to the Internet, desktop video, home office connections, and links between LANs.

Another key to ISDN's popularity is that it is an international standard. Therefore, digital telephone calls and data transmissions can be made to more countries across the globe when using ISDN.

How ISDN Works

An ISDN line uses two kinds of channels:

- B (bearer) channels do the real work of carrying signals. Each B channel carries 64 Kbps, and an ISDN line may have either 2 or 23 B channels.

- The D channel carries control information that organizes the B channels. Each ISDN line has one D channel.

BRI

ISDN-Basic Rate Interface (BRI) is a circuit-switched digital service that can be carried over a single pair of copper wires, which makes it attractive to home users and small businesses. ISDN-BRI consists of two B channels of 64 Kbps each, plus one D channel of 16 Kbps, as illustrated on the ISDN-BRI Channels Diagram.

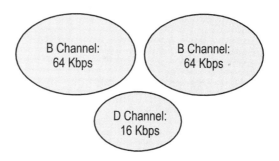

ISDN-BRI Channels

Each of the two B channels can carry digital voice, data, or video. Therefore, we can talk on one channel while sending computer data on the other, or use one channel for voice and the other for video. These two channels can also be combined or "bonded" into a single 128-Kbps channel.

The single D channel is used for control signaling. The D channel can also be used as a separate data channel for fax or packet data applications, such as Internet access. In addition, in many cases, you can now order just a D channel for low-speed, point-of-sale applications, such as communication links for credit card verification and cash register connections.

ISDN-BRI is often used for basic dial-up connectivity for home and small business connectivity, typically connecting individual computers or small LANs over the public switched network. This is shown on the ISDN Basic Connectivity Diagram.

ISDN Basic Connectivity

A device called a "terminal adapter (TA)" is required to attach a non-ISDN device to an ISDN network. The Home ISDN Connectivity Diagram shows how a TA is used to connect a telephone and personal computer (PC) to an ISDN-BRI line. If a voice conversation is not active, the PC can transmit information at the full 128-Kbps bandwidth. After a telephone call is initiated, the 128- Kbps bandwidth is shared between the telephone call and data transfer.

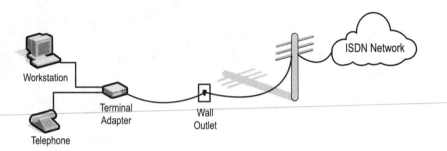

Home ISDN Connectivity

PRI

ISDN-Primary Rate Interface (PRI) is the industrial-strength version of ISDN, often used as a point-to-point connection between LANs, business telephone systems, or both. ISDN-PRI is a Data Link Layer technology that uses the Physical Layer services of a T-carrier. Thus, ISDN-PRI provides the same bandwidth as T1 service.

ISDN-PRI consists of 23 B channels of 64 Kbps each, plus 1 D channel of 64 Kbps. This setup is illustrated on the ISDN-PRI Channels Diagram.

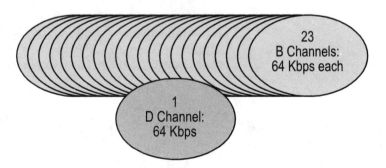

ISDN-PRI Channels

ISDN-PRI operates the same way as ISDN-BRI. Each B channel can carry voice, data, or video. The D channel is used for control signaling and can also be used as another channel for packet data applications.

Channel Bonding

Like T1 channels, 64-Kbps ISDN channels can be bonded, or combined to form a single large channel. ISDN channel bonding is performed by the D channel as part of its control signaling function. The technical term used for ISDN channel bonding is "non-facility-associated signaling (NFAS)." When channels are not bonded, the ISDN line is using facility-associated signaling (FAS).

NFAS offers many practical advantages to ISDN-PRI customers, because each D channel can control up to 20,000 B channels. A customer with 10 ISDN-PRI lines can designate 1 D channel to control all other B channels, and assign a second D channel as a backup to the first. The eight unused D channels can then be converted to additional B channels, providing even more transmission bandwidth.

This principle is even more powerful when combined with channel bonding. A customer with multiple ISDN-PRI lines can convert unused D channels to B channels, then bond the B channels to support high-bandwidth applications such as video conferencing, high-capacity data transfers, or high-speed Internet access.

SONET

Synchronous Optical Network (SONET) is a Physical Layer standard that provides rules for converting electrical signals to pulses of light, moving the light signals over fiber optic cable, and converting the signals back to electrical form at their destination.

Like the T-carrier system, SONET defines a method of multiplexing, as well as the bandwidth required to accomplish the multiplexing. Also, like the T-carrier system, each SONET signal can be multiplexed into a larger signal. Put it all together and we have the Optical Carrier (OC) hierarchy shown in the OC Hierarchy Table.

OC Hierarchy

SONET (OC) Level	Bandwidth	Number of T1 Lines	Number of 64-Kbps Channels
OC-1	52 Mbps	28	672
OC-3	155.5 Mbps	84	2,016
OC-9	466.5 Mbps	252	6,048
OC-12	622 Mbps	336	8,064
OC-18	933 Mbps	504	12,096
OC-24	1.2 Gbps	672	16,128
OC-36	2 Gbps	1,008	24,192
OC-48	2.5 Gbps	1,344	32,256
OC-96	5 Gbps	2,688	64,512
OC-192	10 Gbps	5,376	129,024

Notice that OC-1 is designed to carry the same number (672) of 64-Kbps channels as a T3 circuit. However, the bandwidth requirement is different for T3 (45 Mbps) and OC-1 (52 Mbps). The difference is because SONET uses more bandwidth for the control information necessary to keep its multiplexed signals in synch.

Notice also that, beginning with OC-24, we are no longer talking about bandwidth in Mbps. At OC-24 and above, SONET carrier lines handle gigabits per second (Gbps), or billions of bits.

SONET Rings

SONET is a ring network technology. It can be built as a true ring, using two parallel rings that carry signals in opposite directions. The same signal is sent simultaneously over both rings, thus both rings carry identical traffic. This redundancy ensures that if one ring fails, a signal will still get through.

A SONET network can also use a point-to-point physical topology. However, signals still flow in a logical ring.

SONET was originally developed to provide high-speed connections between telephone company CO switches across entire regions. However, the SONET standard also extends down to the office desktop. Today, telephone companies offer SONET connections to their large customers that need high-speed optical transmission in their business networks.

However, how can an individual business network connect to a public network that operates at Gbps data rates? The SONET architecture provides what are called "virtual tributaries" of channels, just as a large river is fed by smaller tributaries, and sometimes divides into smaller side streams. A SONET network uses MUXs to add and remove smaller signals from the main data flow. A MUX also cross-connects communication channels, so that one customer location can be connected to a communication channel at another customer location.

Activities

1. If you need 30 FT1 channels between Los Angeles and San Diego, it is easiest to order an E1 line. True or False

2. Leased lines offer less flexibility than dial-up services. True or False

3. A router can connect two remote LANs; however, a bridge is used to connect LANs located in a metropolitan area. True or False

4. LANs can be connected using both point-to-point networks and packet-switched networks. True or False

5. All dial-up lines are point-to-point connections. True or False

6. What is the top speed of a modem used for dial-up?

   _____

7. If a receiving modem demodulates an analog signal, what did the sending modem do to the original digital information?

   _____

   _____

   _____

   _____

8. List at least three characteristics of analog dial-up services.

   _____

   _____

   _____

   _____

9. List three advantages of leased-line services over dial-up services.

   _____

   _____

   _____

10. How many 64-Kbps circuits are available on a T1 line?

_____

11. If you lease FT1 service at a 10-channel capacity, how much aggregate bandwidth will you have?

_____

12. What equipment is used to connect a single PC to an analog line?

_____

13. What three components are required to connect a LAN to a T-carrier line?

_____

14. Draw a diagram illustrating a point-to-point network connecting two sites.

Extended Activities

1. Go to various Web sites and find information on 56-Kbps modems. Try **http://www.3Com.com**, **http://www.hayes.com**, and others. Discuss your findings.

_____

_____

_____

2. Go to various Web sites and find information on cable modems. Try **http://www.mot.com** (Motorola), **http://www.ibm.com**, **http://www.intel.com**, and others. Discuss your findings.

_____

_____

_____

3. Find and discuss information on the V.90 modem standard. What problems does this standard solve?

_____

_____

4. What is the effective top speed of a 56-Kbps modem? Why this limitation?

_____

_____

_____

_____

5. As a class, find all the terms introduced in this unit. Type or print each complete term (not just the acronym) on a small piece of paper, then place the pieces in a container. Have each student draw a term. (Add some terms from previous units if there are not enough terms for everyone.) Each person will research the term and informally describe what it means, providing examples where appropriate.

Lesson 2—Switched WAN Services

Point-to-point services are often used to connect two or three remote locations using long-distance facilities. There are advantages to using point-to-point services; however, at some point, it becomes more advantageous to use a switched facility.

As we learned earlier in this course, the number of point-to-point lines in a full mesh network increases sharply with the number of nodes. Switched services provide more flexibility in connecting WAN nodes. Dial-up or dedicated connections are still necessary to reach the switched network; however, after the switched network is accessed, you have any-to-any connectivity.

In addition, private lines are engineered to meet peak traffic rates. In other words, a network designer must buy enough point-to-point bandwidth to carry the network's highest expected level of traffic. During nonpeak times, however, unused transmission capacity goes to waste. Switched services can provide variable capacity, at rates that vary according to the bandwidth actually used.

Thus, the emphasis in wide area networking is shifting from dedicated networks to switched alternatives. Public switched networks, such as frame relay and asynchronous transfer mode (ATM), are highly reliable, fast, and efficient. This lesson introduces these services, which are the most popular switched WAN technologies used today. We will also introduce the structure of the Internet, which is becoming a popular wide area link for businesses of all sizes.

Objectives

At the end of this lesson you should be able to:

- Explain the advantages a switched service offers over a point-to-point service

- Describe the basic features of frame relay and ATM

- Name the types of traffic and applications that are best carried by each of these services

- Explain what a virtual private network (VPN) does

 **Key Point**

Switched service provides greater connectivity options.

Types of Switched Services

Packet-switched services fall into two broad categories: connection-oriented networks and connectionless networks. The Packet-Switched Network Options Table provides a summary of the most common switched services offered in networks today.

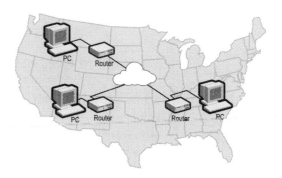

Packet-Switched Network Options

Service	Link Speed	Type of Service
X.25	300 bps to 56 Kbps	Connection-oriented
Frame relay	56 Kbps to 1.544 Mbps	Connection-oriented
ATM	155 Mbps to 2.48 Gbps	Connection-oriented
The Internet	Varies widely	Connectionless

X.25

X.25 was the first switched network service. An X.25 network, whether public or private, is typically built largely upon the leased-line facilities of the public telephone network. It uses a Network Layer address (telephone number) so that switches can route packet traffic over multiple paths.

X.25 only provides data rates up to a maximum of 56 Kbps. It is still used to switch packet traffic over a wide area. However, it is quickly being replaced by faster technologies, such as frame relay and ISDN, which were built upon the foundation of X.25.

X.25 is connection-oriented, and offers two types of service:

- Permanent Virtual Circuits (PVCs)—This is the X.25 equivalent of a leased line, statically defined and always available as long as a network is up. Unlike leased lines, however, more than one virtual circuit can share a physical link.

- Virtual Connections—This is the X.25 equivalent of a dial-up connection. A network establishes a connection on a virtual circuit, transfers packets until the application is finished, and then releases the connection.

The X.25 standard predates the Open Systems Interconnection (OSI) model. (The first version of X.25 was issued in 1976.) X.25 is now considered a connection-oriented Network Layer protocol because it provides error-free service to the Transport Layer. However, the overhead associated with the necessary error checking is proving to be unacceptable in today's highly reliable digital networks.

Frame Relay

Frame relay is a connection-oriented packet-switched network service that works at the Data Link Layer. A frame relay network carries traffic over virtual circuits.

The term "frame" is used because frame relay builds data frames and can asynchronously multiplex these frames from multiple virtual circuits (endpoints) into a single high-speed data stream. The term "relay" is used because each frame relay device forwards the frames as they move through the network without examining the frame's payload or demultiplexing the data stream.

Logically, a frame relay is an electronic switch or switches running frame relay software. Physically, it is a box that connects to three or more high-speed links, and routes data traffic between them. The Frame Relay Diagram illustrates the operation.

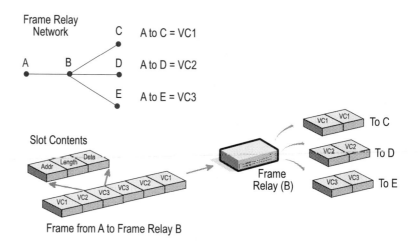

Frame Relay

Assume that virtual circuits have been established as shown on the diagram: VC 1 from MUX A to MUX C, VC 2 from MUX A to MUX D, and VC 3 from MUX A to MUX E. All three circuits flow through Frame Relay B.

Next, assume data for all three circuits flows into MUX A. The MUX places them into the frame, storing an address and length with the data. (This diagram was simplified by showing all data the same length.) The frame is transmitted from MUX A to MUX B. MUX B must demultiplex the frame and then create frames to be sent to MUXs C, D, and E.

Another view of a similar network is shown on the Frame Relay Network Diagram. Here routers feed a frame relay network. VC1 could be a path from Router 1 to Router C. VC 2 could be a path from Router 1 to Router D, and VC3 could be a path from Router 2 to Router E.

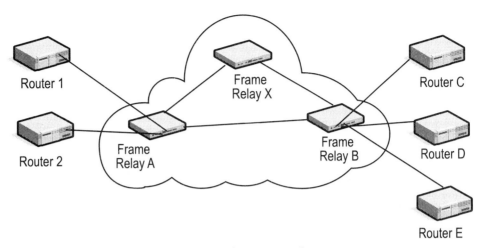

Frame Relay Network

The device that attaches a LAN to a frame relay network encapsulates each LAN data frame or packet inside a frame relay frame before sending it over the frame relay network. This is shown on the Frame Relay Encapsulation Diagram.

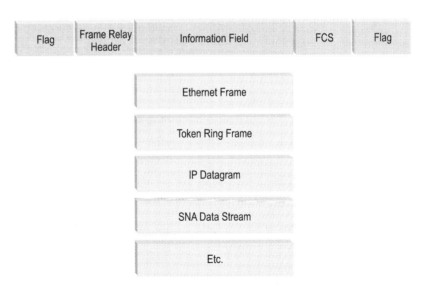

Frame Relay Encapsulation

At the other end of the network, the receiving device decapsulates the frame relay frame and sends the data toward its destination.

**Frame Relay
Characteristics**

The significant frame relay characteristics are as follows:

- Bandwidth up to T1—Frame relay typically uses T1 as the Physical Layer service. (The switches are connected by T1 lines.) Therefore, a frame relay virtual circuit can provide bandwidth up to approximately 1.5 Mbps.

- Fault tolerance—Frame relay switches can monitor network status and take corrective action when necessary, such as rerouting traffic into new virtual circuits. Typical private lines do not have this capability.

- Connection-oriented service—All data in the same virtual circuit travels over the same physical path for the duration of a transmission (unless one of the switches fails or some other network problem occurs).

- No end-to-end error detection or correction—A frame either makes it across the network or it does not. A frame relay switch discards damaged frames without notifying the sender or receiver. It assumes the physical links are reliable, and leaves error recovery to higher layer protocols such as Transmission Control Protocol/Internet Protocol (TCP/IP).

- Bandwidth on demand—Frame relay does not require that a link be up and dedicated at all times. Rather, it uses bandwidth only when there is data to be sent. Other, more traditional WAN transports, such as T1, use TDM, which requires dedicated bandwidth. Thus, a TDM service must be up and running even during times when the network is passing no data.

Most local and long-distance carriers offer frame relay, which was designed to handle various types of LAN traffic. It is ideal for sending data over a wide area because of its speed and flexibility. However, its variable-length frames are not well suited for voice or video, which require a steady data stream.

Frame Relay Implementation

To set up a private frame relay network, a corporation must install a frame relay switch at each site, then connect pairs of switches with point-to-point connections, such as T1 lines. The end of each T1 terminates at a customer's CSU/DSU. The DSU connects directly to the frame relay switch, which connects to the customer's network at each site.

Many corporations prefer to simply access a public frame relay network. To do this, an organization purchases a frame relay access device (FRAD), or installs a software upgrade to a router or bridge to allow that device to generate frame relay frames. The company then sets up a dedicated line (often a T1) between its CSU/DSU and the telecommunication carrier's nearest frame relay switch. The corporation can then subscribe to the frame relay service, usually from a telecommunication carrier.

ATM

ATM is an international standard for a high-speed, connection-oriented, cell-switching technology. ATM operates at both the Physical and Data Link Layers of the OSI model to transmit voice, video, and data across LANs, MANs, and WANs.

ATM transmits data in units called "cells." A cell is essentially the same as a packet, because it consists of data plus a protocol header. However, a cell is always the same size (53 bytes for ATM), while the size of a packet can vary.

The ATM Network Diagram illustrates an ATM "cloud" network. Similar to a frame relay network, an ATM network consists of a number of switches that provide virtual circuits between multiple inputs. ATM switches forward data very quickly, and the fiber optic links that usually connect ATM switches operate at 155 Mbps.

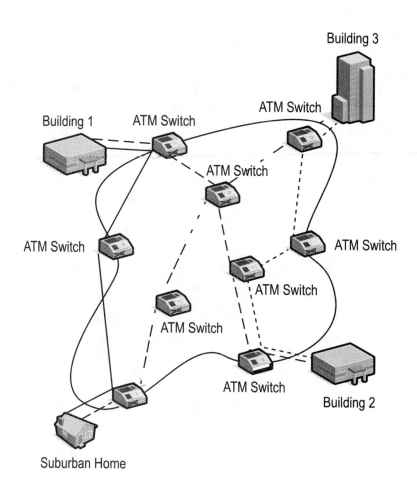

ATM Network

Fiber optic transmission is not the only Physical Layer technology that ATM runs over. ATM is media-independent, because it is not tied to any particular Physical Layer. However, most implementations of ATM use high-speed optical transmission to get the full benefits of this technology.

The Development of ATM

In the mid-1980s, telecommunication researchers began to investigate technologies that would serve as the basis for the next generation of high-speed voice, video, and data networks. The result of this research was the development of Broadband ISDN (B-ISDN) standards. B-ISDN was designed to support subscriber services that require both constant and variable bit rates. These services include data, voice, video, imaging, and multimedia applications. The ultimate goal of B-ISDN is to replace the current public network infrastructure and become the universal network of the future. ATM is the foundation on which B-ISDN is to be built.

Transfer Modes

A transfer mode specifies a method of transmitting, multiplexing, and switching data in a network. Three transfer modes were considered as possible candidates for B-ISDN, including:

- Synchronous Transfer Mode (STM)—"Synchronous" means that data communication is organized by a microprocessor clock; a receiving node can detect the beginning and end of a signal because signals start and stop at particular times. Services that use STM, such as T1/E1, divide each transmission frame into a series of time slots, and then allocate particular time slots to each user.

  STM is ideal for transmission of voice and video, because it provides a constant-bit-rate service. In contrast, data transmissions are typically bursty, because a user is idle for relatively long periods of time between short periods of intense data-transfer activity. STM is inefficient for data communications because the same time slot in each frame is reserved for a particular user, regardless of whether the user has data to transmit. When a user is idle, the time slot is wasted, because STM does not reassign unused time slots to other users.

- Packet Transfer Mode (PTM)—In a PTM network technology, such as Ethernet or frame relay, data is broken into variable-size units of data (packets, datagrams, or frames). Each unit contains both user data and a header that provides information for routing, flow control, and error correction. Instead of establishing a dedicated physical connection between the source and destination station, the network relays packets from one node to another, often in multiple parallel paths, until they reach their final destination.

PTM is excellent for bursty data applications because a station only consumes bandwidth when it needs to transmit data. When a station is idle, its share of network bandwidth can be used by other stations. However, PTM does not provide the guaranteed network access required by constant-bit-rate applications such as voice or video.

- ATM—ATM combines the strengths of STM (constant transmission delay and guaranteed capacity) and PTM (flexibility and ability to handle intermittent traffic) in a single high-speed transfer mode that allows voice, video, and data applications to run across a single integrated network.

ATM Characteristics

There are several important characteristics of ATM as follows:

- Connection-oriented transmission—In an ATM network, a pair of source and destination nodes establishes a virtual connection before the source begins transmitting data. All cells transmitted between a pair of source and destination nodes follow the same virtual path. A later transmission between the same source and destination may follow a different path; however, the path will not change for the duration of the transmission. This approach improves overall transfer speed, and reduces delay, by making it simpler and faster to switch cells through intermediate nodes.

- Fixed-length cells—ATM organizes transmission by formatting data into fixed-size units called "cells." Each cell contains 53 bytes that are divided into a 48-byte payload (data) field and a 5-byte header. The use of fixed-length cells provides the steady data flow that multimedia applications require. It also allows switch hardware to be faster and simpler, by allowing the switch logic to be implemented in firmware instead of software.

- Efficient use of bandwidth—ATM's cell-switching approach allocates cells to applications only as needed. Thus, an ATM station only consumes bandwidth when it has data to transmit.

In computing, the term "asynchronous" usually means that data transmission is coordinated through start and stop signals, without the use of a common clock. However, ATM networks use "asynchronous" to describe how network bandwidth is assigned to user applications. ATM assigns network access to users based on demand, which means that locations in the synchronous data stream are assigned to users in a random or asynchronous pattern.

- No error correction—ATM does not support error correction or flow control on a link-by-link basis. This means that if a physical link introduces a bit error or is temporarily overloaded resulting in the loss of a cell, no corrective action is taken. An ATM network does not support a facility that allows the node at one end of a point-to-point physical link to request the retransmission of lost or corrupted cells from the node at the other end of the physical link. However, ATM typically runs over fiber optic facilities, which offer very low error rates. And upper layer protocols, such as TCP, can handle error correction and retransmission. Because an ATM network can concentrate on just switching cells and not worry about error correction, cell throughput at each switching node is substantially increased.

The Internet

The Internet is not a single WAN technology, like frame relay or ATM. Instead, it is a hybrid combination that uses most of the wide area transmission systems we have discussed thus far. However, we include it as a type of switched WAN solution, because many companies are now using the Internet as a wide area backbone. As the speed and reliability of Internet transmission increases, this trend is likely to continue.

The Internet is a global network of computer networks. Although the idea is simple, its implications are enormous. One of the main features of the Internet is its ability to allow dissimilar computer systems, and even networks of dissimilar systems, to communicate with each other by means of two common protocols: TCP and IP. These two protocols function as a common language that PCs, mainframes, and minicomputers can all use to talk to each other over the Internet.

The Internet could not function without additional standards that provide other details, from the structure of an electronic mail (e-mail) message to rules for building Web pages. Independent organizations govern the Internet by creating and updating these standards and protocols. However, no one organization or government owns the Internet as a whole.

Internet Structure	Internet services, like telephone calls, travel over the telephone network infrastructure. The Internet backbone is the relatively small number of high-volume, high-speed trunks owned by the major telephone interexchange carriers (IXCs). In addition, most countries have their own backbones, each connected to the other.

The Internet is arranged in an informal hierarchy. The biggest corporations, and the largest ISPs, connect their networks directly to this main transmission backbone. The big ISPs, in turn, provide access to smaller service providers and corporations, which in turn provide access to individual users and small businesses. We will discuss various types of Internet access in Unit 8.

Internet, Intranet, and Extranet

New Internet terminology emerges almost daily. One source of confusion is the use of the terms "Internet" (capitalized), "internet" (not capitalized), "intranet," and "extranet."

- The Internet (capitalized) is generally considered the global TCP/IP network. In other words, the Internet connects the world.

- The term "internet" (not capitalized) refers to any interconnection of two or more networks, when the connection uses TCP/IP technology and protocols. This "internet" does not mean that a network is connected to the global Internet.

- An Intranet is a "private Internet." It is a private, internal network that uses Internet applications, tools, and protocols. However, it is designed for private use by company personnel. For example, many company intranets store commonly used information as Web pages, and their employees use Web browsers to retrieve and view the documents.

- An Extranet includes both Internet and intranet capabilities. It is a private intranet shared between closely aligned organizations. While it is external to each organization, it is not available to the general public. For example, a manufacturing company might work closely with a parts supplier for a specific product. Information about parts inventories could be stored in an extranet accessible to both companies.

VPNs

Data packets move across the Internet by being forwarded from one network's router to another until they reach their destinations. Because Internet traffic can be intercepted by any router that forwards it, basic Internet transmission is inherently insecure. To ensure privacy, companies that use the Internet as a WAN backbone often set up a VPN.

A VPN is a connection, set up over a shared network, that behaves like a dedicated link. VPNs use end-to-end network encryption to establish a secure connection from machine to machine. Many encrypted data streams travel over the same public network, such as the Internet, each in a separate secure "envelope" formed by different encryption/key combinations.

The Internet is still not well suited to the time-sensitive traffic that ATM handles so well. However, a company can enjoy a great deal of flexibility with a VPN, because traveling workers and home-officed employees can use their normal Internet connections to access the corporate network.

Activities

1. WANs are shifting away from switched services and increasingly using dedicated network services. True or False

2. Frame relay networks use ATM as the Physical Layer service. True or False

3. In a WAN with many nodes, a frame relay network is more cost effective because it uses fewer lines than a T1 mesh. True or False

4. ATM is a connectionless service. True or False

5. A common ATM link speed is _____ Mbps.

6. Describe the difference between a point-to-point network and a switched network.

   _____

   _____

   _____

   _____

7. How is frame relay similar to an ATM network? How do they differ?

   _____

   _____

   _____

   _____

8. What is a VPN and why is it necessary?

   _____

   _____

   _____

   _____

9. Draw a T1 mesh network that connects seven geographically dispersed offices. There are LANs on the other side of the routers at all locations. Remember, a mesh network connects the networks to all the other networks in a point-to-point topology. How many T1 lines are being used?

10. If those seven offices were connected by a frame relay network, how many T1 lines would be necessary?

Extended Activities

1. Visit the Frame Relay Forum site at **http://www.frforum.com**. What is the latest news about this technology?

   _____

   _____

   _____

2. Visit the ATM Forum site at **http://www.atmforum.com**. What is the latest news at this site?

   _____

   _____

   _____

Lesson 3—Choosing WAN Products and Services

How do we decide what WAN service is best to connect two or more LANs? As with most technology decisions, cost and performance are critical factors when selecting WAN facilities. However, there are many other factors to consider, which makes the process of choosing a WAN technology very complex. This decision is complicated by the fact that there are many service providers, and the range of offerings and prices vary widely.

This lesson introduces some of the most important factors a WAN designer must consider when choosing a transmission service, or combination of services.

Objectives

At the end of this lesson you should be able to:

- Compare the cost and performance of WAN services

- Calculate file transfer times for various data rates

- Discuss some of the factors to consider when choosing a WAN solution

 **Key Point**

A WAN must provide the greatest throughput at the lowest cost, while meeting other key requirements.

The Many Trade-Offs of WAN Design

Earlier in this course, we learned that there is no single best type of LAN cable, Data Link protocol, or internet working device. That principle applies to WANs as well. The choice of a WAN technology depends on a combination of many factors. Some of these factors are more important to some organizations than others, which makes each WAN design a highly customized solution. A few of the most important factors that influence a WAN technology decision include:

- Number of nodes—A switched network is an obvious choice when many nodes must be interconnected. However, to use a switched service, each of those sites must have a point-to-point connection to the switched cloud. Thus, if only a few sites must be interlinked, it may make better sense to connect them with dedicated links.

- Location of nodes—If a node is located far from the switched network, it may be cheaper to use a dedicated line to link that site to another part of the network.

- Private versus public—Deciding between a public and private network is one of the first decisions a WAN designer must make. A private network is built with dedicated leased lines, such as T1, or privately owned transmission media, such as a fiber optic line between two buildings. A public network is implemented over a public telecommunication switching system. Most large WANs combine the two to create a hybrid network. This is why a WAN designer must evaluate the public switched telephone network services side by side with private services.

- Type of traffic—File transfers and "bursty" traffic, such as Web interaction, is well suited to packet networks, such as frame relay, and connectionless systems, such as the Internet. However, multimedia applications, such as video conferencing or digitized telephone traffic, require consistent and predictable transmission technology, such as ATM.

- Availability—Not all WAN technologies are available everywhere. For example, even FT1 local access is not available in all metropolitan areas. In many cases, government regulations dictate what services a telecommunication company may offer and where. Simple economics also dictates that expensive services must go where the most customers are, in large cities and developed countries.

- Security—For most businesses, standard encryption systems and VPNs provide enough security to use public switched networks. However, some organizations may need the additional security provided by private leased lines or lines that they own themselves.

- Reliability—Some WAN technologies are more reliable than others. For example, in crowded city centers, connecting buildings with short-range infrared links is much cheaper than arranging rights of way and digging up a street to install new cable or fiber. However, infrared transmission is often disrupted by heavy rain, fog, or snow. If only low-priority traffic crosses that link, occasional disruptions may be acceptable. However, if a mission-critical application must run over a vulnerable link, then a backup link must be in place to take up the slack.

- Redundancy and fault tolerance—To increase the reliability and fault tolerance of a WAN, designers usually provide redundant links that use different technologies or physical paths. This ensures that a problem that affects the primary link does not also affect the secondary link. Thus, a good backup to a fog-bound infrared link might be a dial-up ISDN line.

  FT1 services provide designers the ability to divide traffic among different paths. For example, instead of concentrating traffic over a single 24-circuit T1, a designer can purchase two 12-circuit FT1s that travel over different routes. For even more disaster recovery protection, a designer can buy the two FT1 services from two different carriers.

- Cost versus performance—WAN links are the most expensive type of network connections. Thus, in addition to considering all of these points, a WAN designer must try to get the highest throughput and best performance for the lowest cost. The rest of this lesson focuses on the vital trade-off of cost and performance.

Cost

When a WAN link is implemented over public facilities, its cost depends on the type of service it offers. The price of switched services, such as frame relay, varies according to the volume of data the network carries. Dedicated links, such as T1, are leased for a flat fee.

One of a designer's challenges is determining cut-over costs between public and private line services. For example, a full T1 circuit can become economical when a business has grown to need 5 to 10 dial-up lines or FT1 circuits. The relatively low cost of T1 service (compared to other WAN services) is often a major factor in network planning. It is tempting to link many sites with T1 facilities simply because of the low marginal costs for full T1 networking.

When evaluating the cost of a WAN service, it is important to consider the total cost of a particular technology, including:

- Equipment—A low price for a link may be offset by the need to buy expensive devices to use it.

- Maintenance—For financial reasons, some companies prefer to own as much of their communication equipment as possible. However, ownership also requires ongoing maintenance and upgrades. Thus, many companies find it worth the expense to subscribe to a switched service, and let the telecommunication company worry about repairs and improvements to network devices and transmission media.

- Management—The more control a company has over its WAN, the more experienced people it needs to keep it running. If a company is unwilling to hire experienced WAN technicians, or if those people are unavailable, a switched service can be an attractive choice. A switched service provider handles all of the details of configuring and optimizing the network, and can provide reports and statistics on a company's WAN usage patterns.

Performance

WAN links come in a wide variety of data rates. These are summarized in the Point-to-Point Link Table. Typically, as speeds increase, cost increases.

Point-to-Point Link

Technology	Data Rate	Physical Media	Application
Dial-up	14.4 to 56 Kbps	Twisted Pair	Home and Remote Low-Speed Access
Leased Line (Analog)	56 Kbps	Twisted Pair	Small Business Low-Speed Access
FT1	56-Kbps Increments	Twisted Pair	Small, Medium Business Internet Access Point-to-Point Networks
DSL	Variable	Local Loop	Home or Small Business
ISDN-BRI	128 Kbps	Local Loop	Home or Small Business
Satellite (DirecPC)	400 Kbps (downlink) 33.6 Kbps (uplink)	Radio Spectrum (downlink) Local Loop (uplink)	Small Business Moderate Speeds

Point-to-Point Link (Continued)

Technology	Data Rate	Physical Media	Application
Microwave	Varies, to greater than 250 Mbps	Radio Spectrum	Medium, Large Business Point-to-Point Networks
ISDN-PRI	1.544 Mbps	Twisted Pair, Optical Fiber	Medium Business Internet Access Point-to-Point Networks
T1	1.544 Mbps	Twisted Pair, Optical Fiber	Medium Business Internet Access Point-to-Point Networks
E1 (Europe)	2.048 Mbps	Twisted Pair, Optical Fiber	Medium Business Internet Access Point-to-Point Networks
T3	45 Mbps	Coaxial Cable	ISP to Internet Infrastructure Large Business
E3 (Europe)	34.368 Mbps	Twisted Pair or Optical Fiber	16 E1 Signals
OC-1	51.84 Mbps	Optical Fiber	Backbone, Campus, Internet ISP to Backbone
OC-3	155.52 Mbps	Optical Fiber	Large Company Backbone Internet Backbone
OC-24	1.244 Gbps	Optical Fiber	Internet Backbone High-Speed Corporate Backbone
OC-48	2.488 Gbps	Optical Fiber	Internet Backbone
OC-96	5 Gbps	Optical Fiber	Internet Backbone Telephony Infrastructure
OC-192	10 Gbps	Optical Fiber	Internet Backbone Telephony Infrastructure

Switched services provide more flexibility in connecting WAN nodes. Dial-up or dedicated connections are still necessary to reach the switched network; however, after the switched network is accessed, you have any-to-any connectivity. The Switched Networks Table summarizes the data rates offered by the most common switched services.

Switched Networks

Technology	Data Rate	Physical Media	Application
X.25	300 bps to 56 Kbps	Coaxial	Small Business Low Speeds
Frame relay	56 Kbps to 1.544 Mbps	Twisted Pair	Small to Medium Business
ATM	51.84 Mbps to 2.488 Gbps	Fiber Optic	Large Business
The Internet	Varies widely	Any (depends on ISP)	Home, Small Business, Large Business

Comparing File Transfer Times

These data rates clearly show which services are faster than others. However, without some first-hand experience with different types of connections, a speed figure alone does not tell us much about the performance a user can expect.

Thus, when comparing WAN services, it is often helpful to compare their performance on a common task. For example, assume a bank transfers many files between its two offices in the same city. These files average approximately 5 megabytes (MB) in size, thus a network designer could evaluate various WAN services by calculating the time each one would require to move 5 MB.

Bits vs. Bytes   As we have seen, network data rates are expressed in Kbps and Mbps. However, file sizes are expressed in KB and MB. Thus, before we can do the simple math to figure a file transfer time, we must first convert the file size into the same units as our data rate. We could use bits; however, kilobits (Kb) is just as useful.

Megabytes to Kilobits

First, let us remember the basic computer numbering system:

- One MB equals 1,024 KB.

- One KB equals 1,024 bytes.

- One byte equals 8 bits.

We can convert our 5-MB file to Kb:

5 MB * 1,024 KB/MB * 8 bits/byte = 40,960 Kb

If a data rate is already expressed in Kbps, then we are ready to calculate. For example, the time necessary for a 56-Kbps connection to transfer our file is:

40,960 Kb / 56 Kbps = 731 seconds or approximately 12 minutes

Megabits to Kilobits

If a data rate is measured in Mbps, it is a one-step conversion to Kbps. We can express the bandwidth of a T1 line in Kbps as follows:

1.544 Mbps * 1,024 Kb per megabit (Mb) = 1,581 Kbps

Now we can see how fast our T1 line can transfer that 5-MB file, assuming we use all 24 channels for the task:

40,960 Kb / 1,581 Kbps = 25.9 seconds

Signaling Overhead

In the last example, we assumed that the entire capacity of a T1 line (1.544 Mbps) would be used to transfer the file. However, as we learned earlier in this unit, some of a T1's bandwidth is used for control signaling.

Thus, when comparing WAN services, it is important to know the effective throughput of each type of connection. Even if a technology offers an impressive data rate, we must remember that not all of that bandwidth is available for our use.

ATM is a good example of this principle. Each 53-byte ATM cell carries 48 bytes of "real" data. The other 5 bytes are used by the cell header. Thus, roughly 9 percent of ATM's bandwidth is unavailable for real traffic.

Activities

1. Point-to-point services are used when you require more flexibility in connecting WAN nodes. True or False

2. Services like frame relay and ATM are used in both private and public networks. True or False

3. A frame relay network can operate at OC-48 speeds. True or False

4. Match each service with a speed from the list below.

    a. OC-3

    b. T3

    c. OC-48

    d. T1

    e. Dial-up analog

    f. ISDN-BRI

    45 Mbps

    128 Kbps

    2.488 Gbps

    56 Kbps

    1.544 Mbps

    155.52 Mbps

5. Using the method shown in this lesson, calculate the time needed to transmit a 15-MB file using the following link speeds:

    a. 56 Kbps _____

    b. ISDN-BRI (both B channels) _____

    c. T1 _____

    d. T3 _____

    e. OC-3 _____

Extended Activities

1. Break into focus groups.

    a. List the benefits and drawbacks of private versus public networks.

    _____

    _____

    _____

    _____

    b. List some advantages of a hybrid network.

    _____

    _____

    _____

    _____

    c. What sort of requirements would lead a company to choose an ATM network (more expensive option) over a frame relay network?

    _____

    _____

    _____

    _____

2. Determining Telecommunications Bandwidth Requirements:

The following table lists options available in a typical WAN arrangement.

Service Type	Line Speed	Equipment
4.8 Analog	4,800 bps	Modem
9.6 Analog	9,600 bps	Modem
14.4 Analog	14,400 bps	Modem
28.8 Analog	28,800 bps	Modem
19.2 Analog	19,200 bps	Modem
56 K DDS	56,000 bps	CSU/DSU
FT1	336 Kbps	CSU/DSU or MUX
T1	1.544 Mbps	T1 MUX
T3	45 Mbps	T3 MUX

a. How long would it take to transmit a 200-KB file with each of these options?

Service Type	Line Speed	File Size	Total Bits	Time
4.8 Analog	4,800 bps	200 KB	1,600,000	
9.6 Analog	9,600 bps	200 KB	1,600,000	
14.4 Analog	14,400 bps	200 KB	1,600,000	
28.8 Analog	28,800 bps	200 KB	1,600,000	
19.2 Analog	19,200 bps	200 KB	1,600,000	
56 K DDS	56,000 bps	200 KB	1,600,000	
FT1	336 Kbps	200 KB	1,600,000	
T1	1.544 Mbps	200 KB	1,600,000	
T3	45 Mbps	200 KB	1,600,000	

b. How long would it take to transmit a 20-MB file with each of these options?

Service Type	Line Speed	File Size	Total Bits	Time
4.8 Analog	4,800 bps	20 MB	160,000,000	
9.6 Analog	9,600 bps	20 MB	160,000,000	
14.4 Analog	14,400 bps	20 MB	160,000,000	
28.8 Analog	28,800 bps	20 MB	160,000,000	
19.2 Analog	19,200 bps	20 MB	160,000,000	
56 K DDS	56,000 bps	20 MB	160,000,000	
FT1	336 Kbps	20 MB	160,000,000	
T1	1.544 Mbps	20 MB	160,000,000	
T3	45 Mbps	20 MB	160,000,000	

c. If the files above were compressed by 25 percent (75 percent of their original size), how long would it take to transfer the files across the network? What if the files were compressed by 67 percent (33 percent of their normal size)?

Summary

Unit 7 introduced the various types of transmission technologies used to connect LANs across a metropolitan or wider area.

Two primary types of connections are used to create WANs: point-to-point and switched services.

Point-to-point services include many Physical Layer services and protocols such as dial-up networking, ISDN-PRI, FT1, and T1. These point-to-point links connect networks in a secure fashion; however, they offer limited options for connectivity. If a WAN needs any-to-any communication among nodes, the number of point-to-point links increases sharply with the number of endpoints.

Switched services provide more flexibility than point-to-point services, and are used to connect many networks in a large WAN. Two of the most common WAN switching protocols are frame relay and ATM. These public switching networks can set up permanent or temporary virtual circuits between any combination of endpoints. Many companies are also using the Internet as a WAN backbone. While the Internet is inherently insecure, corporations can use encryption to create VPNs across the public network.

The type of hardware a WAN requires depends on the type of service used to provide connectivity. Analog connections require a modem at each end of the line. A T1 or FT1 line requires a CSU/DSU to convert signals from the format used by the telephone system to that used by a LAN. In addition, a router is usually placed between a LAN and its WAN link, to keep unnecessary traffic off the expensive wide area connection.

WAN services are significantly more expensive than LANs, and the cost of a WAN link is directly related to its bandwidth and quality. A WAN designer always tries to get the highest bandwidth at the lowest cost; however, one must also consider other factors that may be more important than price. Thus, many organizations use more costly services that provide greater security, or better support for time-sensitive traffic.

Unit 7 Quiz

1. What distinguishes a LAN from a WAN or MAN?

   a. Distance

   b. Use of public or private systems

   c. Use of routers, modems, and bridges

   d. All of the above

2. Which of the following is not a WAN connection type?

   a. Leased

   b. Public data

   c. Dial-up

   d. Ethernet

3. Which of the following is the unit of data transferred by an ATM network?

   a. Frame

   b. Packet

   c. Cell

   d. Message

4. Which of the following is another name for a CO?

   a. Local exchange

   b. PBX

   c. Local loop

   d. MUX

5. Which of the following is the primary difference between a public and private network?

   a. Who owns and maintains the network

   b. The distance between communicating devices

   c. The cost of the equipment

   d. The number of nodes in the network

6. Which of the following devices are not used to connect a LAN to a WAN?

   a. Bridges

   b. Routers

   c. Modems

   d. Hubs

7. Which of the following WAN services usually provides the highest bandwidth?

   a. T1

   b. T3

   c. DDS

   d. SONET

8. Which of the following is a disadvantage to using modem technology?

   a. Cost

   b. Any-to-any connectivity

   c. Transfer rate

   d. Availability of equipment

9. FT1 might be used instead of T1 because of which of the following (choose two)?

   a. Cost

   b. Speed requirements

   c. Ease of use

   d. Equipment availability

10. ATM is better for multimedia because of which of the following?

    a. All cells are the same size.

    b. Cells are small.

    c. ATM runs over fast fiber optics.

    d. All of the above

11. Normally, what portion of a WAN is analog?

    a. Trunk lines between COs

    b. Cable between computer and modem

    c. Local loop between CO and customer site

    d. LAN

12. Microwave systems are often used instead of land lines because of which of the following?

    a. Right-of-way issues

    b. Security issues

    c. Speed issues

    d. Compatibility issues

13. Which of the following statements is usually true?

    a. Leased lines are the fastest technology in use today.

    b. T1 lines are no longer common in computer networking.

    c. The faster the technology, the higher the cost.

    d. The more expensive the technology, the more stable it is.

14. WANs are shifting away from switched services and increasingly using dedicated network services. True or False

15. Frame relay networks use ATM as the Physical Layer service. True or False

16. A frame relay network uses fewer lines than a T1 mesh, and is therefore more cost effective. True or False

17. Frame relay, unlike ATM, uses fixed-length frames. True or False

18. ATM is a connectionless service. True or False

19. Frame relay outperforms X.25. True or False

20. Technologies such as frame relay and ATM can be used in both private and public networks. True or False

21. It is more economical to run two 12-circuit FT1 lines than one full T1 line. True or False

22. A frame relay network can operate at OC-48 speeds. True or False

23. ATM requires fiber media to run. True or False

24. What is the total raw speed of each of the following link services?

    a. ISDN-BRI _____

    b. T1 _____

    c. DirecPC satellite downlink _____

    d. One FT1 fraction (one DS0) _____

25. List three types of point-to-point WAN link services.

    _____

    _____

    _____

26. List three types of packet-switched WAN link services.

    _____

    _____

    _____

Unit 8
Integrating the Course Elements

This unit reviews the major concepts presented in this course, and shows how they work together in several real-world situations.

We begin by walking through the process of building a small peer-to-peer network, like those used in many small businesses. We then discuss the upgrades and enhancements that are common in the transition from a peer-to-peer network to a client/server network.

You will also learn how one local area network (LAN) connects to another, with particular attention to Internet connectivity. We then bring all of these elements together by discussing how data flows within a workgroup, across a LAN backbone, and over a wide area link. You will see how many processes, protocols, and networking devices work together to move information between two computer applications.

Lessons

1. Building a Small Peer-to-Peer Network
2. Expanding the Small Network
3. Connecting Networks
4. Data Flow Across Networks

Terms

Address Resolution Protocol (ARP)—ARP is a protocol that allows a host to use a logical (network) address to obtain the hardware (NIC, MAC) address for a remote station. ARP is used only across a single physical network, and is limited to networks that support hardware broadcasts.

bridge—A bridge is a device that operates at the Data Link Layer of the OSI model. It can connect several LANs or LAN segments of the same media access type, such as two Token Ring segments, or different LANs, such as Ethernet and Token Ring.

broadcast frame—A broadcast frame is a frame addressed to all nodes on a network. The frame address is a special number that tells all nodes that receive the frame to process it.

client—A client is any program that requests a service or resource from another program, either on the same computer or a different one. This term is often used to refer to the computer that hosts the client program; however, a client program can also run on a computer that normally functions as a server. See server.

coder/decoder (codec)—A codec is a hardware/software device that takes an analog signal and converts (codes) it to digital format for compression and transmission. On the receiving end, the digital signal is put back (decoded) into the original analog signal.

common carrier—A company that must offer its services to all customers at the prices and conditions outlined in a public record is referred to as a common carrier.

default gateway—A default gateway is a router that provides access to all hosts on remote networks. Typically, a network administrator configures a default gateway for each node on a network.

Domain Name System (DNS)—DNA is the online distributed database system that maps human-readable computer names to IP addresses.

firewall—A firewall is a controlled access point between sections of the same network, designed to confine problems to one section. A firewall is also a controlled access between a private network and public network (such as the Internet), usually implemented with a router and special firewall software.

frame relay—A frame relay is a packet-forwarding WAN protocol that normally operates at speeds of 56 Kbps to 1.5 Mbps.

High-Level Data Link Control (HDLC)—A HDLC is a Data Link Layer protocol for point-to-point and point-to-multipoint communication. The HDLC protocol suite represents a wide variety of Data Link Layer protocols, such as SDLC, LAPB, LAPD, frame relay, and PPP.

hub—Also called a wiring concentrator, a simple hub is a repeater with multiple ports. A signal coming into one port is repeated out the other ports.

Hypertext Transfer Protocol (HTTP)—HTTP is the Application Layer protocol used to request and transmit HTML documents. HTTP is the underlying protocol of the Web.

Integrated Services Digital Network (ISDN)—ISDN is a WAN technology used to move voice and data over the telecommunication network. ISDN operates at speeds of 144 Kbps to 1.5 Mbps.

Internet—The term "Internet," capitalized, refers to the global internetwork of TCP/IP networks.

Internet Protocol (IP)—IP is a Network Layer protocol responsible for routing a packet (datagram) through a network. It is the "IP" in "TCP/IP."

Internet service provider (ISP)—Companies that provide Internet access to individuals and businesses are referred to as ISPs. ISPs typically provide a range of services necessary to provide corporate networks and other users with dedicated or dial-up access to the Internet.

Internetwork Packet Exchange (IPX)—IPX is a Novell NetWare's proprietary Network Layer protocol.

intranet—An intranet is a network that uses Internet applications, but is designed for use only by the personnel of a company or organization; that is, it is a "private internet."

local loop—A local loop is the pair of copper wires that connects a customer's telephone to the LEC's CO switching system.

modem—Modem is a contraction for modulator/demodulator. Modems are used to convert binary data into analog signals suitable for transmission across a telephone network.

NetBIOS Extended User Interface (NetBEUI)—NetBEUI is a Network and Transport Layer protocol designed to work within a single physical LAN. (It does not provide packet routing between networks.) NetBEUI is typically integrated with NetBIOS.

435

network interface card (NIC)—A NIC is a workstation or PC component (usually a hardware card) that allows the workstation or PC to communicate with a network. A NIC address is another term for hardware address or MAC address. The NIC address is a unique value built into the NIC.

peer-to-peer—Two programs or processes that use the same protocol to communicate and perform approximately the same function for their respective nodes are referred to as peer processes. With peer processes, in general, neither process controls the other, and the same protocol is used for data flowing in either direction. Communication between them is referred to as "peer-to-peer."

Point-to-Point Protocol (PPP)—PPP is an Internet standard communication protocol that offers support for multiple network protocols, data compression, host configuration, and link setup. PPP is based on the HDLC standard.

router—A router is a Layer 3 device, with several ports that can each connect to a network or another router. A router examines the logical network address of each packet, then uses its internal routing table to forward the packet to the routing port associated with the best path to the packet's destination. If the packet is addressed to a network that is not connected to the router, the router will forward the packet to another router that is closer to the final destination. Each router, in turn, evaluates each packet, then either delivers the packet or forwards it to another router.

Sequenced Packet Exchange (SPX)—SPX is a Novell NetWare's proprietary Transport Layer protocol.

Serial Line Internet Protocol (SLIP)—SLIP is not an official Internet standard, but a de facto standard included in many implementations of TCP/IP. It was originally developed for use over dedicated circuits or leased lines, and therefore does not include provisions for establishing a connection over the telephone network.

server—A server is any program that provides a service to a client program. This term is often used to refer to the computer that hosts the server program; however, a server program can also run on a computer that normally functions as a client. See client.

subnet—A subdivision or section of a network, where users are grouped logically based on their network address is referred to as a subnet.

switch—A switch is a device that operates at the Data Link Layer of the OSI model, using hardware addresses to forward frames between ports. Like a bridge, a switch can connect LANs or LAN segments of the same media access type, such as two Token Ring segments, or different types, such as Ethernet and Token Ring. Unlike a bridge, a switch dedicates the entire media bandwidth, such as 10-Mbps Ethernet, to each port-to-port connection.

Transmission Control Protocol (TCP)—TCP is a Transport Layer protocol that provides reliable, full-duplex communication between two software processes on different computers. TCP normally uses IP to transmit information across the underlying network.

virus—A virus is a self-replicating malicious program that spreads by attaching itself to a file. Viruses can spread quickly through a network, with effects that range from mildly irritating to highly destructive.

Lesson 1—Building a Small Peer-to-Peer Network

Peer-to-peer networks are very common. They are used to share resources between a small number of users, and do not rely on a network server. Generally, a peer-to-peer network contains 10 or less nodes, usually within a small business or home office. All popular desktop operating systems (OSs) have built-in capabilities for peer-to-peer networking, thus creating a small network is a fairly simple and straightforward job.

In this lesson, you will use standard Ethernet components and the Microsoft Windows 98 OS to build a small network. Follow the steps in this lesson for each computer that you want to connect to your test network.

Objectives

At the end of this lesson you should be able to:

- Build a small peer-to-peer network

- List the components necessary for operation of a peer-to-peer network

- Diagram a typical protocol stack that can be used to transfer information between two clients in a peer-to-peer network

 **Key Point**

Most desktop OSs have built-in support for peer-to-peer networking.

What You Will Need

To build your network, you will need several components:

- At least two computers, with OSs capable of peer-to-peer networking. In our examples, we will use Windows 98.

- An Ethernet network interface card (NIC) installed in each computer. The details of installation vary from one computer to the next, thus this lesson assumes a NIC is already in place in each machine, and that its software driver has been installed.

- Unshielded twisted pair (UTP) cable, with RJ-45 connectors on both ends.

- An Ethernet hub, at a speed that matches the NICs.

- One hub port for each computer in your network. To provide more ports by connecting two hubs to each other, review the information on hubs in Unit 6, Lesson 1.

Overview of the Process

In general, you will build your network by working your way up the Open Systems Interconnection (OSI) model. The Data Link Layer is already established because you (or someone else) installed the NIC and its driver. You will begin this lesson at the Physical Layer, by using cable to make the physical connections between computers. Then you will move up to higher layers by installing peer-to-peer networking software and the Transmission Control Protocol/Internet Protocol (TCP/IP) protocol stack.

Connect the Cables

If you only need to network two computers, you can use a single Ethernet crossover cable to connect one NIC directly to another (this is different than a standard Category 5 patch cable). However, your class will probably use a hub so that more computers can participate in the network.

Use one UTP cable to attach each computer's NIC to one port of the hub. This is demonstrated on the Peer-to-Peer Network Diagram.

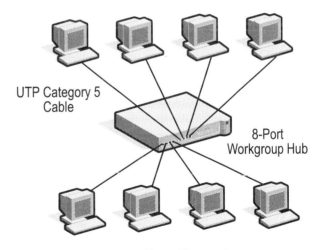

UTP Category 5 Cable

8-Port Workgroup Hub

Peer-to-Peer Network

If you have network-capable peripherals, such as printers, do not attach them to the hub. For now, only connect peer computers to the hub.

Now supply power to the hub. The hub is a repeater, thus it will not function unless it is plugged in.

Set Up Client for Microsoft Networks

Client for Microsoft Networks is an application that allows a computer to communicate with its peers over a network. All of your computer's network settings will be configured within this application, thus you must install and set it up first.

1. From the **Start** menu, select **Settings**, then **Control Panel**.

2. In the Control Panel, select **Network**. In the Network dialog box, shown on the Network Dialog Box Screen Diagram, the list of components should include your computer's NIC. If it does not appear in this list, see your instructor before continuing.

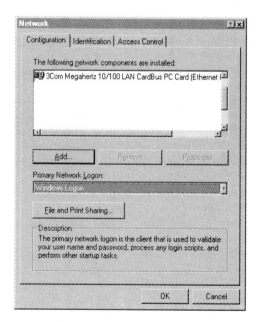

Network Dialog Box Screen

3. In the Network dialog box Configuration tab, click **Add**.

4. In the Select Network Component Type dialog box, highlight **Client**, then click **Add**.

5. In the Select Network Client dialog box, shown on the Select Network Client Dialog Box Screen Diagram, highlight **Microsoft**, then highlight **Client for Microsoft Networks**. Click **OK**.

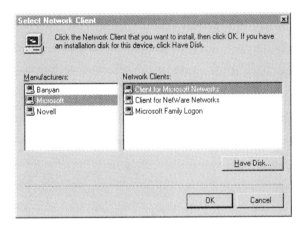

Select Network Client Dialog Box Screen

Note: You may be prompted to insert a disk or point to the location of an installation file. Your instructor will provide these.

Client for Microsoft Networks now appears in the network components list of the Network dialog box.

Network and Transport Layers: Bind Protocols to Each NIC

When you installed the Ethernet network driver for your NIC, the TCP/IP, Network Basic Input/Output System (NetBIOS) Extended User Interface (NetBEUI), and Internetwork Packet Exchange/ Sequenced Packet Exchange (IPX/SPX) protocols were installed by default. Now you must tell Client for Microsoft Networks which of these protocols you want to use. This process is called "binding" a protocol to the NIC.

1. In the Network dialog box Configuration tab, click **Add**.

2. In the Select Network Component Type dialog box, highlight **Protocol**, then click **Add**.

3. In the Select Network Protocol dialog box, shown on the Select Network Protocol Dialog Box Screen Diagram, highlight **Microsoft**, then highlight **TCP/IP**. Click **OK**.

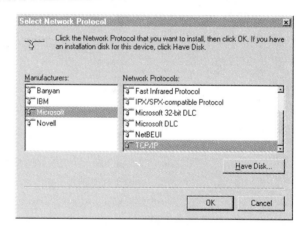

Select Network Protocol Dialog Box Screen

TCP/IP now appears in the network components list of the Network dialog box. It is also bound to the NIC installed in your computer. To verify this:

1. In the Network dialog box Configuration tab, highlight your NIC and click **Properties**.

2. In the dialog box for your NIC, click the **Bindings** tab. It should show that TCP/IP is now associated with the installed NIC. An example of this is shown on the NIC Properties Bindings Tab Screen Diagram.

NIC Properties Bindings Tab Screen

Note: Each peer computer in your network must run the same protocol stack. Bind all NICs to TCP/IP.

Network and Transport Layers: Configure TCP/IP

1. In the Network dialog box Configuration tab, highlight **TCP/IP** (bound to your NIC) and click **Properties**.

2. In the TCP/IP Properties dialog box, click the **IP Address** tab.

3. In the IP Address tab, select **Specify an IP address**. The fields for IP Address and Subnet Mask are activated.

The details of IP addressing and subnet masking are beyond the scope of this course; however, the basics are presented next so you will understand what you need to enter into this dialog box.

IP Addresses

Each computing device or "host" on a TCP/IP network is assigned a unique IP address. Each IP address is a binary number 32 bits long.

To make it easier for people to read and understand IP addresses, the addresses are often written as four decimal numbers, each separated by a dot. This format is called "dotted decimal notation." Each of the decimal numbers is the equivalent of the 8-bit binary number in one field.

For example, the following binary IP address:

10000001 00001111 00010001 00000011

the dotted decimal version of the same address is:

129.15.17.3

An IP address is divided into two parts: the right part identifies an individual host, and the left part identifies the network on which the host resides. Some addresses use 8 bits for the network portion of the address, and use the other 24 bits for the host portion. Other addresses use 16 bits for the network and 16 bits for the host, or 24 bits for the network and 8 bits for the host.

In this exercise, we will use an IP network address portion that is reserved for testing, or for local networks not connected to the Internet: 192.168.xxx.xxx. The "xxx" identifies the host portion of this address. You can insert any numbers there, as long as the number is between 000.001 and 255.254, and each computer uses a unique host address.

Note: For simplicity, we are not dividing this network into subnets.

Subnet Mask   The subnet mask is a separate 32-bit pattern that marks the network portion and host portions of an IP address. As you can see on the Subnet Mask Diagram, each bit of the subnet mask corresponds to 1 bit of the IP address. A "1" in the subnet mask means that the corresponding bit in the IP address is part of the network portion. A "0" in the subnet mask means that the corresponding IP address bit is part of the host portion. Subnet masks use dotted decimal notation just as IP addresses do.

	Network Portion		Host Portion	
IP Address	129	15	17	3
	1 0 0 0 0 0 0 1	0 0 0 0 1 1 1 1	0 0 0 1 0 0 0 1	0 0 0 0 0 0 1 1
Subnet Mask	255	255	0	0
	1 1 1 1 1 1 1 1	1 1 1 1 1 1 1 1	0 0 0 0 0 0 0 0	0 0 0 0 0 0 0 0

Subnet Mask

Assign IP Addresses and Subnet Masks

Now that you understand the basics of IP addresses and subnet masks, you can continue configuring TCP/IP.

1. In the IP address tab shown on the IP Address Tab Screen, enter the following address into the first three fields of the IP Address:

    192.168.0

    In the last field of the IP Address, enter a unique number between 1 and 254.

Note: Each computer in your network must have a different number in the IP Address field.

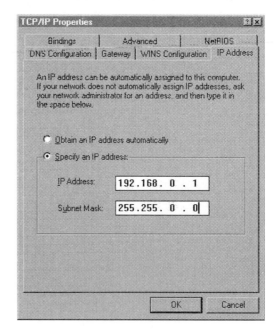

IP Address Tab Screen

2. In the Subnet Mask, enter the following address:

    255.255.0.0

Note: Each computer in your network must have the same number in the Subnet Mask field.

3. Click **OK** to return to the Network dialog box.

Upper Layers: Configure Workgroup and Resource Sharing

Thus far in this process, you have set up the first four OSI layers of your network:

- Physical Layer—Use UTP cable to connect each NIC to a hub port.

- Data Link Layer—Install the Ethernet NIC and its driver.

- Network and Transport Layers—Bind the TCP/IP protocol stack to each NIC, and assign each node a unique IP address.

Now that you have established the communication foundation of your network, it is time to configure the following two settings that allow Client for Microsoft Networks to interact with your applications and other network nodes:

- Assign each node a computer name and workgroup name

- Define access to your files or printer

Assign Each Node a Computer Name and Workgroup Name

Your computer's IP address uniquely identifies it to other machines. However, to help human users recognize your computer, you should assign it a common name.

1. In the Network dialog box, click the **Identification** tab. The Identification tab screen will appear as shown on the Identification Tab Screen Diagram.

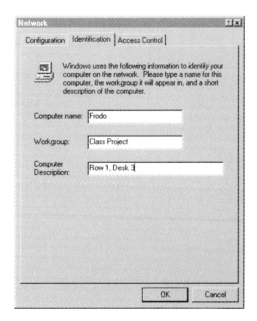

Identification Tab Screen

2. In the Computer Name field, enter a unique, easy-to-remember name that does not include spaces.

3. In the Workgroup field, give your peer-to-peer network a name. In a business environment, you might set up separate workgroups for Accounting, Sales, or other departments. For your class project, all computers must belong to the same workgroup.

Note: All computers in your peer-to-peer network must have the same name in the Workgroup field.

4. The Computer Description field is optional. It captures additional information that helps identify each computer.

Define Access to Your Files or Printer

In a Windows peer-to-peer network, you can decide whether to allow other users to access your hard drive or attached printer. However, you cannot assign different access rights to particular users or groups of users. This default level of control is called "share-level access."

1. In the Network dialog box, click **File and Print Sharing**.

2. In the File and Print Sharing dialog box, select both options, then click **OK**, as shown on the File and Print Sharing Dialog Box Screen Diagram.

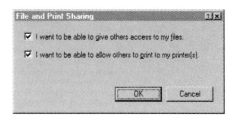

File and Print Sharing Dialog Box Screen

In the Network dialog box, the components list now includes a new entry called "File and printer sharing for Microsoft networks." With this component installed, you can define different types of access for each of your drives, folders, or printers. You can also set a password for any of these resources.

Virus Prevention and Detection

Viruses are destructive and self-replicating applications that are often disguised within an innocent-looking application, such as a game. When a user runs the application, the virus copies itself to the user's system, then performs the job it was designed to do. Some viruses only display a political message. Others erase entire hard drives. A single virus can infect an entire network within minutes, thus virus prevention software is essential for every node on a network.

Excellent applications are available to detect and eliminate viruses; however, all virus prevention programs are blind to new viruses that use new and unknown techniques. When a new virus is discovered anywhere in the world, the developers of virus control software quickly create a software plug-in that allows their application to recognize and eradicate the new threat.

A user can usually prevent problems by promptly downloading and installing each new "signature" file. However, some unfortunate victim must always be the first to discover a new virus. If you do not want that dubious honor, a few simple procedures will reduce the chance that you will get a virus:

- Install virus detection software and keep it up to date. As we just explained, software cannot protect against a radically new threat it cannot recognize. However, most viruses, even new ones, use the same well-known basic techniques.

- Once your software is installed, use it. It takes a little extra time to scan all incoming floppy disks; however, it is time well spent.

- Be wary of electronic mail (e-mail) attachments. Many of the most famous viruses of the past few years have been spread through e-mail systems. Once in a computer, a virus simply mails copies of itself to every entry in a user's e-mail address book. Thus, if you receive an e-mail with an attached executable file, even from a friend, do not launch that program until you verify what it is. If you are not totally sure of an attachment, simply delete the entire message. A virus is an application, thus it does not become active until a user runs it.

- Be wary of downloadable software. Reputable World Wide Web (Web) sites that provide free downloadable applications do everything they can to ensure that their content is virus-free. However, for all the reasons we have discussed, it is impossible to be totally sure. Some users who enjoy downloading programs and games set up a non-networked computer as a quarantine area. All new programs are tested on that platform before being used on the "real" system.

Most businesses are willing to install and maintain antivirus software; however, they do not want to spend the extra time and effort necessary to quarantine downloadable applications. Thus, many companies have rules that prohibit employees from downloading applications to the company network, or even bringing in floppy disks. Some companies, especially those who have had virus problems in the past, may even dismiss employees who violate those rules. At first, this seems overly harsh. However, when you consider that a single virus outbreak can cost a company thousands or millions of dollars, it is easier to understand that releasing a virus can be as costly as setting off a bomb.

Activities

1. Which of the following uses the computer name assigned within Client for Microsoft Networks?

   a. TCP

   b. IP

   c. Ethernet

   d. Users

2. Bob has a color printer that the other users of the peer-to-peer network want to occasionally use. However, Bob does not want to let Jane use the printer, because she often prints downloaded cartoons and digital photos of her grandchildren. When Bob configures his printer as a shared resource, he can specifically block Jane from accessing it. True or False

3. When you assign an IP address to a computer, why must you also provide a subnet mask?

   _____

   _____

4. What will happen if you disconnect a hub from its power source?

   _____

   _____

5. Diagram the protocol stack of a peer-to-peer network that uses TCP/IP. Also draw the structure of a frame on that network, showing all encapsulated headers.

Extended Activities

1. When your peer-to-peer network is set up and operating properly, practice sharing the following resources between peers:

    a. Folders

    b. CD-ROM

    c. Floppy drive

    d. Printers

2. Transfer files from one peer to another. In the case of a printer, print files to the print share.

3. Are there any other devices that can be shared? Discuss.

4. Even though File and Printer Sharing is enabled, you can restrict access to certain folders or drives. After you have set up your peer-to-peer network, confirm that you can access all of the other hard drives on your network. Then have one-half of the class restrict access to their hard drives by following these steps:

   a. In Windows Explorer, right-click the drive to be restricted.

   b. From the shortcut menu, select **Properties**.

   c. In the Properties dialog box, click the **Sharing** tab.

   d. In the Sharing tab, select **Not Shared**, then click **OK**.

   Have the other one-half of the class assign a password to their hard drives by selecting the Depends on Password option in the Sharing tab. Assign a simple password to each computer.

5. Now explore the network again. As soon as you have noted the changes in the network, have everyone restore full access and remove all passwords. Use a Web search engine and find utilities available for a peer-to-peer networking environment. Also try **http://www.download.com** and **http://www.shareware.com**.

6. Can a peer-to-peer network be constructed if two groups of peers are geographically separated? Explain.

   _____

   _____

   _____

   _____

7. From your experience with your peer-to-peer network, when do you think it would make sense to use a full-blown client/server network operating system (NOS) instead of a peer-to-peer network?

   _____

   _____

   _____

   _____

Lesson 2—Expanding the Small Network

As a network grows, it is usually necessary to provide additional options and services for both network users and administrators. As with most network issues, both software and hardware are generally required when a small network graduates to become a larger LAN.

A peer-to-peer network usually upgrades to a full client/server network operating system (NOS) when the network needs specialized servers. A full NOS is also necessary as the number of users grows, and administrators want finer control over user access rights.

Also, a steady increase in user traffic will eventually degrade network performance, just as too many cars on a highway create traffic jams. Thus, when a network grows beyond a certain point, a network administrator usually adds devices to segment the network and isolate traffic within workgroups. This lesson discusses both of these issues, which are common when a network outgrows its peer-to-peer architecture.

Objectives

At the end of this lesson you should be able to:

- Name and describe the most common types of dedicated network servers

- Explain why the function of a server should determine its position in a traffic isolation plan

 **Key Point**

When a peer-to-peer network grows, it often requires dedicated servers and a client/server NOS.

Servers and NOSs

At some point it becomes burdensome to use peer computers, and a dedicated resource may be required for both convenience and performance purposes, as illustrated on the Database Server Diagram.

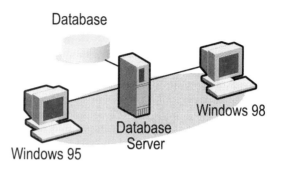

Database Server

Network servers, as the name implies, provide many different services to users of computer networks. Common types of network servers include:

- File servers
- Database servers
- Print servers
- Remote access servers (RASs)
- Web servers

File Servers

File servers contain application software and data files that are downloaded to workstations on request. A file server's job is to make sure that shared resources are accessed in an orderly, non-conflicting way. Working with application programs, servers ensure concurrent file admission when it is needed, and prevent it when inappropriate. File servers control access through a variety of NOS security mechanisms; NOSs vary widely in their ability to provide security.

Personal computers (PCs) and workstations become file servers with the addition of specialized software. Because of the heavy demands placed on file servers, they are designed for higher performance than ordinary workstations. Consolidating power, memory, and disk space in the server reduces workstation hardware requirements.

Database Servers

A database server application controls multiple access to a single shared data repository. In response to requests from various clients, the central database management application will retrieve, add, delete, or update records.

Unlike a basic file server, a database server must run the database management application that works with the database files. A file server is like a self-serve library, where users store files for simple retrieval. A database server is like a specialized research library, where all requests for information must be handled through a librarian who searches the collection and delivers answers.

Print Servers

A print server allows multiple clients to efficiently share a single printer. All print requests are sent to the print server, thus each user's computer is freed for other work. The print server prints each job in turn, and notifies each client when its print job has been completed.

Depending on the intensity of the traffic it must handle, a print server may be a special server platform or basic desktop computer. However, each may require third-party software. All software-based servers require central processing unit (CPU) cycles from the server platform, which affects performance. The Print Server Diagram illustrates this type of server.

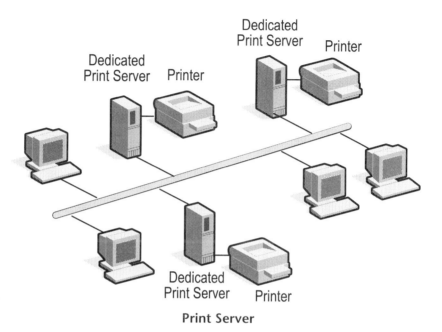

Print Server

A print server can improve the performance of the network's workstation nodes by freeing them to do other work. However, if the print server is turned off or fails, print services disappear until the machine is turned on again.

RASs

We create separate communication servers for many of the same reasons we use print and file servers. These servers, often called RASs, allow pooling of communication resources, such as modems and telephone lines. The RAS Diagram illustrates this type of server.

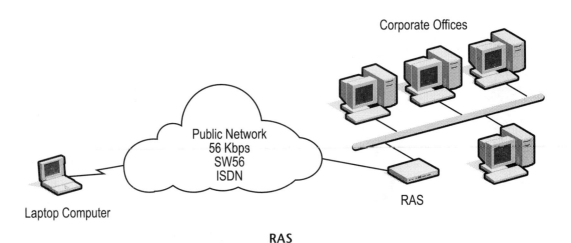

Corporate Offices

Public Network
56 Kbps
SW56
ISDN

Laptop Computer

RAS

RAS

A RAS server is also an important security feature for networks that allow dial-up connections from remote employees. The RAS computer acts as a receptionist or security guard, because it does not allow access to the main network until it has verified the identity and access rights of each user who dials in.

Like printing, communication has its own set of technical requirements. Multiple serial ports are usually needed to accommodate simultaneous connections from several users. Buffering and management of the communication link is necessary. Communications is inherently less reliable than printer sharing, thus some LAN administrators prefer to isolate this possible problem function on a separate server.

Web Servers

A Web server is a computer program that delivers documents to Web clients (browsers) that request them. When we use a browser to surf the Web, each hyperlink we click sends a request to some Web server, which then transmits the pages we see.

The same Web server applications are used to create private intranets, extranets used by close business partners, and publicly accessible sites on the Web. The degree of public or private access is the only thing that distinguishes intranets, extranets, and Web sites.

However, while the same software can be used for all of these, server hardware varies according to the volume and type of traffic the Web server handles. For example, if a mid-sized company's intranet provides a moderate volume of basic Web pages, its internal Web server probably does not need to be much more powerful than a good desktop machine. However, a popular public Web site that handles thousands of simultaneous requests must have extremely powerful servers that are specially designed for intense use. Large sites even share the workload across multiple identical servers.

Traffic Isolation

As we learned in Unit 6, it is often necessary to divide a growing network into physical segments to manage traffic more effectively. As performance becomes an issue, networks can be physically segmented with devices such as switches and routers. By dividing computers and servers into logical workgroups, and isolating the workgroups with such devices, the network becomes more efficient and overall network bandwidth is increased.

We have just discussed how a growing network often creates multiple servers to perform various functions. Some of these servers are specific to various groups or departments, while others are shared by the entire organization. This is shown on the Multiple Servers Diagram. For example, the intranet server and print server are used by all clients; however, the other two servers are each used by a different department.

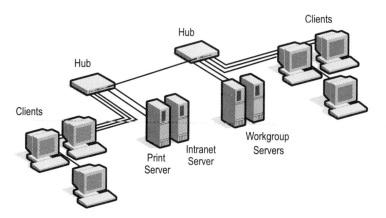

Multiple Servers

This network configuration provides all nodes equal access to the intranet server and print server. However, when a client communicates with its specialized workgroup server, all nodes receive that traffic as well. If each workgroup server handles many requests, the specialized traffic can degrade performance on the rest of the network.

Adding a Switched Backbone

In a typical migration path (upgrade), the network administrator ties the two hubs together with a switch, and attaches each commonly shared server to its own switch port. This divides the network into two logical workgroups, as shown on the Switched Backbone Diagram.

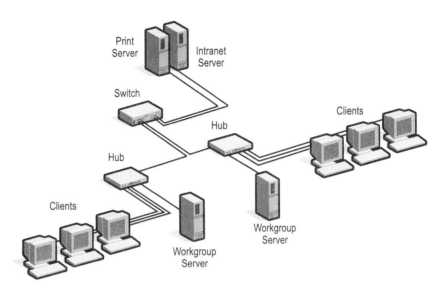

Switched Backbone

Now, when a client sends data to a server in the same workgroup, that traffic is isolated to that segment of the network. The information will not cross the switch boundary. Also, if a client in one workgroup accesses the intranet server or print server, that traffic will not be transmitted to the other workgroup.

A router may also be used in this configuration, instead of a switch. Like a switch, a router will isolate traffic in individual workgroups when information is being sent between members of the same workgroup. Likewise, information destined for the intranet server or print server will not be visible in the other workgroup. However, a router will not forward broadcast traffic out all ports, as a switch will.

Wireless Bridges   A small network may also begin the process of segmentation when it adds wireless access for its mobile nodes. As we learned in Unit 5, a wireless access point forwards traffic between the hard-wired network and mobile nodes. This arrangement is shown on the Wireless Access Point Diagram.

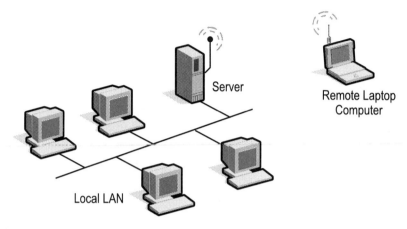

Wireless Access Point

Some wireless access points function as a Layer 2 bridge, thus the hard-wired network forms one workgroup, while the wireless nodes form another.

Activities

1. A small group of users running a popular desktop OS have outgrown their peer-to-peer network and wish to upgrade to a client/server environment. In addition to transferring company files over to a server, the users also require access to two laser printers, a high-end plotting device, and the Internet. Some of the users have requested that remote access from their home PCs be available on the new system. The printers and plotter all have a built-in TCP/IP stack and Ethernet NIC. They run a handful of standard applications, such as word processing, spreadsheets, and e-mail, as well as two custom applications for the plotting device.

   Draw a network diagram illustrating the new client/server system, making sure all user requirements are fully met. Show the position of any new devices you think this network needs. Assume five users currently, with growth to four more users in the next six months.

   Label all the components, including all hardware and software. Include the server OS as well as the clients' OS. Be sure to label the Internet access device as well. Note any additional software installed at the server and clients, such as networking software. Be thorough.

2. Consider the following network diagram:

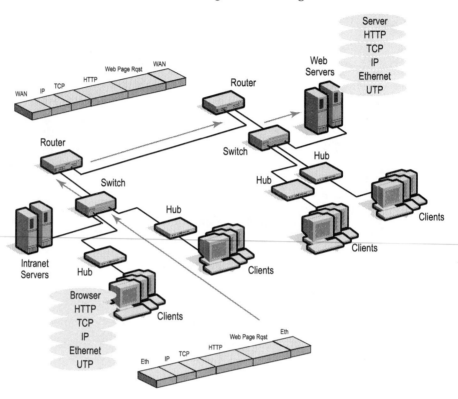

a. What part of this frame does the switch use to move information to the intranet server?

_____

_____

b. What part of the data does the router use to move information through the network?

_____

_____

c. Two routers are connected by a local cable, thus this network forms a single LAN. What device(s) form the backbone of this network?

_____

_____

3. Consider the following network diagram:

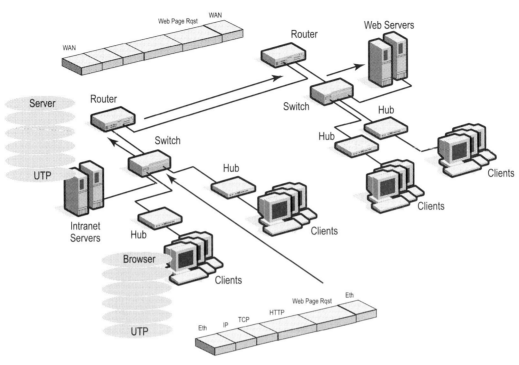

a. Each server is connected to its own switch port. Is the switch-performing port (device) switching, segment switching, or both?

_____

_____

b. Trace the path from one of the clients on the left to the intranet Web servers. Does traffic from this client reach the right-most hub?

_____

_____

c. Fill in the blank ovals representing the protocol stacks of the clients and intranet servers (HTTP servers).

_____

_____

Extended Activities

1. Perform the following exercise that demonstrates the differences between using hubs and switches. This exercise is intended for a Windows 98 peer-to-peer environment with sharing enabled on all clients.

   a. Transfer a large file (more than 25 megabytes [MB]) from one client to another client without going through a central hub. (Connect two peer computers directly to each other.) Record the time it takes to transfer the file.

      _____

      _____

   b. Transfer a large file to and from each client (or multiple clients) connected by means of a hub. Record the time it takes to transfer the file. Because multiple files are transferred simultaneously, average the time.

      _____

      _____

   c. Tie all workgroup hubs together into a central hub and transfer the same number of files between clients as in Step b of this exercise. Record the time it takes to transfer the files. Discuss the results.

      _____

      _____

   d. Replace the central hub with a switch and repeat Step c. Record the time it takes to transfer the files. Discuss the results.

      _____

      _____

2. If one is available, log on to a client/server network. Enter a user name and password to access the server. Can a single user name and password be used for everyone?

   _____

3. Compare functions a peer-to-peer network supports versus functions a client/server supports. What are some functions/ supports that are only available in a client/server environment? Discuss.

_____

_____

_____

_____

4. The Network Layer protocols of various communication architectures do not forward broadcast packets, thus routers keep broadcast messages behind a "firewall." Can a bridge also be used to isolate broadcast messages? A switch? Discuss.

_____

_____

Lesson 3—Connecting Networks

As an organization grows, it may need to connect several small networks over local or wide area links. A company may also choose to divide a single LAN into several subnetworks to provide greater traffic isolation and security.

For all of these reasons, routers are the most common tool used to connect individual networks to each other. This lesson shows how routers are used to connect networks, and how information flows between routers and network boundaries.

Objectives

At the end of this lesson you should be able to:

- Describe how routers isolate traffic in a network

- Explain why routers are used to connect LANs to other LANs

- Describe the configuration of a typical home Internet connection

Key Point

Routers divide networks at Layer 3 and offer more features than simpler devices.

Routers and Traffic Isolation

In the previous lesson, we saw how switches isolate traffic within individual segments or workgroups, and serve as a network backbone. Switches are Layer 2 devices, because they use a frame address to decide whether to forward a frame from one segment to another.

A network with a router backbone looks very similar to a switched backbone network. Like a switch, a router isolates local traffic within individual segments. However, a router uses a packet address to make its routing decisions. To inspect the packet address, a router removes the frame header and trailer from each packet. If the packet is destined for another segment of the network, the router builds a new frame around the packet, and forwards it out the correct router port.

There are both advantages and disadvantages to using either switches or routers for traffic isolation:

- Switches are very fast. Switches are faster than routers, because they do not analyze packets or rebuild frames. Also, more of a switch's function is provided in high-speed hardware.

- Routers provide more functionality. Because routers are software-intensive devices, they take longer to process each frame. However, routers can be programmed to make a wide range of sophisticated routing decisions, thus they are much more flexible than a switch. And, because routers do not forward broadcast packets, they use wide area network (WAN) connections more efficiently than a bridge.

Thus, for traffic isolation, a company may use either a switch or a router. However, routers are widely used to connect a LAN to other networks, as shown on the Router Backbone Diagram. Alternatively, a router can be used in conjunction with switches. The switches provide traffic isolation within the LAN, and the router provides outside connectivity when needed.

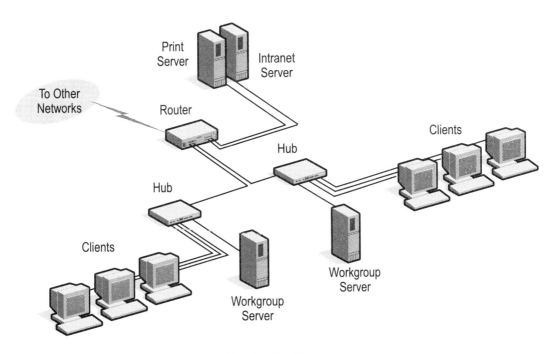

Router Backbone

**LAN-to-LAN
Connectivity**

On the LAN-to-LAN Communication Diagram, a router is used both as a network backbone and for access to other networks. In this example, the router is used by clients in one network to access files on a remote file server in another network.

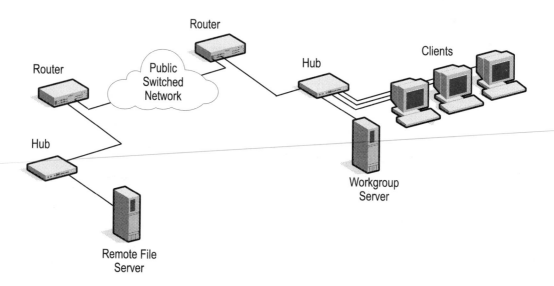

LAN-to-LAN Communication

The router receives a frame from one of the clients in the LAN on the right side of the diagram. The router removes the frame header and trailer, and checks the destination address of the packet to see whether the destination node is on the local network or a remote network.

If the packet is destined for a node within the first network, the router does not forward it. By the time the packet reaches the router, it has already been forwarded to its destination by the hub. However, if the packet is addressed to a remote network, the router forwards it to another router across the switched network. The address of this "next hop" is stored in the router's routing table.

Connecting to the Internet

Internet access has become an indispensable tool for businesses of all sizes. Even if a small peer-to-peer network never needs to link to another LAN, it usually must provide some sort of connection to the Internet.

Fortunately, this process has become simpler. In the early days of the Internet, each organization was completely responsible for learning the Internet's rules and procedures, and installing the equipment necessary to connect to the worldwide network. However, today, telecommunication companies and independent Internet service providers (ISPs) simplify this process for their customers by handling many technical details of Internet access, providing valuable advice, and selling the necessary hardware.

Home Dial-Up Access

An individual user normally accesses the Internet by means of a modem with a dial-up connection over an analog local loop. That connection links the user to an online information service, such as America Online, or a local ISP, as illustrated on the Individual Internet Access Diagram.

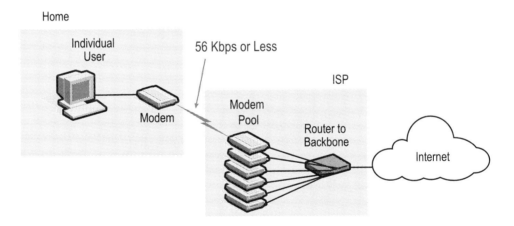

Individual Internet Access

Home Internet connections generally have the following basic components:

- Local loop connection (telephone line).

- Modem.

- ISP account provides Internet access for a monthly fee, and basic services such as e-mail boxes.

- ISP connection software is normally provided by the ISP. The software provides an interface for Internet access and the software that uses the modem to access the Internet. Normally, the dial-up software calls a number to access the ISP, and the ISP then provides access to the backbone of the Internet.

- Web browser application displays Web pages and handles file downloads.

- Specialized software, either a freestanding application or a browser plug-in, provides support for special multimedia functions. For example, with an audio coder/decoder (codec) and microphone, a user may use the Internet to make telephone calls.

Two special protocols, Serial Line Internet Protocol (SLIP) and Point-to-Point Protocol (PPP), are used to transfer IP packets across a serial link. These two protocols are widely used by ISPs to provide dial-up Internet connections for home or small business users.

SLIP

SLIP is a simple encapsulation of an IP datagram asynchronously transmitted over serial lines using an RS-232 interface. At the user's computer, the IP packet is encapsulated between two SLIP control characters (hexadecimal C0), and the resulting SLIP frame is sent to the modem. The modem transmits the information across the telephone network to the ISP modem. The ISP's modem is attached to a router that decapsulates the SLIP frame. The router then encapsulates the original IP packet in a WAN protocol frame, and routes it across the Internet to the proper destination.

A SLIP frame is formed by adding the same control character (a hexadecimal "C0") to both the beginning and end of an IP packet. In other words, the packet is inserted between the two characters, that are called SLIP delimeters.

There are several drawbacks to SLIP:

- There is no protocol header that can contain information about the type of data being transported, thus a SLIP connection can only support one network protocol at a time.

- Each end must know the other end's IP address, because there is no way to exchange this information in the protocol.

- There is no checksum to allow for error detection on noisy telephone lines, which means the higher layers are responsible for error detection and recovery.

Despite these limitations, SLIP is a proven protocol that is very easy to implement. Its simplicity is very attractive on slow links, such as analog local loops.

PPP

PPP is a more robust and flexible serial protocol. This Internet standard protocol offers multiprotocol support, data compression, host configuration, and link setup. PPP is used by higher layer protocols, such as TCP/IP, to provide simple WAN connectivity between users. It replaces SLIP and solves some of its inefficiencies. PPP supports either asynchronous (character-oriented) or synchronous (bit-oriented) transmission links.

PPP is based on the High-Level Data Link Control (HDLC) standard, which deals with LAN and WAN links and operates at the Data Link Layer of the OSI model. PPP starts with the HDLC frame format; however, it adds a protocol field to identify the Network Layer protocol of each frame. This is what allows a PPP link to carry data for multiple network protocols.

Business Internet Access

There are two ways to connect a business customer to the Internet:

- Nondedicated access is any connection that is not continuous. The connection is established at the time it is desired and released when no longer needed. The connection is usually made through a switched network, typically the telephone system. The most common method to access the Internet is to use an existing telephone line, although Integrated Services Digital Network (ISDN) provides much better performance if available.

- Dedicated access, at a minimum, requires a permanent analog telephone number for a dial-up modem connection. However, the analog connection speed is primarily controlled by the modem speed which, as you have seen, is slow. Thus, businesses that need dedicated access usually opt for dedicated digital services, such as T1, fractional T1 (FT1) (DS0), or ISDN. Because of the additional expense of these services, ISPs tend to provide a higher level of service and support to their permanently connected corporate clients.

Some technologies, such as dial-up lines and ISDN, can be used for both dedicated and nondedicated installations. The difference between the two is the type of equipment used to make the connection. For example, the Dedicated vs. Nondedicated Access Diagram illustrates how an ISDN line might be used for either a dedicated or nondedicated application.

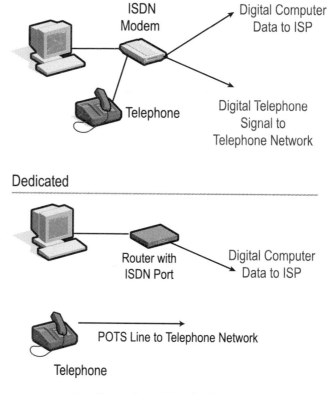

Dedicated vs. Nondedicated Access

When a business uses a dedicated line to connect to an ISP, the permanent connection makes it possible for the business to use a domain name and dedicated IP address. This is typically necessary if the corporation wants to establish a Web site.

Private line Internet connections generally have the following basic components, as shown on the Dedicated Connection to ISP Diagram:

- Common carrier connection—A connection such as FT1, T1, frame relay, and so on is required.

- Channel service unit/data service unit (CSU/DSU)—A CSU/DSU is required to terminate a multiplexed common carrier connection such as a T1 line.

- Router—The routers employed on the Internet are capable of accommodating multiple speeds, channels, protocols, and transmission paths. Some routers may have a built-in CSU/DSU.

- Internet domain name—Even though a business may have no plan to create a Web site in the near future, it is best to reserve a domain name to prevent someone else from registering the preferred domain name first.

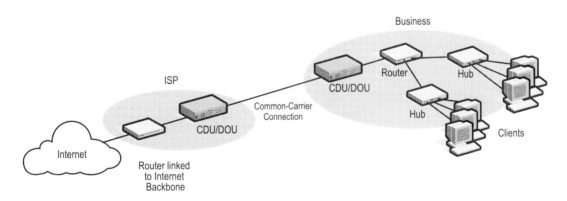

Dedicated Connection to ISP

Activities

1. Which of the following is not used for a home dial-up Internet connection?

   a. Modem

   b. Local loop

   c. CSU/DSU

   d. Web browser

2. Which of the following is the main reason routers are used for wide area connectivity?

   a. They keep all unnecessary traffic off the expensive connection.

   b. Routers transmit data faster than bridges.

   c. Routers are less expensive than switches.

   d. If you install a router, you do not need a CSU/DSU.

3. A switch looks at the network address to decide where to forward the data. True or False

4. Routers are normally used to interconnect remote LANs. True or False

5. Where possible, it is faster to route traffic than switch traffic. True or False

6. Most ISPs use PPP for home dial-up connections. True or False

Extended Activities

1. Research the prices of common carrier services (T1, frame relay, Asynchronous Transfer Mode [ATM], and so on) that can be used to interconnect routers across WANs. What services are available in your area? What is considered "low-end" service? What is considered "high-end" service?

   _____

   _____

2. Visit **http://www.networksolutions.com** and see how much it costs to register an Internet domain name. Think of a name and see whether it is already taken.

3. Research and explain the speculative practice often called "cybersquatting" or "domain name squatting."

Lesson 4—Data Flow Across Networks

In Unit 5, we followed the flow of a client/server interaction across a single workgroup segment. This lesson traces the flow of information across a network that includes hubs, switches, routers, and wide area links. As we will see, the same principles govern data flow in both simple and complex networks.

Objectives

At the end of this lesson you should be able to:

- Describe the process of transmitting a message across a segmented network

- Explain what data changes as it flows across a network and what does not

- Describe the function of ARP

 **Key Point**

Each network device uses frame or packet header data to decide whether to forward a frame or packet.

Common Network Configuration

Many networks use a combination of hubs, switches, and routers to move information from source to destination. A common configuration of two LANs is shown on the Common Network Configuration Diagram. In each of these two networks, users are connected to hubs, and each hub is attached to one port of a backbone switch. Each shared server also has its own switch port. A router controls traffic that flows between the networks over a wide area link.

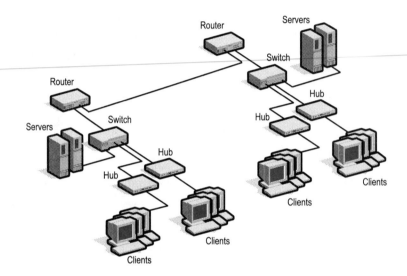

Common Network Configuration

Information Flow on a Hub

When one client sends a message to another client attached to the same hub, that Ethernet frame flows to all clients on the same hub; however, it does not pass the switch. Only the client with a NIC address that matches the frame's destination address will process the information inside the frame.

After the NIC processes the frame, the node's Network Layer process examines the packet's destination address to see whether it matches the node's Network Layer address. In this case, the addresses match, and the packet contents are passed up to the Transport Layer. The Transport Layer process checks the Transport Layer header to see what port number the message is addressed to, then passes the message to the application or process that corresponds to that number.

During transmission of this frame, no other clients attached to the hub can transmit information because they all share the same physical segment. Other clients on the rest of the network can transmit, because the switch does not allow the frame to travel to other parts of the network.

Information Flow Across a Switched Backbone

Now let us see what happens if the frame is addressed to a destination on a segment attached to a different switch port. On the Client to Intranet Server Diagram, we see how data flows from a client to an intranet server in the same network.

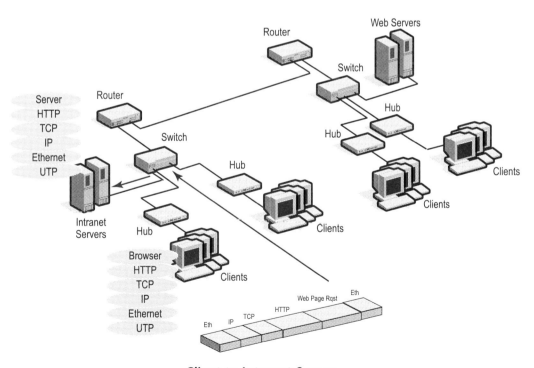

Client to Intranet Server

The stacked ovals represent the protocol layers of the client and server. As you can see, the only difference between them is the application running at the Application Layer. On the client, the application is a Web browser, such as Netscape Communicator. On the server, the application is a Web server software package. Both of these applications use the Hypertext Transfer Protocol (HTTP) to communicate with each other. HTTP, in turn, uses the services of TCP, which uses IP, and so on down the protocol stack that should be familiar to you by now.

When the user of the client node clicks a hyperlink to view a Web page, the client browser sends an HTTP request to the intranet server that contains that document. The bottom of the diagram shows the structure of the frame that the client transmits. As you can see, each of the encapsulated headers corresponds to one layer of the client's protocol stack.

As before, the client's hub repeats the frame to all other nodes attached to that hub. The frame is not addressed to any of those nodes, thus they ignore it.

The switch recognizes that the frame is addressed to the NIC in the intranet server, thus it forwards the frame out the port that is connected to the intranet server. The frame does not pass through any other switch ports, thus the frame does not travel through the rest of the network. The server's NIC receives the frame, recognizes its own NIC address, and processes the frame.

The server's Network Layer process (IP) sees that the packet's destination address matches the server's IP address. IP then passes the packet contents up to the Transport Layer. TCP sees that the message is addressed to the well-known port number assigned to HTTP. It then passes the message to the intranet server software, which is using HTTP.

 **Key Point**

IP packet addresses identify the destination computer.

Information Flow Across a WAN

Now we will see how a message travels from a client in one network to a Web server in another network. As we can see on the Web Server Request Diagram, the client's request must first cross its local network, then travel over the wide area link between the two routers. The message must then cross the distant network to arrive at the destination Web server.

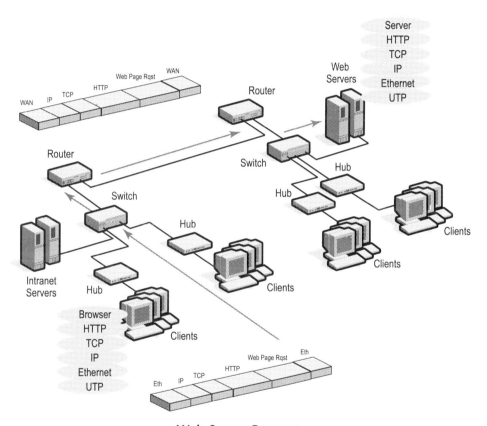

Web Server Request

To simplify this example, we will assume that the client node knows the complete IP address of the destination Web server. When the client sends a message to a server in another network, the client's IP process recognizes that the network portion of the packet's destination IP address does not match the network portion of the sending node's IP address. That means that the destination is on some distant network. The client's IP process does not know how to reach that distant network, thus it addresses the frame to the router that serves as its default gateway.

Thus this time, the client transmits a frame addressed to the router. However, that frame contains a packet addressed to the distant Web server. Once again, the hub broadcasts the frame, which the other clients ignore. The switch recognizes the frame address of the router, and forwards the frame only to the port connected to the router. The destination address of the frame matches the NIC in the router, thus the router's NIC sends the IP packet up to its IP process.

The router's IP process recognizes that the network portion of the destination IP address does not match the network portion of its own IP address. The router checks its routing table, and finds an entry for the destination network. That table entry tells the router what router port is connected to a link that leads to the destination network. That link may be either directly or indirectly connected to the destination; however, that port will eventually get the packet where it needs to go, and that is all the router cares about.

In this case, the correct router port is connected to a wide area link, such as a frame relay virtual circuit. The router now builds a frame relay frame to encapsulate the IP packet, then transmits the new frame over the physical wide area link. The frame relay frame is addressed to the frame relay address of the router connected to the destination network. (You will learn the details of frame relay addressing in later courses; however, that is close enough for now.)

The router at the other end of the frame relay connection removes the frame relay header and trailer, then evaluates the IP packet address. It recognizes that its network number matches the network portion of the destination IP address, thus it knows that the packet must go somewhere within its own network. To build a frame that will get the packet to the server, the router now needs the NIC address of the server.

If the router does not already know the NIC address, it broadcasts an Address Resolution Protocol (ARP) request frame. The ARP request asks for the NIC address that corresponds to the IP address. When the server broadcasts its NIC address in an ARP reply, all nodes, including the router, record that address in their ARP cache, which is a list that maps IP addresses to NIC addresses. Each node checks its cache first when it needs the NIC address of a destination.

The router then encapsulates the packet within an Ethernet frame addressed to the Web server's NIC. The router transmits the new Ethernet frame over the router port that leads to its local network. The switch forwards the frame to the switch port that is connected to the Web server. The Web server's NIC processes the frame, and the client's original Web request message is finally passed up the server's protocol stack to the Web server application.

DNS

Earlier, we simplified this example by assuming the Web client knew the full IP address of the destination Web server. In many cases this is true, especially in a corporate intranet. However, in the Web, it is rare for a client node to know a server's address. New servers are constantly added to the worldwide system, and Web content is often moved from one server to another.

The Domain Name System (DNS) provides a way to navigate the Web without knowing each server's IP address. Clients use easy-to-remember domain names, such as "westnetinc.com." A computer called a "DNS server," or name server maps these alphanumeric Internet addresses to binary IP addresses.

DNS servers (or software that provides DNS functionality) are found in virtually every network that uses TCP/IP as the networking protocol. The Internet's DNS servers regularly exchange new and changed addresses. Within a few days, a change in an Internet address is received by every DNS server around the world.

Thus, when a router receives a packet addressed to "westnetinc.com," it asks the nearest DNS server to supply the IP address that corresponds to that domain name. The name server looks up the name in its database, then returns an IP address in binary format. The router then forwards the packet as we described above.

Activities

Consider the following network:

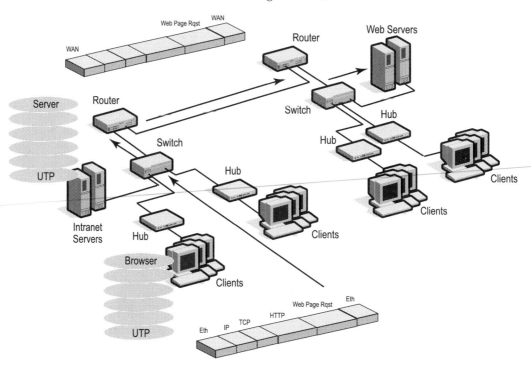

1. Assuming both networks use Ethernet over twisted pair, list the protocol stacks on the server and client.

   _____

   _____

   _____

   _____

2. Describe the flow of a request between the Web browser and Web server.

   _____

   _____

   _____

   _____

3. What kind of UTP cabling would most likely be used in the LAN?

   _____

4. If this LAN originally ran at 10 Mbps, could you increase its speed to 100 Mbps by just replacing the NICs? Explain.

   _____

5. The frame shown traveling between the routers has a WAN header. What happened to the Ethernet header and trailer?

   _____

   _____

   _____

6. What type of WAN protocols could be used between the routers?

   _____

   _____

7. The first time a router must forward a packet to a node, it uses ARP to ask the node for its NIC address. A short time later, the router must forward another packet to the same node. Does it use ARP again? Why or why not?

   _____

   _____

Extended Activities

1. Divide into focus groups and discuss the following:

   a. The differences between hubs, switches, and routers, and the way they work together in the network configurations shown in this lesson. How would traffic flow change by removing any one of these devices?

   b. Where network bottlenecks are likely to occur, and what might be done about alleviating potential network congestion. (Consider the server load.)

2. Research the DNS and prepare a short report that summarizes its operation.

Summary

Unit 8 discussed the practical applications of the various concepts we have covered in this course. We explained how to build a simple peer-to-peer network, and related each part of that process to a layer of the OSI model.

Many peer-to-peer networks become client/server networks by adding NOSs to create servers. However, both peer-to-peer traffic and client/server traffic can exist in the same network. When two clients are communicating directly, it is peer-to-peer communication. When a client requests services from a NOS, it is client/server communication.

As networks grow, the increased traffic may create performance problems. Devices, such as switches and routers relieve network congestion by isolating traffic to logical groupings of network devices. The choice of whether to switch or route is dependent on the functionality required by the network. A switch is used for performance boosts and is more efficient than a router. A router is used to provide connectivity to other networks and for specialized security functions, such as Internet firewalls.

We then traced the path and format of data as it travels across local and remote boundaries. We explained how a new frame is built to cross each type of link, carrying packets from source to destination. We saw how applications communicate through software ports, including client application port to network application port. Most important, we saw that the same basic concepts and processes are used to carry data across workgroups and LANs, over wide area links, and across the worldwide Internet.

Unit 8 Quiz

1. Which of the following best describes the function of a frame address?

   a. Transmits a frame to the next NIC in the data's path

   b. Transmits a packet to the correct port

   c. Transmits a frame to the final destination

   d. Transmits a frame to the correct socket

2. Which of the following is processed at the Network Layer of a protocol stack?

   a. Datagram or packet

   b. Frame

   c. Bit or byte

   d. Logical unit

3. What unit of information does a bridge operate on?

   a. Bit

   b. Byte

   c. Frame

   d. Packet

   e. Socket

4. What unit of information does a router operate on?

   a. Bit

   b. Byte

   c. Frame

   d. Packet

   e. Socket

5. In a client/server arrangement, where are requests normally generated?

   a. Client

   b. Server

   c. Either of the above

   d. NIC

487

6. A computer that allows users to connect to a LAN from outside an organization is called which of the following?

   a. RAS

   b. Backbone

   c. Firewall

   d. Hub

7. A router connects a frame relay network to an Ethernet LAN. When a frame comes in from the frame relay network, what does the router do before it forwards the data to a node on the LAN?

   a. It does nothing to the frame.

   b. It removes the frame relay frame header, and builds a new Ethernet frame.

   c. It encapsulates the frame relay frame within an Ethernet frame.

   d. It discards the frame relay frame and forwards the packet.

8. Node A has a packet to send to Node B. Both nodes are on the same network. If Node A does not have the NIC address of Node B, what does Node A do?

   a. Broadcasts the packet to all nodes

   b. Refuses to send the data, and alerts the user to find the address

   c. Broadcasts an ARP request for the NIC address of Node B

   d. Broadcasts an ARP request for the NIC address of all nodes

9. Which of the following is the main purpose of a backbone switch?

   a. To increase performance by isolating traffic within separate segments

   b. To improve security by preventing unauthorized access

   c. To reduce the level of broadcast traffic in a network

   d. To link a LAN to a wide area connection

10. You are part of the network staff of a large company. Your network administrator wants you to set up a workstation for a new employee, and tells you to "bind the NIC." What should you do?

    a. Look for a roll of duct tape.

    b. Disconnect the workstation from the hub.

    c. Use the workstation's network client software to associate the adapter card with the networking protocols used by your company.

    d. Use an administrative software utility to assign a NIC address to that workstation.

11. The IP address of a host is 155.221.120.1. If the network number of the LAN is 155.xxx.xxx.xxx, what is the subnet mask for the host?

    a. 255.255.0.0

    b. 0.0.255.255

    c. 155.221.0.0

    d. 255.0.0.0

12. Your class builds a peer-to-peer network. All connections are complete and all client software is configured properly. However, none of the nodes can "see" any of the others. Which of the following problems is the most likely cause?

    a. The hub is not plugged into a power source.

    b. You used Category 3 cable instead of Category 5.

    c. All of the nodes have a virus.

    d. None of the nodes knows the NIC addresses of the others.

13. You receive an e-mail message with an application file attached. The message says, "Be one of the first 50 people to try our new game, and we will pay you $100!" You should do which of the following?

    a. See when the message was sent. If it is more than a few hours old, you will not be one of the first 50 people.

    b. Delete the message and attachment, without running the game.

    c. Make sure your virus software is up to date, then try the game.

    d. Forward the message to your friends, thus they have a chance at the money.

14. Which of the following statements is true about virus protection software?

    a. Antivirus programs stop all malicious programs.

    b. Antivirus programs can stop malicious programs they are programmed to detect.

    c. Antivirus programs can restore files damaged by a virus.

    d. Antivirus programs stop infected files from entering a computer.

15. You need to connect to your ISP over a standard telephone line. What protocol is best suited to transmit data over this link?

    a. SONET

    b. PPP

    c. ATM

    d. SLIP

16. A router is a cost-effective solution to traffic isolation.
    True or False

17. A switch looks at the network address to decide where to forward the data. True or False

18. Routers are normally used to interconnect remote LANs.
    True or False

19. Where possible, it is faster to route traffic than switch traffic.
    True or False

20. List the components you need to build a small peer-to-peer network.

COURSE QUIZ

1. What type of device is used with UTP cabling to create an Ethernet star network topology?

   _____

2. Which of the following best describes the function of a MAC address?

   a. It transmits a frame to the next NIC.

   b. It transmits a packet to the correct port.

   c. It transmits a frame to the final destination.

   d. It transmits a frame to the correct socket.

3. Name the two types of fiber optic cables used to transmit data.

   _____

4. Name the type of cable most commonly used to wire new Ethernet networks.

   _____

5. Which of the following is found at the Network Layer of a protocol stack?

   a. Datagram or packet

   b. Frame

   c. Bit or byte

   d. LU

6. Which of the following is true?

   a. Each OSI layer adds its own trailer to the data that is passed down to it.

   b. Each OSI layer adds its own header to the data passed up from below.

   c. Each OSI layer adds its own header to the data that is passed down to it.

   d. Each OSI layer converts data as it processes it.

7. What is the main difference between a LAN and WAN?

   _____

8. What does MAC stand for?

   _____

9. Which of the following uses CSMA/CA?

   _____

   a. Ethernet

   b. Token Ring

   c. Wireless LANs

   d. Frame relay

10. The MAC sublayer is part of what OSI layer?

    _____

11. What does NIC stand for?

    _____

12. What does MAU stand for?

    _____

13. Which of the following is a connectionless protocol?

    a. Frame relay

    b. ATM

    c. ISDN

    d. IP

14. Name the three main types of physical transmission media.

    _____

    _____

    _____

15. Which of the following is not a client/server NOS?
    a. Windows NT
    b. Windows 98
    c. Novell NetWare
    d. UNIX

16. In a 10BaseT network, a hub-centered star topology functions logically as which of the following?
    a. Bus
    b. Ring
    c. Mesh
    d. Cloud

17. What is modulation?
    a. Scrambling a bit stream so only the intended recipient can understand it
    b. Altering an analog carrier wave to represent information
    c. Converting an analog signal to digital
    d. Allowing multiple signals to take turns using one physical medium

18. What unit of information does a bridge operate on?
    a. Bit
    b. Byte
    c. Frame
    d. Packet
    e. Socket

19. What is the difference between a 10Base2 network and a 10BaseT network?

    a. Cabling

    b. Bandwidth

    c. Data Link protocol

    d. MAC

20. What unit of information does a router operate on?

    a. Bit

    b. Byte

    c. Frame

    d. Packet

    e. Socket

21. What does a repeater do?

    _____

    _____

22. Which of the following is most like a repeater?

    a. Switch

    b. Patch cable

    c. Hub

    d. Router

23. Why is a switch used in a network?

    a. To improve network performance

    b. To keep broadcast traffic off a WAN link

    c. To convert upper layer protocols

    d. To forward Internet messages

24. Name the layers of the OSI model from top to bottom.

    _____

    _____

25. What is the biggest challenge to the growth of wireless networking?

    a. The cost of the equipment

    b. The supply of usable electromagnetic frequencies

    c. Sunspots

    d. Low demand from potential users

26. Why is it expensive to install fiber optic cable?

    a. It is very thin.

    b. It is brittle and inflexible.

    c. It attracts lightning strikes.

    d. It must be shielded from interference.

27. What part of the electromagnetic spectrum do wireless LANs use?

    a. Gamma rays

    b. Ultraviolet

    c. Infrared

    d. Microwaves

28. CSMA/CD is most like which of the following?

    a. A systematic discussion in which each person has a periodic opportunity to speak

    b. An informal conversation in which each person speaks when the opportunity presents itself, but only one person speaks at any time

    c. A formal meeting in which a chairman must grant each person permission to speak

    d. A crowded room with multiple conversations going on at the same time

29. Which of the following causes the propagation delay of a GEO satellite link?

    a. The height of the satellite's orbit

    b. The frequency assigned to GEO satellites

    c. The orbital speed of the satellite

    d. The protocol used for the satellite link

30. What is frame relay used for?

    a. To move frames across a switch

    b. To transmit frames from one LAN node to another

    c. To link the floors of a building

    d. To connect LANs over a metropolitan or wide area

31. When you surf the Web from home, what protocols are you most likely to use?

    a. HTTP, PPP, IP

    b. SMTP, IP, SLIP

    c. Ethernet, TCP, IP

    d. ATM, POTS, ISP

32. Which will carry a signal the greatest distance without a repeater?

    a. Multimode

    b. Single-mode

    c. UTP cabling

    d. STP cabling

33. A MAC address is the same as which of the following?

    a. Network address

    b. NIC address

    c. Internet address

    d. Port number

34. The IEEE 802.3 standard defines which of the following?

    a. Token Ring

    b. Wireless LANs

    c. Token bus

    d. Ethernet

35. In a client/server arrangement, where are requests normally generated?

    a. Client

    b. Server

    c. Either of the above

    d. NIC

36. What is the main difference between a standard switch and a bridge?

    a. Switches do not forward broadcast frames.

    b. Bridges are faster than switches.

    c. Switches effectively multiply the network's bandwidth.

    d. Bridges operate at Layer 3.

37. The most common topology for corporate WANs is which of the following?

    a. Mesh

    b. Cloud

    c. Ring

    d. Hybrid

38. How many point-to-point links are needed to build a mesh network of four nodes?

    _____

39. In the term "10BaseT" what does the "T" mean?

    a. Thicknet

    b. Twisted pair

    c. Thinnet

    d. Terminated

40. Light stays within a fiber optic cable by bouncing off what part of the fiber?

    a. Cladding

    b. Coating

    c. Core

    d. Jacket

41. Each layer of the OSI model provides a service to which of the following?

    a. Its peer process

    b. The layer above it

    c. The layer below it

    d. The user

42. An Ethernet NIC adds a header and trailer to data before it transmits it. This is an example of which of the following?

    a. Modulation

    b. Decapsulation

    c. Encapsulation

    d. Multiplexing

43. Which type of address is unique anywhere in the world?

    a. Port address

    b. IP address

    c. Subnet mask

    d. NIC address

44. Data compression is handled by what OSI layer?

    a. Compression Layer

    b. Presentation Layer

    c. Data Link Layer

    d. Application Layer

45. The Network Layer moves data in which of the following ways?

    a. End-to-end

    b. Point-to-point

    c. NIC-to-NIC

    d. User-to-ISP

46. The biggest obstacle to high-speed Internet access is which of the following?

    a. Government regulations

    b. T1 multiplexing

    c. Competing telecom companies

    d. Analog local loops

47. The binary number 01001011 is equivalent to what decimal number?

48. The hexadecimal number E is equivalent to what decimal number?

49. On a Token Ring network, what happens when the number of communicating nodes decreases?

    a. Network bandwidth increases.

    b. Each node has more tokens to use.

    c. Network performance does not change.

    d. The token moves more quickly around the ring.

50. On a 10BaseT network, what happens when the number of communicating nodes decreases?

    a. Network bandwidth increases.

    b. The hub works faster because fewer ports are in use.

    c. Network speed does not change.

    d. Network performance increases because of fewer collisions.

51. What protocols are primarily used across the Internet?

    a. SPX and IPX

    b. TCP and IP

    c. NetBIOS and NetBEUI

    d. T1 and T3

52. When a router forwards data from a frame relay network to an Ethernet network, what happens?

    a. It repeats the frame without changes onto the Ethernet network.

    b. It removes the frame relay header and trailer, and transmits the packet onto the Ethernet network.

    c. It removes the frame relay header and trailer, inspects the packet header, builds a new Ethernet frame around the packet, and transmits the frame onto the Ethernet network.

    d. It builds an Ethernet frame around the frame relay frame and transmits the frame onto the Ethernet network.

53. In a network that uses the CSMA/CD method of MAC, what does a sending node do if it detects a collision?

    a. Stop transmitting, wait a random length of time, then check to see if the medium is silent

    b. Keep transmitting because it was first

    c. Pass the token to the next node

    d. Stop transmitting then wait for the next Clear to Send signal

54. The UNIX protocol stack, which includes TCP and IP, does not correspond exactly to the OSI reference model. Why?

   a. UNIX is a proprietary system.

   b. The OSI model was developed after UNIX.

   c. UNIX developers wanted a more efficient layering system.

   d. The OSI model is not widely used in the networking industry.

55. All popular NOSs and peer-to-peer applications support which of these protocols?

   a. NetBIOS and NetBEUI

   b. ATP and DDP

   c. SPX and IPX

   d. TCP and IP

Glossary

100VG-AnyLAN—100VF-AnyLAN is a 100-Mbps LAN technology standard that directly competes with 100BaseT Ethernet. The IEEE 802.12 committee is currently investigating this standard. The access method used by this standard is different from the CSMA/CD method used by 10-Mbps Ethernet and Fast Ethernet. However, the MAC frame format stays the same. The new access method is called "demand priority."

address—An address is a unique value that identifies source or the destination of data being transmitted across a communication link. A single item of data may have different addresses that identify a station's place in a network, the computer hardware itself, and the address of a software process.

Address Resolution Protocol (ARP)—ARP is a protocol that allows a host to use a logical (network) address to obtain the hardware (NIC, MAC) address for a remote station. ARP is used only across a single physical network, and is limited to networks that support hardware broadcasts.

American National Standards Institute (ANSI)—ANSI is a U.S. voluntary organization that develops and publishes standards for data communications, programming languages, magnetic storage media, office systems, and encryption. ANSI represents the United States as a member of ISO and IEC.

American Standard Code for Information Interchange (ASCII)—ASCII is one of the most widely used codes for representing keyboard characters on a computer system. ASCII uses 7 bits to represent 128 elements. For example, when the character "A" is pressed on the keyboard, the ASCII binary representation is 100 0001. The other major encoding system is EBCDIC. See Extended Binary Coded Decimal Interchange Code (EBCDIC).

amplitude—Amplitude is the height of a wave, or how far from the center it swings.

analog—A signal transmitted as a pattern of continually changing electromagnetic waves is referred to as an analog signal.

architecture—The design and method of construction of a particular entity is referred to as its architecture. Different computer network architectures were developed for particular purposes. Examples of network architectures include IBM's SNA and Apple's AppleTalk.

asynchronous—Asynchronous operation means that bits are not transmitted on any strict timetable. Transmitting a start bit indicates the start of each character. After the final bit of the character is transmitted, a stop bit is sent, indicating the end of the character. The sending and receiving modems must stay in synchronization only for the length of time it takes to transmit the 8 bits. If their clocks are slightly out of synch, data transfer will still be successful.

Asynchronous Transfer Mode (ATM)—An ATM is a connection-oriented cell relay technology based on small (53-byte) cells. An ATM network consists of ATM switches that form multiple virtual circuits to carry groups of cells from source to destination. ATM can provide high-speed transport services for audio, data, and video.

authentication—Authentication is the process of accurately identifying a computer user, usually done through passwords.

backbone—A backbone is the portion of a network that carries the most significant traffic. It is also the part of the network that connects many smaller networks to form a larger network.

bandwidth—Bandwidth is a measure of the information-carrying capacity of a channel. In analog networks, bandwidth is the difference between the highest and lowest frequencies that can be transmitted across a communication link. Analog networks measure bandwidth in cycles per second (Hz). Digital networks measure bandwidth in Kbps, Mbps, and Gbps.

baseband—Baseband is a form of digital modulation in which one signal takes up the entire available bandwidth of the communication channel.

beta test—A beta test is the final stage of software testing in which volunteers use a new application or OS under real-world conditions.

binary—Binary refers to the base 2 numbering system used by computers to represent information. Binary numbers consist of only two values: 1 and 0. In a binary number, each position is two times greater than the position to its right.

bit—"A bit, also referred to as a binary digit, is a single value that makes up a binary number. A bit can be either 1 or 0. See binary.

bits per second (bps)—The number of binary bits transmitted per second is measured in bps. For example, common modem speeds are 28,800 bps and 54,000 bps. Another way of writing 28,800 bps is 28.8 Kbps, because "kilo" means 1,000.

Bluetooth—"Bluetooth" is an open standard (IEEE 802.15.1, under development) for short-distance wireless personal area networking between handheld computers, peripheral devices, and other smart electronic appliances. It uses frequency hopping spread spectrum radio transmission in the 2.4-GHz range.

BNC connector—BNC connectors are small devices used to connect computers to a thin coaxial cable bus (10Base2) or terminate the ends of a bus. There are several different types of BNC connectors. A BNC barrel connector joins two Thinnet cables. A BNC terminator is used to terminate the end of a cable. It acts as a resistive load that absorbs the signal that reaches one end of the bus. (Two terminators are needed on each bus.) BNC adapters connect different types of cable, such as Thinnet to Thicknet.

bridge—A bridge is a device that operates at the Data Link Layer of the OSI model. It can connect several LANs or LAN segment of the same media access type, such as two Token Ring segments, or different LANs, such as Ethernet and Token Ring.

broadband—Broadband is a communication medium with enough bandwidth to carry multiple signals simultaneously. A broadband analog system assigns each signal to a different band of frequencies. A broadband digital system uses multiplexing to carry multiple signals.

broadcast domain—A broadcast domain is the area of a network that will receive broadcast packets. Routers and Layer 3 switches create network segments that are separate broadcast domains, because they do not forward broadcast packets from one segment to another.

broadcast frame—A broadcast frame is a frame addressed to all nodes on a network. The frame address is a special number that tells all nodes that receive the frame to process it.

broadcast storm—Due to differences between nodes and bridges in different parts of a network, a broadcast frame can sometimes be misinterpreted. This leads to another broadcast frame by the bridge that misinterpreted it. The second broadcast frame is again misinterpreted, and so on. The result is a "storm" of broadcast frames that can severely degrade network performance. Sometimes storms can persist and eventually bring down an entire network.

bus—An external bus connects a computer to its peripheral devices. An I/O bus connects the central processor of a PC with the video controller, disk controller, hard drives, memory, and other I/O devices. See serial bus and parallel bus.

byte—One byte is equal to eight bits. See bit.

capacity—The term "capacity" refers to using the data-carrying capability of a component or communication link. It is the number of bits the component or link can process in a period of time.

carrier wave—A carrier wave is a consistent waveform that can be modulated to carry a signal. To receive a signal, a receiver must be tuned to the same carrier wavelength used by the transmitter.

cell—A cell is a unit of data similar to a frame. It is very small (53 bytes for ATM) and fixed in length. Cells are typically associated with ATM technology.

central office (CO)—A CO is a telephone company facility where local loops are terminated. The function of a CO is to connect individual telephones through a series of switches. COs are tied together in a hierarchy for efficiency in switching. Other terms for a CO are "local exchange," "wiring center," and "end office."

channel—A portion of the total bandwidth of a physical transmission path, used to carry a single signal is referred to as a channel. Channels are also called links, lines, circuits, and paths. A physical connection, such as a cable, may support more than one channel.

channel service unit (CSU)—A CSU is a device that connects to the end of a T1 or T3 line, between the line and a DSU. The CSU maintains an electrical connection on the line and functions as a repeater, regenerating and amplifying both incoming and outgoing signals. A CSU is usually combined with a DSU in a device called a "CSU/DSU."

cladding—Cladding is the clear plastic or glass layer that encloses the light-transmitting core of a fiber optic cable. The cladding has a lower refractive index than the core, and reflects the light signal back into the core as the light propagates down the fiber.

client—A client is any program that requests a service or resource from another program, either on the same computer or a different one. This term is often used to refer to the computer that hosts the client program; however, a client program may also run on a computer that normally functions as a server. See server.

coder/decoder (codec)—A codec is a hardware/software device that takes an analog signal and converts (codes) it to digital format for compression and transmission. On the receiving end, the digital signal is put back (decoded) into the original analog signal.

collapsed backbone—A collapsed backbone is a network topology that uses a multiport device, such as a switch or router, to carry traffic between network segments or subnets. This is in contrast to the original backbone that, in the case of Ethernet, consisted of a single common bus cable to which nodes were connected.

collision domain—The portion of a network where all nodes receive every frame transmitted is referred to as collision domain. A bus, hub, or group of interconnected hubs forms a single collision domain.

common carrier—A company that must offer its services to all customers at the prices and conditions outlined in a public record is referred to as a common carrier.

compiler—A compiler is an application that converts code written in a programming language (source code) into machine-level instructions (an executable program).

compression—The process of reducing the number of bits required to represent data, without altering the information conveyed by the data, is referred to as compression. The primary reason for using compression techniques is to optimize the use of a communication channel.

connectionless—Connectionless transmission treats each packet or datagram as a separate entity that contains the source and destination addresses. Connectionless services can drop or deliver packets out of sequence.

connection-oriented—A connection-oriented data communication mode is one in which the sending and receiving computers stay in contact for the duration of a session, while packets or frames are being sent back and forth

core—The innermost layer of a fiber optic cable, made of clear glass or plastic, is the core. It carries light signals down the fiber.

criminal hacker (cracker)—A cracker is someone who gets fun or profit from breaching a secure system and possibly stealing information or damaging data.

daisy chain—A daisy chain is a type of bus topology created by connecting each device to the next device with a separate cable. Node A connects to Node B, Node B to Node C, and so on in a line. In an AppleTalk network, the daisy-chain topology is created using PhoneNet connectors and twisted pair wiring (regular telephone wire). A daisy-chain configuration must be terminated at both ends using terminating resistors.

Data Link Control (DLC)—DLC is a generic term that refers to a protocol, such as Token Ring or Ethernet, used to transfer data across a single physical link.

data service unit (DSU)—A DSU is a device that converts a binary signal from the format used on a LAN to that used by a T1 line. It resolves differences in the way each system represents binary numbers. It sits between a CSU and a T1 MUX, and is usually combined with a CSU in a device called a "CSU/DSU."

datagram—The term "datagram" is another word for a Network Layer packet.

de facto—De facto standards are standards that are not developed by an official standards-making organization, and are usually created by a single vendor or group of vendors. Nevertheless, they are widely accepted and used, usually to allow interoperation with a popular system.

decapsulation—As a data transmission is passed up through the protocol stack of a receiving computer, each protocol layer first removes the header that was added by its peer process on the sending computer, then passes the remaining data to the protocol layer just above. This process is referred to as decapsulation.

decryption—The process of unscrambling encrypted data to restore the original meaningful message is referred to as decryption.

default gateway—A default gateway is a router that provides access to all hosts on remote networks. Typically, a network administrator configures a default gateway for each node on a network.

device driver—A device driver is a program that controls hardware devices attached to a computer, such as a printer or hard disk drive.

digital—A digital signal is transmitted as a pattern of binary bits. Information is represented as a series of 1s and 0s, high or low electrical voltages, or the absence or presence of light.

digital access cross-connect switch (DACS)—A DACS is a connection system that establishes semipermanent (not switched) paths for voice or data signals. All physical wires are attached to the DACS once, then electronic connections between them are made by entering instructions.

Digital Subscriber Line (DSL)—DSL is a modem technology that converts existing twisted pair telephone lines into high-speed data lines that can also carry separate telephone communications. Variants of DSL include ADSL, RADSL, ADSL Lite; IDSL, and VDSL.

Domain Name System (DNS)—DNA is the online distributed database system that maps human-readable computer names to IP addresses.

duplex—The process of transmitting data in two directions is referred to as duplex transmission. There are three modes of transmission: simplex, half-duplex, and full-duplex. In simplex transmission, a signal can only be transmitted in one direction. In half-duplex transmission, the signal can travel in both directions, but not simultaneously. Full-duplex transmission allows signals to travel in both directions simultaneously.

Electronic Industries Association (EIA)—EIA is a U.S. trade organization that publishes hardware-oriented standards for data communications.

encapsulation—As a data transmission is passed down through the protocol stack of the sending computer, each protocol layer adds its own header to the data it receives from the layer above. This is known as encapsulation. When a message is physically transmitted from a sending computer, it includes a header for each of the protocols that processed it.

encoding—Encoding is the process of translating binary data (1s and 0s) into signals to be transmitted across a physical link. The most common signaling forms are electrical signals, light signals, and radio signals. Encoding also describes the process of using binary values to represent symbols or keyboard characters. Two of the most common encoding systems for keyboard characters are ASCII and EBCDIC.

encryption—Encryption is the process of scrambling data by changing it in a series of logical steps called an encryption algorithm. Most encryption algorithms use a numeric pattern or "key" to guide the scrambling process. Different keys and algorithms will each produce data scrambled or encrypted in different patterns. The recipient of a message uses the same algorithm and key to restore the original message.

Ethernet—The Ethernet protocol, originally developed in the 1970s by Xerox Corporation, in conjunction with Intel and DEC, is now the primary protocol for local area networking. The original Ethernet provides 10-Mbps through-put. Fast Ethernet (100 Mbps) and Gigabit Ethernet (1,000 Mbps) use the same basic technology, but at higher speeds.

Extended Binary Coded Decimal Interchange Code (EBCDIC)—EBCDIC is the IBM standard for binary encoding of characters. It is one of the two most widely used codes to represent characters, such as keyboard characters. (ASCII is the other.) See American Standard Code for Information Interchange (ASCII).

Extended Industry Standard Architecture (EISA)—EISA is a 32-bit bus technology for PCs that supports multiprocessing. EISA was designed in response to IBM's MCA; however, both EISA and MCA were replaced by the PCI bus. See Peripheral Component Interconnect and bus.

facilities—The term "facilities" refers to the physical media that are necessary to provide a telecommunication service. For example, twisted pairs of copper wire, or fiber optic cables, are facilities. Private facilities are owned and used by a private organization. Public facilities are leased from a telecommunication carrier, such as a local telephone company or long-distance service provider.

File Transfer Protocol (FTP)—FTP is an Application Layer protocol used in TCP/IP networks. FTP is commonly used to transfer files between hosts on the Internet.

firewall—A firewall is a controlled access point between sections of the same network, designed to confine problems to one section. A firewall is also a controlled access between a private network and public network (such as the Internet), usually implemented with a router and special firewall software.

FireWire—FireWire is a new external bus that can connect up to 63 devices and transfer up to 400 Mbps. FireWire is good for real-time applications, such as video, because it transfers data at a guaranteed and predictable rate. FireWire is a trademark of Apple Computer, who developed the technology. Other companies market the same technology under different names.

flow control—Flow control is the process of controlling the volume of data sent between two computer systems. Practically every data communication protocol contains some form of flow control to keep the sending computer from sending too much data to the receiving node.

fractional T1 (FT1)—FT1 is a telephone company service that provides data rates from 64 Kbps to 1.544 Mbps, by allowing a user to purchase one or more channels of a T1 link. If the customer needs less bandwidth than 1.544 Mbps, FT1 is a low-cost alternative to purchasing a full T1.

frame—A frame is a unit of information processed by the Data Link Layer. Each frame contains the hardware address (NIC address) of its destination node. Control frames are used to set up and manage a communications link. Information frames contain packets from the Network Layer above. The format of each frame depends on the Data Link Layer protocol in use (for example, Ethernet or Token Ring).

frame relay—A frame relay is a packet-forwarding WAN protocol that normally operates at speeds of 56 Kbps to 1.5 Mbps.

frequency—Frequency is the number of times per second that a wave swings back and forth in a cycle from its beginning point to its ending point. It is the number of wave crests or cycles that passes a fixed point during a particular period of time.

gateway—The term "gateway" can have two definitions in the context of networking. 1. A gateway can be a protocol converter. This type of gateway converts data between two distinct types of protocol architectures, often at the higher layers of the OSI model. 2. A gateway can also be a router used to connect a private network to a public network, typically the Internet.

hacker—A hacker is a very skilled, curious, experimental programmer. A hack is an unorthodox, often elegant, solution to a programming problem. See criminal hacker.

half-duplex—See duplex.

handshake—An exchange of signals and data that prepares two devices to communicate with each other is referred to as a handshake.

header—A header is part of a message that contains information necessary to send the message from one node to another. The header normally contains a field specifying the length of the encapsulated message, together with at least one field providing information about the message. If, for example, the message is a segment of a larger message, the header might specify the relative position of the segment in the complete message and probably the total number of segments in the message.

hertz (Hz)—The frequency of an analog signal is measured in cycles per second or Hz. One Hz is 1 cycle per second; 1,000 cycles per second is 1 kHz; and 1 million cycles per second is 1 MHz.

High-Level Data Link Control (HDLC)—HDLC is a Data Link Layer protocol for point-to-point and point-to-multipoint communication. The HDLC protocol suite represents a wide variety of link layer protocols, such as SDLC, LAPB, LAPD, frame relay, and PPP.

host—A host is any computer system that provides a resource over a TCP/IP network. A host may be a PC, UNIX workstation, networking device, or supercomputer.

hub—Also called a wiring concentrator, a simple hub is a repeater with multiple ports. A signal coming into one port is repeated out the other ports.

Hypertext Markup Language (HTML)—HTML is a text-based language used to generically format text for Web pages. HTML tags different parts of a document more in terms of their function than their appearance. A Web browser reads an HTML document and displays it as indicated by the HTML formatting tags and the browser's default settings.

Hypertext Transfer Protocol (HTTP)—HTTP is the Application Layer protocol used to request and transmit HTML documents. HTTP is the underlying protocol of the Web.

Industry Standard Architecture (ISA)—ISA is an older PC bus technology used in IBM XT and AT computers. See bus.

Internet—The term "Internet," capitalized, refers to the global internetwork of TCP/IP networks.

Institute of Electrical and Electronics Engineers (IEEE)—IEEE is a professional organization composed of engineers, scientists, and students. Founded in 1884, IEEE publishes computer and electronics standards, such as the 802 series that defines shared-media networks such as Ethernet and Token Ring.

Integrated Services Digital Network (ISDN)—ISDN is a WAN technology used to move voice and data over the telecommunication network. ISDN operates at speeds of 144 Kbps to 1.5 Mbps.

interexchange carrier (IXC)—An IXC is a long-distance company that provides telephone and data services between LATAs.

International Electrotechnical Commission (IEC)—A voluntary organization, chartered by the United Nations, IEC defines standards for electrical and electronic technologies. ANSI represents the United States in IEC.

International Standards Organization (ISO)—ISO is a voluntary organization, chartered by the United Nations, that defines international standards for all fields other than electricity and electronics (IEC handles that). ANSI represents the United States in ISO.

International Telecommunication Union-Telecommunications Standardization Sector (ITU-T)—ITU-T is an intergovernmental organization that develops and adopts international telecommunication standards and treaties. ITU was founded in 1865 and became a United Nations agency in 1947.

Internet Protocol (IP)—IP is a Network Layer protocol responsible for routing a packet (datagram) through a network. It is the "IP" in "TCP/IP."

Internet service provider (ISP)—Companies that provide Internet access to individuals and businesses are referred to as ISPs. ISPs typically provide a range of services necessary to provide corporate networks and other users with dedicated or dial-up access to the Internet.

internetwork—A complex network that may combine smaller networks in different physical locations, based on different types of network architectures is referred to as an internetwork.

Internetwork Packet Exchange (IPX)—IPX is Novell NetWare's proprietary Network Layer protocol.

intranet—An intranet is a network that uses Internet applications, but is designed for use only by the personnel of a company or organization; that is, it is a "private internet."

latency—Latency is the transmission delay created as a device processes a frame or packet. It is the duration from the time a device reads the first byte of a frame or packet, until the time it forwards that byte.

light-emitting diode (LED)—An LED is a device that converts electrical signals into light pulses.

local area network (LAN)—A network typically confined to a single building or floor of a building is referred to as a LAN.

local loop—A local loop is the pair of copper wires that connects a customer's telephone to the LEC's CO switching system.

megahertz (MHz)—One hertz equals one cycle of a wave per second. One MHz equals 1 million cycles per second.

modem—The term "modem" is a contraction for modulator/demodulator. They are used to convert binary data into analog signals suitable for transmission across a telephone network.

modulation—Modulation is the process of modifying the form of a carrier wave (electrical signal) so that it can carry intelligent information on some sort of communications medium.

Moving Pictures Experts Group, Layer-3 (MP3)—MP3 stands for MPEG Layer-3, which is an extension of the Motion Picture Experts Group (MPEG) standards for compressed digital video. MP3 is the most popular compression format for digital audio files, and is commonly used to distribute music over the Internet.

multiplexer (MUX)—A MUX is a device that transmits multiple signals over the same physical medium. Multiple signals are fed into a MUX and combined to form one output stream.

multiplexing—Multiplexing is a technology that allows multiple signals to travel over the same physical medium. Multiple signals are fed into a multiplexer and combined to form one output stream.

multistation access unit (MAU)—A MAU is a device used in Token Ring networks to provide connectivity between individual workstations. It is also called a Token Ring hub.

National Electrical Code (NEC)—The NEC is a set of safety standards and rules for the design and installation of electrical circuits, including network and telephone cabling. The NEC is developed by a committee of ANSI, and has been adopted as law by many states and cities. Versions of the NEC are dated by year; each local area may require compliance with a different version of the NEC.

NetBIOS Extended User Interface (NetBEUI)—NetBEUI is a Network and Transport Layer protocol designed to work within a single physical LAN. (It does not provide packet routing between networks.) NetBEUI is typically integrated with NetBIOS.

NetWare Core Protocol (NCP)—NCP is the proprietary protocol used by the NetWare OS to transmit information between clients and servers. NCP messages are transmitted by means of IPX, NetWare's Network Layer protocol.

Network Basic Input/Output System (NetBIOS)—NetBIOS is a software system originally developed by Sytek and IBM to allow a NOS to communicate with computer hardware. NetBIOS has been adopted by Microsoft Windows NT and Novell NetWare, and has become the de facto standard for application interface to all types of LANs. Thus, many LANs are described as "NetBIOS compatible."

Network File System (NFS)—NFS is a file management system commonly used in UNIX-based computer systems.

network interface card (NIC)—A NIC is a workstation or PC component (usually a hardware card) that allows the workstation or PC to communicate with a network. A NIC address is another term for hardware address or MAC address. A NIC address is a unique value built into a NIC.

Network News Transfer Protocol (NNTP)—NNTP is a protocol used to post and retrieve USENET news group messages.

open source—Open-source software is software that may be used and redistributed without paying a licensing fee, and includes a copy of its source code. Vendors may sell distributions that include both the open-source software and their own added-value components (including technical support). Open-source software is popular with large organizations that often need to customize an application or OS.

operating system (OS)—An OS is the basic system software of a computer that provides low-level services to applications.

packet—A unit of information processed by the Network Layer is referred to as a packet. The packet header contains the logical (network) address of the destination node. Intermediate nodes forward a packet until it reaches its destination. A packet can contain an entire message generated by higher OSI layers or a segment of a much larger message. A packet is sometimes called a "datagram."

parallel bus—A parallel bus is an I/O bus that carries multiple bits simultaneously. See bus and serial bus.

peer—Two programs or processes that use the same protocol to communicate, and perform approximately the same function for their respective nodes are called "peer processes." With peer processes, in general, neither process controls the other, and the same protocol is used for data flowing in either direction.

peer-to-peer—Two programs or processes that use the same protocol to communicate and perform approximately the same function for their respective nodes are referred to as peer processes. With peer processes, in general, neither process controls the other, and the same protocol is used for data flowing in either direction. Communication between them is referred to as "peer-to-peer."

Peripheral Component Interconnect (PCI)—PCI is a 64-bit local bus that allows up to 10 expansion cards to be installed in a computer. PCI technology is capable of transferring data across a PC bus at very high rates.

peripherals—Peripherals are parts of a computer that are not on the primary board (motherboard) of a computer system. Peripherals include hard drives, floppy drives, and modems.

personal area network (PAN)—A PAN is a short-distance wireless network that connects a user's personal electronic devices, such as a cell phone, PDA, and headphones. It is also called a WPAN. See Bluetooth.

personal digital assistant (PDA)—PDAs are small, handheld devices that provide a subset of the operations of a typical PC. They are used for scheduling, electronic notepads, and small database applications.

piconet—A piconet is a Bluetooth PAN that links up to eight devices. Each piconet is controlled by one master device, and up to seven slave devices at any one time. Any device may be a member of more than one piconet, changing its membership as a user moves from one area to another. See Bluetooth.

Point-to-Point Protocol (PPP)—PPP is an Internet standard communication protocol that offers support for multiple network protocols, data compression, host configuration, and link setup. PPP is based on the HDLC standard.

Point-to-Point Tunneling Protocol (PPTP)—PPTP was developed by MicroSoft for VPNs using Microsoft Windows 95/98 and Windows NT. PPTP can support tunneling of IP, IPX, NetBios and NetBEUI protocols inside IP packets.

port—There are two primary ways the term "port" is used in networking. Port can refer to a physical port in a device, such as a port on a switch or MUX. Port can also refer to a software port, a number typically used to identify a software process within a computer.

proprietary—A proprietary network solution is one that is designed and implemented using equipment and protocols specific to one vendor. Purchasing equipment from one vendor typically creates proprietary networks. The opposite of a proprietary network is an "open" network, which is based on industry standards.

protocol—A protocol is a defined method of communication between computers or computer applications.

reassembly—Reassembly is the process of recombining a segmented transmission to restore the original message. See segmentation.

redirector—A redirector is a client software component that decides whether a request for a computer service or resource (for example, read a file) is for the local computer or another computer on the network. Each software vendor uses a different name for this function, such as "shell," "requestor," or "client."

regulation—Technical or operational rules that protect health, safety, national security, or environmental cleanliness are referred to as regulations. Because they deal with such important human needs, regulations are backed by the force of law.

repeater—A device that regenerates and boosts electrical or radio signals is referred to as a repeater. It can be used to lengthen a wire or a wireless transmission path.

RJ-45 connector—An RJ-45 connector is a snap-in connector for UTP cable, similar to the standard RJ-11 telephone cable connector.

router—A router is a Layer 3 device, with several ports that can each connect to a network or another router. A router examines the logical network address of each packet, then uses its internal routing table to forward the packet to the routing port associated with the best path to the packet's destination. If the packet is addressed to a network that is not connected to the router, the router will forward the packet to another router that is closer to the final destination. Each router, in turn, evaluates each packet, then either delivers the packet or forwards it to another router.

RS-232—RS-232 cables are used for connecting a computer to a modem. The RS-232 specification details the electrical and mechanical interface between the computer and modem.

segment—A physical portion of a network is referred to as a segment. A network is composed of one or more physical segments.

segmentation—The process of dividing a long data transmission into smaller chunks that lower layer processes can handle is referred to as segmentation. See reassembly.

Sequenced Packet Exchange (SPX)—SPX is Novell NetWare's proprietary Transport Layer protocol.

serial bus—An I/O bus that carries 1 bit at a time is referred to as a serial bus. See bus and parallel bus.

Serial Line Internet Protocol (SLIP)—SLIP is not an official Internet standard, but a de facto standard included in many implementations of TCP/IP. It was originally developed for use over dedicated circuits or leased lines, and therefore does not include provisions for establishing a connection over the telephone network.

server—A server is any program that provides a service to a client program. This term is often used to refer to the computer that hosts the server program; however, a server program may also run on a computer that normally functions as a client. See client.

Server Message Block (SMB)—SMB is an Application/Presentation Layer protocol used between clients and servers on a LAN. Functions requiring LAN support, such as retrieving files from a file server, are translated into SMB commands before they are sent to the remote device. Applications use SMB "calls" to perform file operations across a network.

Simple Mail Transfer Protocol (SMTP)—SMTP is a protocol and set of processes that use the protocol to transfer e-mail messages between user mailboxes.

simplex—See duplex.

source code—Source code refers to the programming instructions a programmer writes using a programming language. The source code of most applications and OSs is compiled into a machine language format that computers can use (but people cannot read or alter). The compiled version of a program cannot be edited; however, the original source code can be changed and recompiled.

stack—A stack is a group of protocols that work together to provide data communication. In a stack, each protocol uses the services of the protocol below it, and provides services to the protocol above it.

standard—Standards are the technical specifications and working methods necessary for different vendors' equipment to interoperate. Standards enhance efficiency and usability; however, they generally do not protect life or limb.

subnet—A subnet is a subdivision of a network, in which users are grouped logically based on their network address. Subnets are formed by routers, thus each subnet is a separate broadcast domain.

switch—A switch is device that operates at the Data Link Layer of the OSI model, using hardware addresses to forward frames between ports. Like a bridge, a switch can connect LANs or LAN segments of the same media access type, such as two Token Ring segments, or different types, such as Ethernet and Token Ring. Unlike a bridge, a switch dedicates the entire media bandwidth, such as 10-Mbps Ethernet, to each port-to-port connection.

synchronous—Synchronous communication is data communication controlled by a microprocessor clock, so that signals are permitted to start and stop at particular times. To use synchronous communication, the clock settings of the sending and receiving systems must match.

Synchronous Data Link Control (SDLC)—See High-Level Data Link Control (HDLC).

Synchronous Optical Network (SONET)—SONET is an optical transmission standard that defines a signal hierarchy. The basic building block is the STS-1 51.84-Mbps signal, chosen to accommodate a T3 signal. The STS designation refers to the interface for electrical signals. The optical signal standards are correspondingly designated OC-1, OC-2, and so on.

Systems Network Architecture (SNA)—SNA is IBM's architecture for computer networking. It was designed for transaction processing in mission-critical applications, often involving a large number of "dumb" terminals communicating with a mainframe. Typical transactions perform inquiries and update information in a database. For example, a commercial bank might have a number of 3270-type display units and printers in each of hundreds of branch offices that are used to access a central database in the home office.

T1—T1 is one of the T-carrier telecommunication standards for multiplexing digitized voice signals. A T1 channel operates at 1.544 Mbps. Each T1 channel (64 Kbps) was designed to carry a digitized representation of an analog signal (a telephone call) that has a bandwidth of 4,000 Hz. Originally, 64 Kbps was required to digitize a 4,000-Hz voice signal. Current technology has reduced that requirement to 32 Kbps or less; however, a T-carrier channel is still 64 Kbps.

T1 multiplexer (MUX)—A T1 MUX is a device that breaks an outgoing bit stream into T1 time slices, and reassembles incoming time slices into a continuous bit stream. It sits between a LAN and a DSU (or DSU side of a CSU/DSU).

Telecommunications Industry Association (TIA)—TIA is a subgroup of EIA that focuses on electronic products for data communications.

Telnet—Telnet is an Application Layer protocol that provides a remote login capability to another computer on a network.

time-division multiplexing (TDM)—TDM is a technology that allows multiple signals to travel over the same physical medium by guaranteeing each signal a fixed amount of bandwidth on a rotating basis.

Token Ring—Token Ring is a LAN protocol for ring topologies that operates at 4 and 16 Mbps.

Transmission Control Protocol (TCP)—TCP is a Transport Level protocol that provides reliable, full-duplex communication between two software processes on different computers. TCP normally uses IP to transmit information across the underlying network.

Universal Serial Bus (USB)—USB is an external bus that can transfer up to 12 Mbps. Up to 127 peripheral devices can be connected to a single USB port.

UNIX-to-UNIX Copy Program (UUCP)—UUCP is a protocol used for communication between consenting UNIX systems.

unroutable protocol—A unroutable protocol is a network protocol that does not support routing at OSI Layer 3, such as NetBIOS or DEC-LAT. This type of protocol does not create packets, thus Layer 3 devices, such as routers, cannot be used.

User Datagram Protocol (UDP)—UDP is a Transport Layer protocol (an alternative to TCP) that provides a simple, connectionless datagram delivery service, without error checking, for certain specialized application services that do not require the full services of TCP.

virtual circuit—A virtual circuit is a communication path that appears to be a single circuit to the sending and receiving devices, even though the data may take varying routes between the source and destination nodes.

virtual private network (VPN)—VPNs use end-to-end network encryption to establish a secure connection from machine to machine. Each VPN is an encrypted data stream that travels over a public network, such as the Internet.

virus—A virus is a self-replicating, malicious program that spreads by attaching itself to a file. Viruses can spread quickly through a network, with effects that range from mildly irritating to highly destructive.

World Wide Web (Web)—The Web is the global collection of HTML documents (Web pages) made available for public access by means of the Internet. To retrieve Web pages, a user must have a browser application.

X.25—X.25 is a connectionless packet-switching network, public or private, typically built upon leased lines from public telephone networks. In the United States, X.25 is offered by most carriers. The X.25 interface lies at OSI Layer 3, rather than Layer 1. X.25 defines its own three-layer protocol stack, and provides data rates only up to 56 Kbps.

Xerox Network System (XNS)—XNS is the protocol suite developed by PARC for their first versions of Ethernet networks. Several of the major LAN vendors (notably Novell and Banyan) have based portions of their network architectures on the XNS model.

INDEX